Kees Hengeveld, Heiko Narrog, Hella Olbertz (Eds.)
The Grammaticalization of Tense, Aspect, Modality and Evidentiality

Trends in Linguistics
Studies and Monographs

Editor
Volker Gast

Editorial Board
Walter Bisang
Jan Terje Faarlund
Hans Henrich Hock
Natalia Levshina
Heiko Narrog
Matthias Schlesewsky
Amir Zeldes
Niina Ning Zhang

Editor responsible for this volume
Walter Bisang

Volume 311

The Grammaticalization of Tense, Aspect, Modality and Evidentiality

A Functional Perspective

Edited by
Kees Hengeveld
Heiko Narrog
Hella Olbertz

DE GRUYTER
MOUTON

ISBN 978-3-11-065567-4
e-ISBN (PDF) 978-3-11-051938-9
e-ISBN (EPUB) 978-3-11-051742-2
ISSN 1861-4302

Library of Congress Cataloging-in-Publication Data
A CIP catalog record for this book has been applied for at the Library of Congress.

Bibliographic information published by the Deutsche Nationalbibliothek
The Deutsche Nationalbibliothek lists this publication in the Deutsche Nationalbibliografie;
detailed bibliographic data are available on the Internet at http://dnb.dnb.de.

© 2019 Walter de Gruyter GmbH, Berlin/Boston
This volume is text- and page-identical with the hardback published in 2017.
Typesetting: Compuscript Ltd., Shannon, Ireland
Printing and binding: CPI Books GmbH, Leck
♾ Printed on acid-free paper
Printed in Germany

www.degruyter.com

Contents

Kees Hengeveld, Heiko Narrog and Hella Olbertz
A functional perspective on the grammaticalization of tense, aspect, modality, and evidentiality —— 1

Kees Hengeveld
A hierarchical approach to grammaticalization —— 13

Riccardo Giomi
The interaction of components in a Functional Discourse Grammar account of grammaticalization —— 39

Heiko Narrog
Relationship of form and function in grammaticalization – the case of modality —— 75

Sophie Villerius
Modality and aspect marking in Surinamese Javanese: Grammaticalization and contact-induced change —— 111

Lotta Jalava
Grammaticalization of modality and evidentiality in Tundra Nenets —— 133

Shadi Davari and Mehrdad Naghzguy-Kohan
The grammaticalization of progressive aspect in Persian —— 163

Carlos García Castillero
Grammaticalization as morphosyntax and representation: Mood from tense markers in the Old Irish and Romance conditional —— 191

Jimena Tena Dávalos
The end of a cycle: Grammaticalization of the future tense in Mexican Spanish —— 215

Aude Rebotier
The grammaticalization of tenses and lexical aspect – the case of German and French perfects —— 241

Hella Olbertz and Wim Honselaar
The grammaticalization of Dutch *moeten*: modal and post-modal meanings —— 273

Names index —— 301

Language index —— 305

Subject index —— 307

Kees Hengeveld, Heiko Narrog and Hella Olbertz
A functional perspective on the grammaticalization of tense, aspect, modality, and evidentiality

1 Introduction

The book to which this chapter is an introduction collects a number of studies on the grammaticalization of tense, aspect, modality, and evidentiality written from a functional perspective. In this introductory chapter we address a number of issues relevant to the general topic of this volume, which surface in different ways and combinations in the following chapters. After that we will explain the structure of this book in view of these issues. The overarching issues that we will address in the following sections are the following.

A functional approach to grammaticalization addresses the question how grammaticalization paths reflect changes in the function of a linguistic element, either in terms of its denotation (semantics) or in terms of its communicative function (pragmatics). It furthermore looks for explanations of these changes in the communicative function of language and the contexts in which language is used. In Section 2 we have a closer look at these properties of a functional approach to grammaticalization.

Grammaticalization, however, obviously does not only involve the function of the grammaticalizing element but also has a formal counterpart that needs to be accounted for. A principled functional approach to grammaticalization therefore needs to strictly separate functional and formal aspects of the grammaticalization process. This issue is addressed in Section 3.

Many functional approaches to language are concerned to develop a grammatical theory that is equally applicable to languages of all possible types, based on the results of extensive cross-linguistic research. This has led to a close, though certainly not exclusive connection between functional theory formation and studies in language typology. The relation between grammaticalization processes and typological differences between languages is discussed in Section 4.

An important issue in recent functional studies of grammaticalization is the idea that grammaticalization is a scope-widening process, such that processes of

---

Acknowledgment: Heiko Narrog's research activity was supported by grants number 24520450 and 16H03411 by the Japanese Society for the Promotion of Science.

DOI 10.1515/9783110519389-001

grammaticalization can be systematically described and predicted in a number of small steps along a pathway that ranges from narrow to wide scope. This idea is again not exclusive to functional approaches, but the pathways proposed in functional approaches are based on functional notions in a hierarchical relationship rather than on structural positions. This issue is further explored in Section 5.

Conclusions to this chapter are presented in Section 6. The conclusion will be followed by a brief explanation of the structure of this book in Section 7.

2 Functionalism and grammaticalization

Functional theories of grammaticalization differ from formal ones in at least two respects, which will be discussed in this section. The differences concern the priority given to either contentive or formal changes on the one hand, and the explanations provided on the other.

Functional theories of language have in common that they try to understand and describe grammatical systems in terms of the extralinguistic requirements imposed on those systems. In Dik's (1986: 10) words, these requirements can be divided into: "(i) the aims and purposes for which natural language expressions are used; (ii) the means by which natural languages are implemented; (iii) the circumstances in which natural languages are used." Dik then argues that a possible natural language is defined as one that complies with the various requirements mentioned above and continues: "Indirectly, the functional prerequisites define the notion 'possible linguistic change': a possible linguistic change must lead from one possible language to another possible language" (Dik 1986: 10). Language is thus primarily seen as an instrument, and its structure should be understood in terms of the functions this instrument is used for. A change in the instrument should not lead to a situation in which it can no longer carry out its functions.

Requirement (i) corresponds to pragmatics; (ii) to syntax, morphology, phonology, and phonetics; and (iii) partly to semantics. Here a clear difference with formal approaches to grammaticalization emerges. As noted by Nykiel (2014: 12), "minimalist grammaticalization describes change at the level of phrases and interpretations in terms of phrase structure come into play. For functionalists grammaticalization is conceived of as not only morphosyntactic change but also, if not primarily, semantic, pragmatic, and phonetic." Narrog (this volume) is a bit more careful when he draws attention to the fact that certain changes that are generally considered functional in functionalist approaches may be derived from structural configurations in formal approaches, as shown for instance in van Gelderen (2011).

What follows from the above is that in a functional approach to grammaticalization pride of place is given to semantic and pragmatic change, which may be subsumed under the term contentive change, while formal change is seen as a consequence of or concomitant with contentive change. In formal approaches, on the other hand, pride of place is given to formal change, and contentive change is seen as a consequence of or concomitant with formal change. In Section 3 below we will return to the question how the interaction between contentive and formal change is dealt with in functional approaches.

A second aspect distinguishing functional from formal approaches to grammaticalization concerns the kind of explanation that is offered for the process. In formal approaches, a grammar can only change during the process of (first language) acquisition. This is, for instance, the position taken in Roberts & Roussou (2003), who claim that in child language acquisition grammaticalization steps are taken that lead to simpler underlying structures, or by van Gelderen (2004), for whom children's language acquisition is guided by economy principles. In functional approaches, it is generally maintained that 'grammar emerges out of usage' (Harder & Boye 2011: 58). Hopper & Traugott (2003: 44) argue explicitly against children being the primary drivers of change. For them, adolescents and adults play at least an equally if not more important role. Giomi (this volume) formulates it this way: "there is a general consensus that the phenomenon is essentially rooted in language usage." And Davari & Kohan (this volume) when discussing the rise of the progressive in Persian use exactly this kind of explanation, when they state: "We suggest that the progressive function arose through context-induced reinterpretation based on metonymic relations."

3 Grammaticalization of form and function

It has long been assumed in grammmaticalization studies that there is co-evolution of form and function in grammaticalization. This has been called the 'parallel path hypothesis' (Siewierska & Bakker 2005; see van Rijn (2016) for more details) and is defended in e.g. Bybee et al. (1994: 20). The parallel path hypothesis entails that every formal change would be accompanied by a contentive change, and the other way around. Formal changes would then develop along clines such as the one in (1) (cf. Siewierska 2004: 262):

(1)   Ø < fusional form < agglutinative affix < clitic < grammatical word < content item

It is not difficult to come up with counterexamples to the parallel path hypothesis. Many languages, for instance, exhibit highly grammaticalized question particles. Consider the following example from Hatam (Reesink 1999: 69):

(2) *A-yai   bi-dani   mem   di-ngat   i.*
    2SG-get   to-me   for   1SG-see   INT
    'Would you give it to me so that I can see it?'

The sentence final particle *i* 'INT' would on all counts qualify as highly grammaticalized from a contentive perspective: it is strongly abstract in meaning, and it has the widest possible scope. Yet the formal category that expresses this abstract meaning is that of the grammatical word, which is only the second category in the cline in (1).

On the other hand, from early on, Heine and collaborators entertained a 'meaning-first' hypothesis, in which functional (semantic) change is the core and primary in grammaticalization, and may or may not be accompanied by formal changes. Heine & Reh (1984: 62) hypothesized that "[d]esemanticization is the process which is responsible for most other developments", and Heine et al. (1991: 15) write that "functional processes chronologically precede both morphosyntactic and phonetic processes; that is, if a linguistic unit undergoes both desemanticization and cliticization, then the former is likely to precede the latter in time." Likewise, in Heine & Kuteva (2002: 3), the authors make clear that "grammaticalization, as conceived here, is above all a semantic process", and "new grammatical meanings arise, and it usually takes quite some time before any corresponding morphological, syntactic, and/or phonetic changes can be observed. In many languages, [....] tense or aspect auxiliaries may still behave morphosyntactically largely like lexical verbs even if they have lost their lexical semantics and serve exclusively as functional categories."

Bisang (2004) is the first publication to highlight a systematic disconnection between functional and formal change in grammaticalization in a specific group of languages as an areal phenomenon. It is not surprising that the languages Bisang discusses are of the isolating type, where formal adaptations of the kinds assumed in (1) do not go well with the morphological type of the language, to the extent that they go beyond the stage of the grammatical word.

In this volume several authors similarly reject the parallel path hypothesis. They argue that contentive change and formal change are two different processes that should each be described in their own right. Often the two processes will occur hand in hand, but this is not necessarily the case in the process of grammaticalization. This alternative approach is most clearly formulated in Narrog (this volume) when he states: "The claim is that formal and functional grammaticalization proceed unidirectionally in the sense that we expect that in the vast majority of cases of grammatical development at least either form or function advance along parameters of grammaticalization while neither of them should regress. On the other hand, the entry point in grammaticalization and the pace of development differ marker by marker, construction by construction. Therefore it is not possible to expect every marker and construction that is functionally more grammaticalized to be also formally more grammaticalized than a functionally less grammaticalized item, and vice versa." Furthermore, he suggests that "the core of grammaticalization is functional. Formal changes (in a functional sense of "formal"), at least to the extent that they are reflected in written language, are merely optional."

Similarly, Hengeveld (this volume) claims: "Grammaticalization is seen as a combination of contentive and formal change, and, crucially, it is argued that these need not go hand in hand, though there are restrictions on how they combine." Hengeveld then continues to specify these restrictions.

Giomi (this volume) makes the issue more precise by separating pragmatic and semantic change on the contentive side and morphosyntactic and phonological change on the formal side using the model of Functional Discourse Grammar. He concludes: "By mapping directional universals explicitly onto the structure of the four levels, the FDG approach gains a decisive advantage over most functionally oriented theories of grammaticalization: that of showing how language change is not only compatible with general cognitive principles, but directly reflects the same underlying grammatical hierarchy as is observable synchronically across the languages of the world. In this way, it provides precise grammar-internal constraints on possible and impossible patterns of grammaticalization."

In her study of the grammaticalization of the perfect in French and German, Rebotier (this volume) shows that, whereas an exclusively formal view on this matter leads to the conclusion that the English perfect should be more grammaticalized than the German one, a contentive view on this relation reveals exactly the contrary, i.e. that the German perfect is much more grammaticalized than the English one.

4 Grammaticalization and language typology

In order to uncover the principles underlying processes of grammaticalization at the highest possible level of abstraction, it is important to study these processes in languages of maximally different types and affiliations. This way generalizations may be arrived at that would be missed if we would restrict ourselves to the study of grammaticalization in a single language or in a limited number of mutually related languages. Among the competing approaches to grammaticalization theory, particularly the lines of research by Heine (e.g. Heine 1997a, b) and of Bybee (e.g. Bybee et al. 1994) have made systematic use of typological data. The idea pursued in both lines of research is to find explanations for synchronic typological patterns in the paths that led to their grammaticalization. As Heine (1997a: 2) writes, "[l]anguage is a historical product and must be explained first of all with reference to the forces that have shaped it." Similarly, Bybee (2006: 187) claims that "the very robust and very specific paths of development shown above constitute much stronger cross-linguistic statements than any statements we could devise about synchronic states" (Bybee 2006: 187).

Conversely, insights from typology may help predict patterns of grammaticalization or of language change in general. Furthermore, synchronic typological patterns may also constrain grammaticalization in a specific language. For an overview of the literature on both directions of potential influence and constraints, see Narrog (in press).

To start with the importance of typology for the study of grammaticalization, it is important to mention the contribution of Greenberg (1978), who introduces the notion of 'dynamic typology'. The basic idea is that typological hierarchies predict possible languages. Every change in a language can be interpreted as the change from one possible language to another possible language. Therefore, diachronic changes can be seen as steps along the same typological hierarchies that are used to describe synchronic variation. Hengeveld (1991) provides an example of this, arguing that the typological hierarchy defining the extent to which languages allow different types of non-verbal predication is reflected in the pathway along which the Latin verb *stare* 'stand' developed into a copula in the Ibero-Romance languages.

In the current volume the point mentioned in the beginning of this section, however, i.e. the importance of the study of grammaticalization processes in widely divergent languages, is more prominently present. The languages studied include some that have not received much attention so far in the grammaticalization literature. This is true, for instance, for Tundra Nenets. Jalava (this volume) shows that insubordination (Evans 2007), a process the relevance of which has been demonstrated for several languages, has given rise to an evidential marker in Tundra Nenets as well. Similarly, García Castillero (this volume) contributes to our body of knowledge on grammaticalization by studying the rise of the conditional form in Old Irish. He shows that the counterfactual meaning arose out of the combination of future and imperfect tense markers in indirect speech, just as it did in e.g. Spanish and several other Romance languages.

Other studies in this volume show that proposals in the literature on the theory of grammaticalization can be applied fruitfully to languages not considered so far. For instance, Olbertz & Honselaar (this volume) show that the division of modalities into volitive and non-volitive ones, as proposed in Narrog (2005), is the appropriate one in describing the behaviour of the Dutch modal *moeten* 'must'. As another example, Rebotier (this volume) discusses Leiss' (1992) statement that lexical aspect is intimately related to grammaticalization, and fruitfully applies this idea to the German and French present perfect, thus explaining both the differences and the similarities between the corresponding grammaticalization processes.

Finally, the study of grammaticalization in a wide range of typologically diverse languages may lead to the discovery of processes hitherto unattested. This is the case of the 'possessive progressive', a cross-linguistic rarity attested in Persian, as described in Davari & Kohan (this volume).

5 Grammaticalization and layering

In many different frameworks grammatical categories are organized in layers, such that the higher the layer, the wider the scope of the grammatical category. Clear evidence for the reality of layering comes from strictly agglutinating languages such as Japanese, where the morpheme closest to the stem has the narrowest scope and the one farthest from the stem has the widest scope (Narrog 2009: 37). Hengeveld (1989: 142) was probably the first to give a diachronic interpretation to the notion of layering, when he hypothesizes that diachronic developments in the field of TAM expressions will go from lower to higher scope, and not the other way round. In other words, grammaticalization is predicted to proceed in such a way that a certain category may assume a function one layer up, but the opposite process would not be expected to occur. This idea is applied in Hengeveld (2011) to the development of Tense and Aspect categories. As an example of a process predicted by the theory he discusses the development of the verb *haber* 'have' in Peninsular Spanish, as presented in Olbertz (1993). *Haber* started out as a lexical verb of possession. It then came to express resultative aspect at the lowest layer of grammatical analysis. Subsequently it developed into a marker of anterior relative tense, moving one layer up. Finally, it started to express absolute tense in a number of restricted contexts, again moving one layer up.

The layering hypothesis gives rise to a large set of predictions, the exact nature of which of course depends on the definition of layers in a specific theory, as most clearly shown in Narrog (2009). Reversely, studies of layering and scope expansion in grammaticalization phenomena can be used to evaluate the validity of competing hypotheses on layering, as also suggested in Narrog (2009) and

Narrog (2012). A possible functional explanation of the phenomenon of layered scope increase would be that this process reflects an increase in speech-act orientation, that is, change towards categories that are more speaker-oriented (especially those that are speaker-deictic), hearer oriented, and finally speech-act, or discourse-oriented at the highest layers (cf. Narrog 2012; Narrog, this volume).

Many papers in this volume touch upon the idea of scope increase. Hengeveld (this volume) sets out a general theory of grammaticalization as a hierarchical process using the model of Functional Discourse Grammar. Giomi (this volume) expands on this theory by explicitly connecting it to contextual factors. Narrog (this volume) shows the relevance of this approach for modality in general and in Japanese, while Olbertz & Honselaar (this volume) show the relevance of this approach more concretely for the analysis of the grammaticalization of the Dutch modal *moeten* from modal to illocutionary functions; Tena Dávalos (this volume) studies the development of future reference in Mexican Spanish from that same perspective; and Villerius (this volume) applies this idea to Heritage Javanese spoken in Suriname.

6 Summary

We have discussed a number of issues that are distinctive of the various contributions in this volume. First of all, we argue that functional approaches to the grammaticalization of tense, aspect, modality and evidentiality take the instrumentality of language as their starting point, which means that semantic and pragmatic changes are assigned primary importance as compared to formal changes, such that the latter may but need not co-occur with the former. Secondly, and following from the previous point, the papers in this volume do not assume, and some even explicitly argue against, the idea that change in meaning and change in form have to go hand in hand. Thirdly, the studies in this collection present a wide array of genetically different languages, and some general studies explicity address typological facts, thus providing the ground for more broadly supported explanations of grammaticalization than those that consider the properties of closely related languages only. Finally, the idea of layering is being advanced, i.e. the hypothesis that grammaticalization proceeds in such a way that the scope of a grammatical item increases as it further grammaticalizes.

Given the wide range of functional theories of language, it is not surprising that not every functional approach to grammaticalization adheres to all of these distinctive features of this volume, but each of the chapters of this book clearly manifests at least one of them.

7 The structure of this book

This book is divided into two parts. The first part contains three general studies, and the second seven language-specific studies.

In the opening chapter of the first part *Kees Hengeveld* discusses a wide range of grammaticalization phenomena from typologically different languages in order to elaborate on the idea that grammaticalization is a matter of scope increase (see Section 5), using the theory of Functional Discourse Grammar. *Riccardo Giomi* focuses on the role of context (see Section 2) and its formalization in Functional Discourse Grammar in processes of grammaticalization, thus reconciling Heine's (2002) idea of the importance of "bridging contexts" with the highly formalized framework of Functional Discourse Grammar. *Heiko Narrog's* primary concern is to show that formal and contentive change do not necessarily go hand in hand (see Section 3), but that functional change is essential whereas formal change is accidental and highly language specific. Using examples from the domain of modality he argues that by default formal and functional changes do not correlate negatively, but that in the exceptional cases in which they do, it is the form rather than the function that is being degrammaticalized.

In the second part of this book, the grammaticalization of tense, aspect, modality and/or evidentiality categories in languages from various genetic stocks is studied, the relevance of which was discussed in Section 4. The chapters of this part are ordered in such a way that, starting from non-Indo-European languages, we proceed to lesser known Indo-European languages and end with West-Germanic. *Sophie Villerius* compares Javanese (Malayo-Polynesian) with its heritage variety spoken in Surinam as regards different realizations of modality and aspect, one of the findings being that in the domain of modality there is scope increase from participant-oriented to event-oriented modal categories in the Surinamese variant. *Lotta Jalava* studies the grammaticalization of evidentiality and modality in Tundra Nenets (Samoyedic). She argues that there are two main grammaticalization paths of modal and evidential suffixes in Tundra Nenets, the verbalization of participles and insubordination, both of which probably represent an areal pattern. *Shadi Davari* and *Mehrdad Kohan* investigate a typologically rare grammaticalization path in Persian (Indo-Aryan), in which a verb of possession comes to be used as a progressive auxiliary. *Carlos García Castillero* compares the rise of the conditional in Old Irish (Celtic) with that in Old Spanish, Spanish being representative in this respect of most Romance languages. *Jimena Tena Dávalos* traces the development of the 'go'-future in Mexican Spanish (Romance) from the lexical expression of movement through prospective aspect and near future to the expression of absolute future tense and argues that the synthetic future, which is based on a modal-like expression in Latin, is presently acquiring a modal meaning again. *Aude Rebotier* studies the role of lexical aspect in the grammaticalization of the perfect in French (Romance) and German (West-Germanic), in both of which the perfect expresses past tense meanings. She argues that the crucial difference in the grammaticalization processes is due to the fact that French has grammatical aspect, which German lacks. *Hella Olbertz* and *Wim Honselaar*, finally, apply the framework of Functional Discourse Grammar in their diachronic and synchronic study of the the Dutch (West-Germanic) modal *moeten*, in which they describe the development of modal meanings into illocutionary functions, i.e. from modal possibility to optativity in the Middle Ages and from modal necessity to imperativity in 20th century.

References

Bisang, Walter. 2004. Grammaticalization without coevolution of form and meaning: The case of tense-aspect-modality in East and mainland Southeast Asia. In Walter Bisang, Nikolaus P. Himmelmann & Björn Wiemer (eds.), *What makes grammaticalization: A look from its fringes and its components*, 109–138. Berlin & New York: Mouton de Gruyter.

Bybee, Joan L. 2006. Language change and universals. In Ricardo Mairal & Juana Gil (eds.), *Linguistic universals*, 179–194. Cambridge: Cambridge University Press.

Bybee, Joan, Revere Perkins & William Pagliuca. 1994. *The evolution of grammar*. Chicago: University of Chicago Press.

Davari, Shadi & Mehrdad Naghzguy Kohan. This volume. The grammaticalization of progressive aspect in Persian.

Dik, Simon C. 1986. On the notion 'Functional Explanation'. *Working Papers in Functional Grammar* 11.

Evans, Nicolas. 2007. Insubordination and its uses. In Irina Nicolavea (ed.), *Finiteness: Theoretical and empirical foundations*, 366–431. Oxford: Oxford University Press.

Gelderen, Elly van. 2004. *Grammaticalization as economy*. Amsterdam & Philadelphia: John Benjamins.

Gelderen, Elly van. 2011. Grammaticalization and generative grammar. A difficult liaison. In Heiko Narrog & Bernd Heine (eds.), *The Oxford handbook of grammaticalization*, 43–55. Oxford: Oxford University Press.

Giomi, Riccardo. This volume. The interaction of components in a Functional Discourse Grammar account of grammaticalization.

Greenberg, Joseph. 1978. Diachrony, synchrony, and language universals. In Joseph Greenberg (ed.), *Universals of human language*, Vol. 1, 61–91. Stanford: Stanford University Press.

Harder, Peter & Kasper Boye. 2011. Grammaticalization and functional linguistics. In Heiko Narrog & Bernd Heine (eds.), *The Oxford handbook of grammaticalization*, 56–68. Oxford: Oxford University Press.

Heine, Bernd. 1997a. *Cognitive foundations of grammar*. New York: Oxford University Press.

Heine, Bernd. 1997b. *Possession: Sources, forces, and grammaticalization*. Cambridge: Cambridge University Press.

Heine, Bernd. 2002. On the role of context in grammaticalization. In Ilse Wischer & Gabriele Diewald (eds.), *New reflections on grammaticalization* (Typological Studies in Language, 49), 83–101. Amsterdam & Philadelphia: John Benjamins.

Heine, Bernd, Ulrike Claudi & Friederike Hünnemeyer. 1991. *Grammaticalization*. Chicago: The University of Chicago Press.

Heine, Bernd & Tania Kuteva. 2002. *World lexicon of grammaticalization*. Cambridge: Cambridge University Press.

Heine, Bernd & Mechthild Reh. 1984. *Grammaticalization and reanalysis in African languages*. Hamburg: Buske.

Hengeveld, Kees. 1989. Layering in Functional Grammar. *Journal of Linguistics* 25(1). 127–157.

Hengeveld, Kees. 1991. Tipología, sincronía, diacronía. In Henk Haverkate, Kees Hengeveld, Gijs Mulder & Hella Olbertz (eds.), *Exploraciones semánticas y pragmáticas del español* (Foro Hispánico 2), 81–94. Amsterdam: Rodopi.

Hengeveld, Kees. 2011. The grammaticalization of tense and aspect. In Bernd Heine & Heiko Narrog (eds.), *The Oxford handbook of grammaticalization*, 580–594. Oxford: Oxford University Press.

Hengeveld, Kees. This volume. A hierarchical approach to grammaticalization.

Hopper, Paul J. & Elizabeth C. Traugott. 2003 [1993]. *Grammaticalization*. 2nd edn. Cambridge: Cambridge University Press.

Jalava, Lotta. This volume. Grammaticalization of modality and evidentiality in Tundra Nenets.

Leiss, Elisabeth. 1992. *Die Verbalkategorien des Deutschen: Ein Beitrag zur Theorie der sprachlichen Kategorisierung*. Berlin & New York: Walter de Gruyter.

Narrog, Heiko. 2005. Modality, mood, and change of modal meanings: A new perspective. *Cognitive Linguistics* 16(4). 677–731.

Narrog, Heiko. 2009. *Modality in Japanese: The layered structure of the clause and hierarchies of functional categories*. Amsterdam & New York: John Benjamins.

Narrog, Heiko. 2012. *Modality, subjectivity, and semantic change: A cross-linguistic perspective*. Oxford. Oxford University Press.

Narrog, Heiko. In press. Typology and grammaticalization. In Alexandra Y. Aikhenvald and R.M.W. Dixon (eds.), *The Cambridge handbook of of linguistic typology*. Cambridge: Cambridge University Press.

Narrog, Heiko. This volume. Relationship of form and function in grammaticalization – the case of modality.

Nykiel, Jerzy. 2014. Grammaticalization reconciled: Functionalist and minimalist insights into the development of purpose subordinators in English. *Language Sciences* 42(1). 1–14.

Olbertz, Hella. 1993. The grammaticalization of Spanish *haber* plus participle. In Jaap van Marle (ed.), *Historical Linguistics 1991: Papers from the 10th International Conference on Historical Linguistics*, 243–263. Amsterdam & New York: John Benjamins.

Olbertz, Hella & Wim Honselaar. This volume. The grammaticalization of Dutch *moeten*: modal and post-modal meanings.

Rebotier, Aude. This volume. The grammaticalization of tenses and lexical aspect: The case of German and French perfects.

Reesink, Ger P. 1999. *A Grammar of Hatam, Bird's Head Peninsula, Irian Jaya*. (Pacific Linguistics, Series C, 146.) Canberra: Australian National University.

Rijn, Marlou van. 2016. The grammaticalization of possessive person marking: A typological approach. *Transactions of the Philological Society* 114(2). 233–276.

Roberts, Ian & Anna Roussou. 2003. *Syntactic change: A minimalist approach to grammaticalization*. Cambridge: Cambridge University Press.

Siewierska, Anna. 2004. *Person*. Cambridge: Cambridge University Press.
Siewierska, Anna & Dik Bakker. 2005. Inclusive and exclusive in free and bound person forms. In Elena Filimonova (ed.), *Clusivity: Typology and case studies of the inclusive–exclusive distinction*, 151–178. Amsterdam & New York: John Benjamins.
Tena Davalos, Jimena. This volume. The end of a cycle: Grammaticalization of the future tense in Mexican Spanish.
Villerius, Sophie. This volume. Modality and aspect marking in Surinamese Javanese: Grammaticalization and contact-induced change.

Kees Hengeveld
A hierarchical approach to grammaticalization

Abstract: This paper argues that grammaticalization processes can be systematically described using the framework of Functional Discourse Grammar (FDG). Grammaticalization is seen as a combination of contentive and formal change, and, crucially, it is argued that these need not go hand in hand, though there are restrictions on how they combine. It is argued that contentive change always involves scope increase, where scope is defined in terms of the levels and layers distinguished in FDG. Formal change is not defined in terms of specific formal categories, as in earlier grammaticalization hierarchies, but is rather defined in terms of the distributional behaviour of grammaticalized elements. This way, formal change can be defined independently of the morphological type of a language. Finally, it is shown that contentive change and formal change are two independent processes, though their interaction is severely limited, in the sense that when an item moves up along the contentive cline, it cannot move down along the formal cline. Similarly, an item can not move up the formal cline while moving down the contentive cline.

Keywords: grammaticalization, Functional Discourse Grammar, layering, TAME systems

1 Introduction

In this paper I argue that processes of grammaticalization, seen as a combination of contentive and formal change, follow predictable paths: on the content side they entail a stepwise and systematic increase in scope, while on the formal side they entail a stepwise and systematic decrease in lexicality. In defining scope relations I use the framework of Functional Discourse Grammar (FDG), a typologically based theory of language structure (Hengeveld and Mackenzie 2008). This grammatical theory defines scope relations in terms of hierarchical multi-layered structures that are pragmatic and semantic in nature. It furthermore offers new

---

Kees Hengeveld: University of Amsterdam, Amsterdam Center for Language and Communication, Spuistraat 134, 1012 VB Amsterdam, The Netherlands, p.c.hengeveld@uva.nl

DOI 10.1515/9783110519389-002

tools to define degrees of lexicality through its systematic distinction between lexemes, operators, and lexical operators (Keizer 2007). By taking this approach the paper thus also addresses the question whether FDG can serve as a framework to predict, describe and explain processes of grammaticalization.

Section 2 gives a brief outline of relevant aspects of FDG, which are then applied systematically in the following sections. A description of processes of contentive change is provided in Section 3, while processes of formal change are studies in Section 4. Section 5 then looks at the interactions between processes of contentive change and of formal change. The paper ends with a conclusion in Section 6.

2 Functional discourse grammar

2.1 Layering[1]

Since the eighties, a number of grammatical theories[2] have incorporated the idea that grammatical categories are organized in layers. The basic idea may be illustrated with the following example from Hidatsa:

Hidatsa (Matthews 1965)
(1) Wíra   i   ápáari   ki   stao   ski.
     tree   it   grow   INGR   REM.PST   CERT
     'The tree must have begun to grow a long time ago.'

In this example the relative order of the tense, mood, and aspect (TAM) markers with respect to the predicate is ingressive – remote past – certainty. In terms of a layered approach to grammar this may be interpreted as a result of the fact that there are differences in scope between them: ingressive, specifying the internal temporal structure of the event, is within the scope of remote past, specifying the

---

[1] This section is largely based on Hengeveld (2011).
[2] This assumption is prominent in Role and Reference Grammar (Foley & Van Valin 1984), Usage-based Grammar (Bybee 1985), Functional (Discourse) Grammar (Hengeveld 1989; Boland 2006; Hengeveld & Mackenzie 2008), and Generative Grammar (Pollock 1989; Cinque & Rizzi 2010). A major difference between these approaches is that in Usage-based Grammar and Functional (Discourse) Grammar layers are defined in semantic terms, while in Role and Reference Grammar and Generative Grammar they are defined in positional terms. For a detailed comparison between various approaches to layering see Narrog (2009) and for the relation between layering and grammaticalization Narrog (2012: 89f).

external temporal structure of the event. Both are in the scope of certainty, which qualifies the content of the message as a whole. These scope relations may be indicated as in (2):

(2) certainty (remote past (ingressive (predicate+arguments)))

It is not the absolute linear order but the relative order with respect to the predicate that is predicted to correlate with scopal layers. Thus, the order of the relevant TAM markers in the English translation of example (1) is the mirror-image of the one in the Hidatsa original. Note that the correlation between scopal layers and the relative order of TAM (and E: evidentiality) markers holds under restricted conditions, namely only to the extent that TAME markers are expressed using the same morphological strategy. Thus the prediction holds for e.g. all affixal expressions among themselves, all particles among themselves, all auxiliaries among themselves, all clitics among themselves, but not for combinations of e.g. affixes, auxiliaries, and particles.

2.2 Layers

In Functional Discourse Grammar scope relations are defined in terms of different pragmatic and semantic layers. Pragmatic layers together constitute the interpersonal level in this model, while semantic layers together constitute the representational level.

At the interpersonal level scope relations are defined in terms of different pragmatic layers. The ones that are relevant for our argumentation below are, working inside out, the *ascriptive subact* and the *referential subact*, which are the building blocks of the communicated content; the *communicated content* itself, which represents the message transmitted in an utterance; the *illocution*, which specifies the communicative intention of the speaker; and the *discourse act*, which is the basic unit of communication.

At the representational level scope relations are defined in terms of different semantic layers. Working inside out again, the layers that are relevant for the argumentation below are the *property* expressed by a lexical element; the *configurational property*,[3] which consists of the lexical element and its argument(s) and as such provides the basic characterization of a state-of-affairs; the *state-of-affairs*, which is the situated real or hypothesized situation the speaker has in mind; the *episode*, which is a thematically coherent combination

---

[3] In Hengeveld (2011) I used the term 'situational concept' for what was originally called a Configurational Property in FDG. I now believe the original term to be more appropriate.

of states-of-affairs that are characterized by unity or continuity of time, location, and participants; and the *proposition*, which is a mental construct entertained about an episode.

The layers within each level are hierarchically related and so are the levels among themselves. These hierarchical relations are indicated in Fig. 1.

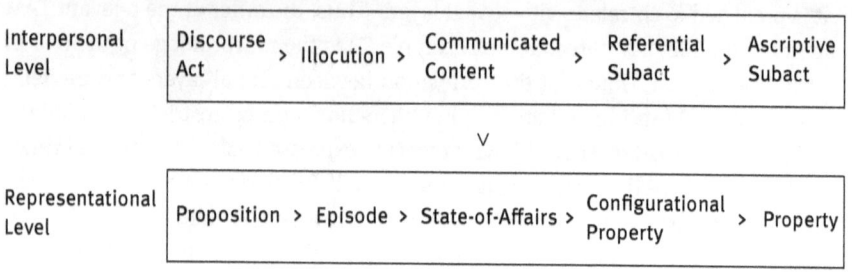

Fig. 1: Scope relations in FDG.

Figure 1 shows the hierarchical relations between layers and levels, with the symbols '>' and '∨' showing the directions in which layers and levels have scope over one another. Thus, the Interpersonal Level has scope over the Representational Level, and within each level layers more to the left have scope over layers more to the right.

2.3 Operators, modifiers, and functions

All layers introduced in Section 2.2 have a basic content which may be further specified by operators, modifiers, and functions. Operators capture specification by grammatical means, as in the case of e.g. TAME expressions; modifiers capture specification by lexical means, as in the case of e.g. modal, temporal, and locative adverbs. Functions, finally, express a relation of the layer under consideration with another linguistic unit, as in the case of e.g. causal and conditional conjunctions. Operators, modifiers, and functions are associated with the layer to which they semantically belong. For instance, expressions of subjective propositional attitudes are associated with propositions, since only propositions can be mentally evaluated; illocutionary adverbs are associated with illocutions as they specify the manner in which the speech act is being carried out; and temporal conjunctions are, depending on their relative or absolute nature, associated with states-of-affairs or episodes respectively. There is no space here to give a full motivation of all distinctions. Table 1 list the ones that have been argued for in Hengeveld and Mackenzie (2008), Hengeveld and Hattnher (2015), and Hattnher and Hengeveld (2016).

Tab. 1: Operators, modifiers and functions in FDG.

Interpersonal Level	Discourse act	Illocution	Communicated Content	Referential Subact	Ascriptive Subact
Operators	illocutionary modification	basic illocution	reportativity, approximation, mirativity	approximation	approximation
Modifiers	style, enumeration	manner of speech act	source, attitude	source, attitude	source, attitude
Functions	motivation, consent, orientation, correction	—	informational status	informational status	informational status

Representational Level	Propositional Content	Episode	State-of-Affairs	Configurational Property	Property
Operators	inference, subjective epistemic modality	absolute tense, deduction, objective epistemic modality	event quantification, relative tense, event perception, event-oriented modality	phasal aspect, (im)perfectivity, participant-oriented modality	directionality, degree
Modifiers	propositional attitude	absolute time	relative time, location, frequency, reality, cause, purpose	additional participants, manner, duration	manner, degree
Functions	condition, concession reason	cause	purpose, consequence	means	—

New in Tab. 1 is the assignment of mirativity to the class of operators that operate on the communicated content.[4] This is warranted by the fact that mirativity has to do with the informational status, more specifically the newsworthiness, of the content of a speech act (see Hengeveld and Olbertz 2012).

3 Contentive change

3.1 Introduction

In grammaticalization processes both the meaning and the form of an element may change, though not necessarily simultaneously, as I will argue below. In this section I look at the contentive changes that an element may undergo in grammaticalization. The main claim is that contentive changes are always changes that lead to an increase in scope, a point also made in Narrog (2012: 89f). As indicated in Fig. 1, and in terms of the FDG framework used here, scope increase may apply in three different ways: within levels, scope increase may take place at (i) the representational level (Section 3.2) or at (ii) the interpersonal level (Section 3.3). Across levels, (iii) scope increase may take place from the representational to the interpersonal level (Section 3.4). Grammaticalization starts out when a lexical element enters the grammatical system. This process will be looked at separately in Section 3.5. The different processes are brought together in an overall model of grammaticalization paths in Section 3.6.

3.2 Scope increase at the representational level

In Hengeveld (1989: 142) I argue that semantic units develop diachronically from lower to higher layers, and not the other way round. This observation provides a more formal characterization of what Traugott (1982: 253) calls a development from 'less personal to more personal' and Bybee (1985: 19) from 'less general to more general'. In terms of the categories discussed above this means that the prediction is that contentive change at the representational level occurs along the following pathway:

(3) Proposition ← Episode ← State-of-Affairs ← Configurational Property ← Property

There are several examples of this development in the literature. A well-known case is that of English *will* (Bybee, Pagliuca and Perkins (1991)). *Will* started out as a lexical verb before becoming an expression of obligation/intention

---

[4] I am grateful to Hella Olbertz for suggesting this to me.

(participant-oriented modality, at the layer of the configurational property), then developed into a posterior marker (relative tense, at the layer of the state-of-affairs), then into a future (absolute tense, at the layer of the episode), and finally acquired suppositional readings (epistemic modality, at the layer of the propositional content). Less well-known is the case of Spanish *capaz*, as described in Grández-Ávila (2010b), that I will describe in some detail here.

Capaz is originally an adjective referring to capacity both in an aptitudinal sense and a spatial sense, as in the following examples from the 15th century:

(4) maestro famoso, sotil e capaz
    master famous keen and skilful
    'a famous master, keen and skilful' (Anónimo, *Danza general de la muerte* [Spain 1430])

(5) otra casa más anchurosa y capaz
    other house more wide and capacious
    'another bigger and more capacious house'
    (Ribadeneira, *Vida de San Ignacio de Loyola* [Spain 1583])

From this lexical use it developed several grammatical uses:

– *Facultative participant-oriented modality.* From 1500 onwards the adjective *capaz* came to express facultative participant-oriented modality (Grández-Ávila 2010: 17). A participant-oriented modality is one that specifies a relation between the potential realization of a state-of-affairs and a participant in that state-of-affairs. This is illustrated in the following example:

(6) Ese hombre es capaz de componer bell-os
    DEM man COP.PRS.3.SG capable of write.INF beautiful-M.PL
    poema-s
    poem(M)-PL
    'That man is capable of writing beautiful poems.'

This type of modality is located at the layer of the configurational property in FDG.

– *Facultative event-oriented modality.* From 1700 onwards *capaz* comes to express another type of facultative modality (Grández-Ávila 2010b: 21), one in which the general enabling conditions of a state-of-affairs are specified, as in:

(7) Solo así, es capaz de form-ar=se una idea de
    only thus COP.PRS.3.SG capable of form-INF=REFL INDF idea of
    lo mucho que ha declin-ado la producción.
    NMLZ much CNJ AUX.PRS.3.SG decline-PST.PTCP DEF production
    'Only in that way, is it possible to form an idea of how much the production has declined.'

This type of modality is located at the layer of the state-of-affairs in FDG.

- *Objective epistemic modality.* From 1800 onwards *capaz* comes to express objective epistemic modality, more specifically, objective epistemic possibility (Grández-Ávila 2010b: 26). In this type of modality a situation is objectively evaluated in terms of its likelihood of occurrence in terms of what is known about the world. This is illustrated in the following example:

(8) Es   capaz   que nadie   vaya   a   su   casa.
    COP.3.SG   capable CNJ nobody   go.SBJV.NONPST.3.SG   to   his house
    'It is possible/likely that nobody visits him.'

This type of modality is located at the layer of the episode in FDG.

- *Subjective epistemic modality.* After 1950 *capaz* acquired a further use, one in which the speaker uses it to express his subjective commitment with respect to the content of his utterance (Grández-Ávila 2010b: 29). This use is illustrated in (14):

(9) Capaz   que   era   un   vago   que   no
    capable   CNJ   COP.PST.IPFV.3.SG   INDF   idler   CNJ   NEG
    quería   hacer   nada.
    want.PST.IPFV.3.SG do.INF   nothing
    'Maybe he was an idler who didn't want to do anything.'

This type of modality is dealt with at the layer of the propositional content in FDG.

Note that the different uses also bring along different formal properties of the constructions in which *capaz* occurs. In the facultative modalities *capaz* is used with the copula and followed by the preposition *de*. In its objective epistemic use it is used with the copula and followed by the conjunction *que*. And in its subjective epistemic use it is followed by the conjunction *que* too, but in this use the copula is absent.

It may thus be concluded that *capaz* developed along the lines predicted in (3), as represented in (10):

(10) Historical development of *capaz* as a modal marker

Proposition	←	Episode	←	State-of-Affairs	←	Configurational Property
Subjective epistemic modality (9)		Objective epistemic modality (8)		Facultative event-oriented modality (7)		Facultative participant-oriented modality (6)

3.3 Scope increase at the interpersonal level

FDG also recognizes an interpersonal level, and it seems attractive to extend the analysis applied in the previous subsection to this level as well. The claim would then be that pragmatic units, too, develop diachronically from lower to higher layers, and not the other way round. In terms of the categories discussed above this means that the prediction is that contentive change at the interpersonal level occurs along the following pathway:

(11) Discourse ← Illocution ← Communicated ← Referential ← Ascriptive
     Act   Content   Subact   Subact

It is much harder to come up with examples of historical evidence for this pathway, as empirical research into the categories that characterize layers at the interpersonal level has not been carried out systematically. Yet there is a phenomenon that can be observed synchronically that seems to support this hypothesized pathway. This concerns the use of *sort of* in English, as described in Hengeveld and Keizer (2011). *Sort of* can be used in three different configurations. The most common use seems to be the one illustrated in (12):

(12) *We're looking for a sort-of manager to book us shows.*[5]

In this use *sort of* directly modifies a lexical element, in this case *manager*, and has the function of indicating that this lexical element only approximately designates what the speaker has in mind. The lexical item *manager* is characterized as not being fully appropriate for what the speaker has in mind. In FDG terms *sort of* is in cases like (12) said to operate at the layer of the ascriptive subact, as it is the appropriateness of the ascription of a property that is at stake here.

This construction may be compared to the following one:

(13) *I think I can more or less understand in general terms what happens up until sort of the impressionist time, maybe just post-impressionist.*[6]

In this example *sort of* precedes the determiner *the*, which is indicative of the fact that in this use it has scope over the entire noun phrase *the impressionist time*, which in this case serves as a measure that is roughly indicative of the end point of the period about which the speaker has some understanding. In FDG *sort of* is,

---

5 http://www.pandahi.com/1016843689.html, consulted 22 April 2015.
6 British National Corpus (BNC).

in such cases, said to operate on the referential subact, as the unit being modified is referential in nature.[7]

A third use of *sort of* is illustrated in (14):

(14) *McCain backtracks on gay adoption, sort of*.[8]

In this example *sort of* modifies the entire preceding utterance, it qualifies this utterance as expressing approximately what the speaker has in mind. In FDG terms, *sort of* modifies the communicated content, the message transmitted by the speaker, in this example.

It does not seem too far-fetched to assume that the use of *sort of* illustrated in (12) is the original one, as it comes closest to the lexical behaviour of *sort of* when directly modifying a noun. From there it could have developed to modify noun phrases as a whole, as in (13), and then would have extended its use to the utterance as a whole, as illustrated in (14). The full hypothesized pathway of the development of the uses of *sort of* may thus be represented as in (15), which covers three of the five interpersonal layers distinguished in (11):[9]

(15) Communicated Content ← Referential Subact ← Ascriptive Subact
     Approximate message   Approximate reference   Approximate ascription

3.4 Scope increase across levels

Hengeveld and Wanders (2007, see also Sweetser 1990: 76ff) state that semantic units may develop diachronically into pragmatic units, and not the other way round. In this case there is vertical scope increase, in the sense that elements from the —lower— representational level develop into elements of the —higher— interpersonal level. This may be represented schematically as in (16):

(16) Interpersonal Level
     ↑
     Representational Level

---

[7] For the general idea that grammaticalization in the noun phrase involves increasing (inter)subjectification see Ghesquière (2014).
[8] http://hotair.com/archives/2008/07/15/mccain-backtracks-on-gay-adoption-sort-of/, consulted 22 April 2015.
[9] There is quite some work on the grammaticalization of *sort of* (e.g. Denison 2005, Brems & Davidse 2010), but these papers do not track the development of the three uses discussed here individually, though Davidse et al. (2013: 57) seem to suggest that the use of *sort of* to modify sentences as a whole is posterior to the other two uses represented in (15).

They also argue that an element does not have to grammaticalize all the way up to the representational level before it can move to the interpersonal level, but can cross over from any intermediate position as well. The vertical development sketched in (16) thus truly interacts with the horizontal developments represented in (3) and (11). The examples they provide concern the use of causal adverbial conjunctions (Hengeveld and Wanders 2007: 221):

(17) *Providing food assistance is not easy* because *the infrastructure is lacking.*

(18) *Watch out*, because *there is a bull in the field!*

In example (17) two pieces of information are causally related: one piece of information (*the infrastructure is lacking*) is used to back up another piece of information (*providing food assistance is not easy*). The relation in (17) can therefore be said to obtain between two propositional contents, mental constructs, that are layers at the representational level.

In (18), on the other hand, two speech acts are causally related: one speech act, the explanation *there is a bull in the field*, is used to motivate another speech act, the warning *watch out*. The fact that we are dealing with two different speech acts is also evident from the fact that the illocutionary values of the two parts are different: the warning takes the form of an imperative, the explanation the form of a declarative. Speech acts are represented in FDG as discourse acts at the interpersonal level.

The prediction, following Hengeveld and Wanders' claim, would then be that (18) is more grammaticalized than (17). And this can indeed be shown to be the case. Consider (19) and (20):

(19) *Providing food assistance is not easy exactly because the infrastructure is lacking.*

(20) **Watch out, exactly because there is a bull in the field!*

Conjunctions that retain (part of) their descriptive use allow modification, a criterion for lexical status that will be presented in Section 4 below. The conjunction *because* allows modification by an adverb of degree in (19), but not in (20). This shows that the occurrence of *because* in (20) displays a higher degree of grammaticalization than the occurrence of *because* in (19), as predicted by (16).

Another example of the same phenomenon is provided by Souza (2009). He studies, among other things, the grammaticalization of *aí* in Brazilian Portuguese, which started out as a locative adverb and acquired many other functions during its history. Originally, these additional functions were all representational in nature, but more recently *aí* has acquired an interpersonal function as well, as illustrated in (21):

(21) um   livro   aí   de   suas   cem   páginas
     INDF.SG.M book   there   of   POSS.3.PL.F hundred pages
     'a book of a hundredish pages'

The function of *aí* illustrated in (21) is an approximative use, like the one illustrated for *sort of* above. By using *aí* the speaker indicates that he/she is not aware of the precise number of pages and that, therefore, the modifier *de suas cem* 'of its hundred' is an approximation. This is captured in FDG through an approximative operator at the layer of the ascriptive subact at the interpersonal level.

3.5 From lexical to grammatical element

Much of the grammaticalization literature (e.g. Lehmann 1982b; Heine 1993; Bybee et al. 1994; Olbertz 1998; Kuteva 2001; Keizer 2007; Krug 2011) focuses on yet another, fourth, pathway of grammaticalization, which involves the fundamental change of a lexical element into a grammatical element. The examples in the previous sections may have suggested that lexical elements turn into grammatical elements only at the lowest possible layers. This is not the case: lexical elements may change into grammatical ones at any point in the hierarchies just presented. This is mainly due to the fact that a common source for grammaticalization is found in complementation constructions, in which the erstwhile complement taking predicate turns into a grammatical element. Now depending on the underlying complexity of the erstwhile complement, the grammatical element will enter the grammatical system at different layers. For instance, a perception verb expressing direct event perception may turn into an operator at the layer of the state-of-affairs, a lexical modal verb expressing an epistemic attitude may turn into an operator at the layer of the propositional content, and a speech act verb may turn in an operator of reportative modality at the layer of the communicated content. A number of concrete examples follow.

Mackenzie (2009) discusses the case of English *fail*. In its lexical use, this verb requires an intentional agent, the one that would like to but does not succeed in reaching a specific goal. This use is illustrated in (22):

(22) *He failed to win the race.*

There is another use, however, in which *fail* does not impose such a restriction. This use is illustrated in (23):

(23) *The bomb failed to explode.*

In this use there is no intentional agent trying to achieve a particular goal. As Mackenzie argues, *fail* is equivalent here to regular negation, as in (24):

(24) *The bomb didn't explode.*

Mackenzie shows that *fail* is a negative operator at the layer of the configurational property. This means that *fail* has entered the grammatical system at that particular layer, rather than at the lowest one, that of the property.

A second example of the process from lexical to grammatical element is that of Spanish *dizque* (Olbertz 2005, 2007; Grández Ávila 2010a). This particle is found in many different varieties of Latin-American Spanish, and derives from the lexical expression *dicen que* 'they say that'. There has thus been a development as sketched in the following examples:

(25) *Dicen   que   Juan   está   enferm-o.*
     say.IND.PRS.3.PL CNJ Juan(M)   COP.IND.PRS.3.SG   ill-M.SG
     'They say that Juan is ill.'

(26) *Dizque   Juan   está   enferm-o.*
     REP   Juan(M)   COP.IND.PRS.3.SG   ill-M.SG
     'Reportedly Juan is ill.'

Note that in this process the construction has changed from a bi-clausal into a mono-clausal one. Reportativity is treated in FDG as an operator at the interpersonal level, more specifically at the layer of the communicated content. The grammatical element here thus enters the system at a hierarchically high level and doesn't pass through any lower steps.

3.6 A model of contentive change

From the combination of all four potential pathways sketched above, the model of contentive change presented in Fig. 2 arises.[10] Figure 2 defines various possible pathways of contentive change, but is at the same time highly restrictive. Lexical items may enter the system at any point, but once this point has been selected they cannot move down to a lower point on the interpersonal or representational scale. Items can move up from the representational level to the interpersonal level at any point, but once they have entered the interpersonal level they cannot move down the interpersonal scale. Note that all examples provided in the previous sections can be translated into contiguous pathways through the combination of clines in Fig. 1.

---

[10] M = move, A = discourse act, C = communicated content, R = referential act, T = ascriptive act, p = propositional content, ep = episode, e = state-of-affairs, f^c = configurational property, f = property, Lex = lexeme.

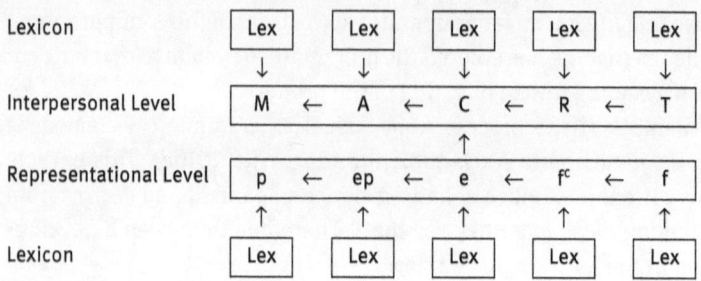

Fig. 2: A model of contentive change.

Figure 2 defines various possible pathways of contentive change, but is at the same time highly restrictive. Lexical items may enter the system at any point, but once this point has been selected they cannot move down to a lower point on the interpersonal or representational scale. Items can move up from the representational level to the interpersonal level at any point, but once they have entered the interpersonal level they cannot move down the interpersonal scale. Note that all examples provided in the previous sections can be translated into contiguous pathways through the combination of clines in Fig. 1.

An interesting illustration of the working of the interacting pathways in Fig. 2 concerns the development of the Spanish auxiliary *haber* (Olbertz 1993, 2012). The development of this auxiliary folllowed different pathways in Peninsular Spanish on the one hand and Ecuadorian Highland Spanish on other.

Haber started out as a lexical verb meaning 'to have/to possess'. It then passed through a number of stages, described one by one in what follows.

– *Resultative*. The first grammaticalized use of *haber* in Spanish is that of a resultative auxiliary, a use it no longer exhibits but that has now been taken over by the verb *tener* 'to hold'. This use of *haber* is illustrated in (27):

(27) vna   muyt   grant   quantidat   de   oro   que   yo
     INDF.F.SG   very   big   quantity(F)   of   gold   that I
     he   prometi-da   a-l   dich-o
     have.1.SG.PRS   promise-PST.PTCP.F   to-DEF.M.SG aforementioned-M.SG
     sacerdote
     priest
   'a very big quantity of gold that I have promised to the priest' (Juan Fernández de Heredia, *Historia troyana* [1376–1396])

This use is aspectual in nature: it describes the current state of the gold in relation to the anterior event of being promised to the priest. Note that the gold is still in the possession of the first person subject, so that there is a link to the original possessive meaning of *haber*. In FDG this use is captured by an operator at the layer of the configurational property, as the operator modifies the internal temporal constituency of a state-of-affairs. We may thus conclude that the lexical verb *haber* entered the grammatical system at the layer of the configurational property. This is shown by means of boldface in Fig. 3.

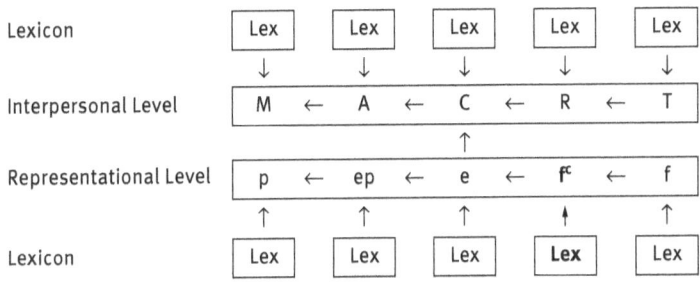

Fig. 3: The grammaticalization of *haber* 1.

- *Anterior*. In the subsequent use of *haber* as an auxiliary it expresses anteriority of an event with respect to another event. It thus expresses a relative temporal value, and can itself be combined with absolute tenses, as illustrated in (28):

(28) *Había   / he   / habré   prepara-do*
     have.PST.1.SG / have.PRS.1.SG / have.FUT.1.SG prepare-PST.PTCP
     una   cena   fenomenal.
     INDF.SG.F   meal(F) terrific
     'I had/have/will have prepared a terrific meal.'

In these examples the combination of *haber* + past participle indicates anteriority with respect to the absolute temporal reference point expressed through the inflection of the auxiliary. Thus in (28) the event of preparing a meal is characterized as having occurred before a past/present/future reference point respectively. In FDG relative temporal distinctions are captured by operators at the layer of the state-of-affairs. Figure 4 shows this further development of *haber*.

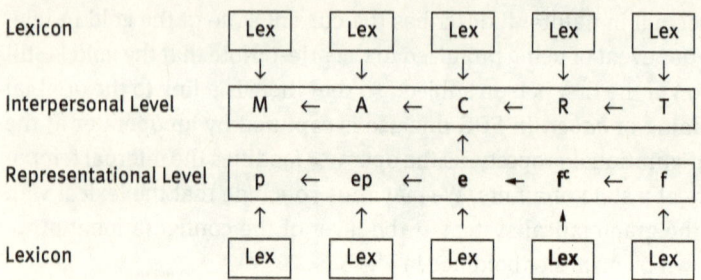

Fig. 4: The grammaticalization of *haber* 2.

- *(Hodiernal/Recent) past.* In Peninsular Spanish, a yet later use of *haber* as an auxiliary is in the expression of absolute hodiernal or recent past tense. This use seems to be present in all dialects of Peninsular Spanish, though the restrictions may be different. Kuteva (2001: 37), citing Schwenter (1994: 93–94), provides the following example from Alicante Spanish:

(29) *Me   he   levanta-do   a   las   siete.*
     1.SG.REFL   AUX.PRS.1.SG   get.up- PST.PTCP at   the   seven
     'I got up at seven o'clock.'

The presence of the absolute temporal modifier *a las siete* here indicates that the sentence has an absolute temporal reference point. In earlier stages of Spanish the auxiliary construction would not be allowed to combine with such a modifier. In FDG absolute temporal distinctions are captured by operators at the layer of the episode. This absolute temporal use is excluded in Ecuadorian Highland Spanish, so Fig. 5 represents the third stage of grammaticalization in Peninsular Spanish only:

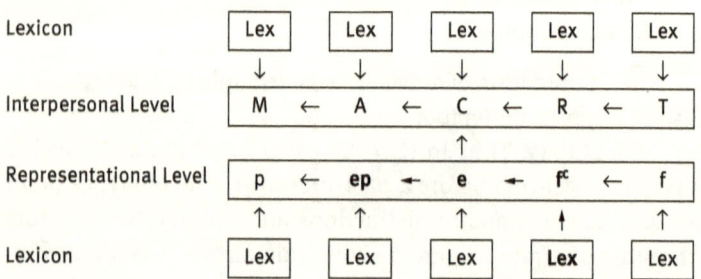

Fig. 5: The grammaticalization of *haber* 3 – Peninsular Spanish.

- *Mirative.* Olbertz (2012) describes yet another use of *haber* in Ecuadorian Highland Spanish, the mirative use, which is illustrated in (30):

(30) Mire,   compr-ó   estos,   los   prob-é ...
     Look   bought-IND.PST.PFV.3.SG   these   them   tried-IND.PST.PFV.1.SG
     y ..   ¡han   sido   peras!
     and   have.IND.PRS.3.PL   COP.PST.PTCP   pears
     'Look, she bought these, I tasted them ... and ... they are pears!'

The construction with *haber* is used in (30) to indicate the surprise the speaker experienced when tasting a fruit that he/she did not suspect to be a pear. The grammatical category expressing surprise is usually called mirativity. In FDG it is located at the layer of the Communicated Content, as this category has to do with the informational status, more specifically the newsworthiness, of the content of a speech act. This mirative use is excluded in Peninsular Spanish, so Fig. 6 represents the third stage of grammaticalization in Ecuadorian Highland Spanish only:

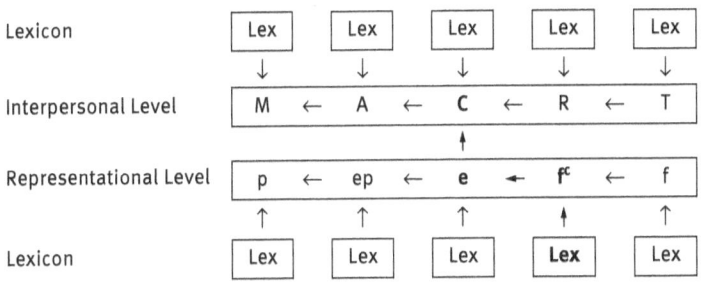

Fig. 6: The grammaticalization of *haber* 3 – Ecuadorian Highland Spanish.

The different developments of the uses of *haber* as an auxiliary in Peninsular and Ecuadorian Highland Spanish thus nicely illustrate the interaction between the different pathways integrated in Fig. 2: while in Peninsular Spanish *haber* in the third stage of its development continued along pathway (3) (scope increase at the representational level), in Ecuadorian Highland Spanish it followed pathway (16) (scope increase across levels), thereby ending up at the interpersonal level.

4 Formal change

It has often been claimed in the literature on grammaticalization that contentive change and formal change go hand in hand. This has been termed the 'parallel path hypothesis' by Siewierska and Bakker (2005) and can be found, for instance, in Traugott (1980: 47), Lehmann (1982a: 239), and Bybee et al. (1994: 21); see also van Rijn (2016) for discussion. The formal changes are then often described in terms of clines such as the one in (31) (cf. Siewierska 2004: 262):

(31) Ø < fusional form < agglutinative affix < clitic < grammatical word < content item

This cline should be read from right to left, and the prediction is that in grammaticalization a content item first changes into a grammatical word, then cliticizes, then agglutinates, then fuses, and finally disappears. The parallel path hypothesis furthermore states that these formal changes are directly related to contentive changes in a one-to-one relationship.

The parallel path hypothesis was challenged in Bisang (2004) and Narrog (2005: 697, 2012: 107–109). The approach defended here is incompatible with the parallel path hypothesis too. First of all, the treatment of pathways of contentive change given above conflicts with the idea of a necessary parallelism between contentive and formal change for an obvious reason: if lexical elements may enter the grammatical system at any layer/level, then there cannot be a one-to-one relation between formal changes and layers/levels. But there is a further reason to not accept clines such as the one in (31), which is that the morphological type of a language severely restricts the possible pathways of formal change. In languages of the isolating morphological type the cline in (31) could never be completed beyond the grammatical word or perhaps the clitic. Yet one would not want to say that there is no grammaticalization in the sense of contentive change in isolating languages, a point made convincingly in Ansaldo and Lim (2004). Similarly, in agglutinating languages the cline in (31) could never be completed beyond the agglutinative affix, and again, this cannot be said to correlate with the lack of a final step of contentive change. In all, (31) suggests that full grammaticalization is only possible in fusional languages.

An alternative approach to formal change takes the functional behaviour of the grammaticalized item into account. Such an alternative is presented in Keizer (2007) who, using the framework of FDG, defines a scale of formal change containing three categories: lexemes, lexical operators, and operators. Lexemes are fully lexical, operators fully grammatical, and lexical operators occupy an intermediate position. Keizer (2007) departs from a long list of partially overlapping characteristics given in the literature on grammaticalization to distinguish between the three categories, but I will take only two here as criterial and distinguishing properties: modification and focalization.

An element that is fully lexical is the head of a phrase and can therefore be modified by other lexical elements. An element that is fully grammatical cannot be focalized as it is 'discursively secondary' (Harder and Boye 2011: 60), in the sense that it expresses secondary information. Now consider the behaviour of the three items *man*, *that*, and *a* in English with respect to their possibilities of being modified and focalized:

(32) lexeme (*man*): modification: an old man
 focalization: (Who did it?) That MAN did it.

(33) lexical operator (*that*): modification: *
 focalization: (Which man?) THAT man

(34) operators (*a*): modification: *
 focalization: *

On the basis of differences in behaviour such as these ones, Keizer (2007) proposes to distinguish the three categories of items in the following way within the FDG framework:

(35) lexeme (man) $(x_i: - man - (x_i): - old - (x_i))$
 'the/an old man'

(36) lexical operator (that) $(\mathbf{that}\ x_i: - man - (x_i))$
 'that man'

(37) operator (a) $(\mathbf{1}\ x_i: - man - (x_i))$
 'a man'

That is, lexical operators are represented like operators in terms of their position, but like lexemes in the fact that they are given in their morphophonemic form rather than in terms of an abstract element.

On the basis of these categories a new cline of formal change may now be defined as in (38):

(38) operators < lexical operators < lexemes

Note that this cline does not make reference to specific form classes, but rather refers to classes with a specific grammatical behaviour. This way it can be applied to languages of all morphological types, without the bias towards fusional languages that is present in clines of formal change such as (31).

5 Contentive and formal change

If the parallel path hypothesis is incorrect, the question is of course if there is a better way to characterize the interplay between pathways of contentive change and those of formal change. In this section I intend to show that there is. The major point to be made is that, as elements move up along a contentive scale, they need not move up along the formal scale; on the other hand, one would not expect an element to move down the formal scale in such circumstances either. In other words, an element that moves up a contentive scale will either move up the formal scale as well or stay where it is at the formal scale. Similarly, as elements move up along the formal scale, they need not move up the contentive scale, though they would not move down that scale either. So an element that moves up the formal scale will either move up the contentive scale as well or stay where it is at the contentive scale. In this way the scales of contentive change and the scale of formal scales may be linked in a relative fashion.

So the important generalizations are that, as elements move up or stay where they are on the contentive scale, they cannot move down the formal scale, and as they move up or stay where they are on the formal scale, they cannot move down the contentive scale. This allows a large number of combinations of contentive and formal change, of which I will illustrate just an expected scenario and two unexpected ones.

In (39) an expected mapping is given between the contentive scale at the representational level and the formal scale. Note that numbers indicate grammaticalization steps of a certain element:

(39) Proposition ← Episode ← State-of-Affairs ← Configurational Property

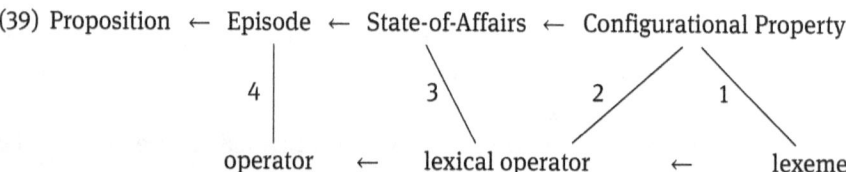

      4   3   2   1

    operator ← lexical operator ← lexeme

In (39) a sitation is depicted in which first a contentive category at the layer of the configurational property, say resultativity, is expressed through lexical means. In the second step the lexeme looses some of its lexical properties and changes into a lexical operator, so it moves up the formal scale. However, it keeps expressing the same resultative meaning, so it does not move up the contentive scale. In the third step the reverse happens: the element under consideration comes to express a contentive category at the layer of the State-of-Affairs, say anteriority, so it moves up the contentive scale. However, anteriority is still expressed through a lexical operator, so it does not move up the formal scale. The fourth step illustrates a parallel change, one in which the element under consideration comes to express a contentive category at the layer of the episode, say past tense, and thus moves up the contentive scale, while at the same time it changes from a lexical operator into an operator, and thus also moves up the formal scale. All the steps given here conform with the generalizations that, as elements move up or stay where they are on the contentive scale, they cannot move down the formal scale, and as they move up or stay where they are on the formal scale, they cannot move down the contentive scale.

In (40) an unexpected mapping is given between the contentive scale at the representational level and the formal scale.

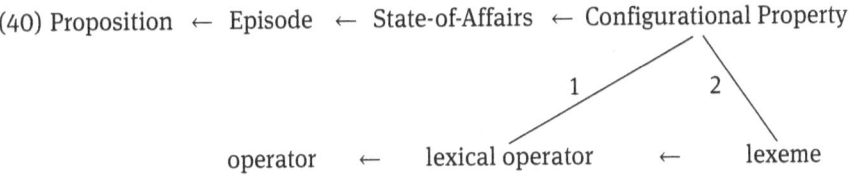

(40) Proposition ← Episode ← State-of-Affairs ← Configurational Property

                                                  1   2

             operator   ←   lexical operator   ←   lexeme

In (40) a sitation is depicted in which first a contentive category at the layer of the configurational property, say intention, is expressed through a lexical operator. In the second step the lexeme gains lexical properties and changes into a lexeme, so it moves down the formal scale. Though it keeps expressing the same intentional meaning, this is a violation of the predicted correlation between contentive and formal change that says that, as elements move up or stay where they are on the contentive scale, they cannot move down the formal scale.

In (41) the reverse happens:

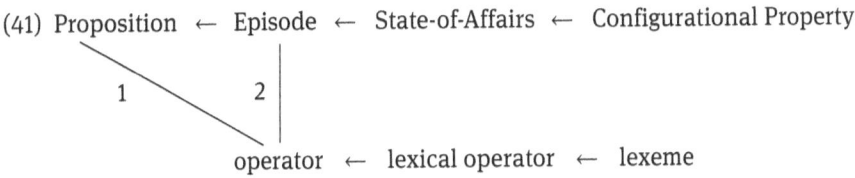

(41) Proposition ← Episode ← State-of-Affairs ← Configurational Property

      1   2

             operator ← lexical operator ← lexeme

In the first step represented in (41) an operator expresses a category at the layer of the proposition, say prediction. In the second step the lexeme comes to express a category at the layer of the episode, say future tense, so it moves down the contentive scale. Though it is still expressed as an operator, this is another violation of the predicted correlation between contentive and formal change that says that, as elements move up or stay where they are on the formal scale, they cannot move down the contentive scale.

Note that various scenarios were illustrated here involving contentive change at the representational level. Using the same principles, similar scenarios could be constructed for contentive change at the interpersonal level and for contentive change across levels.

6 Conclusions

This paper has shown that FDG offers a framework within which known processes of grammaticalization can be captured. Contentive change is predicted, following FDG's hierarchical organization, to be restricted to those processes that lead to scope increase both within and across levels. Formal changes can be captured in a cross-linguistically valid way by adopting Keizer's grammaticalization scale rather than traditional ones. Finally, contentive and formal scales can be linked in a typologically adequate way by assuming a relative rather than absolute relationship between them.

Acknowledgements

I am indebted to Magaly Grández Ávila, J. Lachlan Mackenzie, Heiko Narrog, Hella Olbertz, Marlou van Rijn and Freek van de Velde for comments on earlier versions of this paper. To Magaly Grández Ávila and Hella Olbertz I am furthermore grateful for the help they provided in obtaining the relevant data for this paper.

Uncommon abbreviations

CERT = certainty, CNJ = conjunction, FUT = future, IND = indicative, INGR = ingressive, NONPST = non-past, REM = remote, REP = reportative.

References

Ansaldo, Umberto & Lisa Lim. 2004. Phonetic absence as syntactic prominence. Grammaticalization in isolating tonal languages. In Olga Fischer, Muriel Norde & Harry Perridon (eds.), *Up and down the cline — The nature of grammaticalization*, 345–362. Amsterdam & Philadelphia: John Benjamins.

Bisang, Walter. 2004. Grammaticalization without coevolution of form and meaning: The case of tense-aspect-modality in East and mainland Southeast Asia. In Walter Bisang, Nikolaus P. Himmelmann & Björn Wiemer (eds.), *What makes grammaticalization: A look from its fringes and its components*, 109–138. Berlin & New York: Mouton de Gruyter.

Boland, Annerieke. 2006. *Aspect, tense and modality: Theory, typology, acquisition*. Utrecht: LOT.

Brems, Lieselotte & Kristin Davidse. 2010. The grammaticalization of nominal type noun constructions with kind/sort of: chronology and paths of change. *English Studies* 91(2). 180–202.

Bybee, Joan L. 1985. *Morphology. A study of the relation between meaning and form*. Amsterdam & Philadelphia: John Benjamins.
Bybee, Joan L., William Pagliuca & Revere Perkins. 1991. Back to the future. In Elizabeth C. Traugott & Bernd Heine (eds.), *Approaches to grammaticalization*, Vol. II, 17–58. Amsterdam & Philadelphia: John Benjamins.
Bybee, Joan L., Revere Perkins & William Pagliuca. 1994. *The evolution of grammar: tense, aspect and modality in the language of the world*. Chicago: University of Chicago Press.
Cinque, Guglielmo & Luigi Rizzi. 2010. The cartography of syntactic structures. In Bernd Heine and Heiko Narrog eds, *The Oxford handbook of linguistic analysis*, 51–65. Oxford: Oxford University Press.
Davidse, Kristin, Lieselotte Brems, Peter Willemse, Emeline Doyen, Jessica Kiermeer & Elfi Thoelen. 2013. A comparative study of the grammaticalized uses of English "sort (of)" and French "genre (de)" in teenage forum data. In Emanuele Miola (ed.), *Languages go web. Standard and non-standard languages on the internet*, 41–66. Alessandria: Edizioni dell' Orso.
Denison, David. 2005. The grammaticalisations of *sort of*, *kind of* and *type of* in English. Paper presented at 'New Reflections on Grammaticalization' 3, University of Santiago de Compostela.
Foley, William A. & Robert D. Van Valin jr. 1984. *Functional syntax and universal grammar*. Cambridge: Cambridge University Press.
Ghesquière, Lobke. 2014. *The directionality of (inter)subjectification in the English noun phrase: Pathways of change*. Berlin & New York: De Gruyter Mouton.
Grández Ávila, Magaly. 2010a. Grammaticalization and the issue of scope: The case of *dizque* in Spanish. Paper, University of Amsterdam.
Grández Ávila, Magaly. 2010b. *A functional approach to the subjectification of facultative meaning: The case of* capaz *in American Spanish*. MA thesis, University of Amsterdam.
Harder, Peter & Kasper Boye. 2011. Grammaticalization and functional linguistics. In: Bernd Heine & Heiko Narrog (eds.), *The Oxford handbook of grammaticalization*, 56–68. Oxford: Oxford University Press.
Hattnher, Marize Mattos Dall'Aglio & Kees Hengeveld. 2016. The grammaticalization of modal verbs in Brazilian Portuguese: A synchronic approach. *Journal of Portuguese Linguistics* 15(1). 1–14.
Heine, Bernd. 1993. *Auxiliaries: Cognitive forces and grammaticalization*. New York: Oxford University Press.
Hengeveld, Kees. 1989. Layers and operators in Functional Grammar. *Journal of Linguistics* 25(1). 127–157.
Hengeveld, Kees. 2011. The grammaticalization of tense and aspect. In Bernd Heine & Heiko Narrog (eds.), *The Oxford handbook of grammaticalization*, 580–594. Oxford: Oxford University Press.
Hengeveld, Kees & Marize Mattos Dall'Aglio Hattnher. 2015. Four types of evidentiality in the native languages of Brazil. *Linguistics* 53(3). 479–524.
Hengeveld, Kees & M. Evelien Keizer. 2011. Non-straightforward communication. *Journal of Pragmatics* 43(7). 1962–1976.
Hengeveld, Kees & J. Lachlan Mackenzie. 2008. *Functional Discourse Grammar: A typologically-based theory of language structure*. Oxford: Oxford University Press.
Hengeveld, Kees & Hella Olbertz. 2012. Didn't you know? Mirativity does exist! *Linguistic Typology* 16(3). 487–503.

Hengeveld, Kees & Gerry Wanders. 2007. Adverbial conjunctions in Functional Discourse Grammar. In Mike Hannay & Gerard Steen (eds.), *Structural-functional studies in English grammar: In honor of Lachlan Mackenzie*, 211–227. Amsterdam & Philadelphia: John Benjamins.

Keizer, Evelien. 2007. The lexical-grammatical dichotomy in Functional Discourse Grammar. In Marize Mattos Dall'Aglio Hattnher & Kees Hengeveld (eds.), *Advances in Functional Discourse Grammar*. Special issue of *Alfa – Revista de Lingüística* 51(2). 189–212.

Krug, Manfred. 2011. Auxiliaries and grammaticalization. In Bernd Heine & Heiko Narrog (eds.), *The Oxford handbook of grammaticalization*, 544–555. Oxford: Oxford University Press.

Kuteva, Tania. 2001. *Auxiliation: An inquiry into the nature of grammaticalization*. Oxford: Oxford University Press.

Lehmann, Christian. 1982a. Universal and typological aspects of agreement. In Hansjakob Seiler & Franz Josef Stachowiak (eds.), *Apprehension: Das sprachliche Erfassen von Gegenständen*, vol. 2, 201–267. Tübingen: Gunther Narr.

Lehmann, Christian. 1982b. *Thoughts on grammaticalization: A programmatic sketch*. (Arbeiten des Kölner Universalien-Projekts 48). Köln: Institut für Sprachwissenschaft, Universität zu Köln.

Mackenzie, J. Lachlan. 2009. English *fail to* as a periphrastic negative: an FDG account. *Web Papers in Functional Discourse Grammar* 82. 1–28.

Matthews, George Hubert. 1965. *Hidatsa Syntax*. The Hague: Mouton.

Narrog, Heiko. 2005. Modality, mood, and change of modal meanings – a new perspective. *Cognitive Linguistics* 16(4). 677–731.

Narrog, Heiko. 2009. *Modality in Japanese: The layered structure of the clause and hierarchies of functional categories* (Studies in Language Companion Series 109). Amsterdam & Philadelphia: John Benjamins.

Narrog, Heiko. 2012. *Modality, subjectivity, and semantic change: A cross-linguistic perspective*. Oxford: Oxford University Press.

Olbertz, Hella. 1993. The grammaticalization of Spanish *haber* plus participle. In Jaap van Marle (ed.), *Historical Linguistics 1991: Papers from the 10th International Conference on Historical Linguistics*, 243–263. Amsterdam & Philadelphia: John Benjamins.

Olbertz, Hella. 1998. *Verbal periphrases in a Functional Grammar of Spanish* (Functional Grammar Series 22). Berlin & New York: Mouton de Gruyter.

Olbertz, Hella. 2005. *Dizque* en el español andino ecuatoriano: conservador e innovador. In Hella Olbertz & Pieter Muysken (eds.), *Encuentros y conflictos: Bilingüismo y contacto de lenguas en el mundo andino*, 77–94. Madrid/Frankfurt am Main: Iberoamericana/Vervuert.

Olbertz, Hella. 2007. *Dizque* in Mexican Spanish: the subjectification of reportative meaning. *Rivista di Linguistica / Journal of Italian Linguistics* 19(1). 151–172.

Olbertz, Hella. 2012. The place of exclamatives and miratives in grammar — a Functional Discourse Grammar view. In Maria da Conceição de Paiva & Maria Luiza Braga (eds.), *Análises linguísticas segundo modelos baseados no uso*. Special issue of *Revista Linguística* 8. 76–98 (Rio de Janeiro).

Pollock, Jean-Yves. 1989. Verb movement, universal grammar, and the structure of IP. *Linguistic Inquiry* 20. 365–424.

Rijn, Marlou van. 2016. The grammaticalization of possessive person marking: A typological approach. *Transactions of the Philological Society* 114(2). 233–276.

Schwenter, Scott A. 1994. The grammaticalization of an anterior in progress: Evidence from a peninsular Spanish dialect. *Studies in Language* 18(1). 71–112.

Siewierska, Anna. 2004. *Person*. Cambridge: Cambridge University Press.
Siewierska, Anna & Dik Bakker. 2005. Inclusive and exclusive in free and bound person forms. In Elena Filimonova (ed.), *Clusivity: Typology and case studies of the inclusive–exclusive distinction*, 151–178. Amsterdam & Philadelphia: John Benjamins.
Souza, Edson R. F. 2009. *Gramaticalização dos itens linguísticos* assim, já e aí *no português brasileiro*. PhD Thesis, Universidade de Campinas.
Sweetser, Eve. 1990. *From etymology to pragmatics: Metaphorical and cultural aspects of semantic structure*. Cambridge: Cambridge University Press.
Traugott, Elizabeth Closs. 1980. Meaning-change in the development of grammatical markers. *Language sciences* 2. 44–61.
Traugott, Elisabeth Closs. 1982. From propositional to textual and expressive meanings: Some semantic-pragmatic aspects of grammaticalization. In Winfred P. Lehmann & Yakov Malkiel (eds.), *Perspectives on historical linguistics* (Current issues in linguistic theory 24), 245–271. Amsterdam & Philadelphia: John Benjamins.

Riccardo Giomi
The interaction of components in a Functional Discourse Grammar account of grammaticalization

Abstract: The main goal of this paper is to show how the usage-based nature and pragmatic motivations of grammaticalization can be felicitously accommodated within the framework of Functional Discourse Grammar (Hengeveld and Mackenzie 2008), a typologically-based theory of language structure that conceives the grammar as one component of a wider model of verbal communication, constantly interacting with a Conceptual and a Contextual Component.

Starting from the idea that grammatical meaning diachronically results from the gradual conventionalization of an invited inference (Traugott and Dasher 2002; Heine 2002), the paper suggests that the successive stages into which this process can be broken down differ from each other as to the role played by each component in the selection and interpretation of the grammaticalizing construction. Taken together with Functional Discourse Grammar's capacity to formulate separate clines of grammaticalization for each grammatical level (pragmatics, semantics, morphosyntax, phonology), the proposed model offers a systematic and formalized account of the entire grammaticalization process: from the synchronic inferential mechanisms that trigger it to the ultimate outcomes of the functional and formal evolution of the grammaticalized item. The workings of the model are illustrated through the analysis of concrete cases of grammaticalization, with special focus on TAM markers.

Keywords: grammaticalization, Functional Discourse Grammar, contextual component, grammatical component, invited inferencing, conventionalization

---

Riccardo Giomi: University of Lisbon, Alameda da Universidade, 1600-214, Lisbon, Portugal, CELGA-ILTEC (University of Coimbra), Largo da Porta Férrea, 3004-530, Coimbra, Portugal
giombombo@gmail.com

1 Introduction[1]

One basic assumption of functional linguistics is that a language is first and foremost a social tool and, as such, is shaped in the first place by the ever-changing communicative needs and strategies that arise among the community of its speakers. Accordingly, in the vast functionalist literature on grammaticalization there is a general consensus that the phenomenon is essentially rooted in language usage. In this vein, scholars have often emphasized the role played by cognitive and discourse factors in the rise of new grammatical meanings (e.g. Heine et al. 1991; Bybee et al. 1994; Bybee 2010). In particular, the most pragmatically oriented accounts see the driving force behind grammaticalization in the semanticization of an inference (e.g. Traugott 1988; Traugott and Dasher 2002; Heine 2002). On the other hand, scholars who have addressed grammaticalization from the perspective of the so-called "structural-functional" theories of language,[2] such as Functional (Discourse) Grammar (Dik 1978, 1997a, 1997b; Hengeveld and Mackenzie 2008) and Role and Reference Grammar (Foley and Van Valin 1984; Van Valin and LaPolla 1997; Van Valin 2005), have been mainly concerned with showing how the process reflects the structure of the grammar, as postulated by the respective theories. (See Hengeveld 1989, 2011, this volume, for Functional [Discourse] Grammar, and the papers in Part 1 of Kailuweit et al. 2008 for Role and Reference Grammar.) The main aim of this paper is to develop a comprehensive functional model of grammaticalization, which may be used to describe both the synchronic mechanisms which trigger the process and the ways in which diachronic change reflects the general structure of grammar. I intend to show that the theory of Functional Discourse Grammar (FDG; Hengeveld and Mackenzie 2008) provides a suitable framework for developing such a model, as it conceives the grammar as being one component of a wider theory of verbal interaction which also includes a Conceptual and a Contextual Component. It is in the context of this network of components, I will suggest, that the usage-based nature of grammaticalization can be felicitously accommodated. In order to do so, I will propose that the current FDG approach to grammaticalization be integrated with an explicit account of the emergence and conventionalization of new meanings based on Heine's (2002) model of the contexts of change relevant to grammaticalization.

The paper is organized as follows. The theoretical foundations of FDG are introduced in Section 2 and its approach to grammaticalization presented in

---

[1] I am grateful to the editors of this volume for their inspiring comments and suggestions. I also wish to thank Lachlan Mackenzie for useful discussion on an earlier draft.
[2] This definition is owed to Butler (2003).

Section 3. In Section 4 I develop an extended FDG model of grammaticalization, illustrating its workings with an analysis of the development of proximative aspect markers. Section 5 offers two further applications of the model, with case studies concerning the rise and further development of future tenses. The conclusions of the paper are summarized in Section 6.

2 Functional Discourse Grammar

2.1 Grammar, communicative intentions and context

FDG is a theory of grammar that aims to provide realistic and comprehensive descriptions of linguistic phenomena. Realistic in the sense that FDG "tries to reflect psycholinguistic evidence in its basic architecture", on the assumption that "a model of grammar will be more effective the more its organization resembles language processing in the individual" (Hengeveld and Mackenzie 2008: 1–2). Comprehensive because it does not focus on one particular level of analysis but, as shown in Fig. 1, models the description of natural languages in terms of four hierarchically interrelated grammatical levels. As is evident from this representation, the grammar is conceived as "one component of an overall theory of verbal interaction" (Hengeveld and Mackenzie 2008: 25). This section briefly outlines the mechanisms that ensure the implementation of this model, regulating the interaction between the Grammatical, the Conceptual and the Contextual Components.

Language production is triggered by a communicative intention developed by the Conceptual Component. The Grammatical Component "translates" this non-linguistic input into a full phonological representation, which, in turn, triggers Articulation to produce an acoustically perceivable Output.

The Conceptual Component is "the driving force behind the Grammatical Component" (Hengeveld and Mackenzie 2008: 7). Its tasks are to develop a context-specific communicative goal and an appropriate strategy for pursuing this goal and to organize conceptual material into a pre-linguistic mental representation. Hengeveld and Mackenzie (2008: 11–12, 47–48) illustrate the division of labour between the Conceptual and the Grammatical Components by contrasting direct and indirect speech acts. If a directive illocution is expressed by means of a dedicated imperative marker, the illocutionary value "Imperative" will be inserted at the Interpersonal Level. By contrast, if it is expressed as a question about ability (e.g. *Can you close the window?*), then the fact that this question is being used as a request will not be reflected in the Grammatical Component: the Illocution specified at the Interpersonal Level will be "Interrogative" and a modal

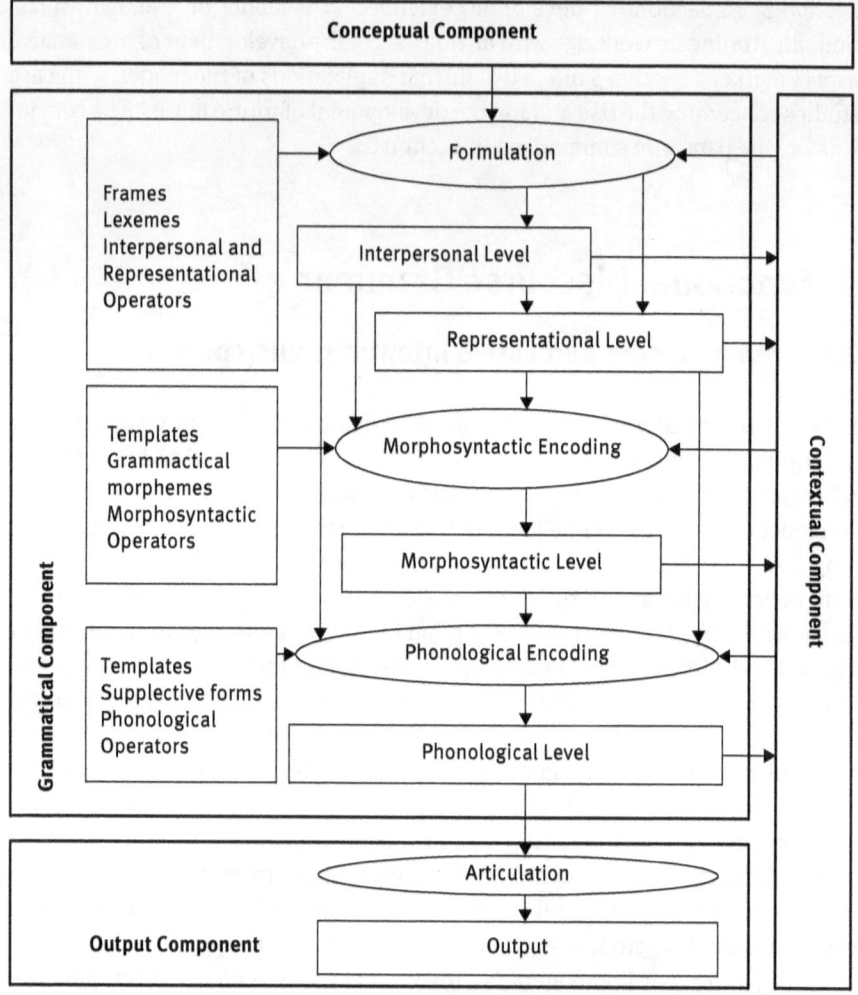

Fig. 1: General layout of FDG (Hengeveld and Mackenzie 2008: 13).

marker of ability will be inserted at the Representational Level. It is a task for the Conceptual Component to select one or the other communicative strategy on the basis of language-external considerations.

The Contextual Component is a storehouse for those aspects of the utterance context that have relevance for some systematic, obligatory grammatical distinction (Hengeveld and Mackenzie 2008: 10, 2014: 205). Since grammatical requirements are by definition language-specific, so is the information contained in the Contextual Component. Consider the Spanish sentence in example (1).

(1) ¡Que   pálid-a   est-ás!
    what   pale-F.SG   COP-IND.PRS.2SG.FAM
    'How pale you look!' (Hengeveld and Mackenzie 2008: 10)

The feminine+singular marking on the predicative adjective *pálida* 'pale' is motivated by the fact that the addressee is a single, female individual and the familiar second person by the informal relationship between the interlocutors. In the presence of these contextual specifications, no other gender, number or social status marker would have been acceptable. By contrast, no corresponding contextual specification is needed for the analysis of English *How pale you look!*, since none of these features is grammatically encoded in the sentence.

Besides storing "Situational Information" of the kind just seen, the Contextual Component is continually updated by the linguistic structures produced at each speech turn. This allows for linguistic phenomena such as anaphora, temporal chaining, "contextual agreement" and the assignment of Topic and Focus (see Hengeveld and Mackenzie 2014: 207–210, 214). In fact, such phenomena can only be explained by assuming that the Grammatical Component of both participants has direct access to the "Discoursal Information" provided by the preceding utterances.

2.2 Levels and layers

Let us now look at the internal organization of the grammatical levels. All levels share "a hierarchically ordered layered organization", where each layer is "restricted by a (possibly complex) head" (Hengeveld and Mackenzie 2008: 14). The head may consist of a (combination of) unit(s) corresponding to a subordinate layer and may be further specified by grammatical operators and lexical modifiers.

Let us briefly illustrate these principles with reference to the Representational Level, which deals with semantic representation. The highest layer of this level is that of Propositional Contents (p), defined as "mental constructs that [...] exist in the minds of those entertaining them". Propositional Contents can be characterized "in terms of propositional attitudes [...] and/or in terms of their source or origin" by means of operators and modifiers expressing subjective modality (epistemic or volitive) and inferential or "generic" (i.e. gnomic) evidentiality (Hengeveld and Mackenzie 2008: 144, 156).

A Propositional Content can contain one or more Episodes (ep). These are combinations of "one or more States-of-Affairs that are thematically coherent" in terms of time, location and participants (Hengeveld and Mackenzie

2008: 157). The specifications relevant at the layer of Episodes are less subjective than those applying to Propositional Contents, but still involve crucial reference to the speaker. They include deictic tense, deductive evidentiality (Hattnher and Hengeveld 2015) and subjective deontic modality (Olbertz and Gasparini Bastos 2013).

States-of-Affairs (e) correspond to real-world entities which "can be said to '(not) occur', '(not) happen', or '(not) be the case'" (Hengeveld and Mackenzie 2008: 166). They can be specified for relative tense, quantificational aspect, location, perception and event-oriented modality. States-of-Affairs can be headed by one or more Configurational Properties (f^c):[3] these are abstract nuclear predications formed by a predicate and its argument(s) and divested of any kind of "situatedness" with respect to the real world or characterization in terms of speaker attitudes. Configurational Properties can be specified for phasal and perspectival aspect and for participant-oriented modality.

Abstracting away from operators and modifiers, the overall structure of the Representational Level is as follows (where 'v' stands for "any semantic category" and 'φ' for "semantic function"):

(2) $(p_1: (ep_1: (e_1: (f^c_1: [(v_1)...(v_{1+n})_\varphi] (f^c_1)) (e_1))(ep_1)) (p_1))$

3 Grammaticalization in FDG

3.1 Directionality and grammatical structure

Probably the most important fact about grammaticalization is that it involves a number of recurrent, patterns of change that affect both the form and the function of linguistic expressions. In recognizing four hierarchically structured levels of description, FDG finds itself in a position to draw testable predictions with respect to the diverse types of change that characterize the phenomenon. In this vein, Keizer (2007: 39) notes that "grammaticalization can be said to involve (potentially at least) changes at each of the four levels."

Within the framework of "traditional" Functional Grammar (Dik 1978, 1997a, 1997b), Hengeveld (1989: 142) suggested that the diachronic evolution of grammatical markers invariably implies widening in semantic or pragmatic scope (see also Olbertz 1993, 1998: 540; Boland 2006: 187–196; cf. Nuyts 2004: 294–295, 2013:

---

3 Sometimes referred to as "situational concept" after Vet (1990: 280) and Cuvalay-Haak (1997).

129–130; Narrog 2012: 100–107).⁴ In FDG terms, this means that, once grammaticalized, an operator (or function) may "climb" up the layers of the Representational or Interpersonal Level, or pass from the former to the latter, but not the other way round (Hengeveld 2011: 583; Hengeveld and Wanders 2007: 224; Souza 2009: 180–181).

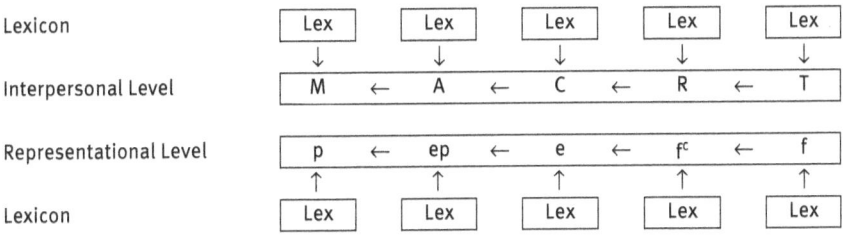

Fig. 2: "A model of contentive change" (Hengeveld, this volume).

Formal change can be described at the Morphosyntactic and Phonological Levels (Keizer 2007: 45–47). For reasons of space, the general structure of these levels will not be presented here. Suffice it to say that, in the long term, grammaticalization can be represented as a downward cline at both levels. Thus, Hopper and Traugott's (2003: 7) famous cline can be quite straightforwardly transposed at the Morphosyntactic Level:

(3) a. Hopper and Traugott:
content item > grammatical word > clitic > inflectional affix
b. FDG:
lexical word or > grammatical word (> affix)⁵
complex lexical expression

---

4 Comparable claims have been formulated in various frameworks, including generative syntax (Tabor and Traugott 1998; Roberts and Roussou 2003; Roberts 2007, 2010; van Gelderen 2004, 2009) and Role and Reference Grammar (Matasović 2008; Kailuweit 2008; Nicolle 2008). The similarities with FDG, however, are especially partial, since, unlike the latter, these theories define scope relations "in positional terms" and not in purely semantic and pragmatic ones (Hengeveld, this volume). The scope-increase hypothesis, in its various formulations, is also largely compatible with the often-noted correlations between grammaticalization, (inter)subjectification and discourse orientation (see Narrog 2012; Boye and Harder 2012; Hengeveld, this volume).
5 The last step is only relevant in fusional and agglutinating languages: the more a language tends toward the purely isolating type, the less likely it is for unbound grammatical formatives to develop into affixes. On the relevance of clitics as a separate stage of grammaticalization, see Keizer (2007: 47).

Similarly, "erosion" (Lehmann 1985: 307) ideally moves down the following scale at the Phonological Level:

(4) phonological phrase > phonological word > (foot >)[6] syllable > phoneme

By mapping directional universals explicitly onto the structure of the four levels, the FDG approach gains a decisive advantage over most functionally oriented theories of grammaticalization: that of showing how language change is not only compatible with general cognitive principles, but directly reflects the same underlying grammatical hierarchy as is observable synchronically across the languages of the world. In this way, it provides precise grammar-internal constraints on possible and impossible patterns of grammaticalization.

However, this is not all that needs to be explained about grammaticalization. A really encompassing model should also include an account of the synchronic processes which trigger the phenomenon and of the mechanisms that lead to the creation of new grammatically encoded meanings. The question, then, is whether these processes and mechanisms can find their place within an FDG theory of grammaticalization.

3.2 The usage-based nature of grammaticalization

In this paper, grammaticalization is regarded as being rooted in the way linguistic expressions are employed in actual discourse practice, that is, at any one moment, in a specific context and with a specific communicative goal in mind. According to this view, grammaticalization is triggered by the conventionalization (or "semanticization") of a pragmatic inference.

Geis and Zwicky (1971: 565–566) are often cited as having been the first to foreshadow that certain pragmatic inferences "can, historically, become part of semantic representation in the strict sense".[7] As for the term "conventionalization", this was inspired by Grice (1975: 58), who incidentally hinted at the possibility that conversational implicatures may "become conventionalized". Accordingly, in the grammaticalization literature, some authors have reserved the term to indicate a

---

[6] While in most stress languages Syllables are systematically grouped into Feet, this layer is never needed for the phonological analysis of tone languages (see Hengeveld and Mackenzie 2008: 452–454).

[7] In the same year, and in a similar vein, Bolinger (1971: 522) claimed that "it is probably a fact that, in the course of time, inferences do become references". In that paper, however, Bolinger investigates a case of lexical change, while Geis and Zwicky explicitly refer to "the association of invited inferences with syntactic form".

diachronic transition between two different kinds of inferences.[8] In this paper, by contrast, "conventionalization" refers to the process whereby a context-specific inferential meaning is reanalyzed as a new grammatically encoded function (cf. Comrie 1985: 26; Dahl 1985: 11). The scenario is, in a nutshell, the following. If the use of a construction to imply a certain, non-literal meaning is found to be particularly successful in specific types of contexts, this meaning can, over time, become firmly associated with the construction in those contexts. It is at this point that, as an effect of frequency, the new form-meaning pairing may acquire the conventional character that is the defining feature of grammatical constructions.[9] If this stage is reached, the new form-meaning pairing will start occurring in new contexts and eventually generalize to a whole variety of contexts (cf. Heine 2003: 587).

In this perspective, it becomes crucial to describe the rise of new constructional meanings in terms of the kinds of contexts associated with each stage of the process. This is the core idea of Heine's (2002) model, which largely inspires the account to be proposed here. As shown in Tab. 1, the new meaning is expressed in each stage through a different communicative strategy.[10]

Tab. 1: "A scenario of how a linguistic expression acquires a new grammatical meaning." (Heine 2002: 86).

Stage	Context	Resulting meaning
I Initial stage	Unconstrained	Source meaning
II Bridging context	There is a specific context giving rise to an inference in favor of a new meaning	Target meaning foregrounded
III Switch context	There is a new context which is incompatible with the source meaning	Source meaning backgrounded
IV Conventionalization	The target meaning no longer needs to be supported by the context that gave rise to it; it may be used in new contexts	Target meaning only

---

8 Such accounts include Traugott (1988) and Traugott and König (1991), who discuss the mechanism by which conversational implicatures turn into conventional ones, as well as Traugott and Dasher (2002: 38), who speak of the "conventionalizing of IINs [invited inferences] as GIINs [generalized invited inferences]" (see Section 4.1).
9 The role of frequency is emphasized in particular by Bybee (1998: 266–267, 2003, 2006: 725, 2010: 107–110).
10 Note that Heine's use of the term "conventionalization" is more restricted than the sense I have described above. As will become evident in Section 4.2, in my approach the conventionalization of new meanings starts out in the "switch context" stage, whereas Heine's Stage IV represents the full completion of this process.

The contextual-pragmatic processes triggering grammaticalization have, to my knowledge, not been the object of any FDG study so far. This should not come as a surprise: FDG is first and foremost a theory of grammar and, accordingly, its accounts of grammaticalization have been mainly concerned with describing diachronic change in terms of underlying grammatical structure. At the same time, however, a distinctive characteristic of the theory is its fundamental concern with psychological and pragmatic adequacy. In keeping with this concern, the grammar is encapsulated within a wider model of verbal interaction, which explicitly recognizes a Conceptual and a Contextual Component. The claim put forth in the remainder of this paper is that this multi-component model offers a suitable basis for accommodating the pragmatic motivations of grammaticalization, precisely because the emergence and conventionalization of new meanings is a process that takes place at the interfaces between context, cognition and grammar.

4 An extended FDG model of grammaticalization

In what follows, I propose what may be regarded as an "FDG version" of Heine's (2002) model of grammaticalization. In Section 4.1 I argue that FDG would have much to gain from a principled extension of the tasks and purport of the Contextual Component. On the one hand, this move would improve our understanding of the interaction between the Contextual and the Grammatical Components. On the other, it allows for a systematic treatment of the specific type of pragmatic inferences that arise in what Heine refers to as "bridging contexts". In Section 4.2, the last two stages of Heine's model are also formalized in FDG terms and the semanticization of inferential meanings is described as a passage from the Contextual to the Grammatical Component.

4.1 Bridging contexts and the role of the Contextual Component in a dynamic FDG

The FDG account of grammaticalization presented in this section rests on the idea that the successive stages summarized in Tab. 1 differ from each other with respect to the role that is played by each component in the selection and interpretation of the construction. However, as should be clear from the brief outline given in Section 1, FDG is not currently set up to deal with contextual-pragmatic mechanisms such as those that may trigger grammaticalization. This is because inferences are by definition a matter of language use, while FDG is solely concerned with language as a system. As stated explicitly by Hengeveld and Mackenzie (2014: 204), the Contextual and Conceptual Components "are ancillary to the Grammatical Component", their sole purport being to ensure the smooth functioning of the grammar (cf. Cornish 2013: 85). Clearly, an explicit account of incipient grammaticalization is only possible if the interaction of components is reinterpreted in a somewhat broader fashion. In particular, this requires (i) that the Contextual Component be reframed as an "implicit common ground", which is jointly constructed by the speech participants as the exchange unfolds (Mackenzie 2012: 427), and (ii) that, besides storing grammatically relevant information, this component also functions as a dynamic interface between the linguistic system and a general, epistemological model of human reasoning.[11]

Proposals for a more dynamic Contextual Component have been advanced, among others, by Connolly (2007, 2014) and Mackenzie (2012, 2014). The latter elaborates on the idea of a "public" component, emphasizing that "participation in a dialogue entails an overlap of minds" (Mackenzie 2014: 253) and involves "creating a common ground through which to interact" (Mackenzie 2012: 431). Connolly's "contextual super-component" includes what he terms the "broader" context, i.e. "the physical and social universe outside of the immediate context" and any conversation-relevant information that may be supplied "by some other discourse or discourses" (Connolly 2007: 15–16). Furthermore, it is responsible for a variety of processes ranging from the very choice of an appropriate dialect or sociolect (Connolly 2014: 241) to the drawing of inferences such as the following:

(5) *I'm going to get my own back on him.*
    →
    '*The man has hurt the speaker in some way.*' (adapted from Connolly 2007: 28)

The position taken in this paper shares aspects of the approaches of both Connolly and Mackenzie. The Contextual Component is regarded as a co-constructed mental space, whose interaction with the grammar is limited to providing "a dynamic support for grammatical processes" (Mackenzie 2012: 428). However, there are cases in which information which, strictly speaking, does not belong to the immediate utterance context also needs to be incorporated into the Contextual Component and I support the idea that *some specific kinds* of inferences should be represented within the model.

---

[11] It is of course not a task for the linguist to elaborate such a model in any detail, for this is not inherently linguistic in nature.

Consider for instance (6):

(6) *Sorry about yesterday. That was silly.*

The identification of the referent of *that* is a probabilistic inferential process which takes as input (i) the inherent semantics of the pronoun and of the adjective *silly*, (ii) the contextual record of the previous utterance and (iii) the shared memories activated by that utterance. The output is of course a mental representation of the inferred referent. It may be argued that the Grammatical Component is not affected by this process and that the nature of the referent does not need to be specified in underlying representation. This, however, would make it impossible to account for such modifications as:

(7) a. *Yes, it was silly of you (to react like that).*
    b. *Yes, reacting like that was silly of you.*

Such structures, in fact, are only available with certain types of referents (see Hengeveld and Mackenzie 2008: 209). If, for instance, the referent of *that* in (6) had been understood as being a concrete entity, the utterer of (7a) or (7b) could not have used the same structure (cf. **Yes, that present was silly of you*). In other words, the class of entities to which the referent belongs constrains the grammatical options available to the speaker. The nature of the referent (a State-of-Affairs) must therefore be reflected in the semantic representation. This means that (the output of) the inferential process described above, though non-linguistic in nature, must be incorporated into the Contextual Component to become accessible to Formulation, so that the appropriate variable can be inserted at the Representational Level.

This example shows that a dynamic interface with the general inferential system and an explicit modelling of the output of certain inferential processes are unavoidable for an effective implementation of the Grammatical Component. I would now like to go one step further and suggest that the specific type of inference involved in Heine's (2002) "bridging contexts" should also be represented within the Contextual Component, where the new meaning is derived as a function of the inherent meaning of the construction and the relevant shared information. This information may be context-situational, co-textual and/or encyclopaedic in nature: at any rate, by virtue of the fact that it is implicitly called upon by the speaker and must necessarily be computed by the addressee in deriving the "target" meaning, this information must also be modelled within the co-constructed Contextual Component.

Let us illustrate this by way of example. One of the case studies proposed by Heine concerns the grammaticalization of Swahili *-taka* ('want') into a "proximative aspect" marker.[12] The process starts out in bridging contexts such as (9), where "a human subject referent cannot really be assumed to 'want' what is described by the relevant predication":

(8) *a-na-taka*   *ku-ni-ita*
    3SG-PRS-want   INF-1SG-call
    'he wants to call me'

(9) *A-na-taka*   *ku-fa*
    3SG-PRS-want   INF-die
    (i) 'he wants to die',
    (ii) 'he is about to die'
    (Heine 2002: 90, my glosses)

While in (8) *-taka* + infinitive can only express the "source" lexical meaning, in (9) a literal interpretation is, in most contexts, highly unlikely. An alternative, more contextually relevant meaning is thus foregrounded by means of an inference and the construction is reinterpreted as an expression of proximative aspect. However, being inferential in nature, this meaning is by definition defeasible, while "an interpretation in terms of the source meaning cannot be ruled out" on semantic grounds (Heine 2002: 84). This means that, in this stage, the source meaning is still part of "what is said" by the construction. It follows that *-taka* must be characterized as a lexical verb of volition in underlying representation. All the same, it is not the volitional meaning, but the implied meaning 'be about to, be on the point of' that represents the actual contribution of the construction to the shared common ground. The latter meaning must therefore be captured in the Contextual Component. This analysis is represented in Fig. 3.[13]

At the Representational Level, the nuclear predication (i.e. the Configurational Property) consists of a predicate and its two arguments. The Lexical

---

[12] Proximative aspect differs from immediate future in that it "indicates a moment shortly before the *possible* occurrence of the given verbal situation" (Kuteva 2009: 19, emphasis added). That is, by using a proximative marker the speaker does not commit him/herself to the actual being the case of the State-of-Affairs: what is at issue is "the aspectual notion of [...] *being on the point of V-ing* rather than temporal deixis" Kuteva (2001: 94).

[13] Recall that, in the FDG formalism, 'f^c' stands for Configurational Property and 'e' stands for State-of-Affairs. Further elements introduced in the Figure are 'f' for "Lexical Property" and 'x' for "Individual" (see Hengeveld and Mackenzie 2008: 215, 236). For ease of reading, only the level and layers relevant to the reinterpretation process are represented.

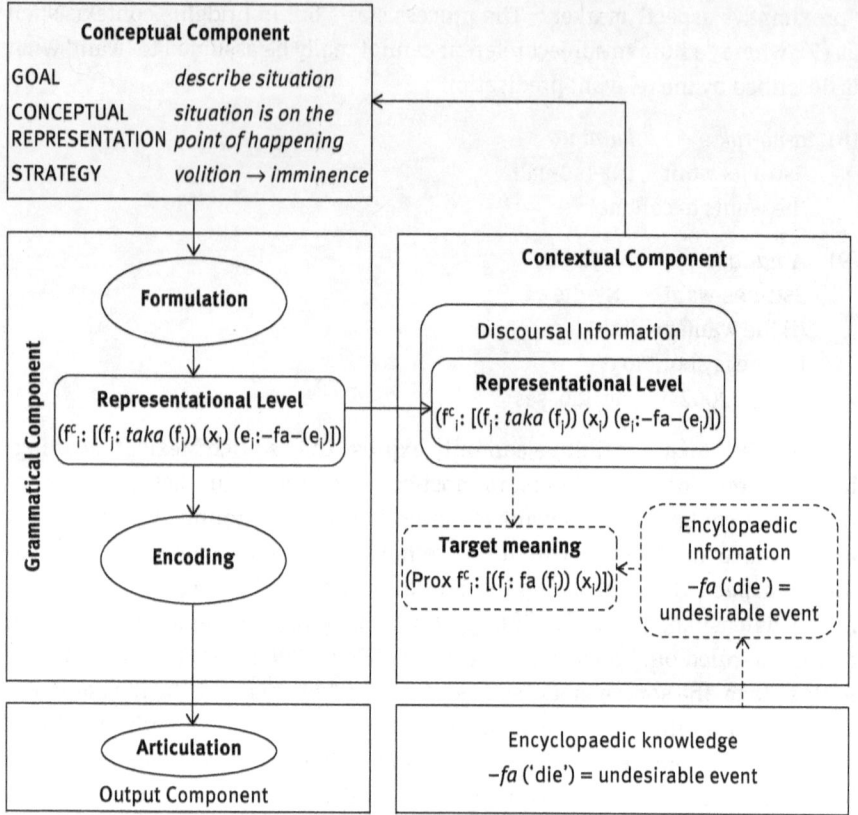

Fig. 3: Bridging contexts in FDG. The reinterpretation of Swahili *-taka* in *Anataka kufa* ('He *wants* to die' → 'He *is about to* die').

Property *-taka* ('want') functions as the predicate and takes as its arguments an Individual (corresponding to the grammatical subject of the clause) and an embedded State-of-Affairs (*-fa*, 'die'). As soon as the utterance is produced, this semantic representation is incorporated as such into the Contextual Component (see Section 2.1). Here, the lexical meaning of *-taka* comes to interact with the shared assumptions associated with the verb *-fa*, 'die'; the clash between these assumptions and the volitional meaning of *-taka* makes the latter highly unlikely, so that a "context-induced reinterpretation" (Heine 2002: 84–86) is activated that foregrounds a more contextually relevant interpretation of the construction.[14] In

---

[14] This clash may of course be overridden by specific factors in particular contexts, which results in the "blocking" of the inference.

this derived, context-dependent interpretation (the target meaning), -fa functions as a one-place predicate with (x) as its argument, while -taka is reanalyzed as expressing "the aspectual notion of *being on the point of V-ing*".[15]

As shown in Fig. 3, the lexical verb -taka is inserted in fulfilment of a, so to speak, indirect communicative strategy. In selecting this strategy, the Conceptual Component must calculate the relevant shared information (as symbolized by the arrow coming in from the Contextual Component). In addition, it must "know" that *volition → imminence* is a highly generalized implicature in Swahili, which will allow the addressee to easily derive the implied meaning. In this sense, inferences occurring in bridging contexts may be understood as "generalized invited inferences", as defined by Traugott and Dasher (2002: 16–17):

> [Generalized invited inferences] are preferred meanings, and conventions of use in language-specific communities, but may be canceled. They are crystallized invited inferences associated with certain lexemes or constructions that are specific to a linguistic community, and can be exploited to imply/insinuate certain meanings.

Let us compare this specific type of communicative strategy with inferences of a considerably different nature, such as particularized conversational implicatures[16] and relatively context-independent inferences of the type exemplified in (5). While these may operate upon the whole content of a sentence, yielding entirely new propositions, generalized invited inferences are associated with one specific word or construction and only affect the meaning of that particular word or construction. This is a *conditio sine qua non* for the semanticization of an inference; therefore, only inferences of this kind should be accounted for in a model of grammaticalization. Moreover, particularized implicatures are language-independent and arise in highly specific, unsystematic context-*tokens*. In contrast, bridging contexts are language-specific and represent context-*types* definable in terms of precise necessary conditions. In Swahili, for instance, the reinterpretation of -taka requires the contextual assumption that the situation described is undesirable for the participant involved (either in general, as in (9), or for more context-specific reasons); but this does not mean that, given this assumption,

---

15 Importantly, the choice to represent the target meaning with the same formalism as used for grammatical representations is dictated by notational convenience and is not intended to suggest that encoded and inferred meaning are in any way similar in nature.
16 Grice (1975: 56) defines particularized conversational implicatures as implicatures that are carried "by saying that *p* on a particular occasion in virtue of special features of the context". With particularized implicatures, "there is no room for the the idea that an implicature of this sort is NORMALLY carried out by saying that *p*" (emphasis in the original).

volitional verbs will be reinterpreted as proximatives in all languages. Thirdly, particularized implicatures and unbound inferences like (5) necessarily involve a certain amount of conscious reasoning; in bridging contexts, however, the target meaning is derived in a much more systematic and automatic fashion, precisely because its association with a specific construction has become crystallized in the context-type at stake. From this point of view, generalized inferences arising in bridging contexts have less in common with the other kinds of inferences considered above than with such phenomena as (e.g.) gender, number and social status marking, anaphorical reference, temporal chaining or Topic and Focus assignment (see Section 2.1). Unlike the latter, the inferential processes at play in bridging contexts do not have a direct influence on the Grammatical Component (at least from the synchronic point of view); however, it is a fact that they share the same automatic, unconscious and language-specific character as the processes taking place at the interface between context and grammar and within the grammatical core itself. In my view, these similarities make it not only possible but very desirable to have these highly routinized, language-specific inferential patterns explicitly modelled in a dynamic Contextual Component.

4.2 From inferential to grammatical meaning

The turning point in the grammaticalization of new meanings is represented by "switch" contexts. It is at this stage that a former generalized inference becomes inalienably attached to the construction, and as such can no longer be cancelled. At the same time, the source meaning is "incompatible, or in conflict" with the context-type concerned and does not provide an available interpretation in that specific cluster of contexts (Heine 2002: 85). The only possible interpretation is now one in terms of the new meaning. This meaning must thus be reflected in underlying representation as a semantic or interpersonal operator (or function).

However, meanings occurring in switch contexts have not yet achieved a sufficient degree of context generalization (see Heine and Kuteva 2002: 2) to be considered *fully* conventional. In this sense, they can be characterized as "protogrammatical": they are inherent to the construction, but still need to be supported by a specific type of linguistic and/or situational context. It is this context that enables the use of the construction with its new grammatical meaning, while ruling out any interpretation in terms of the older meaning. In the grammaticalization of the Swahili proximative, this stage is characterized by contexts "where instead of a human referent there is an inanimate referent" (Heine 2002: 90), which obviously excludes a volitional interpretation leaving only the proximative sense available:

(10) *M-ti   u-na-taka   ku-anguka*
     CLF-tree   CLF-PRS-PROX   INF-fall
     'the tree is about to fall'
     (Heine 2002: 90; my glosses)

As in the bridging-context stage, it is an element of long-term knowledge (the inanimacy of the subject referent) that provides the necessary condition for a proximative interpretation of *-taka*. The crucial difference is that, having grammaticalized into a new representational operator, the proximative function of *-taka* does no longer emerge in the Contextual Component as the result of an "indirect" communicative strategy. Rather, in switch contexts such as (10), a Proximative operator is selected by Formulation in response to the immediate communicative intention to present the event as an imminent one. This is thus not a pre-linguistic choice but a grammatical one. It follows that the factors relevant to the selection of the operator are not computed in the Conceptual Component but directly impact the grammatical operation of Formulation, as shown in Fig. 4.[17]

Finally, full conventionalization is achieved when the construction starts occurring with the new meaning in a variety of new contexts (Heine 2002: 85), including contexts that used to be prototypically associated with the source meaning. The grammaticalization of proximative *-taka* is not complete in Swahili, since with human subjects a volitional interpretation can never be excluded (Heine 2002: 90–91). This, however, is possible in other languages in which a lexical verb of volition has undergone the same development. Consider for instance (11), from Tok Pisin, where "in spite of the fact that [there is] a human subject, a volitional meaning appears to be ruled out" (Heine 1994: 38–39):

(11) *Tif   wan   tek   wi   moni*
     thief want   take   our   money
     'A thief is/was about to take our money.'
     (Heine 1994: 39)

---

[17] Note that, although encyclopaedic in nature, the information concerning the (in)animacy of the referent is recorded in the immediate context as language-specific Situational Information. This is because (in)animacy is systematically relevant to the Swahili grammar for the selection of noun class markers (Contini-Morava 1996: 258; Hengeveld and Mackenzie 2008: 395). Therefore, for Swahili, this information must be assumed to belong by default in the Contextual Component, where it is stored as grammatically relevant Situational Information (see Section 2.1).

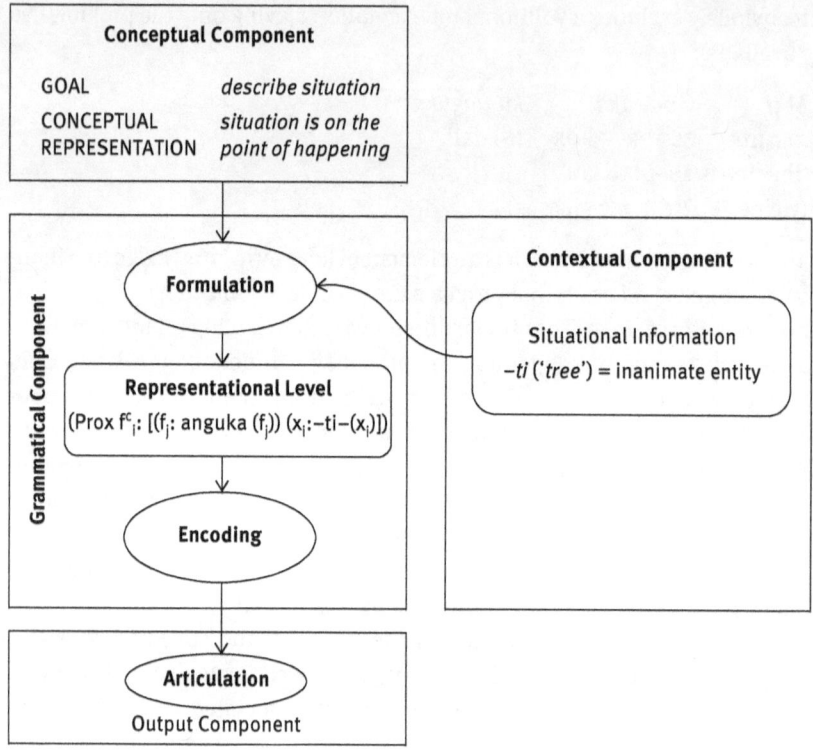

Fig. 4: Switch contexts in FDG. Use of *-taka* in *Mti unataka kuanguka* ('The tree is about to fall').

Other fully conventionalized "de-volitive" proximative markers are Chamus *-yyeu*, Tswana *-batla* (Heine 2002: 95) and Zulu *-cishe* (Kuteva 2009: 20–21). All these morphemes are free from the constraints characteristic of the switch-context stage. In FDG terms, this means that Formulation can insert a Proximative operator without needing to compute any additional linguistic or contextual information (see Fig. 5). The process is now an entirely top-down, grammar-internal one, and as such can be handled without invoking a broader conception of the interaction between components than is commonly assumed in FDG.

In illustrating the model, it has been shown how it can be used to assess the extent to which similar grammaticalization processes have advanced in different languages. In the next section, I will present two case studies on the grammaticalization of future tense markers, this time from an intra-linguistic perspective. Section 5.1 deals with the emergence of the temporal meaning of English *shall* + verb (< *sculan* + infinitive), supporting the analysis with diachronic data from Old and Middle English; Section 5.2 presents an account of the steps through which future tenses may acquire epistemic functions, illustrating this process with examples from Modern Greek.

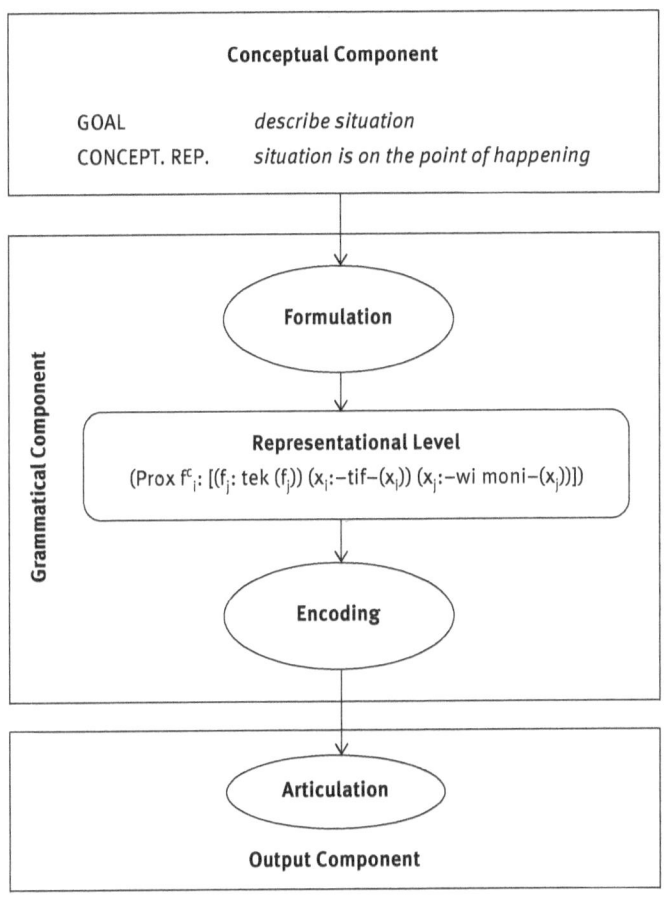

Fig. 5: Fully conventional meaning in FDG. Tok Pisin *wan* as a Proximative operator in *Tif wan tek wi moni* ('A thief is/was about to take our money').

5 Applying the model

5.1 Diachrony

5.1.1 Bridging contexts

As is well known, Old English *sculan* ('owe') first grammaticalized into a modal marker of deontic necessity, and only later acquired purely temporal meanings. Thus, to reconstruct the emergence of the future meaning in bridging contexts, one should look for early occurrences which, in principle, could admit both a modal and temporal interpretation, but where the latter is contextually more appropriate.

According to Traugott (1992: 196–197), "[o]ne of the conditions for the extension of the *scul-* of obligation to prediction" may have been, since Old English, its use in contexts such as the following (an exhortation directed by the Spartan commander Leonidas to his troupes before the final clash of the famous battle of Thermopylae against the Persians). As a matter of fact, despite the proposed translation, the second occurrence of *sculon* can hardly be interpreted as a prototypical deontic marker:[18]

(12) *Uton   nu   brucan   þisses   undernmetes   swa*
     HORT   now   enjoy.INF this.GEN   breakfast.GEN   as
    þa   sculon   þe   hiora   æfengifl   on   helle
    those   must.3PL REL   their   dinner   PREP   hell.DATINSTR
    gefeccean   sculon
    get.INF   must.3PL
'Let us now enjoy this breakfast as befits those who must eat their supper in hell.'
(*Orosius*, tenth century, cited in Traugott 1992: 196; my glosses.)

The sense of "predestination" suggested by this kind of context has sometimes been regarded as a distinct semantic domain through which constructions with certain types of lexical source may come to develop a future tense function (Benveniste 1968: 91; Bybee et al. 1994: 262–263; for OE *sculan*, see Visser 1969: 1581–1582). Predestination uses are indeed cross-linguistically common for modal markers of necessity, independently of whether they have also developed purely temporal meanings or not. However, I am not aware of any construction with predestination uses which cannot also express deontic and/or facultative necessity. This suggests that predestination should not be regarded as a separate semantic domain, but rather as a context-specific reading of constructions with a basic meaning of necessity. Now, participant-oriented deontic necessity (i.e. obligation, see Hengeveld and Mackenzie 2008: 213) was the prime function of *sculan* in Old English (Quirk and Wrenn 1957 [1955]: 78; Lester 1987: 97–99) and remained very frequent throughout Middle English, alongside the more recent temporal and volitional meanings (Gotti 2002: 203; Dossena 2002: 243). Against this background, if it seems rather unlikely that predestination ever represented a separate grammatical function of *sculan*, Traugott may well be right in suggesting that contexts of the type shown in (12) were involved in the emergence of the future meaning of the construction. In such contexts, in fact, the "predestination" reading of *sculan* comes closer to a "neutral" meaning of prediction than to the grammatical meaning of deontic necessity.

---

18 By contrast, the first occurrence of the construction only allows for a modal interpretation.

Another kind of context which could invite a reinterpretation of *sculan* is exemplified by (13), from Middle English. Note that, in this case, an external authority imposing the realization of the State-of-Affairs is mentioned in the preceding discourse, but is no longer on the stage after the change of scene marked by *and there*:

(13) *þe Kyng wille þat þow bene honged & drawe, [...] and þi bowelles brent, and þi body quarterede, and þin heuede smyten of, and sent vnto London;*

and	þere	hit	shal	be	sette	oppon	London	Brigge;
and	there	it	must.PRS	be	set.PTCP	upon	London	bridge
and	þi	iiij	quarters	shal	be	sent	to	iiij
and	your	four	quarters	must.PRS	be	send.PTCP	to	four
tounes	of	Engeland,						
towns	of	England						

þat alle oþere mowe be-ware and chastisede by þe.

'The king ordains that you be hanged and drawn and that your bowels be burned and your body quartered, and that your head be cut off and sent to London. And there it *shall* be impaled on London Bridge. And the four parts of your body *shall* be sent to four towns of England, so that all other men can be warned and chastised by them.'

(*Brut*, 14th-15th century, cited in Gotti 2002: 213; my glosses and translation)

After the semi-colon, a new Episode is introduced which is set in a different location than the preceding one. A modal interpretation of *shal* is of course not impossible but, with this resetting, it seems much more appropriate to interpret the construction as specifying the time of the new Episode – which, crucially, is also different from that of the preceding one – rather than as insisting on the obligatoriness of the action. All the same, that we are still dealing with a contextually determined interpretation of an inherently deontic marker is evident from contexts such as (14), which provides a nice, authentic example of cancellation of the implicature:

(14)
&	Thomas,	as	a	traitoure	ʒe	shull	be
and	Thomas	as	a	traitor	you.NOM.POL	must.PRS	be
hongede	by	resoun,	but	þe	Kyng	haþ	forʒeue
hang.PTCP	by	reason	but	the	king	has	forgive.PTCP
ʒow		þat	gewys	for	þe	loue	of	Quene	Isabell.
you.DAT.POL	DEM	indeed	for	the	love	of	queen	Elizabeth

'And, sir Thomas, as a traitor you *should* by rights be hanged; but, by my faith, the king has spared you that for the love of Queen Elizabeth.'

(*Brut*, cited in Gotti 2002: 214; my glosses and translation.)

By uttering *but þe Kyng haþ forȝeue ȝow þat (...)*, the speaker is announcing that the accused has been spared the punishment normally reserved to traitors, i.e. that he will *not* be hanged. (In fact, the punishment has been commuted from hanging to beheading.) By doing so, the speaker explicitly denies the inference obligation → prediction, which, otherwise, could easily be yielded by the use of *sculan* in the present tense.

With respect to the extended FDG model illustrated above, this stage of the evolution of *sculan* can be represented as in Fig. 6. The grammatical meaning of the construction is still participant-oriented deontic necessity, but, in contexts in which there is no concrete authority to impose an obligation on the target-participant (12), or this authority is somehow backgrounded (13), a temporal interpretation emerges as being more contextually relevant.

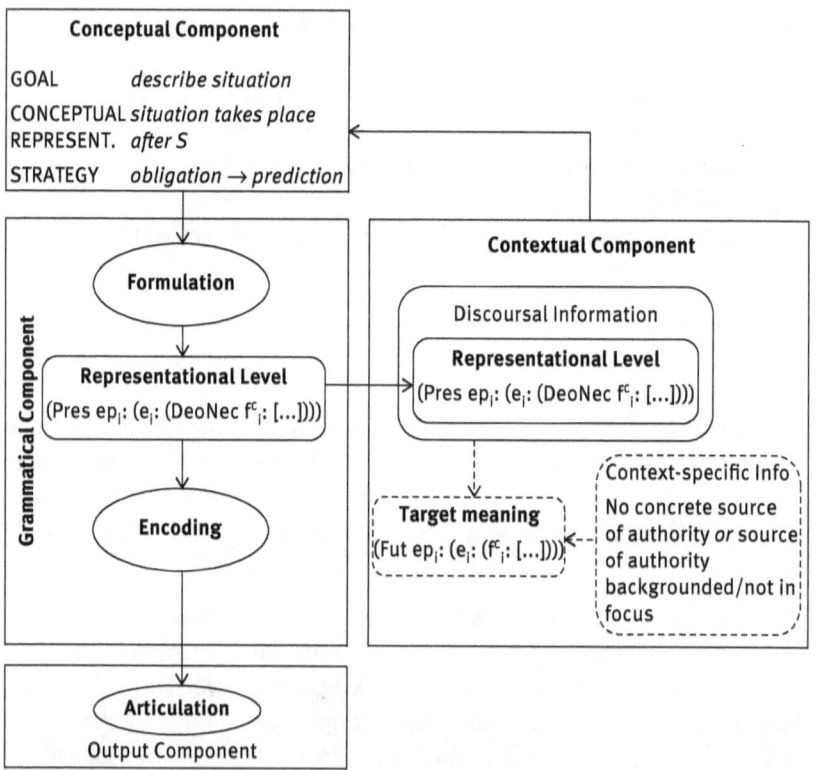

Fig. 6: A bridging context for the reinterpretation of present *sculan* in Old/Middle English.[19]

---

[19] In the Conceptual Component, 'S' stands for "time of speech".

5.1.2 Switch contexts

In Middle English, the construction begins to occur with some frequency in contexts which only admit a temporal interpretation. An extremely clear example is the following, with a past tense auxiliary:[20]

(15) Whanne   this   hadde   herd,   that   Jhesu   schulde   come   fro
     when   this   had   heard   that   Jesus   REP.PST   come   from
     Judee   into   Galilee,   he wente   to   hym,   and   preiede   hym,
     Judea   to   Galilee   he went   to   him   and   begged   him
     that   he   schulde   come   doun,   and   heele   his   sone [...].[21]
     that   he   PST.POST   come   down   and   heel   his   son
     'When this man heard that Jesus had come from Judea to Galilee, he went to him and asked him *to come down and heal* his son [...].'
     (*The Wycliffe Bible*, John 4:47, late 14th century, cited in Dossena 2002: 252; my glosses. Present-day English translation from the *English Standard Version Bible*.)

In this context, it is impossible to cancel the temporal interpretation by foregrounding a modal meaning of necessity, for the latter is logically incompatible with the complement of a verb like Middle English *preien* ('ask, request, implore'). This means that the temporal meaning is no longer derived inferentially: instead, there is a specific contextual setting – the impossibility of identifying an authority or circumstance capable of imposing the State-of-Affairs – which licenses the use of the construction as a grammatical expression of location in time. In the model proposed, the relevant contextual information is computed by Formulation, enabling it to select the appropriate tense operator at the Representational Level. In the case of (15), the construction is analysed as an absolute-relative tense marker, resulting from the combination of an absolute operator Past at the Episode layer and a relative operator Posterior at the State-of-Affairs layer. This analysis yields the representation in Fig. 7.

---

[20] This is not at all a problem for the account proposed here, since the emergence of the temporal function of *schulde* proceeded in parallel with that of *schal* (although with some delay). In both cases, the modal meaning gradually bleaches out in more and more contexts, giving way to a purely temporal meaning in accordance with the schema *present obligation>prediction* (i.e. future); *past obligation>future-in-the-past*. The same types of bridging and switch contexts must therefore be looked at in reconstructing this specific semantic transition.

[21] Notice the reportative use of *schulde* in the first occurrence. This meaning, which is also documented by Traugott (1989: 41–42), represents an independent development of deontic *sculan* (in the past tense only) and is not involved in the rise of the temporal meaning.

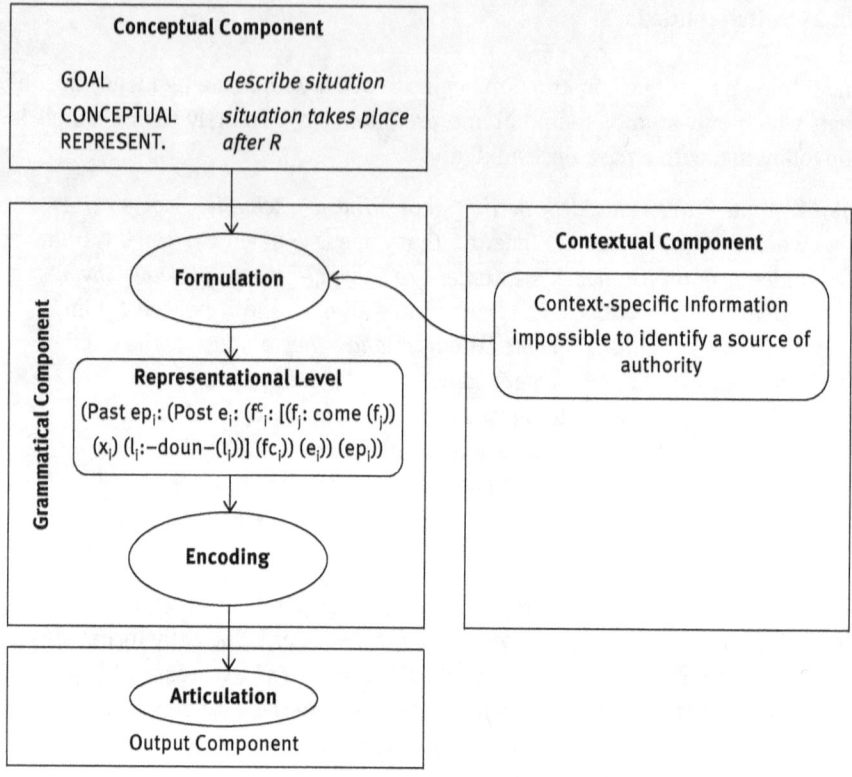

Fig. 7: Switch contexts in FDG. Use of past *sculan* in [*he preiede hym,*] *that he schulde come doun.*[22]

As predicted by the cline of contentive change in Fig. 2, the development from participant-oriented necessity to futurity and posteriority involves an expansion in semantic scope. This change is formalized as a passage of the operator from a lower to a higher layer of the Representational Level:

(16) *schal*:   (Pres ep: (e: (DeoNec f^c [...])))   >   (Fut ep: (e: (f^c [...])))
    schulde: (Past ep: (e: (DeoNec f^c [...])))   >   (Past ep: (Post e: (f^c [...])))

---

[22] In the Conceptual Component, 'R' represents the temporal point of reference (indicated by the Past tense operator); at the Representational Level, 'l' stands for "Location".

5.1.3 Full conventionalization

As we saw in Section 4.2, a strong diagnostic of full conventionalization is the occurrence of unambiguous instances of the new meaning in contexts that, in a previous stage, would have favoured (or at least admitted) an interpretation in terms of the older meaning. It follows that if a full-fledged future marker occurred in a context such as (14) above, it would not be possible to state or imply, in the same sentence, that the traitor will *not* be hanged. This is precisely because a prediction that the State-of-Affairs will come about is the inherent grammatical meaning of fully developed future markers and, as such, cannot be cancelled. Now, this is exactly what happens with present-day English *shall*, as is evident from the oddness of the following constructed example, which recreates the context of (14):

(17) ??*As a traitor you shall be hanged, but the king has spared you that.*

Being now fully grammaticalized, the Future operator no longer requires a specific (configuration of) linguistic and/or contextual factor(s), as was the case in the switch-context stage. In other words, the selection of the Future operator is now an entirely top-down, core-grammatical process, as represented in Fig. 8.

5.2 Synchrony[23]

As noted by Heine (2002: 95), "[i]f a given language is found to have reached a certain stage [...], then it can be expected to also distinguish all preceding stages." This can be observed with respect to the cross-linguistically well documented development from future tense to subjective epistemic modality, as exemplified by the Modern Greek construction *tha* + non-past finite verb (< Ancient Greek *thelo* ['want'] + infinitive). Interestingly, this development took place as early as

---

[23] The examples in this section are taken from the Greek translations of J.K. Rowling's *Harry Potter and the philosopher's stone* and M. Bulgakov's *The master and Margarita*. Both books are included in the parallel corpora ParaSol (Waldenfels 2006, 2011) and ASPAC (http://home.medewerker.uva.nl/a.a.barentsen), which offer an extensive database of aligned translations of the same texts in a variety of languages. For each example, I give a word-by-word translation in the first line and the English version included in ASPAC and ParaSol in the second line.

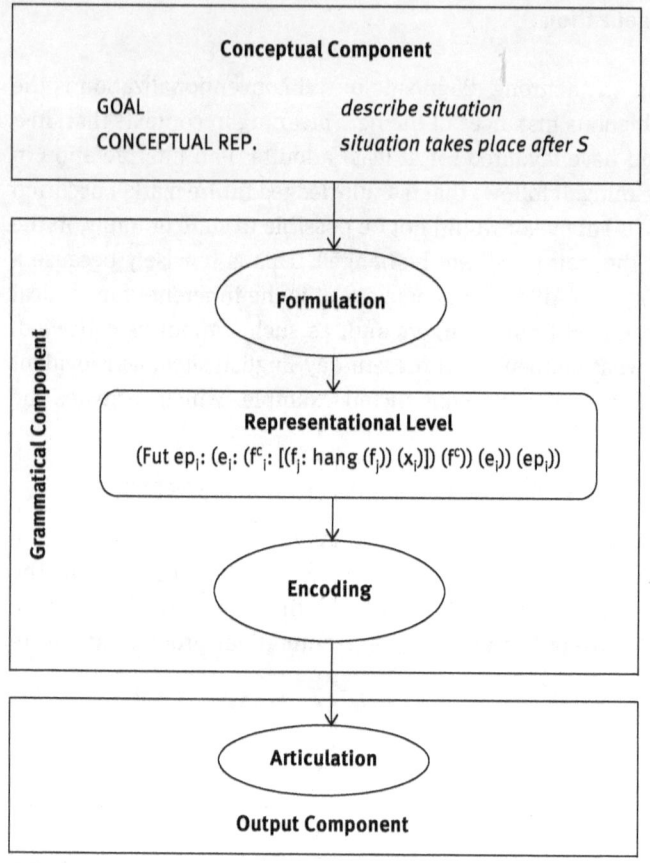

Fig. 8: Fully conventional meaning in FDG. English *shall* as a Future marker in *you shall be hanged*.

in Hellenistic-Roman Greek (Markopoulos 2009: 78), but the temporal function of the construction is still extremely frequent. A clear example is (18), in which *tha* appears in a subordinate temporal clause:[24]

---

[24] Note that the second person future in the main clause gives rise to an indirect speech act of command, but only by virtue of the fact that the speaker has authority over the addressees (cf. Bybee, Perkins, and Pagliuca 1994: 210–211). This could arguably be regarded as an instance of a bridging context between future tense and imperative illocution – an analysis which may be extended to other highly automatized, language-specific implicatures such as *Can/Could/Will you close the window?*, etc.

(18) Tora,   otan   th'   akou-sete   ti   sfyrichtr-a
     now   when   FUT   hear-NPST.PFV.2PL   DEF.F.SG.OBJ   whistle-F.SG
     mou,   tha   klotsi-sete   dynata   to   chom-a (...).
     1SG.OBL FUT   kick-NPST.PFV.2PL   hard   DEF.N.SG   ground-N.SG
     'now, when you will hear my whistle, you will kick the ground hard'
     "Now, when I blow my whistle, you kick off from the ground, hard (...)."
     (*Harry Potter*)

5.2.1 Bridging contexts

It has sometimes been proposed that the subjective epistemic uses of future tenses serve to indicate "that a proposition will turn out to be true in the future", independently of whether the designated State-of-Affairs occurs in the future, in the present or in the past (Boland 2006: 146. See also Rocci 2000: 249–250 and references therein). It is indeed common for futures that have acquired – or are acquiring – proposition-oriented meanings to occur in contexts in which the truth of the proposition is about to be verified. However, a prediction that the proposition expressed "will turn out to be true" cannot be regarded as the inherent function of epistemically used future markers. This is because, as will become evident below, future markers with fully developed epistemic meanings can also be used to express probability, conjecture and the like in contexts in which no future verification is envisaged. What we are left with is the possibility that, though not constituting a separate grammatical domain, the future verification of the proposition expressed plays a role in the process whereby future markers come to acquire epistemic functions. More specifically, *the contextual assumption* that the truth of the proposition will be (immediately) verified in the utterance context may represent a necessary condition for inferring an epistemic meaning in the bridging-context stage. Given this contextual assumption, a prediction that a State-of-Affairs will hold in the future may well be reinterpreted as a supposition about the present. This, however, is only possible if the State-of-Affairs in question is a stative one and thus can be understood as already holding at the moment of speech and continuing into the future:

(19) Bor-ei   na   zouli-chtike   ligo,   alla
     can-NPST.IPFV.3SG   SBJV   squeeze-PASS.PST.PFV.3SG   a.bit   but
     i   gefs-i   tha   einai   entaxei.
     DEF.F.SG.NOM   taste-F.SG   FUT   COP.NPST.3SG   ok
     'it may have been squeezed a bit, but the taste will be OK'
     "I mighta [=might have] sat on it at some point, *but it'll taste all right*."
     (*Harry Potter*)

The contextual saliency of an epistemic interpretation is confirmed by comparison with the other translations of *Harry Potter* included in the ASPAC corpus. Of nineteen other translations of this passage, seven have present temporal reference and contain an unambiguous epistemic expression (either lexical or grammatical). By contrast, only one translator uses an unambiguous future marker (the Czech perfective present), and even in this case there is an accompanying epistemic adverb (*určitě*, 'certainly').[25] However, a future tense interpretation cannot be categorically excluded in (19), while the epistemic interpretation could, in principle, be blocked: if, for instance, the speaker added something like "it'll taste all right, *once you have warmed it up: I guarantee*", then *it'll taste all right* could not be interpreted as a supposition about the present, because the speaker would be explicitly taking responsibility for the future realization of the State-of-Affairs.

As suggested above, the defining features of this type of bridging context can be seen (i) in the assumption that the truth of the proposition will be verified in the context and (ii) in the stativity of the State-of-Affairs. The former is obviously a contextual factor, the latter a linguistic one. The reinterpretation process can thus be represented as in Fig. 9.

5.2.2 Switch contexts

The assumption that the truth of the proposition will be verified in the context does not, by itself, entail that a temporal interpretation must necessarily remain available:[26]

(20) *Paraligo   na   tin   klepsoun   apo   tin*
      nearly   SBJV   3F.SG.OBJ   steal.NPST.PFV.3PL   PREP   DEF.F.SG.OBJ
      trapez-a   Gringotts.   Fantaz-omai   omos   pos   tha
      bank-F.SG   Gringotts   imagine-NPST.IPFV.1SG   however   COMP   FUT
      to   xer-ete   idi   ki   afto.
      3N.SG   know-NPST.2PL   already   and   DEM.N.SG
      '(...) however, I guess you will already know this too'
      "It was almost stolen outta Gringotts – *I s'ppose yeh've worked that out an'all?*" (Harry Potter)

---

25 Four other translations use a construction which has both future and subjective epistemic uses (Bulgarian, Croatian, Serbian and Slovenian). Seven translations have a simple present and no explicit epistemic or future-referring expression.
26 *Tha* is glossed 'FUT' for the sake of notational consistency, but cf. the discussion below.

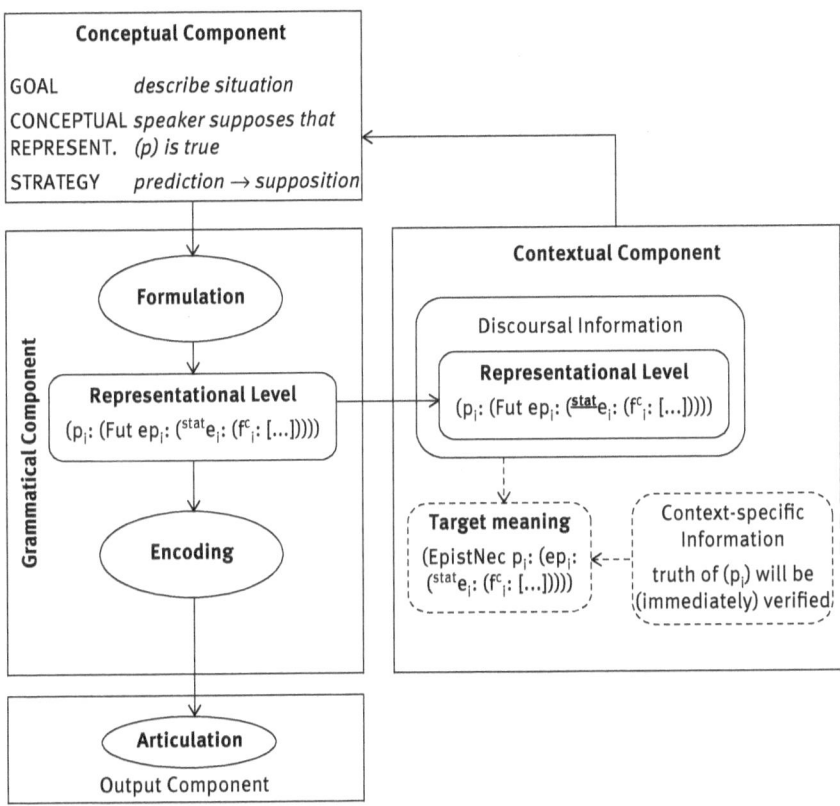

Fig. 9: A bridging context for the reinterpretation of Greek *tha* + non-past.

As in (19), the proposition is about to be verified, since in this kind of statement the addressee is typically expected to confirm or deny the truth of that proposition (cf. the interrogative intonation in the English original). Note also that the State-of-Affairs described by the proposition is again an inherently stative one. Yet, it does not seem possible to force a future tense reading on the construction: the speaker has just finished saying what he guesses the addressees already know at the time of speech, therefore an interpretation in which *tha* expresses a prediction about the future is clearly nonsensical in this context. The only reasonable interpretation is one of supposition about the present.

In sum, the two conditions that are necessary for the emergence of the epistemic meaning in bridging contexts such as (19) can also be relevant at the switch-context stage, as exemplified by (20). First, the speaker assumes that the truth of the proposition will be immediately verified in the context, second he uses the *tha*-construction with a stative predicate. However, as we have just seen, in (20) the construction can only be interpreted as a proposition-oriented epistemic marker, which means that this is now its inherent grammatical meaning. Accordingly, *tha* must be represented inside the Grammatical Component as an epistemic operator on the Propositional Content,[27] and the factors licensing its use with this meaning must be computed by the grammar itself, as shown in Fig. 10. Once again, the scope-increase prediction is respected, with a passage from the Episode layer to that of Propositional Contents.

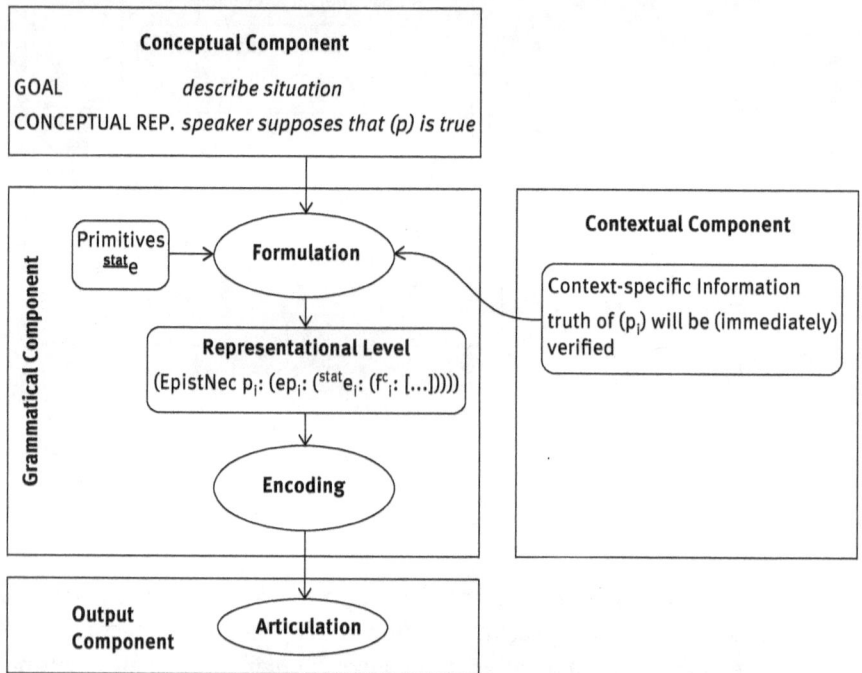

Fig. 10: A switch context for Greek *tha* + non-past as an epistemic necessity marker.

---

27 Although the exact degree of epistemic commitment expressed by the construction may vary quite significantly, Giannakidou (2012: 51) notes that "*tha* is fine with high probability adverbs such as *malon* 'probably/most likely', *sigoura* 'certainly' and *oposdhipote* 'definitely' – but is bad withmere [sic] possibility adverbs such as *isos* 'maybe/perhaps' and *pithanon* 'possibly'". On account of this observation, I follow Giannakidou (2012: 54) in considering that "*tha* behaves like a high-end necessity epistemic modal".

5.2.3 Full conventionalization

Conventional meanings are free from the constraints of the preceding stages and can appear in new contexts. In (21), for instance, neither of the two necessary conditions identified above is satisfied:

(21) *Ma einai toso oraia tora stin Kliazma, kentrise tous parontes o 'Pidaliouchos Zorz', xerontas pos oi viles ton syngrafeon sto Pereligkino, stin Kliazma, apotelousan to evaisthito simeio olon.*

Tora	pou	tha	kelaïd-oun	kai	t'
now	REL	FUT	tweet-NPST.IPFV.3PL	and	DEF.N.PL

aidoni-a	ekeï.
nightingale-N.PL	there

'(...) now even the nightingales will be singing there'
"'It must be nice out at Klyazma now,' said Bo'sun George in a tone of calculated innocence, knowing that the writers' summer colony out at Perelygino near Klyazma was a sore point. *'I expect the nightingales are singing there now.'*" (*The master and Margarita*)

The truth of the proposition cannot be expected to be verified in the context, since the designated State-of-Affairs takes place far away from the current location of the speech participants. The constraint concerning the stativity of the State-of-Affairs also does not hold, since *tha* is now combined with a dynamic predication frame. Nevertheless, the construction can only be interpreted as a present-referring epistemic operator (cf. the adverb *tora*, 'now'). This means that this operator is now fully grammaticalized. It can therefore be inserted by Formulation without taking into account any additional information, in the very same way as was illustrated in Figs. 5 and 8 for Tok Pisin *wan* and English *shall*.

6 Conclusions

In this paper I have proposed a model of grammaticalization which may be used for both diachronic and synchronic research, also lending itself for cross-linguistic comparison and being equally applicable to the grammaticalization of lexical constructions (see Sections 4.1–4.2) and to the further development of already grammatical ones (see Section 5). The model is based on the idea that an effective implementation of FDG requires a dynamic interface with the general, non-linguistic system of human knowledge and inferencing. I have suggested that – at least as concerns the phenomena discussed here – this interfacing function is a task for the shared Contextual Component. This should be seen as the locus for the highly automated, language-specific inferential processes characteristic of bridging contexts, which may trigger the grammaticalization of the construction they are associated with. If this happens, the new meaning will start occurring in switch contexts, where it is no longer achieved through reinterpretation in the Contextual Component but appears as a new representational or interpersonal operator inside the Grammatical Component. It is thus at this point that a former inference can be said to have become semanticized as a new grammatical meaning, although one that, at this stage, can only be used in restricted linguistic and/or situational contexts.

As argued in Section 3.1, grammaticalization is adequately described in terms of underlying grammatical structure by the theoretical and formal apparatus of FDG. It is hoped that, by expanding FDG's account of grammaticalization with a multi-component approach to the conventionalization of new meanings, the model developed in this paper will offer a useful framework for a formal description of the process as a whole: from the synchronic mechanisms which trigger it in specific contexts up to the ultimate outcome of the functional and formal evolution of the grammaticalized construction.

Uncommon abbreviations

DATINSTR = dative-instrumental, FAM = familiar, HORT = hortative, POL = polite, POST = posterior, PREP = preposition, REP = reportative.

References

Benveniste, Emile. 1968. Mutations of linguistic categories. In Yakov Malkiel & Winfred P. Lehmann (eds.), *Directions for historical linguistics*, 83–94. Austin & London: University of Texas Press.
Boland, Annerieke. 2006. *Aspect, tense and modality: Theory, typology, acquisition*. Utrecht: LOT.
Bolinger, Dwight. 1971. Semantic overloading: a restudy of the verb *remind*. *Language* 47. 522–547.
Butler, Christopher S. 2003. *Structure and function: A guide to three major structural-functional theories* (Studies in Language Companion Series 63 and 64). Amsterdam & Philadelphia: John Benjamins.
Bybee, Joan. 1998. A functionalist approach to grammar and its evolution. *Evolution of Communication* 2(2). 249–278.
Bybee, Joan. 2003. Mechanisms of change in grammaticization: The role of frequency. In Brian D. Joseph & Richard D. Janda (eds.), *The handbook of historical linguistics*, 602–623. Oxford: Blackwell.
Bybee, Joan. 2006. From usage to grammar: the mind's response to repetition. *Language* 82(4). 711–733.

Bybee, Joan. 2010. *Language, usage and cognition*. Cambridge: Cambridge University Press.
Bybee, Joan, Revere D. Perkins & William Pagliuca. 1994. *The evolution of grammar: Tense, aspect, and modality in the languages of the world*. Chicago: The University of Chicago Press.
Comrie, Bernard. 1985. *Tense*. Cambridge: Cambridge University Press.
Connolly, John H. 2007. Context in Functional Discourse Grammar. *Alfa: Revista de Lingüística* 51(2). 11–33.
Connolly, John H. 2014. The Contextual Component within a dynamic implementation of the FDG model: Structure and interaction. *Pragmatics* 24(2). 229–248.
Contini-Morava, Ellen. 1996. 'Things' in a noun class language: Semantic functions of grammatical agreement in Swahili. In Edna Andrews & Yishai Tobin (eds.), *Toward a calculus of meaning: Studies in markedness, distinctive features, and deixis*. Amsterdam & Philadelphia: John Benjamins.
Cornish, Francis. 2013. On the dual nature of the Functional Discourse Grammar model: Context, the language system/language use distinction, and indexical reference in discourse. *Language Sciences* 38. 83–98.
Cuvalay-Haak, Martine. 1997. *The verb in Literary and Colloquial Arabic*. Berlin: Mouton de Gruyter.
Dahl, Östen. 1985. *Tense and aspect systems*. New York: Basil Blackwell.
Dik, Simon C. 1978. *Functional Grammar*. Amsterdam: North-Holland.
Dik, Simon C. 1997a. *The theory of Functional Grammar. Part I: The structure of the clause*. Dordrecht: Foris.
Dik, Simon C. 1997b. *The theory of functional grammar. Part II: Complex and derived constructions* (Functional Grammar Series 21). Edited by Kees Hengeveld. Berlin & New York: Mouton de Gruyter.
Dossena, Marina. 2002. Should. In Maurizio Gotti, Marina Dossena, Richard Dury, Roberta Facchinetti & Maria Lima (eds.) *Variation in central modals. A repertoire of forms and types of usage in Middle English and Early Modern English* (Linguistic Insights, Studies in Language and Communication 4), 234–265. Bern: Peter Lang.
Foley, William A. & Robert D. Van Valin Jr. 1984. *Functional syntax and universal grammar*. Cambridge: Cambridge University Press.
Geis, Michael L. & Arnold M. Zwicky. 1971. On invited inferences. *Linguistic Inquiry* 2. 561–566.
Gelderen, Elly van. 2004. *Grammaticalization as economy*. Amsterdam & Philadelphia: John Benjamins.
Gelderen, Elly van. 2009. Feature economy in the Linguistic Cycle. In Paola Crisma & Giuseppe Longobardi (eds.), *Historical syntax and linguistic theory*, 93–109. Oxford: Oxford University Press.
Giannakidou, Anastasia. 2012. The Greek future: epistemic modality and modal concord. In Zoe Gavrilidou, Angeliki Efthymiou, Evangelia Thomadaki & Penelope Kambakis-Vougiouklis (eds.), *Selected papers from the 10th International Conference of Greek Linguistics*, 48–61. Komotini: Democritus University of Thrace.
Gotti, Maurizio. 2002. Shall. In Maurizio Gotti, Marina Dossena, Richard Dury, Roberta Facchinetti & Maria Lima, *Variation in central modals. A repertoire of forms and types of usage in Middle English and Early Modern English* (Linguistic Insights, Studies in Language and Communication 4), 189–233. Bern: Peter Lang.
Grice, Paul. 1975. Logic and conversation. In Peter Cole & Jerry Morgan (eds.), *Syntax and semantics*, vol. 3, 41–58. New York: Academic Press.
Harder, Peter & Kasper Boye. 2012. (Inter)subjectification and pragmaticalization in a functional theory of grammaticalization. In Johan van der Auwera & Jan Nuyts (eds.),

Grammaticalization and (inter)subjectification, 9–20. Brussels: Koninklijke Vlaamse Academie van Wetenschappen en Kunsten.

Heine, Bernd. 1994. On the genesis of aspect in African Languages: The proximative. In Kevin E. Moore, David A. Peterson & Comfort Wentum (eds.), *Proceedings of the Twentieth Annual Meeting of the Berkeley Linguistics Society: Special session on historical issues in African Linguistics*, 35–46. Berkeley: Berkeley Linguistics Society.

Heine, Bernd. 2002. On the role of context in grammaticalization. In Ilse Wischer & Gabriele Diewald (eds.), *New reflections on grammaticalization* (Typological Studies in Language, 49), 83–101. Amsterdam & Philadelphia: John Benjamins.

Heine, Bernd. 2003. Grammaticalization. In Brian D. Joseph & Richard D. Janda (eds.), *The handbook of historical linguistics*, 575–601. Oxford: Blackwell.

Heine, Bernd, Ulrike Claudi & Friederike Hünnemeyer. 1991. *Grammaticalization: A conceptual framework*. Chicago: University of Chicago Press.

Heine, Bernd & Tania Kuteva. 2002. *World lexicon of grammaticalization*. Cambridge: Cambridge University Press.

Hengeveld, Kees. 1989. Layers and operators in Functional Grammar. *Journal of Linguistics* 25(1). 127–157.

Hengeveld, Kees. 2011. The grammaticalization of tense and aspect. In Bernd Heine & Heiko Narrog (eds.), *The Oxford handbook of grammaticalization*, 580–594. Oxford: Oxford University Press.

Hengeveld, Kees. This volume. A hierarchical approach to grammaticalization.

Hengeveld, Kees & John Lachlan Mackenzie. 2008. *Functional Discourse Grammar*. Oxford: Oxford University Press.

Hengeveld, Kees & John Lachlan Mackenzie. 2014. Grammar and context in Functional Discourse Grammar. *Pragmatics* 24(2). 203–227.

Hengeveld, Kees & Marize Mattos Dall'Aglio Hattnher. 2015. Four types of evidentiality in the native languages of Brazil. *Linguistics* 53(3). 479–524.

Hengeveld, Kees & Gerry Wanders. 2007. Adverbial conjunctions in Functional Discourse Grammar. In Mike Hannay & Gerard J. Steen (eds.), *Structural-functional studies in English grammar: In honour of Lachlan Mackenzie* (Studies in Language Companion Series 83), 209–26. Amsterdam & Philadelphia: John Benjamins.

Hopper, Paul J. & Elizabeth Closs Traugott. 1993. *Grammaticalization*. Cambridge: Cambridge University Press.

Kailuweit, Rolf. 2008. Some remarks on RRG and grammaticalization: French verbal periphrases. In Rolf Kailuweit, Björn Wiemer, Eva Staudinger & Ranko Matasović (eds.), *New applications of Role and Reference Grammar: Diachrony, grammaticalization, Romance languages*, 69–86. Newcastle: Cambridge Scholars Publishing.

Keizer, Mathilde Evelien. 2007. The lexical-grammatical dichotomy in FDG. *Alfa: Revista de Lingüística* 51(2). 35–56.

Kuteva, Tania. 2001. *Auxiliation: An inquiry into the nature of grammaticalization*. Oxford: Oxford University Press.

Kuteva, Tania. 2009. Grammatical categories and linguistic theory: elaborateness in grammar. In Peter K. Austin, Oliver Bond, Monik Charette, David Nathan & Peter Sells (eds.), *Proceedings of Conference on Language Documentation and Linguistic Theory 2*, 13–28. London: SOAS.

Lehmann, Christian. 1985. Grammaticalization: synchronic variation and diachronic change. *Lingua e stile* 20(3). 303–318.

Lester, Leland A. 1987.*The modal verbs of Old English*. Austin: The University of Texas at Austin dissertation.
Mackenzie, John Lachlan. 2012. Cognitive adequacy in a dialogic Functional Discourse Grammar. *Language Sciences* 34. 421–432.
Mackenzie, John Lachlan. 2014. The Contextual Component in a dialogic FDG. *Pragmatics* 24(2). 249–273.
Markopoulos, Theodore. 2009. *The Future in Greek: from Ancient to Medieval*. Oxford & New York: Oxford University Press.
Matasović, Ranko. 2008. Patterns of grammaticalization and the layered structure of the clause. In Rolf Kailuweit, Björn Wiemer, Eva Staudinger & Ranko Matasović (eds.), *New applications of Role and Reference Grammar: Diachrony, grammaticalization, Romance languages*, 45–57. Newcastle: Cambridge Scholars Publishing.
Narrog, Heiko. 2012. *Modality, subjectivity, and semantic change: A cross-linguistic perspective*. Oxford: Oxford University Press.
Nicolle, Steve. 2008. Scope and the functions of *be going to*. In Rolf Kailuweit, Björn Wiemer, Eva Staudinger & Ranko Matasović (eds.). 2008. *New applications of Role and Reference Grammar: Diachrony, grammaticalization, Romance languages*, 58–68. Newcastle: Cambridge Scholars Publishing.
Nuyts, Jan. 2004. Remarks on layering in a cognitive-functional language production model. In J. Lachlan Mackenzie & María de los Ángeles Gómez Gonzáles (eds.), *A new architecture for functional grammar*, 275–298. Berlin & New York: Mouton De Gruyter.
Nuyts, Jan. 2013. De-auxiliarization without de-modalization in the Dutch core modals: A case of collective degrammaticalization? *Language Sciences* 36. 124–133.
Olbertz, Hella. 1993. The grammaticalization of Spanish *haber* plus participle. In Jaap van Marle (ed.), *Historical Linguistics 1991: Papers from the 10th International Conference on Historical Linguistics*, 243–263. Amsterdam & Philadelphia: John Benjamins.
Olbertz, Hella. 1998. *Verbal Periphrases in a Functional Grammar of Spanish*. Berlin & New York: Mouton de Gruyter.
Olbertz, Hella & Sandra Gasparini Bastos. 2013. Objective and subjective deontic modal necessity in FDG – evidence from Spanish auxiliary expressions. In J. Lachlan Mackenzie & Hella Olbertz (eds.), *Casebook in Functional Discourse Grammar* (Studies in Language Companion Series 137), 277–300. Amsterdam & Philadelphia: John Benjamins.
Quirk, Randolph & Charles Leslie Wrenn. 1957 [1955]. *An Old English Grammar*, 2nd edn. London: Methuen & Company.
Roberts, Ian. 2007. *Diachronic syntax*. Oxford: Oxford University Press.
Roberts, Ian. 2010. Grammaticalization, the clausal hierarchy and semantic bleaching. In Elizabeth Closs Traugott & Graeme Trousdale (eds.), *Gradience, gradualness and grammaticalization*, 45–73. Amsterdam & Philadelphia: John Benjamins.
Roberts, Ian & Anna Roussou. 2003. *Syntactic change: a Minimalist approach to grammaticalization*. Cambridge: Cambridge University Press.
Rocci, Andrea. 2000. L'interprétation épistémique du futur en italien et en français: une analyse procédurale. *Cahiers de linguistique française* 22. 241–274.
Souza, Edson Rosa Francisco de. 2009. *Gramaticalização dos itens lingüísticos* assim, já *e* aí *no Português Brasileiro: um estudo sob a perspectiva da Gramática Discursivo-Funcional* [The grammaticalization of the linguistic items *assim, já* and *aí* in Brazilian Portuguese: an investigation from the perspective of Functional Discourse Grammar]. Universidade Estadual de Campinas dissertation.

Tabor, Whitney & Elizabeth Closs Traugott. 1998. Structural scope expansion and grammaticalization. In Anna Giacalone Ramat & Paul J. Hopper (eds.), *The limits of grammaticalization*, 227–270. Amsterdam & Philadelphia: John Benjamins.

Traugott, Elizabeth Closs. 1988. Pragmatic strengthening and grammaticalization. *Proceedings of the Fourteenth Annual Meeting of the Berkeley Linguistics Society*, 406–416.

Traugott, Elizabeth Closs. 1992. Syntax. In Richard M. Hogg (ed.), *The Cambridge History of the English Language*, vol. 1, 168–289. Cambridge: Cambridge University Press.

Traugott, Elizabeth Closs & Richard B. Dasher. 2002. *Regularity in semantic change*. Cambridge: Cambridge University Press.

Traugott, Elizabeth Closs & Ekkehard König. 1991. The semantics-pragmatics of grammaticalization revisited. In Elizabeth Closs Traugott & Bernd Heine (eds.), *Approaches to grammaticalization*, vol. 1, 189–218. Amsterdam & Philadelphia: John Benjamins.

Van Valin, Robert D. Jr. 2005. *Exploring the syntax-semantics interface*. Cambridge: Cambridge University Press.

Van Valin, Robert D. Jr. & Randy LaPolla. 1997. *Syntax: Structure, meaning and function*. Cambridge: Cambridge University Press.

Vet, Co. 1990. Aktionsart, aspect and duration adverbials. In Harm Pinkster & Inge Genee (eds.), *Unity in diversity: Papers presented to Simon C. Dik on his 50th birthday*, 279–89. Dordrecht: Foris.

Visser, Fredericus T. 1969. *An historical syntax of the English Language*, vol. 3. Leiden: Brill.

Waldenfels, Ruprecht von. 2006. Compiling a parallel corpus of slavic languages. Text strategies, tools and the question of lemmatization in alignment. In Bernhard Brehmer, Vladislava Zdanova & Rafal Zimny (eds.), *Beiträge der europäischen slavistischen Linguistik (POLYSLAV) 9* [Contributions to European Slavonic Linguistics], 123–138. München: Kubon & Sagner.

Waldenfels, Ruprecht von. 2011. Recent developments in ParaSol: Breadth for depth and XSLT based web concordancing with CWB. In Daniela Majchráková & Radovan Garabík (eds.), *Natural language processing, multilinguality. Proceedings of Slovko 2011*, 156–162. Bratislava: Tribun.

Heiko Narrog
Relationship of form and function in grammaticalization – the case of modality*

Abstract: In this paper I discuss the issue of the relationship between form and function in grammaticalization, claiming that a correlation between formal and functional development only holds in the history of individual markers or constructions. If markers advance either formally or functionally, they will either advance or remain unchanged in the other aspect of their grammaticalization. Since there are also different entry points for lexical items – they may either be grammaticalized as a category low on grammaticalization scales or high – it is impossible to deduce and compare functional grammaticalization based on formal characteristics, and vice versa, even for markers of one grammatical category in one language. I also give an account of why functional grammaticalization is decisive and formal grammaticalization is rather epiphenomenal. This corresponds to the fact that formal degrammaticalization occurs much more easily. Functional grammaticalization is mainly understood in terms of an increase in speech-act orientation, and climbing in hierarchies of grammatical categories. I illustrate the discussion with examples from the grammatical categories of modality and evidentiality.

Keywords: formal grammaticalization, functional grammaticalization, degrammaticalization, speech-act orientation, modality, hierarchical clause structure, layering

1 Introduction

The goal of this paper is to establish the relationship between formal and functional development in grammaticalization from a functional perspective. The claim is that formal and functional grammaticalization proceed unidirectionally in the sense that we expect that in the vast majority of cases of grammatical development at least either form or function advance along parameters of grammaticalization while neither of them should regress. On the other hand, the entry point in

---

*Heiko Narrog's research activity was supported by grants number 24520450 and 16H03411 by the Japanese Society for the Promotion of Science.

Heiko Narrog: Tohoku University, Kawauchi 41, Sendai 980-8576, Japan, narrog@gmail.com

DOI 10.1515/9783110519389-004

grammaticalization and the pace of development differ marker by marker, construction by construction. Therefore it is not possible to expect every marker and construction that is functionally more grammaticalized to be also formally more grammaticalized than a functionally less grammaticalized item, and vice versa, not every formally more grammaticalized item is functionally more grammaticalized. As a result it is impossible to compare the degree of grammaticalization of markers even in the same language and in the same domain by simply comparing how far they have advanced on a scale of formal grammaticalization, as is implied, for example, in scales of grammaticalizations such as Lehmann's (1986:3).

This claim is not particularly original, since I have made it before myself (cf. Narrog 2005a: 697; 2012a: 107–109). Furthermore, Heine (e.g. Heine and Reh 1984: 62, Heine et al. 1991: 15) from early on has claimed the primacy of the semantic aspect of grammaticalization over morphosyntactic changes, also in terms of diachrony. Nevertheless, since the idea that everything that is functionally more grammaticalized must also be formally more grammaticalized, or vice versa, is often tacitly taken for given in grammaticalization studies, I take the opportunity in this paper to elaborate on this claim.

In Section 2 of this paper, I will discuss formal changes in general, in Section 3 functional changes, which are arguably more critical for grammaticalization, in somewhat more depth, before I will discuss the interrelationship between them in Section 4. Section 5 offers a conclusion. The area of grammar from which I will take my examples are modality and evidentiality. The paper will have a typological perspective, but most examples will come from English and Japanese.

Before delving into the topic, I will provide definitions of the topics I am dealing with in this paper. Grammaticalization has been defined by Hopper and Traugott (2003^2: 18) as "change whereby lexical items and constructions come in certain linguistic contexts to serve grammatical functions and, once grammaticalized, continue to develop new grammatical functions", or even shorter as "development from lexical to grammatical, and from grammatical to even more grammatical structures" by Heine (2003a: 577). I believe that this is rather uncontroversial. The definition of modality is more problematic. There are mainly two positions in the current literature, namely, viewing modality in terms of the "speaker's attitude" or "subjective elements" (e.g. Lyons 1968; Bybee et al. 1994), and viewing it in terms of reality status (e.g. Palmer 1999). I take the latter stance and take modality as a category concerning the factual status of a proposition as in the following definition:

(1) "Modality is a linguistic category referring to the factual status of a state of affairs. The expression of a state of affairs is modalized if it is marked for being undetermined with respect to its factual status, i. e. is neither positively nor negatively factual." (Narrog 2005b: 184)

Without going into detail here, I have argued previously (Narrog 2005b, 2012a) that definitions in terms of "speaker's attitudes" or subjectivity by their very nature are not suited to delimit the category. Instead, it is more meaningful to consider subjectivity as an epistemological category independent from modality and interacting with it. This allows for both subjective and objective expressions of modality.

Lastly, when referring to "formal" vs. "functional", unless otherwise mentioned, I mean these terms in a functional sense. In formal linguistics, the territory of what is considered as "formal" is much broader and shifted towards domains that are considered as "functional" in functional linguistics, and vice versa. In functional linguistics, basically only phonological, morphological, and syntactic surface structures can be clearly considered as formal, and this is the understanding I adhere to in this paper. As an example, in Section 3, under the heading of "functional" change, layered structures of grammatical categories will be discussed. These are considered as essentially formal in main stream formal linguistics and as essentially functional in functional linguistics. This reflects the fact that the core of grammar in formal linguistics is considered as formal, while it is considered as functional, or semantic, in functional grammars.

2 Formal changes in grammaticalization

2.1 Changes in general

Famously, Lehmann (2002) has proposed the parameters presented in Tab. 1, which are deduced from the concept of grammaticalization as the decrease in autonomy of a linguistic sign.

Tab. 1: The parameters of grammaticalization (Lehmann 2002: 110).

Parameter	Paradigmatic	Syntagmatic
Weight	Integrity	Structural scope
Cohesion	Paradigmaticity	Bondedness
Variability	Paradigmatic variability	Syntagmatic variability

The six formal processes of grammaticalization that can be derived from the grid of three parameters of grammaticalization and their syntagmatic and paradigmatic dimensions results in, are (i) loss of integrity, i.e. attrition in the case of phonological substance, erosion, and decategorialization in the case of morphosyntax, (ii) increasing paradigmaticity, i.e. paradigmaticization, (iii) loss of paradigmatic variability, i.e. obligatorification, (iv) shrinking of the structural scope of a sign (= condensation), (v) increase in bondedness, i.e., coalescence (also "univerbation"), and (vi) loss of syntagmatic variability, i.e. fixation. Overall, the focus is on change in form, and these changes all imply a reduction in phonological, morphological and syntactic properties of the linguistic sign that changes. It must be noted, though, that semantic changes are also implied. The most salient of these is desemanticization, which is the semantic aspect of loss of integrity.

Another set of criteria has been offered by Heine in various publications, such as Heine and Kuteva (2002). He takes a bottom-up approach and, generalizing over many cases of grammaticalization, defines a set of criteria that is recurrent in grammaticalization as opposed to other types of change. The potentially formal ones among those criteria are listed in (2).

(2) (a) extension (or context generalization) – use in new contexts,
 (b) decategorialization – loss in morphosyntactic properties characteristic of lexical or other less grammaticalized forms, and
 (c) erosion (or "phonetic reduction") – loss in phonetic substance.

(b) and (c) are clearly formal. (a) extension entails the rise of new grammatical meanings when linguistic expressions are extended to new contexts (context-induced reinterpretation). Extension can be considered as relating to both functional and formal factors. Primarily it is a functional criterion, that is, as an expansion of meanings and functions. Extension is theoretically particularly significant, since it stands in contrast to Lehmann's six parameters, which are all reductive. Extension suggests the opposite, namely an increase. However, extension has also a formal side in that the grammaticalized item extends to new morphological and syntactic contexts. Heine and Reh (1984) also cite adaptation, fusion, and loss as phonological changes, and permutation, compounding, cliticization, affixation, fossilization as more concrete morphosyntactic processes involved in grammaticalization. These are elaborations on (b) and (c), and are all reductive.

Although generative grammar will play no major role in the rest of this paper, it is worth-while to note here that the main formal change involved in grammaticalization according to this framework, at least in a more traditional take on grammaticalization, is the loss of movement (also defined as Early Merge by van Gelderen 2004). Roberts (2010: 49) represents this loss of movement as in formula (3) below:

(3) a. $[_{XP} Y + X [_{YP} t_Y]] > $ b. $[_{XP} Y = X [_{YP} ... Y ...]]$

The idea is that at the earlier diachronic stage, Y underwent movement to X, leaving a trace in its launching site. At the later diachronic stage, the element formerly merged as Y is now merged directly as X. The element in Y experiences a shift in category membership from Y to X (cf. also Clark and Roberts 1993: 315–316). This loss of movement as such is formal but it also has an inevitable functional aspect because it requires semantic bleaching in the development of the functional category.

Now if we look at the purely formal criteria proposed by Lehmann and Heine, there is considerable variation in the possible set of changes depending on the structure of the particular language. This makes formal grammaticalization (in terms of functional approaches) a less decisive indicator of grammaticalization than functional/content grammaticalization. This is also the reason why formal grammaticalization is treated in less detail in this section. In Section 2.2, I will briefly review the impact of a number of different morphological and syntactic types of languages on the concrete shape of grammaticalization.

2.2 VO languages (1) – the English modals

The grammaticalization of the modal auxiliaries in English, such as *can*, *must*, *will*, *shall/should*, *may/might*, can be viewed as a typical historical development in a VO language. An auxiliary develops out of a lexical verb in a position preceding the main verb, that is, in head-initial position. In contrast to head-final languages, the grammaticalizing element retains its morphological independence and does not affix to the head. This is in consonance with the "suffixing preference" (cf. Bybee et al. 1990), that is, the cross-linguistic tendency for postposed rather than preposed grammatical material to lose morphological independence. In English, if modals affix at all, they do so to the preceding subject, to which they have no direct structural relationship, rather than to the following verb (e.g. *I'll go* but not *I wi'go*; cf. e.g. Bybee and Thompson 1997). Nevertheless, they form a paradigm (closed class), and their inflection is reduced, including loss of person-number agreement and (partial) loss of tense. The infinitive and the participial form are also lost. Thus, in Lehmann's terms we see a loss of integrity and a rise in paradigmaticity, but little increase in morphological bondedness. However, the ability to take bare infinitives as complements can be interpreted as a higher degree of bondedness compared to lexical complement-taking verbs. Also, the degree of loss of phonetic integrity is moderate. The retention of properties of Old English verbs known as the NICE-properties, especially negation with *not*, and interrogation without *do*-support, can be viewed as fixation.

In Heine's terms, we see decategorialization, i.e. loss of verbal properties such as inflection and certain verb forms, and moderate erosion. We also see an extension of contexts of usage, as the modals historically came to co-occur with a wide range of subjects, including non-animate ones, and propositions (cf. Goossens 1987). However, extension of contexts can also be interpreted as a functional phenomenon.

2.3 VO languages (2) – grammaticalizing verbs in East and Mainland Southeast Asian languages (VO)

East and Mainland Southeast Asian languages, such as Thai or Chinese are not only VO but also historically morphologically isolating, that is, they have very little morphology. Bisang (2011: 110–113), discusses the grammaticalization of 'get' ('come to have') verbs in South East Asian languages, and concludes that they have the following properties with respect to grammaticalization:

(i) Little change in morphology (i.e., little loss of integrity in terms of Lehmann's parameters)
(ii) Reduction of mobility (i.e., loss of syntagmatic variability in terms of Lehmann's parameters)
(iii) No formation of grammaticalization chains because grammatical meanings don't semanticize but instead remain dependent on inference in context

More generally, grammaticalization in these languages is characterized through
(iv) Lack of development of obligatory categories (i.e., little obligatorification in terms of Lehmann's parameters)
(v) Integration into rigid syntactic patterns
(vi) No or very little co-evolution of form or meaning (cf. Bisang 2008: 15)

In essence, then, grammaticalization can formally only be associated with syntactic fixation in specific positions, i.e. Lehmann's sixth criterion of syntagmatic variability. All other parameters are of very limited applicability to languages of this area. Increasing frequency of use can be observed, but this is not a formal criterion.

2.4 OV languages – Japanese and Korean

As we expect in OV languages, modal morphemes in the verbal complexes of Japanese and Korean grammaticalize in a position following the verb. Generally, the head-final nature of the languages in combination with the "suffixing preference" (see above) leads to the characterization of these languages as "agglutinative". In the area of modality as well we find modal markers and constructions as bound material (cf. Narrog 2009: 67–77; Kim-Renaud 2009: 111–113); i.e. there is a relatively high degree of "bondedness" in Lehmann's terms. In Japanese, we can identify the following cline of morphological grammaticalization:

(4) word/construction > (particle) > general suffix (including inflecting suffixes) > inflection
 (Narrog and Ohori 2011: 777)

The development from word to suffix to inflection implies a loss of verbal properties of inflection and derivation of the grammatical item itself. Furthermore, it implies a loss of morphological independence. Words/constructions on the left of the cline in (4) are independent, particles as clitics are only loosely bound to stems, while inflections are most tightly bound to their preceding stem, sometimes involving fusion. The stage of particle is in brackets since it is often skipped or irrelevant for the grammaticalization of a certain category.

A case in point is the secondary grammaticalization of the Japanese future suffix -*am*-, which developed into the hortative inflection -*(y)oo*, losing the ability to inflect itself (cf. Narrog 2007a: 290; 2012a: 130–132). That is, besides bondedness, we see a relatively high degree of decategorialization and erosion as well. In Korean (Rhee 2011), the degree of phonetic erosion is even more salient than in Japanese. The development of suffixes, and then inflections, also implies integration into paradigms, i. e. paradigmatization and loss of paradigmatic variability, while bonding also means loss of morphological scope from phrase to single word.

Despite the 'suffixing preference', not all constructions turn into suffixes quickly. In the domain of Japanese modality, we also find periphrastic postposed constructions such as -*(a)nakereba narana*-, lit. '[it] does not become if [you] don't' for general and deontic necessity and -*ka-mo sirena*-, lit. '[one] does not know if not' for epistemic possibility (cf. Narrog 2009: 82, 103). In such constructions, the primary indicator of grammaticalization is the loss of syntagmatic variability. As Hanazono (1999) showed (cf. also Narrog to appear), grammaticalizing periphrastic constructions, amongst others, lose the ability for permutation, the possibility to insert particles, and the possibility to co-occur with certain adverbs.

2.5 Conclusion

Overall, it is languages like Japanese and Korean to which the formal criteria of Heine and Lehmann apply best. Their application to the East and Mainland

Southeast Asian language type is rather limited, while a language like English lies in between both poles. It is also not clear that there is a single formal criterion of grammaticalization that is indispensable. Writings on grammaticalization in European languages typically stress the importance of paradigmatization (e.g. Diewald 2009; Lamiroy and De Mulder 2011), which is rejected by Bisang (2011) for East and Southeast Asian isolating languages. This seems to leave us with loss of syntagmatic variability only, but this criterion may in turn be much less relevant in languages that don't rely on fixed word order. In light of the observations on isolating languages, it would even seem possible to have functional change without any formal correlates. However, Ansaldo and Lim (2004) show that even in isolating languages grammaticalizing words undergo subtle changes in pronunciation. Indeed we should expect that information that gets downgraded in terms of contents, and that is subject to routinization (cf. Bybee 2003), also gets backgrounded prosodically. Thus we may assume that even if grammaticalization has no reflex in the written representation of the language, it can still have subtle effects on spoken language.

Nevertheless, the cross-linguistic inconsistency of formal change in grammaticalization leads us to conclude that the core of grammaticalization is functional. Formal changes (in a functional sense of "formal"), at least to the extent that they are reflected in written language, are merely optional. However, since it is often the formal changes like affixation (bonding) that stand out in language description, and since they are often easier to pin down objectively, they remain a valid object of interest in grammaticalization studies.

In the rest of this paper, I will mainly discuss examples from Japanese, that is, a language in which the formal aspects of grammaticalization are salient.

3 Functional/contents changes

We start here again with the traditional lists of parameters of grammaticalization and their functional components. Lehmann's loss of paradigmatic integrity (cf. Tab. 1) translates into "desemanticization" in terms of semantics, while increasing paradigmaticity means the shift towards a grammatical meaning that stands in complementary relationship to similar meanings in the same paradigm. Heine and Kuteva (2002) have

(5) (a) desemanticization (or "semantic bleaching") – loss in meaning content, and
    (b) extension (or context generalization) – use in new contexts.

Desemanticization means loss of lexical meaning and acquisition of grammatical meaning/function. Extension, as we have seen above, is a combination of formal and functional factors.

In generative grammar, the core element of grammaticalization is the "diachronic development of lexical heads into functional heads" (Roberts and Roussou 1999: 1011), which entails the reanalysis of lexical as functional material. This has both formal and functional aspects. From a purely semantic perspective Roberts and Roussou (2003) and Roberts (2010) emphasize the process of "bleaching".

Desemanticization and semantic bleaching are rather abstract concepts and they are not uncontroversial. In the more recent research landscape of grammaticalization studies, there is a tendency to emphasize acquisition of new meanings and pragmatic functions over bleaching (cf. Hopper and Traugott 2004: 94–98). In this section, I will focus on two aspects of semantic and functional change that have been especially highlighted in recent research. One is an increase in speech-act orientation. At the core of it is so-called (inter)subjectification, which currently many scholars believe to be the central semantic change in grammaticalization. The other is movement along hierarchies of functional categories, which are, at least from a functionalist perspective, inherently semantic. These two central functional-semantic aspects of grammaticalization will be discussed in Sections 3.1 and 3.2.

3.1 Increase in speech-act orientation

3.1.1 Preliminaries

The idea of increase in speech-act orientation is based on previous research on subjectification and intersubjectification. Two major concepts of subjectification have been offered, a conceptualist one by Langacker (1990, and elsewhere), and an empirically oriented one by Traugott (2003).[1] The latter is also diachronically oriented and therefore of more interest here. Traugott (2003: 126) defines subjectification as "the mechanism whereby meanings come over time to encode or externalize the SP/W [Speaker / Writer]'s perspectives and attitudes as constrained by the communicative world of the speech event." Subjectification is complemented

---

[1] A somewhat detailed comparison of various concepts of (inter)subjectivity and (inter)subjectification is found in Narrog (2012c).

by intersubjectification which is "the semasiological process whereby meanings come over time to encode or externalise implicatures regarding SP/W's attention to the 'self' of AD/R [Addressee / Reader] in both an epistemic and a social sense" (Traugott 2003: 129–130).

Traugott and Dasher (2002: 279) boldly state that, "the main mechanism of semantic change is subjectification (including intersubjectification)." This is the logical consequence of the hypothesis that "the seeds of semantic change are to be found in SP/Ws, drawing on and exploiting pragmatic meanings that arise in negotiated interaction."

In this section, I will approach the issue from a perspective that is similar in spirit to Traugott's but claims to be more inclusive. In a number of publications (Narrog 2012a, b, c; 2015) I have suggested that it is fruitful to realign subjectification and intersubjectification as diachronic processes under a more comprehensive directionality of change towards increased "speech-act orientation", which also includes increased discourse/textual orientation. Semantic change, then, is always towards an increase, or at least, non-decrease in "speech-act orientation" Increase in speech act orientation consists of one or more of the following three tendencies:
– increasing orientation towards the speaker's perspective (increased speaker orientation)
– increasing orientation towards the speech situation including the hearer (increased hearer orientation)
– increasing orientation towards discourse itself (increased discourse/textual orientation)

None of the three tendencies is taken to entail one of the others by definition, unlike intersubjectification in the Traugottian sense, which entails subjectification. The actual sequence of changes is to be empirically established and may vary by domain of grammar.

In the case of modality, I consider speech-act orientation as one of the two important dimensions characterizing the meaning of modal expressions. Note that "event-orientation" is not meant as a contrast to "participant-orientation" but only strictly to speaker- and speech-act-orientation. Participant-orientation is included in event-orientation for reasons outlined immediately below. The other dimension is volitivity, i.e., if the modality contains an "element of will" (Jespersen 1924 [1992]: 313–321) or not. Deontic and boulomaic modalities, for example, do, while dispositional, circumstantial and epistemic modalities don't. In contrast to the dimensions of volitivity and speech-act orientation, I do not consider possibility and necessity, and even less participant-internal vs. -external modalities, as equally relevant for the typological and cross-linguistic description of modality from a diachronic perspective. The reasons for this have been described in detail in Chapter 6 of Narrog (2012a). They may be very relevant for the descriptions of modal categories in specific languages, especially those Indo-European languages that we know very well, but there is no support for assigning them any relevance when it comes to diachronic change from a cross-linguistic perspective. Even the most prominent proponent of the distinction participant-internal vs. participant-external distinction from a typological perspective has frankly admitted this point on the basis of data beyond the core European languages (cf. van der Auwera et al. 2009: 293).

The two dimensions can be represented as in Fig. 1. Figure 1 represents three categories that are closely related to each other, namely, modality proper, mood, which refers to clausal moods such as various types of imperatives, counterfactuals, or subordinating moods like conditionals, and illocutionary modification, which is not strictly modal, because illocutionary modification usually does not change the factuality of a sentence. It is nevertheless included because of close diachronic relationships to modality and mood (cf. Narrog 2012a: Ch. 4). The arrows indicate the overall directionality of diachronic change which is hypothesized to go in the direction of increased speech-act orientation, while there is no specific directionality in the dimension of volitivity, contrary to some earlier claims (for details see Narrog 2005; 2012 a, b, c).

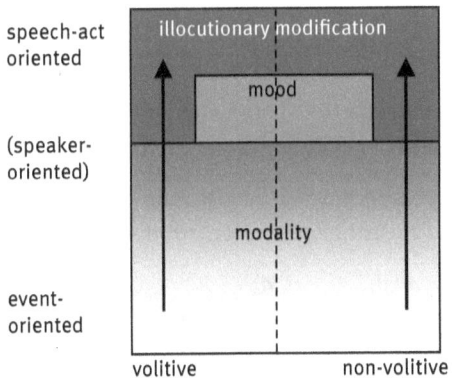

Fig. 1: Model of modality (Narrog 2005a, 2007a, 2012a, c).

In the following sections I will provide three examples of change towards increased speech-act orientation. None of the descriptions of semantic change given here is novel, since I have written about them in various publications that will be cited where appropriate, but they are nevertheless necessary here because these functional changes will be compared with the formal changes involved so as to establish their correlation.

3.1.2 Japanese *be-*

The second example is Japanese *be-*, a highly polysemous modal marker in Old Japanese (see Narrog 2002 for more detail).[2] At that earliest historically documented stage in the development of the language, "appropriateness" and "apparent imminence/inevitability" are the core readings. The former reading, as represented in ex. (6), reminds of English *should*, while the latter, as represented in ex. (7) reminds of English *be about to*, or *will*.[3]

(6) *Umi-tu-di=no   nagi-n-am.u   toki=mo*
    sea-GEN-route=GEN   become.quiet-PRF-FUT.APT   time=FOC
    watar-an-am.u   kaku   tat.u   nami=ni   puna~de
    cross-NEG-FUT.FNP   like.this rise.APT wave=ADV   ship~come.out
    s.u=be.si=ya.
    do.FNP=*be*.FNP=QUE
    'I would like you to go across the sea when it is quiet! Is it appropriate to depart when the waves run high like this?' (MYS 09/1781)

(7) *Imwo=ga   mi.si   aputi=no   pana=pa*
    wife/lover=GEN   see.APT   bead tree=GEN   blossom=TOP
    tiri-n.u=be.si.   *Wa=ga   nak.u   namida   mada*
    fall-PRF.FNP=*be*.FNP   I=GEN   cry.APT   tear   still
    pi-n.aku=ni.
    dry-NEG.NMZ=CNC
    'The blossoms of the bead tree that you saw are about to fall, although my tears haven't dried yet!' (MYS 05/0798)

Readings in contexts with 1st and 2nd person have an implication of intention (1st person) or suggestion (2nd person). The latter is represented in ex. (8)

(8) *Wa=ga   kiki.si   mimi=ni   yo.ku   ni.ru   asi=no*
    I=GEN   hear.APT   rumor=DAT   good.ADV   resemble.FNP   reed=GEN
    *ure=no   asi   pik.u   wa=ga   se   **tutwome~tab.u=be.si#***
    sprout=GEN   leg   drag.APT   I=GEN   man   take.care~do.for=*be*.FNP
    'It is just as I had heard. You, who drags along his leg which is slender like the sprout of a reed, take good care of yourself!' (Man'yōshū 02/0128)

---

[2] Periodization: OJ = Old Japanese (6th–8th c), LOJ = Late Old Japanese (9th–11th c), MidJ = Middle Japanese (12th–18th c), EMJ = Early Modern Japanese (18th–19th c), ModJ = Modern Japanese (late 19th c ~).
[3] Symbols in the glosses: "." in front of an inflection, "=" in front of a particle, "-" in front of any other suffix, "~" between lexemes.

Although still rare, there are also examples with an apparent epistemic reading, that I label here as "conclusion", as in (9).

(9) *Kototop-an.u   kwi=ni=pa   ari=to=mo   urupasi.ki   kimi=ga*
    speak-NEG.APT   wood=ESS=TOP   be=CNC=FOC   noble.APT   lord=GEN
    ta~nare=no   koto=ni=si   ar.u=be.si#
    use.habitually=GEN   koto=ESS-EMP   be.FNP=*be*.FNP
    'You are wood that does not speak, yet you are certainly the koto (Japanese harp) of a noble master that cherishes you.' (Man'yōshū 05/0811)

If we project the meanings of OJ *be-* onto the two-dimensional space of modality, it looks like in Fig. 2.

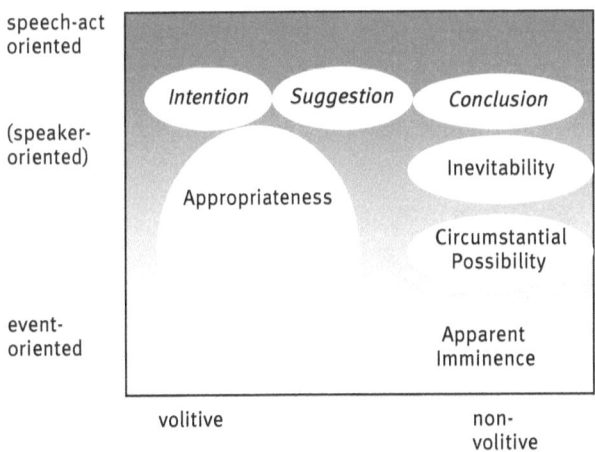

Fig. 2: *be-* in OJ (cf. Narrog 2012: 125).

The two most basic meanings are descriptive and event-oriented. On the volitive side, I consider the "appropriateness" meaning as fairly broad. It is used very frequently and in a large number of contexts, indicating a general necessity. When it is used with 1st and 2nd person subjects it comes close to the domain of speech acts. On the non-volitive side, it is the still rare meaning of "conclusion" that exhibits the highest degree of speaker-orientation.

Later, in the spoken Western Japanese in the Middle Japanese period (which is the documented language of the time) the usage of *be-* declined except for formulaic expressions, but it was continued in Eastern Japanese dialects (which were not documented for many centuries). Here it has become a sentence-final particle with mood and illocutionary force functions, as examples (10) to (12) from Modern Japanese dialects show.

(10) *Kyoo=wa* **arut-te~'g.u=bee**
today=TOP go.on.foot-GER~go.NPS=*be*
'Let's go on foot today!' (Gumma; Hirayama 1992: 532) (hortative)

(11) *Kita~guni=no* *hoo=wa* *koko=yori* **samu-kaN=bee#**
north~country=GEN side=TOP here=ABL cold-VBZ=*be*
'Northern Japan is colder than here, I suppose' (Gumma; Hirayama 1992: 532) (speculative)

(12) *Aizu* **yoN=bee#**
that one read.NPS=*be*
'I'm gonna read that one, (I say)!' (Ibaragi; Hirayama 1992: 2050) (assertive)

Note that the illocutionary force functions have no impact on the factuality of the sentence, and therefore fall outside the categories of modality and mood as defined here. Furthermore, they are a further development of modality and mood functions and not vice versa. In conclusion, the functions in the modern dialects can be arranged on the two-dimensional model of modality as in Fig. 3.

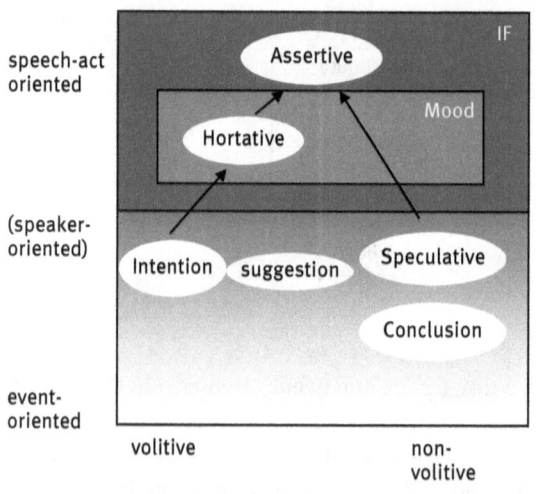

Fig. 3: *bee* in modern eastern dialects (cf. Narrog 2012: 130).

All of the functions left over in Modern Eastern dialects are either speaker-oriented within the modal domain, or belong entirely to the domain of mood and illocutionary force. Thus, over the course of a millennium, there has been a striking shift from event-oriented meanings to speaker- and speech-act-oriented meanings.

3.1.3 Old Japanese –(a)m- to Modern Japanese –(y)oo

This case is presented in even more brevity, since details can be found in Narrog (2012a: 130–132) and Narrog (to appear). Old Japanese –(a)m- was a crosslinguistically common type of future marker (cf. Bybee et al. 1994: Ch. 7), denoting prediction on the one hand, and intention on the other. Occasionally, we find epistemic readings, labeled as "presumptive" here, if the marker occurs with a present (and not future) proposition. In Modern Japanese, its successor –(y)oo[4] has the central function of a hortative, i.e. with the 1st person plural. If it only refers to the 1st person singular, it is a "commissive". The "presumptive" function and "concessive" functions are practically only found in literary language. The "assertive" function is usually realized by *daroo*, which developed from –*am*- suffixed to the copula *da(r)*-. Figure 4 represents the OJ central functions in bold letters, and the modern functions in italics, projected on the two-dimensional model of modality and mood. Again, we find a clear development of more event-oriented functions towards speech-act-oriented functions.

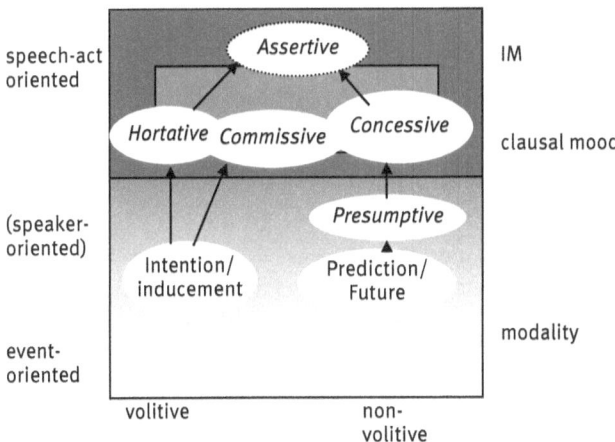

Fig. 4: -(y)oo diachronically.

3.1.4 Japanese -rasi-

This example is presented also only briefly. The semantic changes involved are more subtle and concern evidential categories that are not so well-known from

---
4 Concerning the phonological changes that led from -(a)m- to -(y)oo cf. Narrog (2012a: 130).

the general literature. The Modern Japanese particle adjective *rasi-* has the main function of inferential evidential, that is, a category both modal and evidential, and is occasionally used as a hearsay marker (cf. Narrog 2009: 117–119). One of the earliest examples for use as inferential evidential is represented in ex. (13).

(13) Ano   XX-saN=wa,   onusi=ni   yoppodo   ki=ga
     DEM   (name)-TOA=TOP   2S=DAT   very   feeling=NOM
     ar.u=rasi.i#
     be.NPS=EVI.NPS
     'XX seems to have feelings for you.' (Iroha Bunko 1836–72; Yuzawa 1957: 505)

The meaning of the inferential evidential is that on the basis of some evidence that needs not be mentioned in the sentence, the speaker is drawing a conclusion, of which (s)he cannot be entirely certain. The direct source for this inferential evidential is a morphologically unproductive noun ending in Middle Japanese, as represented in (14).

(14) O.me=wa   hosoboso=to   si.te   **airasi.ku**
     HON.eye=TOP   narrow=STA   do.GER   charming.ADV
     owas.uru=so=ya#
     be(RSP).APT=ILL=ILL
     'Her eyes are narrow, and she looks charming.' (Shasekishū 1, 13th ct)

The noun ending *–rasi-* is found on a limited number of nouns and denotes a factual appearance. The meaning in (14) is not that the speaker is uncertain if the woman he describes is charming or not, but that her appearance is charming. In Narrog (2012a: 139) I have posited a development of *–rasi/rasi-* as in Tab. 2, based on its description in historical dictionaries and papers dealing with its development. A representation in the two-dimensional space as in the examples above is not meaningful since there is only one clearly modal category involved, namely the one at stage IV in the table.

The development sketched out in Tab. 2 took place relatively quickly between the 17th and the 19th century. At the initial stage *-rasi-* denoted a judgment about a property of a referent. This can already be conceived of as a speaker-oriented meaning at a propositional level. However, the end state denotes an epistemic-evidential estimate about a state-of-affairs, which is arguably even more speaker-oriented, since it is non-propositional and bound to the present of the speaking subject (cf. Section 2.3. in Narrog 2012a). *-Rasi-* also underwent a change in morphological status from adjectival ending to particle adjective, as indicated in the middle column of Tab. 2. This is of no further concern here but will be referred to again in Section 4, where we will look at the correlation between formal and functional changes.

Tab. 2: The acquisition of modal meaning by *rasi-*.

stage	Construction	Morphological status	Meaning/function
I	N*rasi*-	Adjectival ending of a small number of words	factual appearance of N-ness
IIa	N-*rasi*- (modification of properties of N)	Suffix adjective	Typicality
IIb	N-*rasi*- (modification of properties of N)	Suffix adjective	False appearance (semblance)
III	N/Adv=*rasi*- (modification of noun/ adverb as a predicate)	Particle adjective	undetermined appearance of identity
IV	V/A/N/Adv=*rasi*- (modification of any clause)	Particle adjective	undetermined appearance that a state-of-affairs holds

3.2 Functional and content changes – hierarchies

An increase in speech-act orientation is a general type of meaning change that is not specifically bound to grammaticalization, but can, for example, also be found in lexical semantic change. Nevertheless, it is probably the most common type of meaning change involved in grammaticalization as well. In contrast, the type of contents change discussed in the Section 3.2.1, namely an ascent in hierarchical clause structure, is an indispensable characteristic of grammaticalization. Furthermore, as argued in Section 3.3 of Narrog (2012a), these changes are usually interrelated, that is, an ascent in category hierarchies is usually accompanied by an increase in speech-act orientation.

In the following I will discuss 'category' climbing from a number of theoretical and empirical perspectives, namely, category climbing in F(D)G and category climbing in Japanese modality and mood (Section 3.2.1), concrete indicators for widening of scope (Section 3.2.2), and cross-linguistically recurring changes along this hierarchy (Section 3.2.3).

3.2.1 Grammaticalization as category climbing

It is difficult to pin down exactly the emergence of the idea of hierarchical clause structures across frameworks of various theoretical convictions, but it is quite possible to pin down when it was first proposed that language change operates along such hierarchical structures. To my knowledge, this was first done by

Hengeveld (1989). The model on which his claim was based was called Functional Grammar (FG) by then, and is called Functional Discourse Grammar (FDG; Hengeveld and Mackenzie 2008) now. The basic idea of the model at that time is represented in Fig. 5.

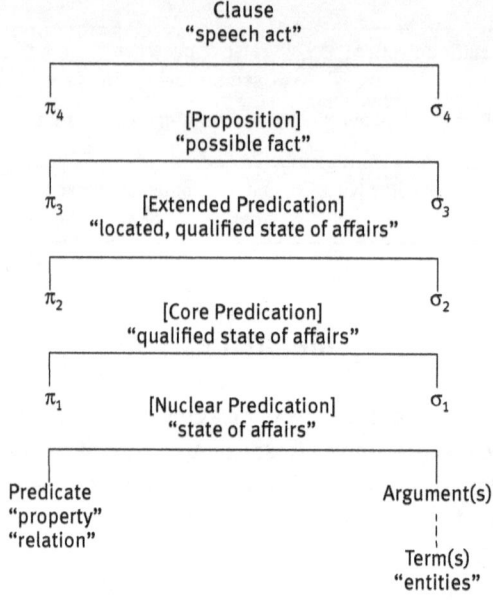

Fig. 5: Layered structure of the clause in FG (cf. Dik 1997: 50).

This model has four layers of the clause, built by grammatical operators (π) and lexical satellites (σ) appropriate for that layer. The motivation for the layers is semantic, although they also have formal aspects. Now, decisively, Hengeveld (1989: 142) claimed that "[d]iachronic developments in the field of operators tend to follow the direction $\pi 1 > \pi 2 > \pi 3 > \pi 4$". That is, there is a movement "upwards" in the clause structure, in which operators can "move up" to higher layers, but will not "move down" to become operator at a lower layer. Hengeveld has recently elaborated on this idea (Hengeveld 2011), but since his work is represented in this volume, it is not necessary to elaborate any further here.

Within functional theories of grammar, RRG (Van Valin and LaPolla 1997) have proposed a similar hierarchical structure of the clause. I have suggested an application to grammaticalization studies that would lead to a similar hypothesis and similar results as in F(D)G (Narrog 2012a: 102), but I am not aware of studies that have actually implemented this kind of research. As for generative grammar, it goes without saying that any research on grammaticalization should inevitably relate to the hierarchical syntactic structure, and this is what we actually see (e.g. van Gelderen 2004, Roberts and Roussou 1998, Roberts 2010; cf. also Narrog 2012a: 103).

While hierarchical structures of clause have a claim to universality, based on the idea that the syntactic and/or semantic categories on which they are based are universal, or at least the scope relationships between them have to be universal, there is still a long way to actually establish this universality as an empirical fact. In a large-scale corpus study of Modern Japanese modal markers and their interaction with categories of other markers (Narrog 2009, 2010b), I have tried to establish a hierarchy of grammatical categories in Modern Japanese centering on modality on purely empirical grounds. A number of complications emerged when trying to combine volitive and non-volitive modal categories in one hierarchy. Therefore, I first identified two hierarchies of modal categories in relation to other interacting categories, one for volitive and one for non-volitive modality. They are displayed in Tab. 3 and Tab. 4, respectively, below. Note that Modern Japanese has several deontic and epistemic modal categories, as Modern English, but they are not identical to the English ones. For details on each category, see Ch. 10 of Narrog (2009).

The differentiation between a volitive and a non-volitive hierarchy of modal categories corresponds to the differentiation between directive and representative (assertive) utterances, which is especially relevant when modal categories are used performatively. The reason why I posited two hierarchies is that scope properties of volitive and non-volitive categories differ fundamentally. For example, volitive modal categories are never able to overtly scope over tense, even if they

Tab. 3: Hierarchy of categories with volitive modalities (cf. Narrog 2012: 98).

Non-modal categories	Modal categories
	Illocutionary modification
	Moods (imperative, hortative)
Tense, (Internal) Negation	Deontic modality 2 (valuative obligation, recommendation)
Perfective/Imperfective aspect	Deontic modality 1 (necessity)
Phasal aspect	Boulomaic modality
Benefactives	
Voice	

Tab. 4: Hierarchy of categories with non-volitive modalities (cf. Narrog 2012: 98).

Non-modal categories	Modal categories
	Illocutionary modification
	Epistemic modality 3 (speculative), (epistemic mood)[5]
Tense	Evidentiality 3 (reportive)
	Epistemic modality 2 (epistemic possibility)
(Internal) Negation	Evidentiality 2 (inferential evidentiality)
	Epistemic modality 1 (epistemic necessity/expectation)
Perfective/Imperfective aspect	Evidentiality 1 (predictive appearance)
Phasal aspect	Dynamic modality
Benefactives	
Voice	

are entirely speech-act-oriented, that is "performative",[6] and at the "top" of all functional categories of a clause. This is because they have an inherent future-orientation, which is pragmatically, and therefore also semantically, incompatible with past events. Thus, their semantics makes differentiation of tense in their scope unnecessary.[7] On the other hand, since there is normally no problem with tense scoping over volitive modalities in descriptive use, this descriptive use tends to get generalized, and therefore volitive modalities tend to be located low in hierarchies (e.g. Cinque 1999: 106; van Valin and LaPolla 1997: 49), irrespective of their potential for performative use.

While it is difficult to build a layering of modal categories containing both volitive and non-volitive modal expressions that is free of contradictions in scopal properties of the individual expressions, volitive and non-volitive modal

---

[5] "Epistemic mood" refers to the epistemic use of the mood inflection -(y)oo. It was not included in previous studies (Narrog 2009a, 2010b) because this use is not fully productive anymore in Modern Japanese, and is also associated with a number of "frozen" (idiomatic) uses which obscure more regular patterns. It can be assumed, though, that in its regular use it is essentially at the same level as its Modern Japanese successor, "Epistemic modality 3" *daroo*, since *daroo* is morphologically derived from -(y)oo, and has to a large extent taken over its functions.

[6] "To the extent that a linguistic form qualifies a proposition with respect to the current speech situation (including speaker and hearer), it is used performatively. To the extent that it does not qualify a proposition with respect to the current speech situation, it is used descriptively" (Narrog 2012a: 42).

[7] For more details on the different scopal behaviour between volitive and non-volitive modal categories see Narrog (2010b).

categories interact diachronically as we have seen above. Therefore, from a diachronic perspective a hierarchy that combines both types of modal elements that contains as few contradictions as possible, is indispensable. This hierarchy is presented in Tab. 5. The arrow in the middle indicates the directionality of diachronic change, from lower to higher (or, inner to outer) layer.

Tab. 5: The modal category hierarchy dynamicized (cf. Narrog 2012: 104).[8]

Non-modal categories	Modal categories
	Illocutionary modification
	Volitive moods (imperative, hortative)
	Epistemic modality 3 (speculative, epistemic mood)
Tense	Evidentiality 3 (reportive) Epistemic modality 2 (epistemic possibility) Deontic modality 2 (valuative obligation, recommendation)
(Internal) Negation	Evidentiality 2 (inferential evidentials) Epistemic modality 1 (epistemic necessity/ expectation)
Perfective/Imperfective aspect	Deontic modality 1 (necessity) Evidentiality 1 (predictive appearance)
Phasal aspect	Boulomaic modality Dynamic modality
Benefactives Voice	

Here the question is to which degree this hierarchy might also be applicable to other languages. If we take the non-modal categories, which are not described in much detail here, I do not see a contradiction to Hengeveld (2011) or to Dik (1997). However, if we look at the fine details concerning modal categories, conflicts with F(D)G, RRG and with Cartography of Syntactic Structures emerge, which, incidentally, also partially contradict each other. I have described details of these conflicts in Narrog (2009: Ch. 19). At least some of these conflicts may be resolved if we accept that modal (and probably also temporal and aspectual) categories differ in their details across languages. For example, the Japanese modal categories are not entirely identical to the English ones, and the properties of Japanese

---

[8] Epistemic modality 3 and epistemic mood is ranked below the volitive moods because they have more flexibility to be used in subordinate positions than volitive moods.

evidentials are not captured well in any of the theories, probably because of the relative lack of knowledge about evidential categories in main stream linguistics, due to their scarcity in European languages. Some conflicts may be more fundamental, but here is not the place to discuss them.

Now, if we project the presumptive change of *-be-* (Section 3.1.2) onto Tab. 5, the result is roughly as in Tab. 6. The OJ core uses can be identified with the "predictive appearance" and "valuative obligation" categories, and the modern dialectal use (dotted line) with volitive moods and illocutionary modification. This is only an approximation since the OJ modal categories and their scopal behaviour are not necessarily identical with the Modern Japanese ones, but the overall directionality should be uncontroversial.

Tab. 6: Development of *-be-* in the hierarchy.

Non-modal categories	Modal categories
	Illocutionary modification
	Volitive moods (imperative, hortative)
	Epistemic modality 3 (speculative, epistemic mood)
Tense	Evidentiality 3 (reportive)
	Epistemic modality 2 (epistemic possibility)
	Deontic modality 2 (valuative obligation, recommendation)
(Internal) Negation	Evidentiality 2 (inferential evidentials)
	Epistemic modality 1 (epistemic necessity/expectation)
Perfective/Imperfective aspect	Deontic modality 1 (necessity)
	Evidentiality 1 (predictive appearance)
Phasal aspect	Boulomaic modality
	Dynamic modality
Benefactives Voice	

3.2.2 Indicators for widening of scope

In the preceding section, I have made some general claims about the development of modal categories within a layered model of grammatical categories. In this subsection I want to substantiate my claim that the scope of the modal categories actually gets wider. Furthermore, I want to point out that this is not a plain, straightforward development, but has some interesting quirks. In this discussion it is important to distinguish between categories over which some modal category can take scope – I will call this "active scope" here – and categories under which it takes scope. The latter phenomenon can be labeled as "passive scope".

To start out with *-be-/-bee*, this morpheme is suffixed to the same non-past verb form in Modern Japanese that it was suffixed to in Old Japanese. It is bound to this position and can in essence not take scope over tense, as we expect from volitive modality. It is also not able to tag onto a negated proposition. Thus, the "active" scope remained the same. However, the "passive" scope properties did change. OJ *-be-* took scope under tense (e.g. *be-kari-si* '*be*-VBZ-PST"), as shown in (15).

(15) ...*omofi~nayam.u   koto=mo   na.ku=te=wa   **faberi-n.u=be-kari.si***
     think-worry-NPS   thing=FOC   be.not-GER=TOP   be-PFV-NPS=*be*-VBZ-PST
     yo=no   naka=ni=mo... (Genji, Usugumo; 10thc)
     world=GEN   inside-LOC=FOC
     'Even at a time when I should not have worried about things...'

Modern Eastern Japanese *-bee* cannot take scope under tense (**-bee-ta* '*bee*-PST'). It is a sentence-final particle with nothing following it. Given what we wrote in the previous section about the scope properties of volitive modalities, this is not unexpected. Even in performative use, the active scope of volitive modality is tightly constrained. It is in their passive scope that volitive modal markers exhibit differences in layering.

Next, we will take a look at *-am-*. If we map its OJ and Modern Japanese main functions onto the layers of modal categories, Tab. 7 should be the best approximation.

Again, while it is not unproblematic to project the historical modal categories onto the modern ones, the core functions of OJ *-am-* can be identified with boulomaic modality and epistemic necessity, while the core function of Modern Japanese *-(y)oo* is hortative mood and speculative, epistemic mood in the written language.

Now, how have the scope properties changed? In terms of active scope, again, not much. *-(y)oo* is suffixed to the same verb form in Modern Japanese that *-(a)m-* was suffixed to in OJ, namely the verb stem. Both the new and the old form therefore tag onto a state-of-affairs without tense and mood. It should be mentioned, though, that in the epistemic meaning, a periphrastic form (particle) *dar.oo*, with the intervening copula verb *da(r-)* developed. This form can be suffixed to a wide range of tense- and mood-marked propositions. It is hard to say, though, whether the development of *dar.oo* should be seen as a direct strategy for widening the scope of *-am-*, since it is also the result of a more fundamental change in Japanese clause structure: adnominal/nominalized verb forms came to be used clause-finally, thus allowing a clause-final copula on verbal predicates. The passive

Tab. 7: Development of -*am*-/-*(y)oo* in the hierarchy.

Non-modal categories	Modal categories
	Illocutionary modification
	Volitive moods (imperative, hortative)
	Epistemic modality 3 (speculative, epistemic mood)
Tense	Evidentiality 3 (reportive)
	Epistemic modality 2 (epistemic possibility)
	Deontic modality 2 (valuative obligation, recommendation)
(Internal) Negation	Evidentiality 2 (inferential evidentials)
	Epistemic modality 1 (epistemic necessity/expectation)
Perfective/Imperfective aspect	Deontic modality 1 (necessity)
	Evidentiality 1 (predictive appearance)
Phasal aspect	Boulomaic modality
	Dynamic modality
Benefactives	
Voice	

scope properties have changed, however. OJ -*(a)m.u* still had inflection, with past (as irrealis) -*si*, conditional -*(ur)e*, and nominalizing -*(ura)ku* following it, and taking scope over it. Modern J -*(y)oo* is only followed by illocutionary force-indicating particles and quotatives, which can embed whole utterances in direct quotation. Especially in the written language, -*(y)oo* is also habitually embedded in idiomatic subordinate constructions, -*(y)oo-ni-mo* 'even if one wants to', or -*(y)oo tame* 'in order to' etc., which make it subjunctive mood-like.

Lastly, we will take a look at the development of -*rasi*-, whose original and modern functions can be mapped onto the modal layering as in Tab. 8. There is no equivalent to its pre-Modern function, which is probably to be classified as lexical rather than grammatical. We have assigned it to the lowest layer on the table. The modern functions are inferential evidential and reportive.

Now, in terms of concrete indicators of scope, at the first stage (cf. Tab. 2), -*rasi*- took scope over a noun. In FDG terms this corresponds to the lowest layer of "individual". At the second stage, as nouns are used predicatively, it comes to scope over equational clauses, in FDG terms "configurational properties". These clauses are at least initially individual-level statements and have no tense and mood. At the third stage, -*rasi*- comes to attach to any predicate and has scope over full clauses ("states-of-affairs"). So, in this case, we see a distinct change

Tab. 8: Development of -*rasi*- in the hierarchy.

Non-modal categories	Modal categories
	Illocutionary modification
	Volitive moods (imperative, hortative)
	Epistemic modality 3 (speculative, epistemic mood)
Tense	Evidentiality 3 (reportive)
	Epistemic modality 2 (epistemic possibility)
	Deontic modality 2 (valuative obligation, recommendation)
(Internal) Negation	Evidentiality 2 (inferential evidentials)
	Epistemic modality 1 (epistemic necessity/expectation)
Perfective/Imperfective aspect	Deontic modality 1 (necessity)
	Evidentiality 1 (predictive appearance)
Phasal aspect	Boulomaic modality
	Dynamic modality
Benefactives	
Voice	

in active scope properties. In contrast, the change in passive scope properties is more subtle. Both pre-modern and modern -*rasi*- can take scope under tense. They don't take scope under aspect, which is not possible because -*rasi*- as an adjective is already stative, and marked aspect in Japanese is stative. However, noun-modifying -*rasi*- could/can be negated while sentence-modifying -*rasi*- cannot. So, here we also see some change in its passive scope properties.

Overall, then, the concrete manner in which scope properties change seems to rely on the specific modality and the individual construction.

3.2.3 Cross-linguistically recurring changes along this hierarchy

In this subsection I will show a number of cross-linguistically common changes within the domain of modality, as identified by Bybee et al. (1994), play out in relation to the hierarchy of categories. Again, the modal categories identified in Japanese are not necessarily identical with the cross-linguistic categories identified by Bybee et al. (1994), but we assume here that they are close equivalents.

First, Bybee et al. (1994) found that in four languages ability/root possibility extended or shifted to epistemic possibility. This can be mapped onto the hierarchy as in Tab. 9.

Tab. 9: Development of ability/root possibility to epistemic possibility.

Non-modal categories	Modal categories
	Illocutionary modification
	Volitive moods (imperative, hortative)
	Epistemic modality 3 (speculative, epistemic mood)
Tense	Evidentiality 3 (reportive)
	Epistemic modality 2 (epistemic possibility)
	Deontic modality 2 (valuative obligation, recommendation)
(Internal) Negation	Evidentiality 2 (inferential evidentials)
	Epistemic modality 1 (epistemic necessity/expectation)
Perfective/Imperfective aspect	Deontic modality 1 (necessity)
	Evidentiality 1 (predictive appearance)
Phasal aspect	Boulomaic modality
	Dynamic modality
Benefactives Voice	

Likewise in four languages, Bybee et al. (1994) found a shift or extension from obligation to imperative. This can be represented in relation to the hierarchy as in Tab. 10.

Tab. 10: Development of obligation to imperative.

Non-modal categories	Modal categories
	Illocutionary modification
	Volitive moods (imperative, hortative)
	Epistemic modality 3 (speculative, epistemic mood)
Tense	Evidentiality 3 (reportive)
	Epistemic modality 2 (epistemic possibility)
	Deontic modality 2 (valuative obligation, recommendation)
(Internal) Negation	Evidentiality 2 (inferential evidentials)
	Epistemic modality 1 (epistemic necessity/expectation)
Perfective/Imperfective aspect	Deontic modality 1 (necessity)
	Evidentiality 1 (predictive appearance)
Phasal aspect	Boulomaic modality
	Dynamic modality
Benefactives Voice	

In Narrog (2010a), based on grammatical descriptions in a 200-languages sample, I showed that quite often voice categories take on functions of modality. Especially common are spontaneity (middle voice) and passives as potential (dynamic modality), and passives as necessity (deontic modality). This is represented in Tab. 11.

Tab. 11: Development of voice to dynamic modality.

Non-modal categories	Modal categories
	Illocutionary modification
	Volitive moods (imperative, hortative)
	Epistemic modality 3 (speculative, epistemic mood)
Tense	Evidentiality 3 (reportive)
	Epistemic modality 2 (epistemic possibility)
	Deontic modality 2 (valuative obligation, recommendation)
(Internal) Negation	Evidentiality 2 (inferential evidentials)
	Epistemic modality 1 (epistemic necessity/expectation)
Perfective/Imperfective aspect	Deontic modality 1 (necessity)
	Evidentiality 1 (predictive appearance)
Phasal aspect	Boulomaic modality
	Dynamic modality
Benefactives	
Voice	

As for the relationship between increase in speech-act-orientation (Section 3.1) and moving up on a hierarchy of categories, I have hypothesized in Narrog (2012a) that these two developments go hand-in-hand, and probably constitute the essence of functional change in grammaticalization.

4 Correlation between functional and formal changes

In this section, we finally try to correlate formal and functional changes. I have suggested that functional grammaticalization is usually correlated to an advance in formal grammaticalization or at least no observable change in formal features, and that formal grammaticalization is accompanied by functional grammaticalization or at least no change in the functional domain (cf. Narrog 2005: 697; 2012a: 107–109). Functional grammaticalization accompanied by formal de-grammaticalization is rare, and formal grammaticalization accompanied by functional de-grammaticalization should be extremely rare if existent at all. If the latter change occurs, it is a veritable exception. Furthermore, I have emphasized that the degree of formal and functional grammaticalization is a matter of the history of the individual marker or construction. In the same grammatical domain, we may have a construction that is functionally highly grammaticalized, that is, semantically speech-act oriented, occupying a high position on a layered model of categories, but is formally only weakly grammaticalized, that is, is still a morphosyntactically independent word. In contrast, there may be another marker/construction in the same domain that is formally further grammaticalized, that is, it is for example a suffix, but is functionally still relatively event-oriented and not high up on the layering of categories. A language like Japanese, where formal grammaticalization is fairly regular and evident through agglutinization (mainly suffixation) offers plenty of material to support this observation (cf. Narrog 2009: Ch. 19; 2010b).

Let us check the above hypotheses by taking a brief look back at the three grammatical markers and constructions discussed in Section 3.1. First, we want to check whether formal and functional grammaticalization indeed proceeded together. The first two items, *-be-/bee* and *-am / -(y)oo* conform to our expectations and show "well-behaved" parallel formal and functional grammaticalization (at least from a macro-perspective).

Japanese *be-/bee* lost inflectional properties as an adjective, underwent phonological fusion (*be-ki* > *be-i* > *bee*), developed speaker- and hearer-oriented uses, and, metaphorically speaking, climbed up the tree of functional categories.

Japanese *-am- / -(y)oo* likewise lost inflectional properties as a suffix verb, underwent phonological fusion and shortening, developed speaker-, hearer-oriented, and text-oriented uses, and also climbed up the tree of functional categories.

In contrast, the development of *–rasi-*, as outlined in Section 3.1.4, shows some complications. *–rasi-* did not lose adjectival properties. In fact, it gained morphological independence and syntactic variability by developing as a particle (clitic) from a noun ending that was more tightly bound to the stem. Morphologically speaking, this is exaptation rather than grammaticalization (cf. Narrog 2007b). On the other hand, functionally, it developed speaker- and hearer-oriented uses, and its functions extended in upward direction on the hierarchy of functional categories. That is, overall *-rasi-* underwent functional grammaticalization but some formal degrammaticalization, that is, an exceptional development.

However, as already argued in previous literature (Heine 2003b; Norde 2009), purely formal degrammaticalization comes relatively cheap in comparison to functional degrammaticalization. This conforms with the observation made in

Section 2 that formal changes in grammaticalization are secondary to functional grammaticalization, as can be already seen by the fact that they heavily depend on the concrete typological characteristics of the language. Formal degrammaticalizations are still exceptions, but in current work on grammaticalization, few scholars would consider them as serious counter-examples to the directionality of grammaticalization.

As for the second point, namely, that the relationship between formal and functional grammaticalization differs item by item, one salient factor involved in the resulting gaps is that both in formal and in functional grammaticalization, various entrance points are possible. In principle, a lexical item does not have to go through a ladder of categories but can enter directly at any spot in the hierarchy without undergoing previous formal grammaticalization. A case in point is the contrast between *I'm sure* vs. *can* (cf. Narrog 2005: 697–698; 2012a: 109), to the extent that one acknowledges a grammatical function of *I'm sure* as an epistemic construction. Besides its function, its positional properties in parenthetical use (cf. Kaltenböck 2007), which is bound to the first person subject (*I'm sure* vs. e.g. *you're sure*), indicate only a moderate degree of formal grammaticalization. However, functionally it is located higher on the hierarchy than *can*, which has undergone a thousand or so years of grammaticalization with salient formal aspects (cf. Section 2.2). Parentheticals and discourse markers, which are prone to cooptation, that is which are often recruited for utterance level functional uses from purely lexical status (cf. Heine 2013), can provide extreme examples. But some regularly grammaticalized TAME markers from Japanese can also illustrate the point nicely. For instance, the evidential *-rasi-* discussed in Section 3.1.2 is formally less grammaticalized than the evidential *-soo*(1), although it clearly expresses two categories with wider semantic scope, and higher in the hierarchy of categories than the latter (cf. Narrog 2009: 227, 242). Overall, the degree of formal grammaticalization is not a very reliable indicator for functional grammaticalization. Only within the polyfunctionality or historical change of a single item (maker/construction) can we expect that a higher degree of formal grammaticalization should correspond to a higher degree or no change in functional grammaticalization (cf. Narrog 2012a: 109).

The above discussion raises a number of questions deeper-going questions about formal and functional grammaticalization. Perhaps the most fundamental of them are:

– Do formal and functional grammaticalization share the same motivations?
– Are they really correlated, or is the fact that they often advance together coincidence?
– Why is functional grammaticalization more strictly unidirectional than formal grammaticalization?

I do not dare to pretend to be able give a full satisfactory discussion of these questions here. First of all, doing so would mean to roll up the whole range of grammaticalization literature of thirty or more years that has been concerned with the question of directionality. My answers here are short and inevitably partially speculative. To the extent that one subscribes to the idea that grammaticalization involves change along a hierarchy of functional categories that is defined by scope, it involves change in mental representations that are shared across speakers, and is thus bound to cognition and categorization. While the details of these categorizations may be language and even speaker-specific, the principles behind these categorizations seem to be near universal, and thus the directionality of changes is also largely universal. The result, as described above, is an expansion in scope. In contrast, formal grammaticalization is the product of online language processing, the details of which have been particularly convincingly described in the work of Bybee and collaborators (e.g. Bybee 2003, 2011). Phonological and morphological changes like phonological erosion and fusion are the almost mechanically predictable result of high-frequency usage. But these phonological and morphological changes are not limited to grammaticalization. They also occur in other phenomena involving high-frequency collocations (e.g. Bybee 2003: 617–618), including lexicalizations (Brinton & Traugott 2005: 48–51). On the other hand, grammaticalization can occur also without high frequency use and therefore need not accompany formal changes typical for high-frequency collocations (cf. Heine and Kuteva 2007: 38–39). Thus, the reason that functional grammaticalization often is accompanied by formal grammaticalization is that grammaticalization often leads to high-frequency use (rather than vice versa; cf. Traugott 2010: 282). But the emphasis here is on "often". Routinization and automatization in both form and meaning can effectively go hand in hand as form and meaning change, but they need not.

In this view, cognition and creativity are essential for grammaticalization (cf. Heine et al. 1991: 30–32; Heine and Stolz 2008), and unlike reductive formal processes, grammaticalization is not the mechanical outcome of online language processing, even if the decisive cognitive actions take place in online discourse (cf. Ariel 2008: Chs. 4, 5). This creativity also enables language users to revert formal grammaticalization processes; that is, exempt suffixes or clitics and start to use them as more independent word forms, if this is useful for the construction of discourse, or give inflection back to word forms that have lost inflection or create inflection with words that were never inflecting, in analogy to similar word forms.

While the reasons for the formal reduction that often accompanies grammaticalization are pretty well understood through empirical research in phonology and morphology, and may also explain the relative low hurdle of counter-directionality, the reason for the overwhelming unidirectionality of functional grammaticalization cannot be considered as solved at all. In the above paragraph I have suggested that this is due to the fact that functional grammaticalization involves cognitive activity that is not merely mechanical. However, the nature of that cognitive activity is largely speculative. Haspelmath (1999) has offered a prominent explanation in terms of "extravagance" that is somewhat similar to the idea of grammaticalization as a creative act by Heine et al. (1991). Speakers try to be "extravagant poets" in order to be socially successful in communication, and this results in cumulative innovations. Within a generative framework (e.g. Roberts and Roussou 1999, 2003), the (uni)directionality of change in the hierarchical clause structure is given by properties of UG. Since UG only allows movement upwards and never downwards, it follows that grammatical change can also be only upwards. Van Gelderen (2011) cites innate principles of economy, which are by also unidirectional by nature. However, these "explanations" will not satisfy scholars outside these frameworks since they invoke principles that are difficult to prove empirically, leading to the danger of circularity (cf. Börjars & Vincent 2011: 174). Kiparsky (2012) claims that grammaticalization is non-exemplar-based analogy while other changes including apparent degrammaticalizations are exemplar-based. The description of formal degrammaticalizations as exemplar-based analogy has strong appeal, but the distinction with non-exemplar based analogy seems similarly a priori and potentially circular as the principles named in the more common generative approaches. An "explanation" from a totally different corner of linguistics, namely Relevance Theory, also invokes an a priori principle. Nicolle (2011: 408) claims that semantic change can only lead to the addition of procedural (i.e., grammatical) meaning but never to its loss, since "procedural information by definition reduces processing effort and therefore always contributes to optimal relevance", which is the ultimate guiding principle of communication. Lastly, Maslova (2008) has brought forward the interesting idea that the expansive change that I have associated with the functional aspect of grammaticalization in this section has a strong perceptive advantage over reductive change when it comes to selection-level (versus the preceding mutation-level) in change: speakers can perceive an extension of context but hardly a reduction (of course, the same does not hold for phonological or morphological change).

To sum up, in the view presented here, formal and functional grammaticalization do not share the same motivation. Nevertheless they are often correlated, as routinization and automatization, which lead to formal changes, are often also involved in grammaticalization of high-frequency markers and constructions. Lastly, formal degrammaticalization is much "cheaper" than functional degrammaticalization since it presumably does not violate any cognitive principles as functional degrammaticalization would do. However, the nature of the cognitive principles invoked that lead to functional unidirectionality has not been established empirically, and differs widely across linguistic theories. Non-cognitive factors like factors in the spread of innovations may also be involved.

5 Summary

In this paper, I have discussed the correlation between formal and functional grammaticalization from a functional linguistic perspective, and illustrated it with examples from the area of modality. I have shown that the extent and concrete features of formal grammaticalization are rather language-specific and that formal grammaticalization as such cannot be regarded as essential for grammaticalization. It is the functional change that is essential. The most important functional changes are a development towards increased speech-act-orientation, which can be broken up into speaker-, hearer-, and text-orientation, and an increase in semantic scope corresponding to an "ascent" in hierarchies of grammatical categories (and preceding that, a shift from lexical to grammatical). Thus, while formal changes are basically reductive, as described in the earlier grammaticalization literature (e.g. Lehmann 2002; Bybee 2003), functional changes are expansive. Formal and functional changes do not have the same motivations. Nevertheless, since the conditions for formal and functional change often overlap, we can assume as the default that formal and functional changes do not correlate negatively. If there is such a negative correlation, it will most likely be due to the formal side of grammaticalization since formal degrammaticalization is much easier to come by than functional degrammaticalization. The former, unlike the latter, does not violate any cognitive principles. Furthermore, due to the fact that grammaticalization has various "entrance points", and functional grammaticalization is not always accompanied by easily discernible formal changes, the degree of grammaticalization across individual markers and constructions cannot be measured reliably based on formal criteria.

Uncommon abbreviations

ADN = adnominal; APT = adnominal present; CNC = concessive; CPL = complementizer; ESS = essive; FIN = finite; FNP = finite non-past; FPT = finite preterite; GER = gerund; HON = honorific; IM = illocutionary modification; LIM = limitative; NMZ = nominalization; NPS = non-past tense; PN = proper noun; TOA = term-of-address; VBZ = verbalization.

References

Ansaldo, Umberto & Lisa Lim. 2004. Phonetic absence as syntactic prominence: Grammaticalization in isolating tonal languages. In Olga Fischer, Muriel Norde & Harry Perridon (eds.), *Up and down the cline: The nature of grammaticalization*, 345–362. Amsterdam & Philadelphia: John Benjamins.

Ariel, Mira. 2008. *Pragmatics and grammar*. Cambridge: Cambridge University Press.

Bisang, Walter. 2008. Grammaticalization and the areal factor: The perspective of East and mainland Southeast Asian languages. In Maria Jóse López-Couso & Elena Seoane (eds.), *Rethinking grammaticalization: New perspectives*, 15–36. Amsterdam & Philadelphia: John Benjamins.

Bisang, Walter. 2011. Grammaticalization and linguistic typology. In Heiko Narrog & Bernd Heine (eds.), *The Oxford handbook of grammaticalization*, 105–117. Oxford: Oxford University Press.

Boland, Annerieke. 2006. *Aspect, tense and modality: Theory, typology, acquisition*. Utrecht: LOT.

Börjars, Kersti & Vincent, Nigel. 2011. Grammaticalization and directionality. In Heiko Narrog & Bernd Heine (eds.), *The Oxford handbook of grammaticalization*, 163–176. Oxford: Oxford University Press.

Bybee, Joan L., William Pagliuca & Revere D. Perkins. 1990. On the asymmetries in the affixation of grammatical material. In William Croft, Keith Denning & Suzanne Kemmer (eds.), *Studies in typology and diachrony: Papers presented to Joseph H. Greenberg on his 75th birthday*, 1–42. Amsterdam & Philadelphia: John Benjamins.

Bybee, Joan, Revere Perkins & William Pagliuca. 1994. *The evolution of grammar: Tense, aspect, and modality in the languages of the world*. Chicago: The University of Chicago Press.

Bybee, Joan. 2003. Mechanisms of change in grammaticalization: The role of frequency. In Brian D. Joseph & Richard D. Janda (eds.), *The handbook of historical linguistics*, 602–623. Oxford: Blackwell.

Bybee, Joan. 2011. Usage-based theory and grammaticalization. In Heiko Narrog & Bernd Heine (eds.), *The Oxford handbook of grammaticalization*, 225–238. Oxford: Oxford University Press.

Bybee, Joan & Sandra Thompson. 1997. Three frequency effects in syntax. *Proceedings of the twenty-third annual meeting of the Berkeley Linguistics Society: General session and parasession on pragmatics and grammatical structure*, 378–388.

Cinque, Guglielmo. 1999. *Adverbs and functional heads*. Oxford: Oxford University Press.

Clark, Robin & Ian Roberts. 1993. A computational model of language learnability and language change. *Linguistic Inquiry* 24. 299–345.

Coates, Jennifer. 1995. The expression of root and epistemic possibility in English. In Joan Bybee & Suzanne Fleischman (eds.), *Modality in grammar and discourse*, 55–66. Amsterdam & Philadelphia: John Benjamins.

Diewald, Gabriele. 2009. Konstruktionen und Paradigmen. *Zeitschrift für germanistische Linguistik* 37. 445–468.

Dik, Simon C. 1997. *The theory of Functional Grammar. Part 1: The structure of the clause*. Ed. by Kees Hengeveld. Berlin & New York: Mouton de Gruyter.

Gelderen, Elly van. 2004. *Grammaticalization as economy*. Amsterdam & Philadelphia: John Benjamins.

Gelderen, Elly van. 2011. Grammaticalization and generative grammar: A difficult liaison. In Narrog, Heiko & Bernd Heine (eds.), *The Oxford handbook of grammaticalization*, 43–55. Oxford: Oxford University Press.

Goossens, Louis. 1987. The auxiliarization of the English modals: A Functional Grammar view. In Martin Harris & Paolo Ramat (eds.), *Historical development of auxiliaries*, 111–143. Berlin & New York: Mouton de Gruyter.

Goossens, Louis. 1992. *Cunnan, cone(n), can*: The development of a radial category. In Günter Kellermann & Michael D. Morrissey (eds.), *Diachrony within synchrony: Language history and cognition*, 377–394. Frankfurt am Main: Peter Lang.

Hanazono, Satoru. 1999. Jōkenkei fukugō yōgen keishiki no nintei [The recognition of complex conditional verb forms]. *Kokugogaku* 197. 39–53.

Haspelmath, Martin. 1999. Why is grammaticalization irreversible? *Linguistics* 37 (6). 1043–1068.

Heine, Bernd. 2003a. Grammaticalization. In Brian D. Joseph & Richard D. Janda (eds.), *The handbook of historical linguistics*, 575–601. Oxford: Blackwell.

Heine, Bernd. 2003b. On degrammaticalization. In Barry J. Blake & Kate Burridge (eds.), *Historical linguistics 2001: Selected papers from the 15th International Conference on Historical Linguistics, Melbourne, 13–17 August 2001*, 163–179. Amsterdam & Philadelphia: John Benjamins.

Heine, Bernd & Thomas Stolz. 2008. Grammaticalization as a creative process. *Sprachtypologie und Universalienforschung* 61. 326–357.

Heine, Bernd. 2013. On discourse markers: Grammaticalization, pragmaticalization, or something else? *Linguistics* 51 (6). 1205–1247.

Heine, Bernd, Ulrike Claudi & Friederike Hünnemeyer. 1991. *Grammaticalization: A conceptual framework*. Chicago: University of Chicago Press.

Heine, Bernd & Tania Kuteva. 2002. *World lexicon of grammaticalization*. Cambridge: Cambridge University Press.

Heine, Bernd & Tania Kuteva. 2007. *The genesis of grammar: A reconstruction*. Oxford: Oxford University Press.

Heine, Bernd & Heiko Narrog. 2010. Grammaticalization. In Bernd Heine & Heiko Narrog (eds.), *Oxford handbook of linguistic analysis*, 401–423. Oxford. Oxford University Press.

Heine, Bernd & Mechthild Reh. 1984. *Grammaticalization and reanalysis in African languages*. Hamburg: Helmut Buske Verlag.

Hengeveld, Kees. 1989. Layers and operators in Functional Grammar. *Journal of Linguistics* 25, 127–157.

Hengeveld, Kees. 2011. The grammaticalization of tense and aspect. In Heiko Narrog & Bernd Heine (eds.), *The Oxford handbook of grammaticalization*, 580–594. Oxford: Oxford University Press.

Hengeveld, Kees & J. Lachlan Mackenzie. 2008. *Functional Discourse Grammar: A typologically-based theory of language structure*. Oxford: Oxford University Press.

Hirayama, Teruo. 1992. *Gendai Nihongo Hōgen Daijiten* [Grand dictionary of Modern Japanese dialects]. Vol. 1. Tōkyō: Meiji Shoin.

Hopper, Paul J. & Elizabeth Closs Traugott. 2003. *Grammaticalization*. 2nd edn. Cambridge: Cambridge University Press.

Jespersen, Otto. 1992 [1924] *The philosophy of grammar*. Chicago: University of Chicago Press.

Kaltenböck, Gunther. 2007. Spoken parenthetical clauses in English: A taxonomy. In Nicole Dehé & Yordanka Kavalova (eds.), *Parentheticals*, 25–52. Amsterdam & Philadelphia: John Benjamins.

Kim-Renaud, Young-Key. 2009. *Korean. An essential grammar*. London: Routledge.

Kiparsky, Paul. 2012. Grammaticalization as optimization. In Dianne Jonas, John Whitman & Andrew Garrett (eds.), *Grammatical change: Origins, nature, outcomes*, 15–51. Oxford: Oxford University Press.

Lamiroy, Béatrice & Walter de Mulder. 2011. Degrees of grammaticalization across languages. In Heiko Narrog & Bernd Heine (eds.), *The Oxford handbook of grammaticalization*, 302–317. Oxford: Oxford University Press.

Langacker, Ronald W. 1990. Subjectification. *Cognitive Linguistics* 1 (1). 5–38.

Lehmann, Christian. 1986. Grammaticalization and linguistic typology. *General Linguistics* 26 (1). 3–22.

Lehmann, Christian. 2002 [1982]. *Thoughts on grammaticalization*. 2nd edn. (Arbeitspapiere des Seminars für Sprachwissenschaft der Universität Erfurt Nr. 9). Erfurt: Seminar für Sprachwissenschaft der Universität [revision of *Thoughts on grammaticalization*: *A programmatic sketch* (1982), Arbeiten des Kölner Universalienprojekts 49].

Lyons, John. 1968. *Introduction to theoretical linguistics*. Cambridge: Cambridge University Press.

Maslova, Elena. 2008. Unidirectionality of grammaticalization in an evolutionary perspective. In Elisabeth Verhoeven, Stavros Skopeteas, Yong-Min Shin, Yoko Nishina & Johannes Helmbrecht (eds.), *Studies on grammaticalization*, 15–24. Berlin & New York: Mouton de Gruyter.

Narrog, Heiko. 2002. Polysemy and indeterminacy in modal markers – the case of Japanese *beshi*. *Journal of East Asian Linguistics* 11. 123–167.

Narrog, Heiko. 2005a. Modality, mood, and change of modal meanings – a new perspective. *Cognitive Linguistics* 16 (4). 677–731.

Narrog, Heiko. 2005b. On defining modality again. *Language Sciences* 27 (2), 165–192.

Narrog, Heiko. 2007a. Modality and grammaticalization in Japanese. *Journal of Historical Pragmatics* 8 (2), 269–294.

Narrog, Heiko. 2007b. Exaptation, grammaticalization, and reanalysis. *California Linguistic Notes* 32 (1). 1–27.

Narrog, Heiko. 2009. *Modality in Japanese – The layered structure of clause and hierarchies of functional categories*. Amsterdam & Philadelphia: John Benjamins.

Narrog, Heiko. 2010a. Voice and non-canonical marking in the expression of event-oriented modality – a cross-linguistic study. *Linguistic Typology* 14. 71–126.

Narrog, Heiko. 2010b. The order of meaningful elements in the Japanese verbal complex. *Morphology* 20 (1). 205–237.

Narrog, Heiko. 2012a. *Modality, subjectivity, and semantic change: A cross-linguistic perspective*. Oxford: Oxford University Press.

Narrog, Heiko. 2012b. Beyond intersubjectification – textual uses of modality and mood in subordinate clauses as part of speaker-orientation. *English Text Linguistics* 5 (1). 29–52.

Narrog, Heiko. 2012c. Modality and speech-act-orientation. In Johan van der Auwera & Jan Nuyts (eds.), *Grammaticalization and (inter-)subjectification*, 21–36. Brussels: Contactforum.

Narrog, Heiko. 2015. (Inter)subjectification and its limits in secondary grammaticalization. *Language Sciences* 47. 148–160.

Narrog, Heiko. To appear. The morphosyntax of grammaticalization in Japanese. In Masayoshi Shibatani (ed.), *Syntax* (Handbooks of Japanese language and linguistics).

Narrog, Heiko & Toshio Ohori. 2011. Grammaticalization in Japanese. In Heiko Narrog & Bernd Heine (eds.), *The Oxford handbook of grammaticalization*, 775–785. Oxford: Oxford University Press.

Nicolle, Steve. 2011. Pragmatic aspects of grammaticalization. In Heiko Narrog & Bernd Heine (eds.) *The Oxford handbook of grammaticalization*, 401–412. Oxford: Oxford University Press.

Norde, Muriel. 2009. *Degrammaticalization*. Oxford: Oxford University Press.
OED [*Oxford English Dictionary*]. 2nd edn. on CD-Rom. Oxford University Press, 2002.
Palmer, F. R. 1999. Mood and modality: further developments. In Keith Brown & Jim Miller (eds.), *Concise encyclopedia of grammatical categories*, 235–239. Oxford: Elsevier.
Rhee, Seongha. 2011. Grammaticalization in Korean. In Heiko Narrog & Bernd Heine (eds.), *The Oxford handbook of grammaticalization*, 764–774. Oxford: Oxford University Press.
Roberts, Ian. 2010. Grammaticalization, the clausal hierarchy and semantic bleaching. In Elizabeth Closs Traugott & Graeme Trousdale (eds.), *Gradience, gradualness and grammaticalization*, 45–73. Amsterdam & Philadelphia: John Benjamins.
Roberts, Ian & Anna Roussou. 1999. A formal approach to grammaticalization. *Linguistics* 37 (6). 1011–1041.
Roberts, Ian & Anna Roussou. 2003. *Syntactic change: A minimalist approach to grammaticalization*. Cambridge: Cambridge University Press.
Roberts, Ian. 2010. Grammaticalization, the clausal hierarchy and semantic bleaching. In Elizabeth Closs Traugott & Graeme Trousdale (eds.), *Gradience, gradualness and grammaticalization*, 45–73. Amsterdam & Philadelphia: John Benjamins.
Traugott, Elizabeth Closs. 2003. From subjectification to intersubjectification. In Raymond Hickey (ed.), *Motives for language change*, 124–139. Cambridge: Cambridge University Press.
Traugott, Elizabeth Closs. 2010. Grammaticalization. In Silvia Luraghi & Vit Bubenik (eds.), *Continuum companion of historical linguistics*, 271–285. London: Continuum.
Traugott, Elizabeth & Richard Dasher. 2002. *Regularity in semantic change*. Cambridge: Cambridge University Press.
Van der Auwera, Johan, Petar Kehayov & Alica Vittrant. 2009. Acquisitive modals. In Lotte Hogeweg, Helen De Hoop & Andrej Malchukov (eds.), *Crosslinguistic semantics of tense, aspect, and modality*, 271–302. Amsterdam & Philadelphia: John Benjamins.
Van Valin, Robert D. & Randy J. LaPolla. 1997. *Syntax: Structure, meaning, and function*. Cambridge: Cambridge University Press.
Yuzawa, Kōkichirō. 1957. *Zōtei Edo Kotoba no Kenkyū* [Research on the Edo language] Expanded & revised edn. Tōkyō: Meiji Shoin.

Sophie Villerius
Modality and aspect marking in Surinamese Javanese: Grammaticalization and contact-induced change[1]

Abstract: The former Dutch colony Suriname shows intricate patterns of societal and individual multilingualism, and one of the important questions is whether mutual influence between these languages causes grammatical changes. This paper investigates the marking of Tense, Modality and Aspect in Surinamese Javanese, whose speakers are typically also fluent in Sranan Tongo and Dutch. It aims to identify possible changes this system has undergone due to language contact and establish a relative order of stability for these structures. These questions are investigated by comparing the system of baseline (Indonesian) Javanese, based on literature and recordings from Java, with that of Surinamese Javanese, based on recordings from Suriname. Several divergences between the two varieties are observed, which are explained on the basis of the functionalist grammaticalization hierarchy of Hengeveld as well as the borrowability hierarchy of Matras. By comparing the observed changes to structures in Dutch and Sranan Tongo, it is shown that there are both MAT (replication of matter; use of Sranan Tongo *proberi*) as well as PAT (replication of grammatical patterns; increased use of prospective aspect) changes which can be explained by language contact, while other changes (semantic extension of [*p*]*inter*) are best explained as language-internal developments.

Keywords: language contact, heritage language, Javanese, Suriname, Dutch, Sranan Tongo

---

[1] Some parts of this paper and the results on which it reports have been included in an earlier form in Borges et al. (2014). I want to thank Kofi Yakpo, my M.A. supervisors at the University of Amsterdam, the editors of this volume and Pieter Muysken for their comments and further contributions.

Sophie Villerius: Radboud University Nijmegen, Department of Linguistics, P.O. Box 9103, 6500 HD Nijmegen, The Netherlands, s.villerius@let.ru.nl

---

DOI 10.1515/9783110519389-005

1 Introduction

Suriname, a former Dutch colony in the Guianas, offers a fascinating research environment to linguists, as many different mother tongues of different origins are spoken there, including indigenous, creole and immigrant languages. One of these immigrant languages is Javanese, an Austronesian language from Indonesia, which came with the contract laborers from the late 19th century onward. For a long time, this community has been quite closed and conservative, which has led to the preservation of much of its cultural heritage, including the Javanese language. Nowadays however, young Surinamese Javanese are mostly dominant in Dutch and Sranan Tongo (the Surinamese creole and lingua franca), and the domains where Javanese is spoken are becoming restricted to the home and to ritual contexts.

Since Javanese in Suriname is spoken in a highly multilingual context, Surinamese Javanese can be expected to show divergences from its Indonesian roots, under the influence of language contact. The goal of this paper is to provide a first overview of the divergences found in the marking of tense, modality and aspect (henceforth TAM) of Javanese as spoken in Suriname nowadays, and to propose possible explanations for the direction of language change in this domain. By comparing Surinamese heritage language data with Javanese baseline data, changes possibly due to language contact will be identified and explored.

This approach will allow me to address two main questions: (1) Is it possible to predict the direction of language change in the TAM-domain in a language contact situation? (2) Can changes in the TAM-system of Surinamese Javanese be ascribed directly to contact with Dutch and/or Sranan Tongo?

This paper is structured as follows: in Section 2, I will give definitions of the TAM-categories used in this paper, and draw the implications about the direction of change on the basis of different theories, notably Matras (2007) and Hengeveld (2011). In Section 3 a short history and description of the Javanese language in Indonesia and Suriname will be given, as well as an overview of the Javanese TAM-system. I will also explain my methodology and data. Section 4 is dedicated to the results of the comparison between TAM-marking in Surinamese Javanese and Indonesian Javanese, followed by a discussion in Section 5. In Section 6 I will present the conclusions.

2 Change and stability in TAM categories

In this section, I will introduce the types of language change that I distinguish, and make predictions about the direction of language change in TAM categories on the basis of different theories.

2.1 Matter and pattern changes

In order to categorize the changes that may be observed in the TAM-system of Surinamese Javanese, I follow the distinction that Sakel (2007) makes between MAT (matter) and PAT (pattern) changes. Matter borrowing is defined as the replication of "morphological material and its phonological shape" (Sakel 2007: 15). Pattern borrowing, on the other hand, is replication of "the organization, distribution and mapping of grammatical or semantic meaning" (Sakel 2007: 15), without transfer of the form itself. As we will see, both types of linguistic change are relevant in the case of Surinamese Javanese.

2.2 Language change in TAM categories

In a situation of language contact, one of the most notable signs of cross-linguistic influence is the incorporation of loanwords. However, grammatical categories may also be subject to contact-induced change, often in a more subtle way. Based on the borrowability of MAT as well as PAT in the categories of tense, mood and aspect in a 27-language sample, Matras (2007: 46) proposes the hierarchy in (1) for the stability of TAM-categories, in which the category of tense is least often affected by borrowing (most 'stable'), while modality is most often affected. The ordering is based on the number of languages showing either structural or lexical borrowing in these categories.

(1) modality > aspect > future tense > (other tenses)

Matras explains this hierarchy in terms of the degree of speaker control: the lower the speaker control, the more cognitive load the utterance requires, and the more susceptible it will be to borrowing. Low speaker control is taken to mean that the speaker refers to a state of affairs which lies "beyond the speaker's domain of secure knowledge" (Matras 2011: 222). The rationale behind the higher susceptibility to borrowing is that bilingual speakers already need extra cognitive control to keep their languages separate while speaking, which will become more difficult when cognitive load is increased, and therefore transfer effects may be expected. In this respect, tense is regarded as implying a high degree of speaker control, since there is an intimate relationship between the event and the speaker's own perspective, as the event is only located in time, and optionality is very limited. Since the event expressed in the future tense is more uncertain than in other tenses, the speaker has a lower degree of speaker control, leading to a higher probability of using borrowed elements. Speakers have even less immediate control over the expression of aspect, which refers to the qualification of the internal structure of an event. In the domain of modality, speaker control is supposedly the lowest, since this involves the presentation of propositional content in relation to hearer expectations, which leads to more potential tension in the interaction.

Within Functional Discourse Grammar, Hengeveld (2011) proposes a hierarchy of the categories of tense, modality and aspect based on the direction of grammaticalization. The categories of tense, modality and aspect are divided according to semantic layers, which are defined in terms of scope relations, as proposed by Hengeveld and Mackenzie (2008). The semantic aspects of an utterance are located at the Representational Level, one of the four levels of formulation and encoding in the framework of Functional Discourse Grammar. The semantic units that make up the Representational Level are called layers, and these are hierarchically ordered on the basis of the scope of the grammatical elements that operate on each of them.

Moving from low to high scope, these scope relations are defined in terms of the following layers: the Configurational Property[2] is a description of the predicate and its arguments in a State-of-Affairs; the State-of-Affairs is a real or hypothesized situation, which can be located in time and space and evaluated in terms of its reality; the Episode is a thematically coherent combination of States-of-Affairs characterized by unity or continuity of time, location and individuals; the Propositional Content is a mental construct about a set of States-of-Affairs, which can be located neither in space nor in time, but only evaluated in terms of its truth. These different scopes correspond to different grammaticalized TAM-categories, an overview of which is given in Tab. 1. Some representative subcategories are given in brackets.

Tab. 1: TAM-categories in Functional Discourse Grammar, with subcategories bracketed.

	Propositional content	Episode	State-of-affairs	Configurational property
Tense		absolute tense (past/future tense)	relative tense (anterior/posterior tense)	
Aspect			event quantification (habitual/ distributive aspect)	phasal aspect (im)perfectivity (perfective/ resultative)
Modality	subjective epistemic modality (certainty/doubt)	objective epistemic modality (ir)reality	event-oriented modality (purpose)	participant-oriented modality (ability/intention)

---

[2] 'Situational Concept' in Hengeveld (2011).

As for the direction of grammaticalization, Hengeveld (2011) proposes that the grammaticalization of TAM categories follows a path of scope increase, always moving from low to high scope:

(2) configurational property > state-of-affairs > episode > propositional content

According to this hierarchy, a marker of e.g. participant-oriented modality may become grammaticalized further as a marker of event-oriented and epistemic modality, but this will not happen the other way around. From this description, it can be deduced that the categories with narrow scope are less 'stable' than those with wider scope, since categories with low scope are more likely to undergo change (i.e. grammaticalization) towards expressing higher scope meanings.

Although these two theories are both concerned with language change in the area of TAM, they can be said to describe two different 'forces' working on this system: whereas Matras is concerned with language change in the shape of borrowing of forms or structures, in terms of frequencies and tendencies, Hengeveld is concerned with the direction of grammaticalization or extension of the functions of TAM-markers, which is expected to follow a path of scope increase. If we take the two theories together, it would seem that both frameworks would predict participant-oriented modality to be one of the categories most susceptible to language change, either by being more likely to take a borrowed form, or by being the first category susceptible to extending its function towards expressing higher scope (i.e. undergo grammaticalization). In the next few paragraphs, I will show how these predictions match the observations with respect to the TAM-categories of Surinamese Javanese.

In the language contact situation of Surinamese Javanese, speakers follow a specific path of language acquisition, which is different from that of monolingual native speakers. Since the language under consideration (the 'heritage' or cultural language) is used only in restricted domains and situations, speakers may be expected to lose the flexibility to use different structures that native speakers have available, for example in word order (Polinsky and Kagan 2007: 25). This change does not necessarily mean that linguistic structures cease to exist: often, the result is more likely to consist in a change in frequency distribution, or overgeneralization of an existing option (Matras and Sakel 2007: 47). As we will see below, this latter observation is specifically relevant in the case of Surinamese Javanese.

3 The Javanese language

In this section, I will give an overview of the linguistic situation in Indonesia (Section 3.1) as well as Suriname with regards to Javanese (Section 3.2), point out the most relevant linguistic characteristics of this language (Section 3.3), and provide an overview of the TAM-system of Indonesian Javanese (Section 3.4). At the end I introduce my methodology and data (Section 3.5).

3.1 Javanese in Indonesia

The current estimated number of speakers of Javanese in Indonesia is 84.3 million (Lewis et al. 2013), making it the 10th most widely spoken language in the world (Cohn and Ravindranath 2013). It is important to note that the Javanese as spoken on Java is not homogeneous. It has traditionally been divided into three main dialects: western, central and eastern Javanese, although there is considerable variation within these regions. The dialect spoken in Surakarta and Yogyakarta (Central Java) has been generally accepted as Standard Javanese (Dudas 1976: iv; Robson 1992: 4). The most important differences between the Javanese dialects concern phonology and the lexicon. The TAM-system seems to be roughly the same between all of them (except for some allomorphic variation of markers); therefore I will not focus on this division any further.

3.2 Javanese in Suriname

From the beginning of the colonization of Suriname in the seventeenth century, the colonizing nations, first the English, then the Dutch from 1667 onward, established plantations. Initially slaves were imported from Africa to cultivate these plantations, and they worked there until the abolition of slavery in 1863. After that, contract laborers were shipped to Suriname as the new workforce for these plantations, among which a substantial population from Java. Between 1890 and 1939 around 33,000 Javanese came to Suriname, and today they constitute around 16% of the Surinamese population (Carlin and Arends 2002). After the end of their five-year contract, laborers were encouraged to stay in Suriname, and a lot of them stayed on as small farmers. Many Javanese nowadays still live in small communities outside the city, which is one of the reasons why their language has been able to survive in Suriname for such a long time.

Not many sources are available about the initial period of this immigration, and it is therefore difficult to establish the exact origin of the immigrants from Indonesia. However, it is certain that this group did not consist exclusively of Javanese speakers: there were also speakers of Sundanese and Madurese among them. According to a survey by Vruggink (1985), these two groups made up around 5.5% of the total number of immigrants. It is clear that Javanese became the dominant language within this group, since no trace of the other languages is found in Suriname anymore. Concerning the regions of origin, on the basis of a small sample of immigration records Vruggink (1985) calculates that the majority (70%) came from Central Java, 20% from East Java and 10% from West Java.[3]

Nowadays, the official language of Suriname is Dutch, while the English-based creole Sranan Tongo is used as the lingua franca. Apart from these two languages, there are sixteen more mother tongues being spoken in Suriname, including indigenous and immigrant languages. Surinamese Javanese is the fourth to fifth most widely spoken mother tongue in Suriname, depending on the classification of Maroon languages as one or several languages (Kroon and Yagmur 2012: 13). Since Sranan Tongo was the lingua franca on the plantations, its influence on Javanese may be assumed to have started very early on. Bilingualism in Dutch probably started later, since it did not play an important role during the contract labor period (Vruggink 1985). For a long time, the Javanese community has been able to preserve the language as a medium of communication at home, since the Javanese lived in relative isolation. However, this situation has begun to change after the Second World War as a consequence of increasing urbanization. More and more Javanese came to live in the cities and entered into contact with other ethnic groups, where they began to use other languages. In the early 1980s already, it was reported in a survey by Hagoort and Schotel (1982) that only 6.8% of Javanese children conversed with their grandparents in Dutch or Sranan Tongo, but in conversations with peers, 79.4% preferred to use one of these two languages. Together with the fact that Surinamese Javanese is barely written, this indicates that language loss and shift has probably already been going on since or even before the 1980s. Nowadays, we see that the use of Javanese in Suriname is mostly restricted to family environment and religious/cultural institutions, while Dutch is used in school and the government, and Sranan Tongo as a means of inter-ethnic communication.

Previous linguistic research on Surinamese Javanese has been carried out by Vruggink (1985; 2001) and Wolfowitz (1991). Vruggink (1985) concludes that the Javanese as spoken in Suriname differs most notably from original Javanese with respect to the incorporation of loanwords from Dutch and Sranan, but that

---

3 This observation was confirmed by my own survey of the records of 15,709 contract laborers (around half of the total) in the immigration archives (Nationaal Archief 1999), which showed that as many as 66% originated from Central Java, 19% from East Java, 1% from either East or Central Java and only 4% from West Java. For the remaining 10% it has not yet been possible to identify their region of origin, either because the province stated in their record could not be identified on modern maps or because there were multiple provinces with the same name. Further research with additional sources is therefore needed to identify these regions.

there are no notable differences in the phonology, morphology and syntax. Wolfowitz (1991) discusses the social stratification of the Javanese in Suriname, and how this is reflected in the "speech levels". Speech levels constitute a very complicated system in Javanese, ranging from most informal (*ngoko*) to most formal (*krama*), depending mostly on the relative status of the interlocutors. She concludes that the number of different speech levels in the Surinamese variety is reduced in comparison to Indonesia. Since *ngoko* is the most widely used speech style (especially in Suriname), I will use this speech level in the examples cited for the remainder of this paper.

3.3 General linguistic characteristics of Javanese

The basic word order of Javanese is SVO (subject-verb-object), although other orders are possible as well, depending on what the speaker wishes to put forward (Robson 1992). The emphasized element, which may be the predicate as well as the object, is placed at the beginning of the sentence, leading to as many as five possible word order variations of the simple clause *Supari tuku gedhang* (Supari buy banana) 'Supari buys a banana', of which only (3a) is slightly more marginal (Conners 2008: 63):

(3) a. ?*Supari gedhang tuku.*
    b. *Gedhang Supari tuku.*
    c. *Gedhang tuku Supari.*
    d. *Tuku Supari Gedhang.*
    e. *Tuku gedhang Supari.*

A further notable property of Javanese, as evident from the glossed examples in the remainder of this paper, is the marking of 'voice' on the verb. The exact nature of this system is still debated (see e.g. Ewing 1999; Gil 2002; Myhill 1993), but most authors agree that some form of distinction between 'active' or 'actor' and 'passive' or 'undergoer' voice exists in Javanese, and is very prominent, as in many other Austronesian languages (Himmelmann 2005). Actor voice is marked by a nasal prefix (mostly *n-*, *m-* or *ng-*), whereas undergoer voice (which turns the patient of the sentence into the grammatical subject) is marked by the prefix *di-*. In these "passive" clauses, the agent is only optionally present, and can appear either unmarked or marked by using the preposition *karo* 'with' (Vander Klok 2012). Consider the following examples:

(4) aku   m-angan   sego
    1SG   AV-eat   rice
    'I eat rice.'

(5) sego   di-pangan   ((karo)   aku)
    rice   UV-eat   with   1SG
    'Rice is eaten (by me).'

While this system may at first sight seem similar to the active/passive distinction in languages such as English, it is often not described in these terms. As argued by Gil (2002: 243), *di*-marked clauses in Javanese are generally foregrounded and of high transitivity, while prototypical passive clauses in English are mostly backgrounded and of low transitivity. Another argument described by Gil for not considering these clauses as prototypical passives comes from constructions with control verbs (or: verbs with equi-deletion), illustrated by the following example from the Surinamese Javanese corpus.

(6) terus   arep   di-jukuk   maar   ora   inter
    then   want   UV-take   but   NEG   ABIL
    'Then he wants to grab it but he cannot.'

In a prototypical English passive, the subject of the control verb *arep* 'want' would be co-referential with the subject of the passive verb *dijukuk* 'to be taken', which would result in the translation 'It then wanted to be taken but could not', which is not the right translation in this context (the context provided is a movie clip in which two boys aim to reach for a piece of clothing from a tree, but it is too high for them to grab).

3.4 TAM-system

Javanese verbs are not marked for person or number and there is only little morphosyntactic marking for TAM-categories. TAM-categories in Javanese are marked by auxiliary words, occurring in pre-verbal position (Robson 1992: 64). One of the arguments for considering these markers auxiliary words, rather than clitics or affixes, is the fact that they can be separated from the main verb by an adverb. Consider the following example where the auxiliary *bakal* (future/irrealis) and the verb *lunga* are separated by the negative adverb *ora*:

(7) aku   bakal   ora   lunga
    1SG   IRR   NEG   go
    'I will not be going.' (Robson 1992: 66)

Vander Klok (2008), argues that while Javanese auxiliaries share some properties with verbs, they should be considered a separate category on the basis of their different morphosyntactic behavior. The properties that auxiliaries and verbs have in common include the possibility of taking verbal, prepositional and adjectival complements, as in the following examples, with the aspectual marker *wis* (all taken from Vander Klok 2008, with my own glosses):

(8) aku   wis   [_{VP} mangan]
    1SG   PRF   eat
    'I ate.'

(9) kito   wis   [_{PP} nang   warong   kuwi]
    1PL   PRF   to   store   that
    'We have been to the store.'

(10) aku   wis   [_{AP} warèk]
     1SG   PRF   full
     'I'm already full.'

What sets the class of auxiliaries apart from lexical verbs is the fact that they cannot take noun phrase-complements and undergoer voice morphology in the form of the *di*-prefix, which can only be attached to lexical verbs (Vander Klok 2008: 2).

Table 2 provides an overview of TAM-auxiliaries in Javanese, based on different sources (Robson 1992, Adelaar 2011a, Vander Klok 2008, Vander Klok 2010). For reasons of space, I will not go into the details of use of each different marker here, because these will be explained where relevant in the sections on Surinamese Javanese. It should be mentioned that the status of some of the markers is controversial. The marker *wis*, for example, is considered a marker of tense rather than aspect in Vander Klok (2008). In this paper, I will analyze *wis* as a marker of perfect aspect, since the defining element of this marker appears to be the emphasis on the result of the verbal action, and the relevance thereof in the present. Comrie (1976: 12) considers this present relevance of the past situation one of the defining characteristics of perfect aspect. Consider the following example, which I regard as one of the most prototypical uses of *wis*, almost always in a reply to the offering of food (politely refusing):

(11) wis   wareg
     PRF   full
     'I am already full.' (so I don't need to eat anymore)

A similar case is that of *bakal*, which according to Vander Klok (2010: 2) is a tense marker comparable to *arep*. The marker *bakal* will be analyzed as a modal marker of irrealis in this paper, so as to clearly distinguish it from the future marker *arep*. In my earlier fieldwork on Indonesian Javanese, this semantic distinction was pointed out as highly relevant by my informant. This speaker emphasized that the use of *bakal* adds a sense of uncertainty to the clause, and I observed that it was mostly used in non-factive complement clauses, such as the following:

(12) dèké   ora   yakin   nèk   wong   iku   bakal   lunga
     3SG   NEG   sure   COMP   person that   IRR   go
     'He doubts whether she will leave.'

Tab. 2: Overview of TAM-markers (auxiliary words and suffixes) in Indonesian Javanese.

Category	Subcategory	Type	Marker
Tense	Absolute	Future[4]	arep
Aspect	(Im)perfectivity	Progressive	lagi
	(Im)perfectivity	Perfect	wis
Modality	Subjective epistemic	Epistemic 'must'	mesthi
	Subjective epistemic	Epistemic 'may'	mungkin
	Objective epistemic	Irrealis	bakal
	Participant-oriented/ event-oriented	Deontic 'may'	entuk/olèh
	Participant-oriented/ event-oriented	Deontic 'must'	kudu
	Participant-oriented	Ability	isa
	Participant-oriented	Conative	jajal

3.5 Methodology and data

In order to explore the TAM-system of Surinamese Javanese, and investigate the possible changes it has undergone in comparison to the TAM-system of Standard Javanese, I made use of audio-recordings of both Indonesian and Surinamese Javanese.

The recordings of Surinamese Javanese were made in 2011 by Stanley Hanenberg and Kofi Yakpo, and were based mostly on the 'Elicit Kit', an especially compiled set of videos aiming at eliciting TAM-markers. Other recordings were retellings of the 'Frog Story' (Mayer 1969) and interviews about hobbies and personal life. The Surinamese corpus consists of 15 recordings, collected from a

---

[4] Note that although *arep* is generally classified as a tense marker in Javanese, there is reason to analyze it as a prospective aspect marker in my corpus of Surinamese Javanese (see the discussion below).

total of 8 different speakers of different ages, genders and social and linguistic backgrounds. The total size of the Surinamese corpus is 8,799 words.

In 2012, Indonesian Javanese speakers in the Netherlands were interviewed in the same way by Riski Lestiono. This corpus consists of 12 recordings from 4 different speakers. The size of this corpus is 6,463 words.

The recordings were compared for the use of TAM-markers, and possible differences with respect to the forms, meanings and frequencies of the different markers. In the following section, the categories for which relevant differences were observed will be described in turn.

4 Results

In this section, I will give an overview of the most important divergences between Surinamese Javanese and Indonesian Javanese in the marking of modality (Section 4.1) and aspect (Section 4.2).

4.1 Modality

The relevant modal categories are conative (Section 4.1.1) and ability (Section 4.1.2).

4.1.1 Conative modality

One of the developments within the category of participant-oriented modality is the borrowing of modal verbs from Sranan Tongo. Conative modality in Indonesian Javanese is expressed lexically by the use of the lexical modal verb *jajal*,[5] which in Surinamese Javanese is systematically replaced by a borrowing from Sranan, the lexical modal verb *proberi* 'to try' (< Dutch *proberen*). The idea that this is an instance of entrenched language change in Surinamese Javanese is supported by the fact that there is only one occurrence of the native modal *jajal* in the Suriname corpus, against eight occurrences of *proberi*. In the Indonesian corpus, the modal *jajal* is only used twice, but according to Conners (2008) and Adelaar

---

[5] The classification of *jajal* as a lexical verb is supported by the fact that it can take actor voice and undergoer voice morphology in the form of the *N-/di-*prefix respectively (Vruggink 2001: 126), which according to Vander Klok (2008: 2) is a property of the class of lexical verbs.

(2011b) it is a frequent modal in Indonesian Javanese. The syntax of the construction remains unchanged (modal verb + verb/complement) in Surinamese Javanese in (14), as compared to Indonesian Javanese in (13). In (14), the modal verb takes a Sranan verb as its complement (*dyompo* 'jump').

(13) n-jajal   di-uncal   manèh   tetep   aé   sik   gak   isa
     AV-try   UV-throw   again   continuously only   first   NEG   ABIL
     'He tries to throw it again but still doesn't succeed.'

(14) tyahtyah-né   proberi   dyompo
     children-DEF try   jump
     'The children try to jump.'

4.1.2 Modality of ability

As can be seen in Tab. 2, the auxiliary used to express modality of ability (a subcategory of participant-oriented modality) in Indonesian Javanese is *isa*, as in the following example from an Indonesian speaker.

(15) isa   arèk   cilik-é   n-jukuk   kelambi
     ABIL   child   small-DEF   AV-take   clothing
     'The small child can take the clothing.'

Whereas the Indonesian speakers use the form *isa* in 100% of the cases for expressing modality of ability (50 occurrences), Surinamese Javanese speakers prefer the form *inter*. This form is used in 80% of all occurrences (40 out of 50), against only 20% for *isa*. The form *inter* is not a loan from Dutch or Sranan Tongo, but originates from the Javanese lexeme *pinter* 'clever, skilled'. The following is an example of the use of this marker in combination with an action verb, with the meaning of event-oriented modality, since the ability to take the shirt depends on external circumstances (i.e. the length of the plank):

(16) n-jukuk   planga   eindelijk   inter   n-jukuk   kaos-é
     AV-take   plank   finally   ABIL   AV-take   shirt-DEF
     'He takes a plank, and can finally grab the shirt.'

It is often used in combination with the negative adverb *ora*, to express negative event-oriented modality, as in the following two examples. In both examples, the inability of performing the action is caused by external circumstances; in the first example, the fact that the shirt is hanging too high, and in the second example, the mouse cannot sleep because an elephant is making noise.

(17) *terus   arep   di-jukuk   maar   ora   inter*
    then   want   UV-take   but   NEG   ABIL
    'Then he wants to grab it but he cannot.'

(18) *tikus-é   nesu,   ora   inter   turu*
    mouse-DEF   angry   NEG   ABIL   sleep
    'The mouse is angry, he cannot sleep.'

4.2 Aspect

The relevant aspectual distinctions in this context are prospective (Section 4.2.1) and progressive (Section 4.2.2).

4.2.1 Prospective

As can be seen in Tab. 2, the marker *arep* is used in Indonesian Javanese to mark future tense. In Surinamese Javanese however, this marker occurs mostly with a meaning that is slightly different from an absolute future tense. In the cases in which this marker occurs in the Surinamese corpus, apart from its volitional meaning (as 'to want'), it appears to have a prospective meaning, which is more akin to aspect than to tense. Consider the following examples, which are both descriptions of videos. In the video described in example (19), the following happens: we see a water tap, with a person walking towards it, opening the tap, and washing his hands, then drying them. The events described thus begin only after the start of the clip. The same holds for the video described in example (20), which begins with the image of a woman standing, after which she starts moving out through the window.

(19) *wong   lanang   arep   wisuh   tangan-é   karo   banyu,   di-lapi*
    person   male   PROSP   wash   hand-DEF   with   water   UV-wipe
    tangan-é   karo   anduk
    hand-DEF   with   towel
    'A man is going to wash his hands with water, the hands are wiped with a towel.'

(20) *wong   wèdok   arep   metu   tekâ   jendélâ*
    person   woman   PROSP   go.out   from   window
    'A woman is going to go out through the window.'

Considering the contexts of these videos, I propose that the most natural translation for this marker as it is used here would be 'be going to', since it refers to a more immediate future, which actually starts happening during the time of the utterance. Therefore, I would propose that *arep* here is not used as a future tense marker, but rather as a prospective aspect marker.[6]

Surinamese speakers use *arep* much more frequently than Indonesian speakers: 48 occurrences for Surinamese speakers versus only 8 occurrences for Indonesian speakers. Surinamese speakers use this form mostly with the aspectual meaning, and also in contexts in which the Indonesian speakers employ other strategies, most of the time using no auxiliary at all, as in the following example:

(21) wong   ng-umbah   tangan   nèng   kran
     person AV-wash   hand   LOC   tap
     'A man washes his hands under the water tap.'

Although the aspectual use of *arep* is most probably not novel in Surinamese Javanese, since its meaning lies very close to the future tense, this usage is not observed within the Indonesian corpus, and the preference for it therefore seems to be a feature of the Surinamese variety.

4.2.2 Progressive aspect

As described in Tab. 2, progressive aspect can (optionally) be expressed with the auxiliary *lagi* in Indonesian Javanese. The Surinamese speakers in the corpus, however, do not make use of this marker at all. Instead, in utterances describing progressive events, Suriname Javanese speakers prefer to use a construction with the existential verb *ènèk/ènèng* (the Standard Javanese counterpart is *ânâ/ânâk*). Compare the following examples of progressive sentences:

(22) Javanese (eastern dialect)
  a. wong   iku   lagi   ng-gambar   wit
     person that   PROG   AV-draw   tree
     'The person is drawing a tree.'

---

[6] A reviewer points out that the marker could also express immediate future tense instead of prospective aspect, since this distinction is not always easy to make; the data analyzed here does not suffice to give a definite answer to this question, and more research is needed to examine the exact semantics of this marker. For the time being I will assume a prospective reading in these contexts, and use the gloss prosp for this category.

  b. *ibu iku lagi m-otong temon*
   woman that PROG AV-cut cucumber
   'The woman is cutting the cucumber.'

(23) Surinamese Javanese
  a. *ènèk wong n-ulis layang*
   exist person AV-write letter
   'Someone is writing a letter.'
  b. *ènèk wong ng-iris jeruk*
   exist person AV-cut orange
   'Someone is cutting an orange.'

It is difficult to assess whether these phrases should truly be interpreted as progressive constructions, or if they should rather be considered presentational constructions with a relative clause, where the relative pronoun is not expressed. On the latter interpretation, examples in (23) could be translated as follows: 'There is a person who writes a letter' and 'There is a person who cuts an orange'. Recall that the task of the speakers was a video clip description, which is compatible with presentational language use. This latter possibility may be supported by the fact that when the existential co-occurs with the relative pronoun *sing*, this is only used to, in some sense, restrict the subject of the clause, as in the following example:

(24) *ènèk wong lanang loro, sing siji ng-ekèki tas karo liya-né*
   exist person male two REL one AV-give bag with other-DEF
   'There are two men, of which one gives a bag to the other.'

However, as argued by Hengeveld (1992: 265), the existential construction is indeed a very suitable candidate for expressing progressive aspect. This seems to fit the Surinamese context: in the Surinamese creoles, among which Sranan Tongo, the progressive marker *e* originates from a copula that is also used in existential constructions (Borges 2014: 154). Hengeveld argues that this type of clause should be viewed as a construction with an existential verb accompanied by a "circumstantial adverbial clause", with the translation 'There is a person in the circumstance of [verb]ing', which does indeed entail a progressive interpretation.

  The progressive marker *lagi* is not attested in the Surinamese Javanese corpus, and it occurs only four times in total in the Indonesian corpus. And while the existential construction is used by Surinamese speakers in contexts where baseline speakers use *lagi*, the overall relative frequency of existential constructions is still higher in the Indonesian corpus, so there seems to be no indication of overgeneralization of the existential at the expense of the use of *lagi*. In fact, in Indonesian Javanese the existential construction can also have a progressive interpretation according to native informants (Arum Perwitasari, personal communication).

The idea that something is going on with the expression of progressive by heritage speakers is supported by the observation of the use of the Dutch progressive expression *bezig* 'busy', in a Surinamese Javanese context, as in the following example:

(25) ènèk   wong   bezig   nganu   skrifi   brifi   karo   pulpèn
     exist   person busy   like   write   letter   with   ballpen
     'A man is writing a letter with a ballpen.'

However, the usage of this Dutch construction in the corpus is only sporadic (one occurrence). It occurs productively in Surinamese Dutch (Borges et al. 2014).

5 Discussion

Let us now turn to the interpretation of the results laid out in the previous section, which show that different changes have taken place in the TAM-system of Surinamese Javanese as compared to Indonesian Javanese.

Within the domain of modality, divergences between the Javanese varieties have been found in two subcategories: conative modality and modality of ability, which both belong to the category of participant-oriented modality. Both these changes involve the use of a different form by the Surinamese speakers; however the origins and presumed sources of these changes differ. Whereas the use of the Sranan modal *proberi* for conative modality in Surinamese Javanese is clearly a case of lexical transfer from Sranan Tongo, and is thus an instance of contact-induced change, this is not the case with the ability modal *inter*. The idea that the use of *proberi* is caused by language contact is supported by the fact that a similar development has been observed in another Asian immigrant language of Suriname, Sarnami, which is the language of the immigrants from British-India (Borges et al. 2014: 143). Here too, the Sranan modal *proberi* is integrated into a construction with a Sarnami main verb. Since the meaning and syntactic realization of the conative construction remains the same for Surinamese Javanese, this innovation should be categorized as a MAT-change as defined by Matras and Sakel (2007).

The case of *inter* is different however. Since *inter* is derived from a native Javanese form, it cannot be argued that this is a case of transfer from Dutch or Sranan Tongo. In Indonesian Javanese, however, the form *pinter* only functions as an adjective with the meaning 'smart/clever' which can express acquired ability, as in the utterance *anakku pinter maca* 'my child can/knows how to read' (lit. 'my child is clever in reading'). In the Indonesian Javanese dialects for which the modal system has been described⁷, the only modal expressing ability is *(b)isa*, and *inter* is not attested as having a modal use in any of these dialects. The development from *pinter* into *inter*, involving the loss of the initial bilabial, may have been caused by analogy with the alternation between *bisa* and *isa* in Indonesian Javanese, which are used interchangeably (Kofi Yakpo, personal communication). The form *inter* in Surinamese Javanese subsequently seems to have undergone extension from a marker of participant-oriented ability towards a marker of event-oriented (participant-external) ability, as illustrated in (17)–(18), a PAT change. Further research is needed to shed light as to how this extension could have come about, and to what extent language contact has played a role in this development. However, it does fit well into the prediction of Hengeveld, as it seems to be an example of the grammaticalization of a participant-oriented modal towards an event-oriented modal, thus following a path of scope increase (from Configurational Property to State-of-affairs).

As for the aspectual markers in Surinamese Javanese, a pattern change can be observed in the domain of prospective aspect, which is more frequently expressed in Surinamese Javanese than in Indonesian Javanese. The marker *arep*, mostly considered a volitional and future tense marker in Indonesian Javanese, is used more often by Surinamese speakers to express a more certain and immediate future.⁸ This may arguably be related to linguistic facts of Dutch and Sranan Tongo, which both make a distinction between immediate and more uncertain future: *gaan* 'go' vs. *zullen* 'shall' in (Surinamese) Dutch, and *sa* and *o* in Sranan, respectively (Borges 2014: 150). The fact that this distinction occurs in both languages may act as a sort of double reinforcement, which causes the speakers to express this distinction also when speaking Javanese. Further research is needed to indicate whether this distinction is truly more salient in Surinamese than in Indonesian Javanese, and what type of strategy is used to differentiate future tense from prospective aspect.

With regard to the progressive, Suriname speakers use the progressive marker *lagi* less frequently than Indonesian speakers. In contexts where Indonesian speakers may use *lagi*, Surinamese speakers often use an existential construction to

---

7 Standard, Tengger, Peranakan, Tegal and Paciran Javanese, laid out in Vander Klok (2012).
8 This seems contrary to the predictions of Hengeveld that the direction of grammaticalization goes from prospective aspect towards future tense. It may also be the case that this marker was a prospective aspect marker in Indonesian Javanese as well and grammaticalized into future tense further in Indonesia but not in Suriname. Additional research with larger datasets are needed to decide on this matter.

express a sense of progressive meaning. As shown by Hengeveld (1992), it is indeed very well possible to express a progressive meaning with an existential construction.

However, it would be premature to state that there is a shift going on towards this construction to express progressive aspect, since, first, this construction seems not to be used very differently in Surinamese Javanese from the way it is used in standard Javanese and, secondly, the existential construction is still frequently used to express existential meaning or a non-progressive event. Furthermore, *lagi* is not frequent with the Indonesian speakers in the corpus either (only four instances). It must be noted that this also seems to depend on the task and/or specific dialect of Javanese: during my fieldwork with a speaker of the eastern Javanese dialect, *lagi* was actually used quite often, and remarkably the most often in the description of videos. In further research, it would therefore be very helpful to first compare the various Javanese dialects in this respect, to see whether these already exhibit differences.

Although at this point, I still consider the observations in the areas of prospective and progressive aspect as a subject for further research, the attested divergences in the domain of modality seem to confirm the 'forces' of language change as described in Section 2.2. To recall, on the one hand it was predicted that modality would be most susceptible to borrowing, following the hierarchy of Matras.[9] On the other hand, the framework of Hengeveld predicted that language change involving grammaticalization would follow a path of scope increase, with markers taking scope over the Configurational Property to be the first to undergo grammaticalization. Both predictions were borne out by the data: on the one hand, we have an example of a frequently used borrowing (*proberi*) in the domain of modality, and an example of grammaticalization from Configurational Property to State-of-affairs has been attested in the case of the development of *inter* from participant-oriented towards event-oriented modality.

6 Conclusions

In this paper, I have argued that there are contact-induced changes to be found in the TAM-system of Surinamese Javanese. The research questions formulated in section 1 were: (1) Is it possible to predict the direction of language change in

---

[9] One reviewer pointed out that the low-level modal categories discussed here (ability and conative) may not be included in Matras' definition of modality with low speaker control. However, given that Matras is not explicit on this point, I assume in this paper that all modal expressions are covered by the broad label of 'modality' in Matras's hierarchy.

the TAM-domain in a language contact situation? (2) Can changes in the TAM-system of Surinamese Javanese be ascribed directly to contact with Dutch and/or Sranan Tongo?

As for (1), the data studied in this paper would be in support of this, since the innovations described were indeed found to be consistent with the predictions made for borrowability and grammaticalization. Especially the domain of participant-oriented modality turned out to be vulnerable to change, by showing both the use of borrowed forms (*proberi* for conative modality) as well as grammaticalization of a marker towards broader usage (participant-oriented to event-oriented modality for *inter*). However, in order to find out whether these predictions on the direction of language change truly hold, more research with data from many different languages is needed to explore the wider applicability of these hierarchies.

Question (2) can only partially be answered affirmatively: in two of the observed cases, the change is arguably due to transfer. First of all, the MAT change for conative modality, where the modal is taken over from Sranan Tongo. Second, the PAT change for phasal aspect seems to be related to the differentiation made in Surinamese Dutch and Sranan Tongo. However, the change from *isa* to *inter* is more likely to be a language-internal development involving semantic extension, which at this stage cannot be directly attributed to language contact.

This paper is explorative but it shows that combining approaches from different domains of linguistics can lead to new insights in the study of language change. As for Surinamese Javanese, in future work I will work with a larger dataset containing spontaneous speech, and in that way contribute towards a better understanding of the relative structural stability in language change.

References

Adelaar, Alexander. 2011a. Tense, aspect and mood in some West Indonesian languages. Paper presented at the International Workshop on TAM and Evidentiality in Indonesian Languages, Tokyo University of Foreign Studies, 17–18 February.

Adelaar, Alexander. 2011b. Javanese -aké and -akən: A short history. *Oceanic Linguistics* 50 (2). 338–350.

Borges, Robert. 2014. *The life of language: dynamics of language contact in Suriname*. Utrecht: LOT Publications.

Borges, Robert, Pieter Muysken, Sophie Villerius & Kofi Yakpo. 2014. Tense, mood, and aspect in Suriname. In Robert Borges (ed.), *The life of language: Dynamics of language contact in Suriname*, 115–162. Utrecht: LOT Publications.

Carlin, Eithne B. & Jacques Arends. 2002. *Atlas of the languages of Suriname*. Leiden: KITLV Press.

Cohn, Abigail C & Maya Ravindranath. 2013. Local languages in Indonesia: Language maintenance or language shift? Paper presented at the Department of Anthropology, Universitas Indonesia.
Comrie, Bernard. 1976. *Aspect: An introduction to the study of verbal aspect and related problems*. Cambridge: Cambridge University Press.
Conners, Thomas J. 2008. *Tengger Javanese*. New Haven, CT: Yale University dissertation.
Dudas, Karen Marie. 1976. *The phonology and morphology of modern Javanese*. Urbana-Champaign, IL: University of Illinois dissertation.
Ewing, Michael C. 1999. *The clause in Cirebon Javanese conversation*. Santa Barbara, CA: University of California dissertation.
Gil, David. 2002. The prefixes di- and N- in Malay/Indonesian dialects. In Fay Wouk & Malcolm Ross (eds.), *The history and typology of western Austronesian voice systems*, 241–283. Canberra: Pacific Linguistics.
Hagoort, Pieter & Henk Schotel. 1982. Teksten in Sranan, Sarnami en Javaans op school. *Oso, tijdschrift voor Surinaamse taalkunde, letterkunde en geschiedenis* 1(1). 80–90.
Hengeveld, Kees. 1992. *Non-verbal predication: Theory, typology, diachrony*. Berlin & New York: Mouton de Gruyter.
Hengeveld, Kees. 2011. The grammaticalization of tense and aspect. In Bernd Heine & Heiko Narrog (eds.), *The Oxford handbook of grammaticalization*, 580–594. Oxford: Oxford University Press.
Hengeveld, Kees & J. Lachlan Mackenzie. 2008. *Functional Discourse Grammar: A typologically-based theory of language structure*. Oxford: Oxford University Press.
Himmelmann, Nikolaus P. 2005. *The Austronesian languages of Asia and Madagascar: typological characteristics*. In Alexander K. Adelaar & Nikolaus P. Himmelmann (eds.), The Austronesian languages of Asia and Madagascar, 110–181. London: Routledge.
Kroon, Sjaak & Kutlay Yagmur. 2012. *Meertaligheid in het onderwijs in Suriname: een onderzoek naar praktijken, ervaringen en opvattingen van leerlingen en leerkrachten als basis voor de ontwikkeling van een taalbeleid voor het onderwijs in Suriname*. Den Haag: Nederlandse Taalunie. http://taalunieversum.org/sites/tuv/files/downloads/meertaligheid_in_het_onderwijs_in_suriname.pdf (accessed 17 December 2015).
Lewis, M. Paul, Gary F. Simons, and Charles D. Fennig (eds.). 2013. *Ethnologue: Languages of the World, 17th edn*. Dallas, Texas: SIL International. http://www.ethnologue.com (accessed 18 July 2013).
Matras, Yaron. 2007. The borrowability of structural categories. In Yaron Matras & Jeanette Sakel (eds.), *Grammatical borrowing in cross-linguistic perspective*, 31–74. Berlin & New York: Mouton de Gruyter.
Matras, Yaron. 2011. Universals of structural borrowing. In Peter Siemund (ed.), *Linguistic universals and language variation*, 204–233. Berlin & New York: Mouton de Gruyter.
Myhill, John. 1993. Functional type, voice, and the Javanese di-form. *Studies in Language* 17(2). 371–409.
Nationaal Archief. 1999. Javaanse immigranten in Suriname. http://www.gahetna.nl/collectie/index/nt00346 (accessed 4 November 2014).
Polinsky, Maria & Olga Kagan. 2007. Heritage languages: In the 'wild' and in the classroom. *Language and Linguistics Compass* 1(5). 368–395.
Robson, Stuart. 1992. *Javanese grammar for students*. Clayton, Victoria: Centre of Southeast Asian Studies, Monash University.

Sakel, Jeanette. 2007. Types of loan: Matter and pattern. In Yaron Matras & Jeanette Sakel (eds.), *Grammatical borrowing in cross-linguistic perspective*, 15–30. Berlin & New York: Mouton de Gruyter.
Vander Klok, Jozina. 2008. Javanese modals. Paper presented at the Annual Conference of the Canadian Linguistic Association, University of British Columbia, 31 May – 2 June.
Vander Klok, Jozina. 2010. On the semantics of future markers in East Javanese. Paper presented at Austronesian Formal Linguistics Association XVII, Stony Brook University, 7–9 May.
Vander Klok, Jozina. 2012. *Tense, aspect, and modal markers in Paciran Javanese*. Montreal: McGill University dissertation.
Vruggink, Hein. 1985. Het Surinaams Javaans: een introduktie. *Oso, tijdschrift voor Surinaamse taalkunde, letterkunde en geschiedenis* 4(1). 53–62.
Vruggink, Hein. 2001. *Surinaams-Javaans – Nederlands woordenboek*. Leiden: KITLV Press.
Wolfowitz, Clare. 1991. *Language style and social space: Stilistic choice in Suriname Javanese*. Urbana: University of Illinois Press.
Yakpo, Kofi & Pieter Muysken. 2014. Language change in a multiple contact setting: The case of Sarnami (Suriname). In Isabelle Buchstaller, Anders Holmberg & Mohammad Almoaily (eds.), *Pidgins and creoles beyond Africa-Europe Encounters*, 101–140. Amsterdam & Philadelphia: John Benjamins.

Lotta Jalava
Grammaticalization of modality and evidentiality in Tundra Nenets

Abstract: This chapter investigates grammaticalization paths that are suggested to have produced most of the evidential and modal suffixes in Tundra Nenets, a Uralic language spoken in Siberia. The suggested main strategies of development are 1) verbalization or finitization of participle predicates and 2) insubordination, the replacement of a main predicate with a reanalysed construction, which in this case originally consists of a lexical item affixed to a nominalized verb. Verbalization of participles has produced majority of the evidential and modal suffixes in Tundra Nenets, 10 of altogether 16 finite suffixes of the paradigm. Insubordination is a mechanism behind the only first-hand evidential in the language, encoding non-visual direct evidence. The semantic changes in the grammaticalization of modal and evidential suffixes in Tundra Nenets are analogous with many similar tendencies attested in many other languages. These are: 1) resultative → evidential perfect, 2) prospective aspect → necessity → future, 3) similarity → inferred information, the speaker's knowledge of an event on the basis of visual evidence, 4) lexical item meaning 'sound, voice' → first-hand evidentiality. Both of these grammaticalization strategies probably represent an areal pattern, which is encountered also in other Uralic and Siberian languages.

Keywords: Tundra Nenets, finitization, participle, insubordination, reanalysis

1 Introduction

This chapter discusses the origin and grammaticalization paths of modal and evidential suffixes in Tundra Nenets. Tundra Nenets is spoken in an area that extends from the Kanin Peninsula in the European part of Russia to the Taimyr Peninsula in the Siberian part. The language belongs to the Samoyedic branch of the Uralic languages, and it is spoken by approximately 22,000 people.[1] The aim of this

---

[1] The number is based on the 2010 census (PEREPIS 2010), according to which 21,900 people reported that they knew the Nenets language, while the number of ethnic Nenets is 44,640.

Lotta Jalava: University of Helsinki, General Linguistics, Department of Modern Languages, P.O Box 24, 00014 University of Helsinki, Finland, lotta.jalava@helsinki.fi

DOI 10.1515/9783110519389-006

study is to discuss the most important functional and formal changes behind the grammatical categories in Tundra Nenets that express modality and evidentiality. I will argue that two main grammaticalization paths are the verbalization (finitization) of participles and insubordination. The verbalization of participles has produced a rich and complex category of modal and evidential affixes, while insubordination is the process behind the only first-hand evidential in the language.

This study is the first attempt to explain how the grammatical marking of modality and evidentiality has evolved in Tundra Nenets. Previous studies on mood, modality and evidentiality in Tundra Nenets and other Samoyedic languages have concentrated mainly on the structure and the main functions of the grammatical affixes, including observations concerning their origin (see e.g. Labanauskas 1974, 1981, 1982, 1992a, 1992b). In the present study, the focus is on the relationship of formal and functional grammaticalization (see Hengeveld, this volume; Narrog, this volume). In addition to the origin of the affixes, which has this far been the main interest of historical grammar in the field of Samoyedic languages (Janhunen 1982, 1998; Mikola 1988), this study concentrates on changes in syntactic structure and its semantic content. As there are no historical data on earlier stages of Tundra Nenets,[2] the source and target constructions and the direction of change in the grammaticalization processes need to be identified on basis of formal and functional variation of modal and evidential expressions, as well as typological generalizations based on similar tendencies of development attested in other languages (see e.g. Fox 1995: 92–109; Traugott and Dasher 2002: 24–34; Hopper and Traugott 2003: 124–126; Hengeveld 2011, Narrog, this volume). In grammaticalization of modality and evidentiality in Tundra Nenets, functional variation refers to polysemy of the same morphemes, or, different functions of their historical cognates in other Samoyedic languages. Variation in form shows in divergent morphosyntactic behaviour of similar items in different constructions or functions.

The emergence of finite categories from non-finite forms (verbalization) is a pattern that is referred to in Finno-Ugric studies relatively often. In addition to many tense and modal suffixes in many Samoyedic languages (Janhunen 1998: 471), the reanalysis of participles or other nominal predicates as verbal predicates has produced the 3rd-person verbal suffixes in Finnish and Mordvinic (Bartens 1999: 123). Moreover, verbalization has been considered a general areal pattern in Siberian languages (Malchukov 2013). In the case of modal and evidential suffixes in Tundra Nenets, verbalization of participles involves primarily functional change and increase of speech-act orientation, and secondarily syntactic change from non-verbal to verbal predication (see Section 3). Another important concept

---

2 The first folklore materials of the language were collected in the mid-19th century.

in this study is insubordination, the reanalysis of a structural feature associated with subordinate clauses as part of an independent matrix clause, a mechanism suggested by Evans (2007) and applied to Altaic, Transeurasian and Siberian languages by Robbeets (2009) and Malchukov (2013). The example of insubordination of the first-hand evidential in Tundra Nenets (see Section 4) shows both formal and functional features classically related to grammaticalization. It follows the cline of grammaticalization typical to agglutinative SOV-languages such as Tundra Nenets or Japanese, from a lexical word / construction to a grammatical suffix (see Narrog, this volume).

The data in the study consist of texts from different periods of time as well as spoken language recorded during a period of fieldwork.[3] The fieldwork data (NenTay2011)[4] includes spontaneous narratives as well as elicited translation sentences recorded on the Taimyr Peninsula in autumn 2011. The written data consist of Nenets folklore stories and narratives collected by Labanauskas (2001). I have also consulted previous studies on the topic (most importantly Labanauskas 1974–1992b), as well as the first notes taken on the language by M.A. Castrén (Manuscripta) in the 1840s. Additionally, I have used the sample sentences in Labanauskas (1982), Tereščenko (1965) and Lehtisalo (1956) as examples. The study is organized as follows: In Section 2 I give an overview of the grammatical coding of modality and evidentiality in Tundra Nenets and the participial elements in the modal and evidential suffixes. Section 3 discusses different examples of modal and evidential suffixes that have grammaticalized from participial predicates. Section 4 is dedicated to the only first-hand evidential that has developed as a result of insubordination. Finally, my findings are summarized in Section 5.

2 Mood, modality and evidentiality in Tundra Nenets

In Tundra Nenets, like in other Samoyedic languages, modality and non-firsthand evidentiality are mainly encoded with suffixes that belong to the same morphological category, traditionally labelled as *mood*. In addition to these suffixes, Tundra Nenets and other Samoyedic languages have one first-hand evidential, traditionally referred to as the *auditive*.

---

[3] The fieldwork was conducted together with Florian Siegl. I am extremely grateful to him for all of his help and support.
[4] Field recordings collected on the Taimyr Peninsula in autumn 2011 by Lotta Jalava and Florian Siegl.

In terms of Uralic languages, as well as in a cross-linguistic context, the grammatical category of modal and evidential affixes in Tundra Nenets is remarkably rich and complex. Most of the Uralic languages primarily use verbs and particles to express modal and evidential functions, and inflectional systems consisting of more than ten modal and evidential suffixes are found only in the Samoyedic languages. In Tundra Nenets, the category of modal and evidential markers known traditionally as the *mood category* consists of up to 16 individual suffixes (Salminen 1997: 98) that encode different types of modality and non-firsthand evidentiality. The members of the mood category are only used in finite verbal predication, and they are mutually exclusive, combining with all other verbal categories except each other (Salminen 1997: 97). It is characteristic of verbal predicates, such as the predicates marked with mood suffixes in Tundra Nenets, that in negation inflectional suffixes are affixed to the negative auxiliary, while the lexical main verb takes the special non-finite form applied in negation, the connegative. Consider example (1):

(1) ŋaćekī   me-n   ńi-rxa   xərwa-ʔ
    child   food-LAT   NEG-SIMEV.3SG   want-CNG
    'It seems that the child does not want food.' (NenTay2011_AID)

In addition to verbal predicates, illustrated in example (1), Tundra Nenets uses another predication strategy, non-verbal predication. This strategy is used for nouns and other nominal categories in predicate position, and it is also applied to participial predicates, with some of them acquiring modal or evidential functions, as in example (2). In the negation of non-verbal predicates, both the lexical main predicate and the negative auxiliary take personal suffixes, and the copula 'be' is applied to carry the connegative suffix:

(2) məń   ńa-m   temta-wənta-dmʔ   ńī-dm-ć   ŋa-ʔ
    I   bread-ACC   buy-PTCP.FUT-1SG   NEG-1SG-PST   be-CNG
    'I wasn't supposed to buy bread' (NenTay2011_VIZ)

The first-hand evidential, the auditive, differs from the other evidential and modal suffixes in its morpho-syntax (Salminen 1997: 115), and for this reason it is not formally included in the same category (see Section 4 for more details). The auditive encodes non-visual direct evidence, information that is perceived through hearing, but also smelling and feeling. It will be argued in Section 4 that it differs from the modal and non-firsthand evidential suffixes in its grammaticalization path.

The members of the inflectional mood category as well as the auditive evidential are listed in Tab. 1. Those modal and evidential suffixes that are marked in brackets ([werəxa] and [wənta]) are used in non-verbal predicates only, and for this reason they have not been considered as members of the formally defined mood paradigm. However, they are relevant when it comes to the grammaticalization of the modal and evidential suffixes, as will be argued in Section 3.

Tab. 1: The modal and evidential suffixes in Tundra Nenets[5].

Category	Suffix	Main functions[6]	
Indicative	∅	fact, own experience, direct visual	Clausal mood and clause type
Imperatives	xə, ʔ, ja	command	
Interrogative	sa	question in past tense	
Conjunctive	ji	irrealis, request, desire	
Narrative	we	perfect, non-firsthand past	Evidentiality
Similative-evidentials	narəxa ~ rəxa wəntarəxa rəxawe [werəxa]	inference, uncertain visual	
Probabilitative	nake weke	assumption, probability	Modality
Probabilitative II	wanəŋkaba	assumption, probability	
Necessitative	bsu [wənta]	epistemic possibility (future), necessity	
Obligative	bcake	commitment	
Reputative	wəna	disbelief, doubt	
Desiderative[7]	rəwa	desire	
Auditive	w(an)on	direct non-visual	Evidentiality

---

5 The list of the mood suffixes is based on Salminen (1997: 98). The names of the individual suffixes are here presented according to Salminen (1997), except for the similative-evidentials (called the "approximative" [narəxa, wəntarəxa, werəxa] and the "hyperprobabilitative" [rəxawe] in Salminen 1997) and the probabilitative II (called the superprobabilitative in Salminen 1997, following Hajdú 1968: 64). In different studies on Tundra Nenets there has been some variation in the category labels of the mood markers. For example, Nikolaeva (2014: 85–106) uses different labels, although her description on moods is essentially based on Salminen (1997).

6 I use the terms inference (based on visual evidence) and assumption (based on other than visual evidence, such as general knowledge and logical reasoning) as they are defined in Aikhenvald (2004: 63). Hengeveld (this volume) and Hengeveld & Hattnher (2015) use the terms deduction for what is inference here, and inference for what is assumption here.

7 The desiderative suffix is found in older text collections, but it does not seem to be used anymore in contemporary language. In contemporary Tundra Nenets, desire can be expressed by the past tense form of the conjunctive (Jalava 2012: 138–140).

Some of the modal categories, such as the indicative, the imperative and the conjunctive (*clausal moods*, see Narrog, this volume), encode similar functions as corresponding traditional moods in many other languages. These are also the oldest mood markers of the category, as they have been suggested to have existed already either from Proto-Uralic or Proto-Samoyedic in a similar function (Mikola 1988: 246, 248; Janhunen 1982: 36, 1998: 474). The next suffixes in Tab. 1, from the narrative to the obligative, encode different types of non-firsthand evidentiality as well as epistemic possibility, necessity and commitment. The development of these suffixes is the main subject of this paper, as they contain an element that is either synchronically or historically identical to a participial suffix (Labanauskas 1974: 47; 1981; 1982; 1992b: 132). A more detailed analysis of their grammaticalization will be provided in Section 3. Furthermore, in addition to the participial-based suffixes and the old modal markers that derive from the proto-language, there are two additional modal suffixes in the category: the reputative (Salminen 1997: 98), which encodes the speaker's incredulity of someone else's statement or presupposition (Jalava 2012: 135, 139–140) and the desiderative, which is no longer used in contemporary language. As these suffixes do not appear to consist of participial elements, and their grammaticalization does not seem to result from insubordination, their development cannot be included in this study.

3 Participle-based modal and evidential suffixes

Five groups of modal and evidential markers have suffixes that contain an element that in some cases is homonymous with a participial suffix. In the modal and evidential suffixes, the participial elements denote the same temporal meaning as the corresponding participles. These participial suffixes are *-we* (past), *-na* (present), *-bsu* (historical future / necessitative participle) and *-wənta* (future / necessitative participle). The way in which the participial elements appear in the modal and evidential markers (the narrative, the similative-evidentials, the probabilitatives, the necessitative and the obligative) is illustrated in Tab. 2. Those suffixes that are used in non-verbal predicates only, and for this reason are not considered members of the morpho-syntactic category of mood, are marked in square brackets ([*we* + *rəxa*] and [*wənta*]).

Tab. 2: Participial elements in the Tundra Nenets modal / evidential suffixes.

Category	Suffix	Temporal reference	Main modal or evidential functions
Narrative	we	past	evidential perfect
Necessitative	bsu [wanta]	future future	future possibility, necessity
Obligative	bca + ke	future	commitment
Similative-evidentials	na + raxa wanta + raxa [we + raxa] raxa + we	present future past past	inference, uncertain visual
Probabilitative	na + ke we + ke	present past	assumption, probability

First, the suffix homonymous to the past participle -we occurs as the narrative suffix that is used as an evidential perfect (see Section 3.1). Second, the future participle can also be used as a marker of a necessitative predicate, although it is a nominal predicate and cannot therefore be considered a full modal suffix, as was demonstrated in Section 2. In addition to the participial suffixes of contemporary Tundra Nenets, the element -bsu appears in the necessitative suffix and in the compound marker of the obligative. It will be argued in Section 3.2 that this suffix dates back to the Proto-Samoyedic future participle. Third, the similative-evidentials and the probabilitatives both consist of a set of compound suffixes in which the first part of the suffix is a participial element (present, past or future) that defines the temporal reference of the form.

The next subsections deal with grammaticalization of the past, present and future participles to different modal and evidential forms. Central to all these processes is extension in meaning and widening of scope, and for most of the cases, change in predication type from nonverbal to verbal predicate (finitization). The subsections 3.1 to 3.4 are organized as follows: Section 3.1 concentrates on the development of the evidential perfect, the narrative, on the basis of resultative forms. In Section 3.2, I argue that the necessitatives in the Northern Samoyedic languages are also of participial origin. Section 3.3 analyses the similative-evidential, a non-firsthand evidential / epistemic suffix that originates from a similative adjectival suffix affixed to participial elements. In Section 3.4, I briefly discuss the different probabilitatives.

3.1 Resultative aspect > evidential perfect

In Tundra Nenets, -*we* is the suffix of two different categories, the resultative past participle, as in (3), and the so-called narrative[8] (4). In (3), the past participle occurs as a modifier in a noun phrase where the past participle *to-wī*[9] 'come-PTCP.PST' modifies the noun *ŋaćekī* 'child'. As for the narrative, it encodes a variety of meanings, but typically perfect tense and indirect evidentiality, such as reported or inferred information in contexts in which the information source is not specified (see (4)). Usually the narrative refers to past events, but in one specific occurrence when encoding mirativity (i.e. unexpected information) it may denote present events (Jalava 2013).

(3) *wīŋ-kəd   to-wī   ŋaćekī*
    tundra-ABL come-PTCP.PST   child
    'the child who has come from the tundra' (Tereščenko 1965: 846)

(4) *xasawa   ŋaćekī   to-wī*[10]
    man   child   come-NARR
    'the boy has (apparently) come' (Labanauskas 2001: 72)

A predicate affixed with the narrative suffix is verbal. It may be used in all conjugation types, as well as in transitive and reflexive clauses. (Labanauskas 1974; Lyublinskaya and Malchukov 2007: 456–459; Jalava, 2014.) As for the past participle, it can also occur in predicate position as a resultative suffix (see Tab. 3), but in this case the predicate is non-verbal. The formal similarity of the two categories, as well as analogical functional developments in other languages, indicates that the narrative suffix emerged from a reanalysis of the past participle predicate. This development probably took place relatively late in the Nenets languages, because in other Samoyedic languages, similar functional categories seem to be formally of a different origin (Siegl 2013: 263; Helimski 1998: 566; Wagner-Nagy 2002: 114). However, it is possible that also in other Samoyedic languages suffixes of similar categories, such as the perfect and the narrative, have developed from different resultative suffixes or past participles,[11] and, it cannot

---

[8] In Russian studies, this mood has usually been referred to as the "perfect" (Labanauskas 1974; Lyublinskaya and Malchukov 2007: 456–459), but in English it is generally known as the "narrative" (Collinder 1957: 441; Salminen 1997: 98).
[9] ~ -*wī* in the final syllable, affixed to the consonant stems -*me*/-*mī* respectively.
[10] The original form is *tu-wī*, which is used in the eastern Taimyrian variety of Tundra Nenets.
[11] Even in Tundra Nenets, another resultative suffix -*bej* has begun to be used as a perfect in the western varieties of the language (Jalava 2014).

be excluded that in Proto-Samoyedic there was also a narrative form that grammaticalized from the past participle.[12]

In Nenets, nominal predicates such as nouns (but also participles) can take verbal personal agreement without using a copula in affirmative indicative clauses. Consequently, in certain contexts they show the same syntactic structure as finite predicates (see the examples in Tab. 3). For this reason, reanalysis can be expected to have taken place in these contexts. The assumed grammaticalization at different levels of analysis is illustrated in Tab. 3, using examples from Tundra Nenets, although the narrative probably emerged already in an earlier stage of the Nenets languages. In the table, the first rows, illustrating the changes in function and scope, represent the contentive change, that is, functional grammaticalization, while the latter rows, illustrating changes in predicate type and the glossing of the example, represent the changes in morpho-syntax, that is, formal grammaticalization (as understood in Hengeveld, this volume and Narrog, this volume).

Tab. 3: Grammaticalization of the narrative.

Category	Past participle	→	Narrative mood
Function	resultative state	→	past event (perfect, evidential)
Scope	properties of the subject	→	properties of the event
Predicate type	non-verbal predicate	→	verbal predicate
Example	weñako xa-wī		weñako xa-wī
Glossing	dog die-PTCP.PST.3SG	→	dog die-NARR.3SG
Translation	'the dog is dead'	→	'the dog has (apparently) died'

A new category, the narrative suffix, is assumed to have developed from the past participle, which remains in the language also in its original function. In predicate position this past participle is a non-verbal resultative predicate. It encodes state at the reference time that results from a past action or process ('the dog is dead', as in the example in the left column in Tab. 3). The assumed reanalysis of the resultative state as a past event presumes a widening of scope from the subject to the whole proposition, and a change of the focal point from the

---

[12] This functional category may have been lost and recreated from different past participles and resultative predicates in the individual Samoyedic languages and language groups.

current resultative state into the past event that caused the resultative state (see also Hengeveld 2011). The new category, referring to a past event, has begun to be used as a finite predicate.[13]

There are many examples of resultatives, often encoded with past participles, developing into perfects and further into indirect evidentials or past tense markers in many languages of Eurasia and other parts of the world (Bybee et al. 1994: 95; Comrie 2000: 3, 6; Lindstedt 2000). In the Uralic languages, evidentials that originate from past participles are found for example in Khanty and Mansi (Csepregi 2014), Komi and Udmurt (Leinonen 2000: 421–422). Indirect evidential perfects could be considered an evidential strategy typical of the Uralic languages, although these expressions are also common in other languages of Eurasia and other areas (Bybee et al. 1994: 95); a well-known example is the evidentially marked past tense -*mIş* in Turkish (Johanson 2000: 62). In Tundra Nenets, the same participial-based suffix -*we* also appears in past tense variants of the compound markers of evidential categories, which will be discussed in Sections 3.3 and 3.4.

3.2 Prospective participle > necessitative

Another suffix that I will suggest to be originally a participial suffix is the necessitative -*bsu*.[14] The necessitative encodes epistemic and deontic meanings, future probability, and, especially with the first person, necessity or weak obligation (Labanauskas 1992a); its temporal reference is always the future:

(5) *məń   xūńana   to-bsu-dm?*
    I   tomorrow   come-NEC-1SG
    'Tomorrow I will probably / I have to come' (NenTay2011_OJ)

In Tundra Nenets the suffix -*bsu* appears as a modal marker, but in other Samoyedic languages it has cognates that are also participial suffixes. In addition to the Tundra Nenets necessitative, similar suffixes with necessitative function, often referred to as the necessitative or the debitive, are found in all contemporary Samoyedic languages or language groups: in Forest Nenets, the most closely related language, the suffix is -*psu*, -*su* (Verbov 1973: 99); in Forest Enets -*ču*

---

[13] A more detailed analysis of the synchrony and diachrony of the past participle predicate and the narrative mood is provided in Jalava (2014).
[14] -*cu*, -*ću* affixed to a consonant stem.

(Siegl 2013: 284–285); in Nganasan -bsutə (Wagner-Nagy 2002: 116); and in Selkup -psååt / -sååt (Helimski 1998: 566).[15]

A comparison of the necessitative suffixes in different Samoyedic languages indicates that in Proto-Samoyedic there was a suffix *-pso,[16] which encoded obligation or necessity. However, further evidence from the Samoyedic languages indicates that this suffix was originally a participle suffix that appeared in non-finite predicates in Proto-Samoyedic. In Nganasan and Selkup there are cognates to the necessitative suffixes found in participles. The Nganasan necessitative participle with the suffix -"sutə (Wagner-Nagy 2002: 118) and the Selkup future / debitive participle -psååtï'' (Helimski 1998: 569) are clearly related to the finite necessitative (debitive) suffixes.

As participles tend to grammaticalize into modal suffixes in Uralic and other Siberian languages, and not the other way around (Janhunen 1998: 471; Malchukov 2013), it can be assumed that the Proto-Samoyedic suffix *-pso was a participle with future reference. It was reanalysed as a finite modal marker that appears in all modern Samoyedic languages. The necessitative participle suffix *-pso remained in its original participial function in Nganasan and Selkup. In Nenets and Enets it was lost and replaced by another suffix, the future participle with prospective meaning: in Tundra Nenets -wənta[17] (see (6)) and in Forest Enets -uda (Siegl 2013: 329). In Tundra Nenets this future participle occurs in the same positions as the past participle: modifying a noun and in predicate position. In predicate position, however, the future participle often express obligation:

(6) pida   ńań-m   temta-wənta
    S/he   bread-ACC buy-PTCP.FUT.3SG
    'S/he is supposed to buy bread' (NenTay2011_VIZ)

In example (6), the suffix -wənta encodes a modal meaning that is very similar to what is expressed with the necessitative -bsu in example (5) above. This indicates that the original prospective meaning has extended towards necessity. However, the suffix -wənta cannot be considered a verbal mood suffix; given the syntactic properties, the predicate is non-finite (see example (2) in Section 2). Although in affirmative clauses finite and non-finite predicates can be similar in certain contexts, as was demonstrated for the past participle and the narrative in Tab. 3, under negation they differ from each other, as shown in Section 2.

---

15 In Nganasan and Selkup the debitive suffix seems to consist of two suffixes, the first part being a probable cognate for Nenets and Enets suffixes.
16 Labanauskas (1992: 132) has suggested a Proto-Nenets future suffix *-psu on the basis of Nenets data.
17 ~wnta, or -mənta, -mnta affixed to a consonant stem.

It can be assumed that at an earlier stage of the language, the particle with the suffix *-pso was used as a necessitative predicate in the same way as the future participle with -wənta in contemporary Tundra Nenets, and it was then reanalysed as a finite predicate. The assumed development of the necessitative suffix -bsu from the Proto-Samoyedic future / necessitative participial suffix at different levels of analysis is illustrated in Tab. 4. Again, the first rows, illustrating the changes in function and scope, represent the functional grammaticalization, while the rows illustrating changes in predicate type and the glossing of the example, represent formal grammaticalization.

Tab. 4: Grammaticalization of the necessitatives.

Category	Future / Necessitative participle	→	Necessitative mood
function	prospective potential	→	weak obligation, possibility
Scope	properties of the subject	→	properties of the event
Predicate type	non-finite predicate	→	finite predicate (-bsu) non-finite predicate (-wənta)
Example a	*to-pso-mã[18]	→	to-bsu-dm?
Glossing	come-PTCP.FUT-1SG	→	come-NEC-1SG
Translation	'I am the one who is supposed to / will come'	→	'I am supposed to come' → 'I will probably come'
Example b	temta-wənta	→	temta-wənta
Glossing	buy-PTCP.FUT.3SG	→	buy-PTCP.FUT.3SG
Translation	'S/he is the one who is supposed to / will buy'	→	'S/he is supposed to buy'

As a stative non-finite predicate, the Proto-Samoyedic participle with *-pso encoded the properties of the subject during the moment of speech, although its aspectual nature was prospective. In other words, a predicate with *-pso indicated that at the moment of speech the subject had the capacity of being the subject of a future event expressed by the verb, as seen in Tab. 4 in the constructed example (a) 'I am the one who is supposed to / will come'. This is one of the functions of the contemporary future participle with -wənta in Tundra Nenets. The semantic content extended from prospective aspect to modality and the scope changed from the subject to the speech situation. The epistemic meaning of future possibility in Tundra Nenets can be assumed to be a later development, as it is a well-known

---

[18] The form of the personal suffix, according to Mikola (2004: 117).

tendency in different languages that epistemic meaning (probability) arises from the original deontic meaning (obligation); for example, see *should* and *must* in English or *bear* 'need', but also 'must be' in Basque (Bybee et al 1994: 199–205). In the case of *-*pso* > -*bsu* the necessitative form was reanalysed as a finite predicate, the usual predication type to modals. In the case of -*wənta*, however, the form still has the properties of non-finite predicates (as demonstrated in (2)). As -*wənta* is a newer form in the language and its functional grammaticalization represents a later development, it is possible that in the future it will also undergo a similar formal grammaticalization.

The suffix -*bsu* also occurs in another modal suffix in Tundra Nenets, the obligative with the suffix -*bcake*. This suffix encodes obligation and commitment.

(7) məń   xūńana   to-bcake-dm?
    I   tomorrow   come-OBL-1SG
    'Tomorrow I promise to come' (NenTay2011_OJ)

In Castrén's (Manuscripta) material from the 1840s, the mood suffix appears in the form -*bsuki*. It can thus be seen that the compound suffix consists of the necessitative suffix -*bsu* and another suffix -*ke* (~-*kī*) (Labanauskas 1992b: 131–132). The modal suffix -*ke*, affixed to the participial-based part of the compound suffix, additionally occurs in another mood, the probabilitative (-*nake*, -*weke*), which will be discussed in Section 3.4.

3.3 Similative > similative-evidentials

The similative-evidential[19] usually encodes inferred information, the speaker's knowledge of an event on the basis of visual evidence. Consider (8)–(10):

(8) *t́eńewa-narxa-da*
    know-SIMEV-3SG>SG
    'S/he seems to know that' (Labanauskas 1982: 287)

---

19 In earlier literature this is referred to as the "probabilitive" (Hajdú 1968: 64); the "mood of apparent action" (*наклонение кажущегося действия*) (Labanauskas 1982), the "approximative" for the suffixes *narəxa, werəxa wəntarəxa* and the "hyperprobabilitative" for the suffix *rəxawe* (Salminen 1997: 98, 109). The name "similative-evidential" has been adopted from Malchukov's (2000) description of a suffix with a similar function and similar source of grammaticalization in Éven, a Tungusic language spoken in Siberia.

(9) xībaw to-wəntarxa
someone come-SIMEV.FUT.3SG
'Someone seems to be coming' (NenTay2011_LXJ)

(10) xameda-rxawe-da
understand-SIMEV.PST-3SG>SG
'S/he seems to have understood this' (Labanauskas 1982: 289)

The mood has three slightly different suffix variants (-narəxa, -wəntarəxa, -rəxawe),[20] which consist of a participial element and the suffix -rəxa. The choice of the suffix variant depends on the temporal reference of the proposition, and the suffix variant is chosen according to the temporal reference of the equivalent participle: -narəxa for present tense (8), -wəntarəxa for future tense (9) and -rəxawe (10) for past tense (Labanauskas 1982; Jalava 2012). The same participles, -we and -wənta with no additional modal suffix, have grammaticalized into modal markers (see Section 3.1 for the narrative and Section 3.2 for the necessitative). The present participle -na occurs in evidential predicates only as part of compound suffixes, as seen in (8).

In addition to the three suffix variants of the similative-evidential demonstrated in (8)–(10), there is a fourth form consisting of a participle and the suffix -merəxa (~werəxa), as in (11). This form refers to the past tense and acts as a nonfinite predicate, as can be observed in the copular negation:

(11) ŋəmkexərt-m pær-me-rxa ńī ŋa-ʔ
something-ACC do-PTCP.PST-SIM NEG.3SG be-CNG
'As if nothing had been done' (Tereščenko 1965: 377)

This suffix variant serves to demonstrate the non-finite origin of the similative-evidential suffixes. Because it applies the negation strategy of non-finite predicates (see Section 2), it cannot morphologically be considered a finite suffix. Functionally, however, it belongs to the group of similative-evidentials. It is likely that this suffix variant was not grammaticalized into a finite suffix because its function as past tense variant was occupied by the fully verbalized evidential suffix -rəxawe (see example 10 above). Contrary to other similative-evidential suffix variants, in this compound suffix the participial-based element follows the suffix -rəxa instead of preceding it. The explanation for this can be found in the homonymy of the past participle and the narrative. Apparently the suffix -we affixed to the similative -rəxa in the suffix -rəxawe is a narrative suffix instead of

---

20 ~ -tarəxa ~ -tarxa, -məntarxa, -rəxawe when affixed to a consonant stem.

a past participle. One could expect a morpheme order where a derivative suffix precedes an evidential marker, and this structure has developed into the finite past tense variant of the similative-evidential.

The second part of the compound suffixes is a derivative suffix, the similative -rəxa,[21] which can be affixed to nouns, adjectives and participles (Labanauskas 1982). It expresses similarity between the subject and the referent of the word form it is affixed to. The similative forms can be considered adjectives (Jalava 2013: 58–59), as they occur as a modifier in a noun phrase and as stative predicates (12).

(12) xoj ńība-rəxa
    hill needle-SIM.3SG
    'The hill is like a needle' (Labanauskas 1982)

The grammaticalization of the similative-evidential seems to follow similar principles (i.e. the verbalization of participles, discussed in Sections 3.1 and 3.2). In similative-evidential forms, the similative suffix is affixed to a participial form that can be considered as a verbal adjective. The semantic change from similative into evidential requires the reanalysis of the meaning 'like something' as 'looks like something happens', which later develops further into 'it appears that something happens' or 'I think that something happens'. At the same time, the scope properties change from the subject (encoded by the participle) towards the speech situation (encoded by the evidential). This can be best illustrated in example (13a/b), where the stative verb jībeć 'be smart' can be morphologically analysed in two different ways: as a similative derivative of a participle (13a) or as a similative-evidential form.

(13) a. jībe-ta-rxa   →   b. jībe-tarxa
        be.smart-PTCP-SIM.3SG   be.smart-SIMEV.3SG
        'He is like someone who is smart'   'He seems to be smart'
                                              (Tereščenko 1965: 133)

The participle jībe-ta 'smart' ('the one who is smart') affixed with the similative suffix in (13a) represents the original form from which the similative-evidential (13b) has developed. This grammaticalization process is illustrated from different perspectives in Tab. 5.

---

[21] ~-rxa or -laxa ~ -lxa when affixed to a consonant stem.

Tab. 5: Grammaticalization of the similative-evidentials.

Category	Similative suffix	→	Similative-evidential
Function	similar to N 'is like'	→	evidential 'it seems', 'apparently'
Scope	properties of the subject	→	properties of the event
Predicate type	non-finite predicate	→	finite predicate

The similative-evidentials with the suffixes -*narəxa*, -*wəntarəxa* and -*rəxawe* represent both functional and formal grammaticalization, while the form with the suffix -*werəxa* has not undergone changes in the syntactic predication type.

Similar categories, such as the similative derivative suffix 'like' used for nouns and the modal / evidential form consisting of the similative affixed to a participle in the sense of 'it seems', are also found in other Samoyedic languages. In Forest Nenets similarity is expressed with the suffix -*lhaxa*; affixed to a verb stem or a participle, the suffix -*lhaxa* produces epistemic meaning. (Verbov 1973: 48, 99.) In Forest Enets as well, the similative suffix -*raxa* appears in marking in the so-called speculative moods that are constructed of participial markers and the similative suffix (Siegl 2013: 167, 288–289). There are also examples in Nganasan where the similative suffix -*rəku* (Wagner-Nagy 2002: 128) occurs as a modal suffix in verbal predication affixed to a participle (Mikola 2004: 114, citing an example from Helimski 1994: 100). On the basis of Nenets, Enets and Nganasan similative suffixes, Mikola (2004: 114) has reconstructed a common North-Samoyedic similative suffix *-*rə̂kå*. As both functions are found in all Northern Samoyedic languages, it is also possible that the evidential function developed in parallel in the individual languages.

The most probable origin for the similative suffix *-*rə̂kå* can be found in Turkic languages. Cognates of a Turkic comparative suffix occur in many contemporary Turkic languages, and in Old Turkic the suffix of the comparative was -*rAk* (Erdal 1998: 141). When no element of comparison is present, as in the case of Samoyedic similatives, the function of the suffix is to augment or reduce the intensity expressed (e.g. *ajïrak* 'rather big', *gökrek* 'bluish') (Kerslake 1998: 187). This suffix was probably already borrowed by Proto-Samoyedic from Turkic languages, as there is lexical and grammatical evidence of intensive contact between these language groups about 2000 years ago (Janhunen 1977: 126–127; Terent'ev 1999), and for historical and geographical reasons, direct contacts between the Northern Samoyedic languages and the Turkic languages cannot be assumed (Róna-Tas 1988: 742). If the suffix was borrowed already in Proto-Samoyedic, one would expect to find it also in the Southern Samoyedic languages as well, not only in the Northern group. In Kamass, an extinct language of the Southern Samoyedic group, the comparative suffix -*rak* has a similar function, but this suffix is probably of later origin.[22] Donner (1944: 135) considers it a Tatar loan. In Selkup, however, there is a deadjectival derivative LÅÅQÏ=L' *soma-lååqi-lʲ* 'rather good' (Helimski 1998: 572; also Hajdú 1968: 141) that could possibly be traced back to the Proto-Samoyedic similative suffix.[23]

An analogous borrowing of the Turkic comparative suffix *-rAk* in the Uralic languages can be found in Mari, where the comparative suffix *-rak* (e.g. *sairak* 'better', *oshirak* 'whiter') has been considered to be of Turkic origin (Anduganov 1991: 129). Similar paths of semantic change, in which similative expressions have developed into modal and evidential categories, are found in different languages spoken in different parts of the world. For instance, in Yurakaré, an isolate language spoken in Bolivia, the similative suffix *-shi* (usually affixed to nouns) is used as an uncertain visual evidential when affixed to verbs (Gipper 2014), and in Japanese the history of the evidential marker *-rasii* is interwoven with the adjectival suffix *-rasi* (Vovin 2009: 697; see also Narrog, this volume). In Siberian languages, these functional categories – the similative and the similative-evidential – have been described at least in Ėven, where the similative-evidential also consists of a participle and similative suffix. Other Tungusic languages also use less grammaticalized similative-evidential markers. (Malchukov 2000: 461). As the Northern Samoyedic and Northern Tungusic languages are spoken in relatively close proximity to each other, and because they have shared sources, targets and pathways of grammaticalization, the possibility of contact-induced grammaticalization needs to be considered. However, research on early linguistic contacts between the Northern Tungusic and Samoyedic languages does not provide further evidence for this possibility (Hajdú 1963: 54, Helimski 1985). Moreover, the fact that similar grammaticalization paths are attested in different parts of the world indicates that the grammaticalization of the similative-evidentials in Samoyedic and Tungusic is not that uncommon.

---

22 Note that the intervocalic Proto-Samoyedic *k* changes to *g/γ* in Kamass (Mikola 2004: 90).
23 The Proto-Samoyedic **r* regularly remains in Selkup as *r*. However, in a suffixal position, the Proto-Samoyedic **-r/*-l* alternation is represented as *l* in Selkup (for example, in second-person suffixes in determinate conjugation) (Mikola 2004: 119). In a suffixal position, the change PS **r* > Selkup *l* in the deadjectival derivative suffix *lååqï=l'* may present an analogy of this. Otherwise the sound changes appear to be regular (e.g. Proto-Samoyedic **k* > Selkup *q*). (Mikola 2004: 86.)

3.4 The probabilitatives

The probabilitatives express assumption and epistemic probability (see also Labanauskas 1981). In many contexts the function is close to the use of the similative-evidential, as both categories express non-firsthand evidentiality. However, whereas similative-evidentials are often used to express inference based on visual evidence, probabilitatives encode assumption, based on evidence that is not visible.[24] This may include logical reasoning and general knowledge:

(14) *məń   ńūńih   internat-xəna   jar-take-xəh*
     I   child.PL1SG   boarding.school-LOC   cry-PROB-3DU
     'My children probably cry in the boarding school' (NenTay2011_VIZ)

(15) *pidər   internat-xəna   jar-make-n*
     you(2SG)   boarding.school-LOC   cry-PROB.PST-2SG
     'You probably cried in the boarding school' (NenTay2011_VIZ)

Like similative-evidentials, probabilitatives also express different temporal references with different suffix variants. The suffix *-take* (*~nake*), as seen in (14), refers to the present tense, whereas the suffix *-make* (*~weke*), as seen in (15), refers to the past tense. The future tense is expressed using the future tense suffix of the indicative combined with the present tense variant of the probabilitative (Labanauskas 1981). However, as argued in Section 3.2, the obligative suffix *-bcake* consists of the old participle with future reference and the same suffix *-ke*. As a matter of fact, Castrén (Manuscripta) refers to the suffix *-bcake* in the paradigm of the probabilitatives as a future tense variant. Whereas the necessitative and the similative-evidential occur in all Northern Samoyedic languages, the probabilitative and the obligative (i.e. the modal and evidential markers with *-ke*) are innovations in Tundra Nenets, as potential cognates for the suffix have not been attested in other Samoyedic languages. The grammaticalization of the suffixes is probably analogous with the emergence of the similative-evidentials: from non-verbal participle predicate affixed with a derivational suffix to verbal evidential suffixes. However, the original function of the suffix *-ke* that follows the participial elements in the modal and evidential markers remains unclear.

In addition to the probabilitatives *-nake* and *-weke*, another probabilitative suffix *-wanəŋkəba* occurs in Tundra Nenets. This probabilitative II[25] encodes

---

[24] "Inference" and "assumption" as used here and in Aikhenvald (2004) correspond to "deduction" and "inference" respectively in Hengeveld (this volume) and Hengeveld & Hattnher (2015).
[25] Hajdú (1968: 64) and Salminen (1997: 98) call this suffix the "superprobabilitative", but because it doesn't appear to express any higher probability than the probabilitatives, I find this name misleading.

similar epistemic and evidential meanings as the present tense probabilitative -*nake*. This suffix is also one of the newcomers in Tundra Nenets. It has grammaticalized relatively recently, and it does not occur in all varieties of the language. My fieldwork interviews indicate that in the easternmost variety of the language spoken on the Taimyr Peninsula where Nenets has been spoken for only 200 years or so, the suffix is known solely by those Nenets who have intensive contact with speakers of the Jamal variety, the central variety of the language on which the standard language is also based.

Hajdú (1968: 64) suggests that the suffix has grammaticalized from the noun *xəba* 'sign / sense', which is affixed to the lative form of the verbal noun suffix -*wa*. This means that in the original construction the nominalized verb form is in the lative case when preceding the noun *xəba* 'sign / sense', whereas in the target construction the combination of the nominalizer -*wa*, the lative case suffix -*nəh* (→ *ŋ*) and the lexical noun *xəba* (→ *kəba*) are reanalysed as a verbal probabilitative suffix *wanəŋkəba*, as illustrated in Tab. 6 and in example (16) with the Tundra Nenets verb *xæ*- 'leave'.

Tab. 6: Grammaticalization of the probabilitative II.

Category / construction	NMLZ-LAT + 'sign / sense'	→	Probabilitative II
Form / suffix	-*wa-n[ə]h* + *xəba*	→	V-*wanəŋkəba*[26]
Function	'the sign / sense of an action / event'	→	inferential / epistemic

(16) a. **xæ-wa-n[ə]h   xəba*   →   b. *xa-wanəŋkəba*
       leave-NMLZ-LAT sense[.3SG]   leave-PROBII.3SG
       '(It is) the sense for leaving'   'S/he has probably left'

Even though the form of the suffix is relatively transparent with the nominalized suffix and the noun *xəba* 'sign / sense', the syntax of the original construction behind the grammaticalized suffix is not as clear as it can argued to be in the case of the participle-based suffixes. In (16a) the noun *xəba* is assumed to have acted as a nominal predicate of the clause, in which case the grammaticalization would have followed similar principles as the verbalization of participial predicates.

---

26 Note that *wan[ə]h* → *wanəŋ* because of regular preobstruental nasalization of the glottal stop *h* (see Salminen 1997: 43). Furthermore, *xəba* 'sense' → *kəba* can be explained by the regular postconsonantal strengthening of a continuant: $|x| \to k\ /\ C\_$ (Salminen 1997).

Another possibility is that the grammaticalization would have been similar to the development of the auditive evidential, the process of insubordination (see Section 4). In this case the noun *xəba* would have been the subject of the clause, and the original verbal predicate would have been elided. However, this kind of development can be much more convincingly argued for the auditive evidential.

4 Insubordination of the direct non-visual evidential

The direct non-visual evidential in Tundra Nenets, traditionally referred to as the auditive *-won / -wanon*,[27] encodes information received by means of hearing, touch, smell or taste (Tereščenko 1947: 224; 1973: 145–146; Perrot 1996):

(17) *jeśa-ʔ   śep-n-ta   ḿu-ńa   śejra-won-toh*
    money-PL pocket-GEN-3SG.POSS in-LOC   clink-AUD-3PL
    'Coins were clinking in her/his pocket' (Lehtisalo 1956: 435)

The evidential expresses non-visual sensory evidence, whereas direct visual evidence has no specific marker and is typically expressed by the indicative mood. In addition to direct perception, the auditive can also be used for expressing hearsay, especially when referring to events in the present tense. The hearsay use of the auditive is probably an extension of its original use in relation to direct perception.

(18) *man-ćti-ʔ: ńabi   ja[h]   wæ-kana   ńaxar   Tajbəŕi*
    say-HAB-3PL other   land   border-LOC   three   Tajbari
    təńa-won-toh   ŋæ-śti-ʔ
    exist-AUD-3PL   be-HAB-3PL
    'They say there are three members of the Nenets tribe Tajbari living on a border of the other land' (Labanauskas 2001: 35)

The auditive, along with the necessitative and similative-evidentials, is one of the modal and evidential suffixes shared by Nenets, Enets and Nganasan.[28] On the basis of these Mikola (2004: 114) reconstructs the Proto-Samoyedic auditive

---

27 ~-*mon/-manon* affixed to a consonant stem.
28 For the auditive in Enets, see Siegl (2013: 300–301), and in Nganasan, see Gusev (2007: 419–424).

mood *-monon.[29] It has been suggested that the auditive suffix originates from a lexical noun (e.g. Collinder 1957: 442), possibly the common North-Samoyedic word *mun / (?)*mon[30] 'voice' (in Nenets and Enets 'sound') (Künnap 2002: 149). In other languages in different parts of the world, there are many examples for the development of first-hand evidentials from lexical items, mostly verbs that express perception (Aikhenvald 2004: 271–272). However, in some languages there are also parallels to the Samoyedic auditive, namely examples of evidentials grammaticalized from nouns such as 'sound' and 'voice', for example in Ainu (Bugaeva 2013).

Morphologically the auditive has been considered as a non-finite verb form (Salminen 1997: 115), but as it occurs as the main predicate of a clause, its status is more complicated. The auditive differs in its morpho-syntactic features from the modal and evidential markers discussed earlier in this paper. First, it appears only in the third person.[31] Second, it cannot be marked for tense (Tereščenko 1973: 145–146). Third, only one set of personal suffixes can be used with the auditive, whereas the modal and the non-firsthand evidential categories allow personal suffixes of three different conjugation types: subjective, objective and reflexive. The personal suffixes used with the auditive are equivalent to the 3rd-person possessive suffixes which are identical with the objective conjugation suffixes.

(19) pida   3SG   jader-mon-ta   walk-AUD-3SG
     pidʼih   3DU   jader-mon-t'ih walk-AUD-3DU
     pidoh   3PL   jader-mon-toh   walk-AUD-3PL
     'S/he / they was / were walking (behind the door, it was perceived).'
     (NenTay2011_VIZ)

Marking of the person of the subject by means of the possessive suffixes differs not only from the modal and evidential forms but from any finite predicates in Tundra Nenets. Instead, person agreement with the possessive suffixes is typical of subordinate clauses. Furthermore, even though in modern Tundra Nenets the subject of the auditive clause is in the nominative (see examples (17) and (18)), in the closest historically related language, Forest Nenets, the subject of the

---

29 Mikola (2004: 114) points out that this functional category occurs also in Selkup. However, from a historical-comparative point of view the Selkup suffix -kunä is problematic, because the k in Selkup goes back to the Proto-Samoyedic *w, which would produce w and not m~w in Northern Samoyedic.
30 See Janhunen (1977: 95) for the reconstruction.
31 The native speakers usually consider the 2nd-person forms (such as 'you are speaking, it is perceived') acceptable, but there are no naturally occurring examples in text collections or in my recordings.

auditive clause can be in the genitive,[32] which is the default case of the possessor and another characteristic of subordinate clauses in Samoyedic languages. These characteristics of the Samoyedic auditive can be described with Evans' (2007: 367) definition for insubordination: "the conventionalised main-clause use of what, on prima facie grounds, appear to be formally subordinate clauses". This means that any structural feature associated with subordinate clauses may turn up in insubordination (Evans 2007: 370). As a diachronic process, insubordination is a relatively common grammaticalization strategy in languages of the Siberian area, in comparison to other parts of the world (Robbeets and Cuyckens 2013: 4–5; Malchukov 2013). This gives reason to assume that grammaticalization of the auditive is linked to insubordination.

Assuming that the auditive was originally a construction consisting of a noun in genitive (the subject of the auditive clause), a verb form (the predicate in the auditive clause) and the noun 'voice' with a 3rd-person possessive suffix (the auditive suffix), it was most probably originally a noun phrase with the meaning 'X's sound'. In this case the verb (X) was nominalized and acted as a genitive modifier of the possessed noun *mon* representing the structural features associated with subordinate clauses. Arguably, this noun phrase acted as a subject of the clause, with a main predicate that denoted a meaning such as 'to be heard', which appears to be one of the most natural verbs in this context.

The assumed original construction that grammaticalized into the auditive is illustrated in examples (20a–b) with a constructed Tundra Nenets example in (20a), although it should be kept in mind that in reality this grammaticalization took place already in the Proto-Samoyedic period. Example (20b) represents the auditive clause in Tundra Nenets.

(20) a. *ńeba[-h]   jader[-ma-h]   mon-ta   [so]
mother-GEN   walk-NMLZ-GEN   sound-3SG.POSS   be.heard.3SG
'The sound of mother's walking was heard'

→ b. ńeba   jader-mon-ta
mother   walk-AUD-3SG.POSS
'It was heard that mother was walking'

Evans (2007: 370) suggests four steps along the grammaticalization path of the insubordinated clause: 1) subordination, 2) ellipsis, 3) conventionalized ellipsis and 4) reanalysis as a main clause structure. Applying these principles,

---

[32] Tapani Salminen, personal communication. I am grateful to him for this important note.

the processes illustrated in Tab. 7 can be assumed in the development of the Samoyedic auditive.

Tab. 7: Grammaticalization of the auditive evidential.

Subordination			
Example	V-ma-h	mon-ta	so
Gloss	V-NMLZ-GEN	sound-3SG.POSS	be.heard.3SG
Translation	'V-ing's sound was heard'		
Ellipsis	V-ma-h	mon-ta	[so]
	V-NMLZ-GEN	SOUND-3SG.POSS	[be.heard.3SG]
	'V-ing's sound was heard'		
Reanalysis as a main clause	V-m(an)on-ta		
	V-AUD-3SG		
	'It is perceived that it / (s)he V'		

It was argued above and illustrated in example (20) that the auditive suffix *-monon, which the longer suffix variant -wanon (-manon) in Tundra Nenets represents, most likely consists of a Proto-Samoyedic verbal noun suffix *-ma (e.g. jader-ma 'walking' in Tundra Nenets) in the genitive with *-n, *-ma-n, to which the noun *mon 'voice' / 'sound' in 3rd-person possessive form is affixed. By means of the insubordination process, the main verb of the original sentence (example 20a), which is illustrated with Tundra Nenets so 'to be heard', was elided. The original noun phrase started to be used in the same function without the main verb, and the original nominalized verb was reanalysed as the main predicate. At the same time, the noun *mon 'voice' / 'sound' lost its lexical meaning, and it was suffixed to the nominalized verb form. The combination of the nominalizer *-ma-n and the noun *mon was reanalysed as an evidential suffix and reduced. This acquisition of grammatical meaning and context generalization includes both functional and formal factors (see also Narrog, this volume). Finally, in Tundra Nenets, the subject of the auditive clause lost its original genitive marking illustrated in the constructed example (20a) (ńeba [-h] 'mother'), which is probably the original form in the auditive clause.

5 Conclusion

In this study, I have discussed the two main grammaticalization pathways of modal and evidential suffixes in Tundra Nenets. These two paths of development are the verbalization of participles (discussed in Section 3) and insubordination (discussed in Section 4). Both of these grammaticalization paths probably represent an areal pattern encountered in either Uralic or Transeurasian languages or many Siberian languages (Janhunen 1998; Robbeets 2009; Malchukov 2013). First, it is argued that the verbalization of participles is a mechanism that has produced the majority of the modal and evidential suffixes in Tundra Nenets. The evidential perfect (narrative) and the necessitative have developed from the past and future participles by extension of semantic content, whereas the similative-evidentials and probabilitatives consist of derivational forms of participles. Second, it is shown that the other suggested main strategy of grammaticalization, insubordination, reflects a pattern of development behind the only first-hand evidential in the language, the auditive, which represents features generally associated with subordinate clauses and in Tundra Nenets characteristic to nominalizations, such as possessive agreement. The auditive suffix has been suggested to originate from a lexical item, the noun 'voice' / 'sound', which was affixed to the nominalized verbal originally acting as its possessor modifier (e.g. 'the sound of X').

The suggested semantic changes in the grammaticalization of modal and evidential suffixes in Tundra Nenets are analogous with many similar tendencies attested in different languages. These are: 1) resultative → perfect, 2) prospective aspect → necessity → future, 3) similarity → inference based on visual evidence → inference / probability and 4) lexical item 'sound' / 'voice' → first-hand evidentiality. The first three changes apply to those evidentials and modals that grammaticalized by verbalization of participles. In addition to extension of meaning, their grammaticalization involves increase in speech-act orientation. Formally, however, they are less grammaticalized: the formal change shows mainly in change of the predication type from non-verbal to verbal predication (verbalization), but there are exceptions for this tendency among the participle-based modal and evidential forms. In case of first-hand evidentiality, the insubordination of the auditive, both functional and formal changes have taken place. While the main functional change is loss of lexical meaning and acquisition of grammatical evidential meaning, the formal changes include suffixation of the lexical item to the preceding nominalization, phonetic reduction and ellipsis of the original main verb.

In contemporary Tundra Nenets the two different strategies of grammaticalization are reflected by the categorical status of the modal and evidential suffixes. The suffixes that originate from verbalized participles or combinations of a participial and a derivational element are part of the category of modal and evidential suffixes. As for the first-hand evidential, it differs morphosyntactically from the other evidentials and modal markers, being a non-finite form and taking the possessive agreement. The different grammaticalization pathways are also reflected in semantic content. The modal and evidential forms that have verbalized from a participial element encode non-firsthand evidential meanings such as inference and assumption, as well as epistemic and deontic modality, whereas the auditive, originating from a word 'voice' / 'sound', encodes first-hand evidentiality.

Some of the modal and evidential forms have grammaticalized much earlier than others. There are historical cognates for the suffixes of the auditive, -*w(an)on* and the similative-evidential -*rəxa*, in other Northern Samoyedic languages (Enets and Nganasan), as well as the necessitative -*bsu* in Selkup. These appear to be the oldest Samoyedic modal and evidential markers that developed after the Uralic mood suffixes (the imperative and conjunctive). The evidential perfects, which the Tundra Nenets narrative represents, are found in all Samoyedic languages, but they appear to have been created from different resultative participles. The probabilitatives, the other group of compound suffixes after the similative-evidentials, as well as the other necessitative based on the future participle -*wənta* are innovations in Tundra Nenets.

Uncommon abbreviations

1, 2, 3 = person of the subject or possessor (1SG>1SG etc.= objective conjugation: number of the object, person and number of the subject), AUD = auditive, CNG = connegative, LAT = lative, HAB = habitual, NARR = narrative, NEC = necessitative, NEG = negative auxiliary, NMLZ = nominalization (action nominal), OBL = obligative, PROB = probabilitative, PROBII = probabilitative II, SIM = similative, SIMEV = similative-evidential.

Sources of the examples

Labanauskas 2001 = Labanauskas, Kazys. 2001 (ed.). *Ямидхы лаханаку – Сказы седой старины.* [Ямидхы лаханаку - Tales from the old days.] Русская литература. Москва.
Labanauskas 1982 = Labanauskas, Kazys. 1982. Наклонение кажущегося действия в ненецком языке. [Der Scheinhandlungsmodus im Nenzischen.] *Советское финно-угроведение* 18. 283–292.
Lehtisalo 1956 = Lehtisalo, Toivo. 1956. *Juraksamojedisches Wörterbuch.* (Lexica Societatis Fenno-Ugricae 13). Helsinki: Suomalais-Ugrilainen Seura.
NenTay2011 = Field recordings collected on the Taimyr Peninsula in autumn 2011 by Lotta Jalava and Florian Siegl.
Tereščenko 1965 = Tereščenko, N. M. (Н. М. Терещенко). 1965. *Ненецко-русский словарь.* [Nenets – Russian dictionary.] Moscow: Советская Энциклопедия.

References

Anduganov Ju. V. (Ю. В. Андуганов). 1991. *Историческая грамматика марийского языка: синтаксис.* [Historical grammar of Mari: syntax.] Йошкар-Ола: Марийское книжное издательство.

Bartens, Raija. 1999. *Mordvalaiskielten rakenne ja kehitys* (SUST 232). Helsinki: Suomalais-Ugrilainen Seura.

Bugaeva, Anna. 2013. Mermaid constructions in Ainu. In Tasaku Tsunoda (ed.), *Adnominal clauses and the 'Mermaid Construction': Grammaticalization of nouns.* (NINJAL Collaborative Research Project Reports. 13-01), 667–676. The National Institute for Japanese Language and Linguistics.

Bybee, Joan, Perkins Revere, Pagliuca William. 1994. *The evolution of grammar: tense, aspect, and modality in the languages of the world.* Chicago: University of Chicago Press.

Castrén Manuscripta = Castrén, Matias Aleksanteri. 1845. Samoiedica 2–5: Jurak-Samoiedica 1–4. Manuscripta Castreniana. Microfilm copy of a manuscript, National Library of Finland.

Collinder, Björn. 1969 [1957]. *Survey of the Uralic languages.* 2nd edn. Stockholm: Almqvist & Wiksell.

Comrie, Bernard. 2000. Evidentials: semantics and history. In Lars Johanson & Bo Utas (eds.), 2000. *Evidentials: Turkic, Iranian and Neighbouring Languages.* Berlin & New York: Mouton de Gruyter. Empirical Approaches to Language Typology 24. 1–13.

Csepregi, Márta. 2014. Evidentiality in dialects of Khanty. *Linguistica Uralica* L 3. 199–211.

Donner, Kai. 1944 *Kamassisches Wörterbuch nebst Sprachproben und Hauptzügen der Grammatik; bearbeitet und herausgegeben von A. J. Joki* (Lexica Societatis Fenno-Ugricae 8). Helsinki: Suomalais-ugrilainen seura.

Erdal, Marcel. 1998. Old Turkic. In Lars Johanson & Éva Ágnes Csató (eds.), *The Turkic languages*, 138–157. London & New York: Routledge.

Evans, Nicholas. 2007. Insubordination and its uses. In Irina Nikolaeva (ed.), *Finiteness. Theoretical and empirical foundations*, 366–431. Oxford: Oxford University Press.

Fox, Anthony. 1995. *Linguistic reconstruction: An introduction to theory and method.* (Oxford textbooks in linguistics). Oxford University Press.

Gipper, Sonja. 2014. 'Uncertain visual' as an evidential category in Yurakaré: A comparative perspective. Paper read at the 47th Annual Meeting of the SLE, Adam Mickiewicz University, Poznań, September 13, 2014.

Gusev, V. Ju. 2007. Эвиденциальность в нганасанском языке. [Evidentiality in Nganasan.] In Храковский В. С. (ed.), *Эвиденциальность в языках Европы и Азии. Сборник статей памяти Наталии Андреевны Козинцевой.* 415–444. St. Petersburg: Наука.

Hajdú, P. 1963. *The Samoyed peoples and languages* (Indiana University Publications, Uralic and Altaic series 14). Bloomington: Indiana University Press.

Hajdú, Péter. 1968. *Chrestomathia Samoiedica.* Budapest: Tankönyvkiadó.

Helimski E. A. 1985. Самодийско-тунгусские лексические связи и их этноисторические импликации. [The lexical relations of Samoyedic and Tungusic and their ethnohistorical implications.] In *Урало-алтаистика: Археология, этнография, язык.* 206–213. Novosibirsk: Наука.

Helimski E. A. 1994. *Таймырский этнолингвистический сборник.* Материалы по нганасанскому шаманству и языку. [Ethnolinguistic collection from Taimyr. Materials from the Nganasan shamanism and the Nganasan language.] Moskow, РГГУ.

Helimski, Eugene. 1998. Nganasan. In Daniel Abondolo (ed.), *The Uralic Languages*, 480–515 London – New York, Routledge.
Hengeveld, Kees. 2011. The grammaticalization of tense and aspect. In Bernd Heine & Heiko Narrog (eds), *The Oxford handbook of grammaticalization*. 580–594. Oxford: Oxford University Press.
Hengeveld, Kees & Marize Mattos Dall'Aglio Hattnher. 2015. Four types of evidentiality in the native languages of Brazil. *Linguistics* 53 (3). 479–524.
Hopper, Paul J. & Elizabeth Traugott. 2003. *Grammaticalization*. 2nd edn. Cambridge: Cambridge University Press.
Jalava, Lotta. 2012. Tempuksen ilmaiseminen tundranenetsin moduksissa. In Tiina Hyytiäinen, Lotta Jalava, Janne Saarikivi & Erika Sandman (eds.), *Per Urales ad Orientem. Iter polyphonicum multilingue. Festskrift tillägnad Juha Janhunen på hans sextioårsdag den 12 februari 2012* (SUST 264), 131–144. Helsinki: Suomalais-Ugrilainen Seura.
Jalava, Lotta. 2013. "Adjectives" in Tundra Nenets: Properties of property words. *Journal de la Société Finno-Ougrienne* 94. 37–67.
Jalava, Lotta. 2014. Indirectivity and resultativity in Tundra Nenets. *Finnisch-ugrische Forschungen* 62. 207–240.
Janhunen, Juha. 1977. Samoyed-Altaic contacts. Present state of research. *Altaica* (MSFOu 158, Helsinki 1977), 123–129. Helsinki: Suomalais-Ugrilainen Seura.
Janhunen, Juha. 1982. On the structure of Proto-Uralic. *Finnisch-ugrische Forschungen* 44. 23–42.
Janhunen, Juha. 1998. Samoyedic. In Daniel Abondolo (ed.), *The Uralic languages*, 457–479. London & New York: Routledge.
Johanson, Lars. 2000. Turkic indirectives. In Lars Johanson & Bo Utas (eds.), *Evidentials: Turkic, Iranian and neighbouring languages* (Empirical approaches to language typology 24), 61–87. Berlin & New York: Mouton de Gruyter.
Kerslake, Celia. 1998. Ottoman Turkish. In Lars Johanson & Éva Ágnes Csató (eds.), *The Turkic Languages*, 179–202. London & New York: Routledge.
Künnap, Ago. 2002. On the Enets evidential suffixes. *Linguistica Uralica* 38. 145–153.
Labanauskas Kazys. 1974. Ненецкий перфект. [The Perfect in Nenets.] *Советское финно-угроведение* 10. 45–52.
Labanauskas, Kazys. 1981. Предположительное наклонение в ненецком языке. [Der probabilitative Modus im Netzischen.] *Советское финно-угроведение* 17. 49–61.
Labanauskas, Kazys. 1982. Наклонение кажущегося действия в ненецком языке. [Der Scheinhandlungsmodus im Nenzischen.] *Советское финно-угроведение* 18. 283–292.
Labanauskas, Kazys. 1992a. Der Obligativ I im Nenzischen. *Linguistica uralica* 28 (1). 36–43.
Labanauskas, Kazys. 1992b. Der Obligativ II im Nenzischen. *Linguistica uralica* 28 (2). 128–133.
Leinonen, Marja. 2000. Evidentiality in Komi Zyryan. In Lars Johanson & Bo Utas (eds.), *Evidentials: Turkic, Iranian and neighbouring languages* (Empirical approaches to language typology 24), 419–440. Berlin & New York: Mouton de Gruyter.
Lindstedt, Jouko. 2000. The perfect - aspectual, temporal and evidential. In: Östen Dahl (ed.), *Tense and aspect in the languages of Europe*. (Empirical approaches to language typology 20–6), 365–383. Berlin & New York: Mouton de Gruyter.
Lyublinskaya, M. D. & A. L. Malchukov. 2007. Эвиденциальность в ненецком языке. [Evidentiality in Nenets.] In Храковский В. С. (ed.), *Эвиденциальность в языках Европы и Азии. Сборник статей памяти Наталии Андреевны Козинцевой*. 445–468. St. Petersburg: Наука.

Malchukov, Andrej L. 2000. Perfect, evidentiality and related categories in Tungusic languages. In Lars Johanson & Bo Utas (eds.), *Evidentials: Turkic, Iranian and neighbouring languages* (Empirical approaches to language typology 24), 441–70. Berlin & New York: Mouton de Gruyter.

Malchukov, Andrej L. 2013. Verbalization and insubordination in Siberian languages. In Martine Robbeets & Hubert Cuyckens (eds.), 2013. *Shared grammaticalization. With special focus on the Transeurasian languages* (Studies in language companion series 132), 177–208. Amsterdam & Philadelphia: John Benjamins.

Mikola, Tibor. 1988. Geschichte der samojedischen Sprachen. In Denis Sinor (ed.), *The Uralic languages: description, history and foreign influences* (Handbuch der Orientalistik 8: Handbook of Uralic studies 1), Leiden: Brill.

Mikola, Tibor. 2004: *Studien zur Geschichte der samojedischen Sprachen*. (Studia uralo-altaica 45), Szeged: SzTE Finnisch-Ugrisches Institut.

Narrog, Heiko. This volume. Relationship of form and function in grammaticalization — the case of modality.

Nikolaeva, Irina. 2014. *A grammar of Tundra Nenets*. (Mouton grammar library 65), Berlin: De Gruyter Mouton.

PEREPIS 2010 = Всероссийской переписи населения 2010 года. [All-Russia Population Census 2010.] The http://www.perepis-2010.ru/ (accessed 1 april 2014).

Perrot, Jean. 1996. Un médiatif ouralien: L'auditif en samoyède nenets. In Zlatka Guentchéva (ed.), *L'énonciation mediatisee*, 157–68. Louvain & Paris: Peeters.

Robbeets, Martine. 2009. Insubordination in Altaic. *Voprosy Filologii: Serija Uralo-Altajskie Issledovanija* 1. 61–80.

Robbeets, Martine & Hubert Cuyckens. 2013. Towards the typology of shared grammaticalization. In Martine Robbeets & Hubert Cuyckens (eds.), *Shared grammaticalization. With special focus on the Transeurasian languages* (Studies in language companion series 132), 1–20. Amsterdam & Philadelphia: John Benjamins.

Róna-Tas, András. 1988. Turkic influence on the Uralic languages. Denis Sinor (ed.), *The Uralic languages: description, history and foreign influences*, 742–780. Leiden: Brill.

Salminen, Tapani. 1997. *Tundra Nenets inflection* (SUST 227). Helsinki: Suomalais-Ugrilainen Seura.

Siegl, Florian. 2013. *Materials on Forest Enets, an indigenous language of Northern Siberia*. Memoires de la Societé Finno-Ougrienne 267. Suomalais-Ugrilainen Seura, Helsinki.

Terent'ev, V. A. (В. А. Терентьев). 1999. Древнейшие тюркско-самодийские языковые контакты. [The oldest linguistic contacts between the Turkic and the Samoyedic.] *Journal de la Société Finno-Ougrienne* 88. 173–200.

Tereščenko, N. M. (Н. М. Терещенко). 1947. *Очерк грамматики ненецкого (юрако-самоедского) языка*. [A concise grammar of Nenets (Yurak-Samoyed).] Leningrad: Учпедгиз.

Tereščenko, N. M. (Н. М. Терещенко). 1973. *Синтаксис самодийских языков*. [Syntax of the Samoyedic languages.] Leningrad: Наука.

Traugott, Elizabeth Closs & Richard B. Dasher. 2002. *Regularity in semantic change*. (Cambridge studies in linguistics). Cambridge: Cambridge University Press.

Verbov, G. D. (Г. Д. Вербов). 1973. Диалект лесных ненцев. [Forest Nenets dialect.] In *Самодийский сборник*, 3–190. Novosibirsk.

Vovin, Alexander. 2009. *A descriptive and comparative grammar of Western Old Japanese, Part 2: Adjectives, verbs, adverbs, conjunctions, particles, postpositions*. Folkestone, Kent: Global Oriental.

Wagner-Nagy, Beáta (ed.). 2002. *Chrestomathia nganasanica*. Studia uralo-altaica. Szeged / Budapest: SZTE Finnugor tanszék, MTA Nyelvtudományi Intézet.

Shadi Davari and Mehrdad Naghzguy-Kohan
The grammaticalization of progressive aspect in Persian[1]

Abstract: This paper investigates the development of the Persian lexical verb *dâštan* 'have', which has grammaticalized into an auxiliary verb functioning primarily as a progressive aspect marker in durative situations, and which is currently developing into a prospective marker with achievement verbs. Possessive progressives are a cross-linguistic rarity and deserve attention. We suggest that the progressive function arose through context-induced reinterpretation based on metonymic relations. The resulting reinterpretation of *dâštan* 'have' to 'ongoingness of a durative event' represents a conceptual shift, in the form of metaphoric extension, from possessing a physical object to possessing the continuum of an action in a focal point of utterance. We will also illustrate that the progressive's focus on subjective notions leads to its development as an expression of the speaker's attitude that does not describe properties of a situation in the extralinguistic world but rather in the subjective conceptualization of the speaker. The auxiliation process of *dâštan* 'have' in Persian will be analyzed based on the *Auxiliation Dimensions Model* proposed by Davari and Naghzguy-Kohan (forthcoming), which focuses on the force, the source and the degree of auxiliation. We also point out that these changes are in tune with the overall directionality of semantic change in grammaticalization according to Narrog (2012), namely, increase in speaker-orientation.

Keywords: auxiliation, evidentiality, grammaticalization, possessive, progressive, subjectivity, Persian.

---
[1] We would like to thank Kees Hengeveld, Heiko Narrog and Hella Olbertz for their constructive comments on an earlier version of this article.

Shadi Davari: Tehran University of Medical Sciences, Nuclear Medicine Department, Imam Khomeini Medical Complex, Keshavarz Boulevard, Tehran, Iran, Postal Code: 1419733141, sh50d@yahoo.com
Mehrdad Naghzguy Kohan: Bu-Ali Sina University, Department of Linguistics, Faculty of Literature and Humanities Hamedan, Iran., Postal Code: 6517838695, mehrdad.kohan@basu.ac.ir

DOI 10.1515/9783110519389-007

1 Introduction

This paper deals with the periphrastic progressive aspect construction in Persian, a construction that covers a number of conceptually adjacent functions, but mainly serves to express an ongoing dynamic situation. The progressive is formed by the auxiliary verb *dāštan* 'have' and a dynamic, non-punctual verb in the present tense marked with the imperfective / declarative marker *mi-*, as in (1):

(1) *dâr-am   mi-nevis-am*
     PROG-1SG   IMPF-PRS.write-1SG
     'I am writing'

Data show that the use of *dâštan* 'have' with achievement verbs such as *oftâdan* 'fall' leads to the development of a prospective reading. We suggest that the emergence of the progressive construction, and its behavior with specific Aktionsarten that leads to the development of one other grammatical aspect with non-core meaning, can be accounted for with reference to grammaticalization, and specifically to auxiliation. According to Heine et al.'s (1991) functional-cognitive framework of grammaticalization, and Heine (1993), metaphor and metonymy are the major forces underlying grammaticalization. However, in their work, more emphasis is put on the importance of metaphor, while the role of metonymy is downplayed. In contrast, the focus of this paper is on the development of grammatical aspects in Persian through the auxiliation of *dâštan* 'have' based on metonymic processes, as represented in our model of *Auxiliation Dimensions*. Furthermore, we suggest that the change of *dâštan* 'have' can be described in terms of increase in speaker-orientation, one of the three dimensions of speech-act orientation (cf. Narrog 2012). We start with the discussion of the emergence of progressive aspect (Section 2) and its subjective meanings (Section 3), and then continue with the development of the prospective (Section 4). After a brief introduction of the model of *Auxiliation Dimensions*, the auxiliation process of the verb *dâštan* 'have' will be analyzed (Section 5). The paper ends with concluding remarks (Section 6).

2 The emergence of the progressive aspect in Persian

This section discusses in some detail the development of *dâštan* 'have' in Persian as progressive, starting with a section that provides some historical background within the language (Section 2.1), then proceeding to the main part on the development in Section 2.2, and ending in some remarks on the role of metonymy in the process (Section 2.3).

2.1 Preliminaries

Progressive aspect in Modern Persian, expressed by the auxiliary *dâštan* 'have' as in (1), is a periphrastic construction that denotes an ongoing dynamic situation. This construction is apparently not based on the same grammaticalization patterns as the progressives in Western languages. French, English, German and Russian, for example, do not code the progressive notion through a *have-* construction. Although it is impossible to establish the date of the first occurrence of *dâštan* 'have' as an auxiliary in spoken language, its existence in older historical periods is doubtful. The periphrastic progressive in Persian was probably grammaticalized as late as the end of the 19th century. There is no evidence for the presence of this grammatical category in Old Persian (before 4th–3th century BCE), and Middle Persian (from 4th–3th century BCE until 8th–9th century CE), and it is only in the modern period that the periphrastic progressive aspect has become part of the aspectual system of this language. According to Dehghan (1972: 204), the surviving Old Persian texts evince no particular verb form to express action in progress. Here the difference between imperfective [in progress or habitual and iterative] and perfective [definitely terminated] can only be understood from the context.[2] Zhukovski's (1899) quotation of the following passage from a satirical folk song, popular around late 1870s, seems to be the earliest recording of this usage in everyday language (Dehghan 1972: 201):

(2) Poles   sâz   mi-zan-e   dâr-e   mi-raqs-e
     Police   sâz   IMPF-PRES.hit-3SG   PROG-3SG   IMPF-PRS.dance-3SG
     'The police are (in the process of) playing *sâz* (musical instrument), and are (in the process of) dancing'

Following up on Dehghan (1972: 201), however, scholars have not made any effort to find the source of this usage or, to at least determine the date of its first introduction into writing. Dehghan's examination of a substantial amount of Persian writings of the nineteenth century (which represents the simple and objective style of the earlier classical periods and bridges the gap between the spoken language and formal writing) does not show any such usage of *dâštan*.

---

2 In Avestan texts there are a few passages in which *hista-* [<stâ]= NP: istâdan 'to stand'], with an adjective or a participle, assumes the function of an auxiliary in the sense of continuity. There are three such passages, cited by Bartholomae (1961 [1094]: 1601), to which Benveniste (1966: 48) has added a few other comparable examples. These particles obviously have nothing to do with *dâštan* (Dehghan 1972: 204).

The earliest use of the verb *dâštan* in written discourse that has come to notice is in Ali Akbar Dehkhod's satirical essays 'Charand-o-Parand' ["A jumble of words"], which appeared in the newspaper *Sur-e Esrafil* at the outset of the Constitutional Revolution of 1906:

(3) âdam –hâ=ye âqâ   dâr-and   mi-ây-and
    servant-PL=of gentleman PROG-3PL   IMPF-PRS.come-3PL
    'The gentleman's servants are coming'

(4) čub-dâr-ha   dâš-t-and   gusfand=e ziad=i   be šahr
    sheep-dealer-PL   PROG-PST-3PL sheep=of   much-INDF to city
    mi-âvar-d-and
    IMPF-PRS.bring-PST-3PL
    'the sheep dealers were bringing a lot of sheep to the city'

Historically, the morphological encoding of progressiveness (with very low frequency) (7) as well as habituality ((5) and (6)) was achieved in New Persian[3] by the prefix *mi-* (the allomorph of archaic *mē-*), as in (6). The prefix *mi-* in turn is the product of the grammaticalization of *hamē* as in (5).[4]

(5) andar šabâne ruz yek bâr   hamē di-d-ø
    in   night   day one time HAB   PST.see-PST-3SG
    'During night and day, he used to see (him) once'.
    (Tenth century, Tabari 2009: 69)

(6) va   ostâd-ân   naqz ân   râ   mi-tarâš-id-and
    and artisan-PL   well that ACC HAB-PRS.rasp-PST-3PL
    '[...] and the artisans used to rasp it well'
    (Eleventh century, Nasir Khusru Ghubadiyani 2009: 206)

---

[3] The introduction of Islam (since 651 CE) in Iran marks the beginning of New Persian; however, the earliest major extant texts of this language date back to tenth century. It is from this early New Persian that Modern Persian or the Present Day Persian evolved.

[4] It must be noted that *hamē* is also the analytic marker of progressiveness in Middle Persian:
(i) u=m   di-d   ruvân ī   zan=ē   kē=š   uzvân   pad
    and=1SG   PAST.see-PAST spirit-EZ woman-INDF   that-3SG tongue toward
    garden   hamē   keš-id-ø
    neck   PROG   PRS.pull-PAST-3SG
    'and I saw the spirit of a woman whose tongue he was pulling toward her neck' (Gignoux 2003: 68)

(7) zâhed=i   namâz   mi-kar-d-ø   va...   ezhâr=e
    pious=INDF   prayer   IMPF-PRS.do-PAST-3SG   and   showing=of
    ajz   va   niâz...   yek=i   gof-t-ø=aš...
    insuffiency and   need   one=INDF PST.say-PAST-3SG=him
    'a pious was praying and (was) whining... (when) someone told him...'
    (Thirteenth century, Ghaani 2009: 1247)

An interesting point to note concerning the periphrastic progressive construction in Modern Persian is the fact that *dâštan* always co-occurs with the prefix *mi-* as an obligatory element in encoding progressive aspect along with *dâštan* as in (8a). However, prefix *mi-* can also express progressive aspect on its own in context as in (8b).

(8) a. dâr-i   chi   kâr   mi-kon-i?
       PROG-2SG   what   work   IMPF-PRS.do-2SG
       'What are you doing?'
    b. rânandegi   mi-kon-am.
       driving   IMPF-PRS.do-1SG
       'I am driving'

This raises the question what the contribution of *dâštan* in Persian progressive construction is. To address this question, we would like to point out the ambiguity which arises through declarative and progressive uses of *mi-*, since *mi-* is a marker of declarative mood in Persian as well. Accordingly, (8b) can also be interpreted as an assertion or a factual statement on the speaker's ability to drive.

Therefore, the use of *dâštan* both disambiguates the sentence in favor of a progressive interpretation and reinforces the concept of progressiveness. Out of context of the dialogue represented in (8), (8b) is used primarily to make a direct assertion about the real world signaling that the proposition expressed by the speaker's utterance is offered as an unqualified statement of fact. The addition of *dâštan* expresses an incomplete action or state in progress at a specific time, that is, the fact that the subject is actively driving a car.

It must be mentioned that in Modern Persian this prefixed construction with *mi-* is still the unmarked one (as in (8b)), and furthermore, the only possible expression of the concept of progressiveness in negative contexts. The periphrastic progressive counterpart with *dâštan* cannot be negated by the Modern Persian negation marker *na-*(or its allomorph *ne-*) as shown in (10), which is ungrammatical. As Taleghani (2008: 11) states, the negative marker cannot attach to *dâštan*, nor can it attach to the main verb. In contrast, the prefixed counterpart (9), is grammatical.

(9) rânandegi   ne-mi-kon-am
    driving   NEG-IMPF-PRS.do-1SG
    'I am not driving'

(10) *na-dâr-am   rânandegi   mi-kon-am
     NEG-PROG-1SG   driving   IMPF-PRS.do-1SG
     'I am not driving'

Persian linguists and grammarians have put forward varying claims about the function of *mi*-. Some have proposed that *mi*- represents the ongoing character of the event (Ghomeshi 2001: 27). Others suggest that *mi*- refers to a habitual event in present or past tense (Lambton 1979; Windfuhr 1979). We categorize *mi*- as the marker of declarative, habitual and progressive as it denotes declaration (as in (8b), out of the context of the dialogue), habituality (as in (5) and (6)) and progression of an action ((7) and (8)). Since it is an obligatory element in encoding progressive aspect even together with *dâštan*, the Persian progressive seems to have two representations. By its very nature, we refer to the progressive in Persian as a 'double marked' aspect. We will further show that through the development of prospective aspect, together with *dâštan*, *mi*- also functions as the obligatory marker of Persian prospective aspect.

With *dâštan* 'have' as the progressive, both *dâr/dâšt* 'have/had' and the main verbs in the progressive form receive subject agreement. Therefore, the subject can be totally omitted, or it appears just once, as the auxiliary verb construction as a whole expresses a single event (cf. Anderson 2006: 12). This synchronic fact helps us to assume the diachronic path of evolution according to the adjacency of two finite verbs, as elaborated in the following sections.

2.2 Basic assumptions about the grammaticalization path of *dâštan* 'have'

Building on Heine's (1993) concept, we claim that *dâštan* 'have' as a lexical verb in the Persian verbal system has primarily grammaticalized into a progressive marker, being located along the grammaticalization chain extending from full verbs to grammatical inflections. However, until recently, most studies on the grammaticalization of aspect (e.g. Heine and Kuteva (2002) and Bybee et al. (1994)), only report the grammaticalization of progressives through motion verbs such as *go, come*, and *walk* (e.g. Bybee et al. 1994: 128)), statives (such as *be, sit, stand, stay*) and particles of location. Our paper highlights the unusual path of progressive development through a possessive construction in Persian, which contrasts with the 'have' > Perfect path in most Indo-European languages.

Event schemas and the mental processes of metaphor and metonymy form the cognitive basis for the emergence of this unusual aspect marker. This will be outlined in Section 5, where we describe the *Auxiliation Dimensions Model*. In terms of conceptual metaphor, abstract domains such as grammatical categories are expressed by means of more concrete concepts like lexical units referring to physical objects or processes. This cognitive mechanism constitutes a way to conceive and express experiences that demand a higher effort for comprehension in terms of more easily intelligible experiences (cf. Lakoff and Johnson 1980). In (1), the linguistic expression for the abstract temporal notion of progressive aspect, which in itself does not refer to any physical object or kinetic process, is derived from the physical state of possessing a concrete object. According to Heine et al. (1991), this reinterpretation is basically metaphoric in nature. In contrast, we wish to highlight metonymic relations. Metonymy is based on contiguity in the linguistic world of an utterance and gives rise to a new conversational implicature, a process which is referred to as context-induced reinterpretation. From this cognitive point of view, the metaphorical transfer which is based on universal human cognitive schemas and is therefore universally available, has a metonymic basis in the possession > progression path of grammaticalization. Through this path, two entities that are textually contiguous, i.e *dâštan* and another predicate, are perceived as conceptually contiguous leading to an auxiliary verb construction. Before we turn to our synchronic analysis of the emergence of progressive aspect in Modern Persian, a few words have to be said about the semantic evolution of *dâštan* which is of prime relevance to the investigation reported in this paper.

2.2.1 The rise of *dâštan* 'have' in the history of Persian

Historically speaking, and based on our analysis of Persian literary texts, the semantic extension of *dâštan* representing the notion of possession first began in Middle Persian as in (11), and extended to New Persian as in (12) and to Modern Persian as in (13). The possessive meaning of *dâštan* in Middle Persian (Mackenzie 1986: 25) developed through metaphorical extension from the core meanings of 'dwell', 'stay near', and 'be at', according to Skjærvø (2002: 61), as in (14)[5] and (15),

---

5 *dâraya-* (+ place): 'stay near, dwell in/at' (Skjærø 2005: 61).

and 'hold firm' according to Kent (1950: 189)[6] and Skjærvø (2002: 61), as in (16), (17) and (18) in Old Persian.

(11) čē   man   dâr-ēm   bârag   azēr   rân... ud
     since I   PRS.have-1SG horse   under   thigh and
     man   dâr-ēm   tigr   andar kantigr
     I   PRS.have-1SG arrow   in   quiver
     'Since I have horse under thigh... and I have arrow in quiver'
     (Jamasp 1992: 216)

(12) va   Maʔmun...   maneš=e   pâdešâh-ân   va
     and   Mʔmun   behavior=EZ   king-PL   and
     hemmat=e   mehtar-ân   dâš-t-Ø
     endeavor=EZ   elder-PL   PST.have-PAST-3SG
     '...and Maamun had the behavior of kings and the endeavor of elders'
     (Tenth century, Abu-Mansur-alomri 2009: 44)

(13) man   yek   barâdar   dâr-am
     I   one   brother   PRS.have-1SG
     'I have a brother'

(14) kâra   haya   Naditabair-ahayâ   Tigr-âm   a-dâraya-Ø
     army   that   Naditabaira-GEN   Tigr-ACC   IMPERF-dwell-3SG
     'The army that belonged to Nidintu-Bel was by the Tigris' (Skjærvø 2002: 59)

(15) θâ-tiy   Dâryavauš   I   martiya   Martiya   nâma
     PRS.say-3SG Dâryuš   one   man   Martiya   name
     Cicixrâiš   puça   Kuganakâ   nâm-a   vardan-am   Pârsaiy
     Cincikhri   son   Kuganakâ   name-ACC   town-ACC   Persia
     avadâ   a-dâraya-Ø.
     there   IMPERF-abide-3SG
     'Says Darius One man, by name Martiya, son of Cincikhri – a town by name Kuganaka, in Persia – there he abode.' (Kent 1950: 121)

---

[6] We considered both core meanings because the same verb has been translated differently by the authors. However we believe that the meaning of 'hold' is the better equivalent as both arguments namely *Tigr-âm* in (14) and *vardan-am* in (15) are in accusative case.

(16) *Aspacanâ   vaça-bara   isuvâ-m   dâray-atiy*
     Aspacanâ   mace-bearer   battle-ax-ACC   PRS.hold-3SG
     'Aspathines the mace-bearer holds a battle-ax (in his hand)' (Skjærvø 2002: 36)

(17) *vašnâ   Auramazd-âha   ima   xšâç-am*
     by_favor_of   Ahuramazda-GEN/DAT   this   kingdom-ACC
     dâray-âmiy
     PRS.hold-1SG
     'by favor of Ahuramazda, I hold this kingdom' (Kent 1950: 119)

(18) *Θâ-tiy   Dârayavauš XŜ   ima   xšaç-am   taya*
     PRS.announce-3SG   Dârayavauš King   this   kingdom-ACC which
     adam   dâray-âmiy
     I   PRS.hold-1SG
     'King Darius announces: This (is) the empire which I hold'.
     (Skjærvø 2002: 185)

Among the archaic meanings of *dâštan* in Old Persian, the location schema was no longer available in Middle, New and Modern Persian. However, the notion of "to hold something" protracted to Middle Persian as in (19) and (20), and to New Persian as in (21) and (22):

(19) *ud   hargâh   pad   dar-ī   tō   ēst-ēd   va*
     and   every-time   to   door-EZ   you   PRS.stand-3SG   and
     hamēšag   payqâmbar   pad   darī   tō   dâr-ēd
     always   messenger   to   door-EZ   to   PRS.hold-3SG
     'and he stands by your house all the time and always holds a messenger at the door of your house' (Jamasp 1992: 271)

(20) *tan   az   drū,   bazag   ud...   rōspīg   dūr   dâr-ēd*
     body   from   lie,   sin   and   prostitute   far   PRS.hold-2PL
     'Hold (your) body far from lie, sin and prostitute' (Jamasp 1992: 374)

(21) *agar   xâs-t-i   u   râ   be-forux-t-i   va*
     if   PST.want-PST-2SG 3SG   ACC   EMPH-PST.sell-PST-2SG   and
     gar   na   hamē⁷   dâš-t-i
     if   not   EMP   PST.have-PST-2SG
     'If you want, you may sell it or you may hold (it)'
     (Tenth century, Tabari 2009: 69)

---

7 It should be noted that *hamē* in New Persian also functioned as an emphatic marker representing higher frequency than habitual marker.

(22) pas   išân   Yusef   râ   be   kârevân   āvar-d-and
     then   they   Yusef   ACC   to   convoy   bring-PST-3PL
     va   hamē   dâš-t-and
     and   EMPH   PST.hold-PST-3PL
     'Then they brought Yusef to the convoy and held (him) there.'
     (Tenth century, Tabari 2009: 73)

A similar pathway of the rise of 'have'-possession through 'hold' has been attested for Catalan *tener* 'hold', 'keep' (< Old Catalan *tenir*) > 'have', 'own' (Steinkrüger 1997) and also in Basque *eduki*, which formerly meant 'hold', 'hold in one's hand', 'grasp', and still does in the East, while in the West, it has become the ordinary verb 'have' (Heine and Kuteva 2002: 185). In many cases, it can be established that the 'have' verb has been derived – usually by a certain amount of semantic bleaching – from some fully lexical verb that indicates physical control or handling. Givón (1984: 103), as cited in Stassen (2009: 63) claims that, most commonly, a 'have' verb arises out of the semantic bleaching of active possession verbs such as 'get', 'grab', 'seize', 'take', 'obtain' etc., whereby the sense of "acting to take possession" has been bleached, leaving behind only its implied result of "having possession". According to Heine (1997: 48) "non-acquisitive" verbs like 'hold', 'carry', or 'rule' may be the historical source of 'have' verbs. The process of semantic bleaching, by which a verb that denotes a concrete act of acquiring or handling turns into a verb with an "abstract" meaning of possession, has been shown to proceed in a number of successive stages (Heine 1997: 48–50). Given the lexical origin of many 'have' verbs, it is plausible to view the 'have' possessive of alienable possession as a semantic extension of the encoding of temporary possession. After all, physical control verbs like 'hold' or 'carry' are typically used for situations in which the relation between possessor and possessed extends over a certain period of time but is not permanent (cf. Stassen 2009: 63).

The leading assumption advanced in this paper of the emergence of a progressive marker through possession is pertinent to what Stassen (2009: 16) labels as "temporary or physical possession". According to his typological study, temporary possession, expresses control without permanent contact. Thus there is a relation between a possessor and a possessee whereby the former wields control over the latter. This subtype can be illustrated by an English sentence like (23).

(23) *Look out! That guy has a knife!*

In the most prominent reading of this sentence, ownership of the knife in question is not what this sentence is meant to assert but the availability and the physical presence of the possessee at a certain point in time. In other words, what the speaker wants to convey is the fact that, at this moment, a certain person has a knife at his disposal, and the question of whether or not that person is actually the owner of that knife is largely irrelevant (Stassen 2009: 19). The advantage this interpretation has versus simply labeling as possession for the development of *dâštan* as the marker of progression in Persian is the fact that the usage of this subdomain of conceptual space of possession encodes the now existing, being in view or at hand relation of contact between the "possessor" and the "possessee". The relevant point regarding the progressive meaning is the state of something being available for the subject at a certain point of time to undergo an action at that point of time may contribute to the rise of the progressive meaning. On the other hand, during the time span in which the relation holds and the action applies, the possessor can be said to exert control over, or even physically handle, the possessee leading to the semantic distinction between possessor and possessee in terms of "power" in the possessive relationship. Thus it is possible to assign the denotation of 'possession' instead of just 'holding' to *dâštan*, leaving unspecified whether or not this object is the property of the person "having" it. In the reminder of this article, we will propose an alternative account of the rise of *dâštan* as the marker of progressive aspect in Modern Persian with respect to the notion of temporary possession.

2.2.2 The rise of *dâštan* "progressive" in Modern Persian

Based on the notion of temporary possession, and along the lines of Heine (1993: 131), we assume that in the second step of the grammaticalization chain, the schema of temporary possession with two participants in terms of concrete and tangible entities (X has Y (a concrete object): "X is temporarily with Y") as in (24) is bleached to the more abstract schema with the participant Y or the complement in terms of an activity which is more abstract than a concrete object (X has Y (an activity): "X is temporarily with (in the process of) Y" in Modern Persian as in (25):

(24) u   aslahe   dâr-ad.
     3SG   gun   PRS-have-3SG
     '(S)he has a gun.'

(25) u   dâr-ad   mi-rav-ad.
     3SG   PROG-3SG   IMPF-PRS.go-3SG
     '(S)he is going.'

This is a path from "being with something concrete" or the "companion possession" in Heine's and "temporary possession", in Stassen's words, to "being with or in the process of an event". The latter meaning serves as the progressive, which basically represents the notion of 'to be in the process of'. The cline in (26) depicts the proposed pathway of grammaticalization:

(26) Meaning change in the grammaticalization of *dâštan*
1) to be at, to dwell; 2) to hold > possess something (to be with something concrete) > to be with an activity or in the process of an activity

However, Modern Persian data show that the metaphoric meaning of progression did not emerge *ex nihilo*. Based on some instances of colloquial use that lead to contextual ambiguities, such as in (27) and (28), we suggest that contexts in which *dâštan* with its source meaning of (temporary) possession appeared immediately before another verb whose subject was the same as that of *dâštan* led speakers to reanalyze *dâštan* as an element of the second verb, that is, an auxiliary, instead of as an independent verb. Here, our view of meaning change emphasizes reanalysis leading to development of the progressive, which is predictable from the underlying semantic features of *dâštan*, that is, the notion of being temporarily with something:

(27) va   dar=e   jaʔbe=i   ra   ke   dâš-t-Ø   bâz
     and   door=EZ box=INDF   ACC   that PAST.have-PAST-3SG   open
     mi-kar-d-Ø
     DEC-PAST.do-PAST-3SG
     'And the door of the box that he had, he opened it'.

Example (27) can also synchronically be interpreted as: 'And the door of the box that he was opening'. (28) would be another example:

(28) âb=i   ke   dâr-im   mi-xor-im
     water=INDF   that PRS.have-1PL   DEC-PRS.eat-1PL
     'The water that we have, we eat it'.

Example (28) may also have the reading of: 'The water that we are eating'

The ambiguity arises in complex sentences encompassing a relative clause with the verb *dâštan* and its immediate neighbor clause in the form of an inflected verb. This may have happened through metonymy, which is a process on the syntagmatic axis in which a specific context, a switch context, invites inferences to a new interpretation. Switch contexts are characterized by an interaction of context and conceptualization, leading to the rise of new grammatical meaning. In this case, the lexical verb *dâštan* was reanalyzed as an auxiliary, analogical to the

Persian Aux-Lex[8] dominant word order such as (29) in which *gereft* 'took' is an inchoative marker:

(29) *geref-t-am   nešas-t-am*
     PST.take-PST-1SG PST.sit-PST-1SG
     'I began to sit'.

(Compare the Aux-Lex word order in Auxiliary Verb Construction (29) *geref-t-am nešas-t-am* with (27): *dâš-t-Ø bâz mi-kar-d-Ø* and (28): *dâr-im mi-foruš-im*).

Here, the question arises why relative clauses are decisive for what happens on the way from possession to progression? In other words, why do we consider relative clauses to be switch contexts? Isn't it possible or plausible to get the same sort of ambiguity in a main clause environment?

As an answer, a comparison with corresponding English sentences is helpful. As for a verb and object as an appropriate context for change, we can imagine the following sentences in English:

(30) a. *I have crutches and I walk on them.*
to
(30) b. *I am walking on* crutches.

Semantically, the step from (30a) to (30b) makes sense because during the time span in which the possession relation holds (a specific time), the possessor takes the action of walking on the controlled possesses (crutches), which leads to a progressive interpretation. But syntactically, there is a problem with respect to the position of the object, because in the target structure it is spelled out after the second verb, while in the source structure it is spelled out after 'have'. The question arises how we can get from (30a) to (30b) in terms of what happens to the object. The relative clause construction comes up for this fact. Here the object is at the beginning of the clause and shared by both verbs. Thus, its position does not get in the way. This is an important reason why the RC might be the best possible switch context as in (31):

(31) a. *šokolât=i   dâr-am   va   ân   râ   mi-xor-am*
        chocolate=INDF   PRS.have-1SG and that ACC DEC-PRS.eat-1SG
        'I have a chocolate and I eat it'
to
(31) b. *šokolât=i   ke   dâr-am   mi-xor-am*
        chocolate=INDF   that PRS.have-1SG IMPF-PRS.eat-1SG
        'The chocolate that I am eating'

---

8 Auxiliary verb-Lexical verb.

Moreover, we need to consider the contextual requirements and concrete conditions that led to the ambiguity between possession and progressive. They are as follows:

(I) The switch context must have contained a transitive verb as the main verb, because 'have' is transitive as well, and we must assume transitivity harmony between the two verbs;

(II) The main clause must describe a dynamic event; a stative verb would result in a stative progressive, which is usually the most advanced stage of a progressive;

(III) The dynamic verb must overlap in time with the 'have'-clause. Therefore it must be of imperfective aspect;

(IV) The subject of both clauses must be animate, because inanimate subjects are not appropriate as possessors, and as agents for the second verb;

(V) Both verbs need the same subject and the same object, and this object can be deleted for one of the verbs, preferably 'have';

(VI) The object must be salient enough that it makes the speaker say 'I have it (with me) and am doing something with it';

(VII) *dâštan* in the relative clause cannot be negated, because we know that it cannot be used in negated clauses (cf. ex. (10) above). It is difficult to construe a sentence such as (32):

(32) ketab-i   ke   na-dâr-am   mi-xun-am
     book-INDF   that   NEG-PRS.have-1SG   DEC-PRS.read-1SG
     'The book that I don't have, I read'

(VIII) Moreover, the relative clause must contain *dâštan* as its predicate; otherwise the relative pronoun *ke* 'that' separates the two adjacent verbs and obstructs the process of reanalysis and auxiliation as in (33):

(33) xune=i   tu   Rašt   dâr-im   ke   mi-foruš-im (=eš)
     house=INDF   in   Rašt   PRS.have-1PL   that   DEC-PRS.sell-1PL (=3SG)
     'We have a house in Rašt that we sell (it)'

Based on the Modern Persian data, we hypothesize that the extension from possession to progressive has proceeded across different contexts. That is, it has extended from relative clauses to other clause types like main clauses. It also extended to intransitive verbs, to inanimate subjects and to stative verbs except the copula *budan* 'be'.

Examples for such meaning change are not hard to come by in Modern Persian classical novels. (34) and (35) are instances of specific contexts in which contiguity and flow of speech are important and lead to metaphor-based grammaticalization, arising out of (metonymic) semantic proximity. As can be observed in (34) and (35), the predicate is the head of the clause, so the first brackets should be on *parde* 'curtain' in (34) and *tajtobi-ât* 'experiments' in (35).

(34) [parde=i   [ke   dāš-t-and]]   bâz   mi-kar-d-and]
     [curtain=INDF [that PST.have-PST-3PL]]   open   DECL-do-PST-3PL]
     'They opened a curtain that they had.'
     (Hedayat 1977 [1933]: 30)

(35) [tajrobi-ât=i   [ke dāš-t-and]]   enteqâl
     [experiment-PL=INDF   [that PST.have-PST-3PL]] transfer
     mi-dâ-d-and⁹]
     DECL-PST.give-PST-3PL
     'They transferred the experiments that they had.'
     (Hedayat 1977 [1933]: 123)

We hypothesize that in utterances such as (34) and (35), the juxtaposition of the two morphological verbs with identical subjects, *dâštand* '(they) had' and *bâz mikardand* '(they) opened', and *dâštand* '(they) had' and *enteqâl midâdand* '(they) transferred', respectively, invites the conversational inference that the subject was involved in one single event consisting of a main predicate 'to open' in (34a), and 'to transfer' in (35a), and a predicate with a modifying meaning, indicating the continuation of an ongoing dynamic situation (i.e 'to be in the process of'), expressed by *dâštan* (with the basic notion of 'to be with something'). The semantic extension leading to this shift can be delineated in terms of the following scenario representing the ambiguity in terms of the functions of *dâštan*:

(36) Stage I   qazâ   dâr-am [temporary possession schema]
                 food   have-1SG
                 'I have food (with me).'
     Stage II   qazâ   mi-xor-am [action schema]
                 food   HAB-eat-1SG
                 'I eat food.'
     Stage III   qazâ-i   ke   dâr-am   mi-xor-am [relativization]
                 food-INDF that   PRS.have-1SG   DEC-eat-1SG
                 a. 'The food that I have (with me), I eat it'. [relativization involving two events]
                 b. 'I am eating the food' [progressive interpretation through auxiliation involving one event]

This in turn leads to the development of the auxiliary as an affiliated part of the main predicate. Furthermore, in our view, the inference from the contiguous source *dâštan* supports the grammaticalization of *dâštan*. According to (33), the reanalysis involves the rebracketing of [[... *dāš-t-and*] [... *bâz mi-kar-d-and*]] as

---

9 *enteqâal dâdan* 'transfer' is a complex predicate in Persian.

[... *dâš-t-and bâz mi-kar-d-and*], or more schematically as [... *dār*-TNS V-TNS]. The semantic ambiguity of *dāštan* 'have' is important, because the aspectual function cannot develop without moving through an intermediate phase where both readings coexist. That is, we go through the stages of *have* > (*have ~PROG*) > *PROG* (cf. Hopper and Traugott 1993: 36; Heine 1997: 82).

According to Heine (2002), the role of a 'switch context' in the overlapping stage is crucial. In (34) and (35), the sentences may ambiguously describe both imperfect events through the habitual marker -*mi* related to the entities possessed, and an action in progress regardless of the meaning of possession. Since both texts represent events that are in progress at reference time (i.e *bâz kardan* 'to open' and *enteqâl dâdan* 'to transfer)', the element *dāštan* 'have' with the sense of 'be with something' markedly foregrounds the progressiveness 'to be in the process of an event', which is defined as imperfectivity not occasioned by habituality, while the possessive meaning may still be available. This is possible because both possession and progressiveness share a common interpretation: they each refer to a temporary 'being with', involving either an entity in the case of possession, or an activity in the case of the progressive. Thus, we can rebracket (34) and (35) in their new interpretation as follows:

(34) a. *parde=i* [*ke dâš-t-and bâz mi-kar-d-and*]
curtain=INDF [that have.PROG-PAST-3PL open IMPF-do-PST-3PL]
'The curtain that they were opening.'
(Hedayat 1977 [1933]: 30)

(35) a. *tajrobi-ât=i* [*ke dâš-t-and enteqâl mi-dâ-d-and*]
experiment-PL=INDF [that PST.have-PST-3PL transfer IMPF-PST.give-PST-3PL]
'The experiments that they were transferring.'
(Hedayat 1977 [1933]: 123)

2.3 The prominence of metonymy in the development of the progressive marker in Persian

From a semantic and cognitive perspective, the conceptual contiguity of the two parallel events, namely the metonymic component, (*dâštan* 'to have' and doing something with that what you have e.g *bâz kardan* 'to open' or *enteqâsl dâdan* 'to transfer' at the same time) is metaphorized through the mechanism of analogy to the progressive notion of an ongoing event. It means that without an earlier metonymic understanding of the two contingent activities expressed through *dâštan* and the other verb, the process of metaphorization would not have started. As we showed in (34) and (35), evidence from Persian classical novels bears witness to the gravitational force of conceptual metonymy. This compels us to think of metonymy as even more basic than metaphor in language processing. In our opinion, based on the examples in (34) and (35), it is the sequence of the two verbs that is reinterpreted as a single syntactic constituent as schematically presented in the cline (37):

(37) Linguistic contingency > metonymic relation > ambiguity > context-induced reinterpretation > metaphoric relation > new grammatical function

The description in terms of metaphor alone, according to which a possessive schema is mapped onto a progressive situation, would not account for the fact that a stative element is involved in the Persian expression of the non-stative state of affairs. The cline proposed in (37), which crucially includes a mentonymic step, remedies this deficiency. In this account, inferences from the local context of the verb in its linear position within the clause are the main driving factor for change. However, this is not meant to deny the fact that metaphors of progression, which map the locative-based expression of possession 'to hold (be) in a place' or 'to have a concrete entity' onto aspectual meanings like 'being in the process of' or 'to have an abstract activity at the moment of utterance', may provide the conceptual background that supports the development.

Furthermore, the development of prospective aspect function out of the possessive function can be described as an increase of "speaker-orientation", that is, an increasing orientation towards the speaker's perspective. Increase of speaker orientation was identified by Narrog (2012: 105) as one of three elements that characterize an overarching tendency in semantic change in grammaticalization called speech-act orientation. While the possessive expresses an "objective" state-of-affairs, that is, a state-of-affairs that is generally independent of speaker deixis, and is shared with other speakers, the progressive reflects the speaker's own temporal perspectivization of a state-of-affairs. Progressive also have crosslinguistically a tendency towards specialized subjective uses (cf. e.g. Killie 2004). Some of them in Persian are briefly introduced in the following section.

3 Subjective meanings of the progressive aspect

In this section we will make some observations on the non-core meanings of the progressive construction, which are strongly pragmatic in nature and appear to be related to the speaker's attitude and the expression of emotion. Storms (1964: 62)

suggests that "the opposition between progressive vs. non-progressive can quite generally be explained as one of subjectivity vs. objectivity and the use of progressive or simple form will vary according to the emotional make-up of the speaker[...], to momentary influences and momentary fluctuations." The emotional coloring of the progressive is obvious in combination with adverbs of frequency (e.g *hamaš* 'always', *modâm* 'all the time'), and with downtoners (e.g *faqat* 'just') where we can observe a semantic prosody, either positive or negative. However, in our opinion, even in the absence of such adverbs, the speaking subject's stance is directly expressed through the periphrastic progressive, while the simple form is fully conventionalized and does not express the speaker's negative or positive attitude towards a proposition. The invited inferences of irritation, surprise and politeness are illustrated in (38), (39), and (40), respectively:

(38) *hamaš   dâr-am   dard   mi-keš-am*
     always   PROG-1SG   pain   IMPF-PRS.pull-1SG
     'I am always suffering (pain).'

(39) *dah   sâl=e   dâr-e   piano   mi-zan=e*
     ten   year=PRS.BE.3SG   PROG-3SG   piano   IMPF-PRS.hit-3SG
     'He has been playing piano for ten years.'

(40) *faqat   dâš-t-am   komak   mi-kar-d-am*
     just   PROG-PAST-1SG   help   IMPF-PRS.do-PST-1SG
     'I was just helping.'

Having exemplified the subjective meanings of the progressive aspect here, let us now turn to the next step in the grammaticalization chain with another aspectual meaning. Starting from the new meaning of ongoingness of a durative situation, the grammaticalized construction has also metonymically acquired the meaning of prospectiveness when applied to punctual achievement situations. As was mentioned before, we consider this meaning as a non-core meaning of the progressive aspect. Again, we suggest that metaphor is not the essential mechanism of change at work, as the new function emerges through association in the flow of speech, and is entirely context-dependent.

4 The emergence of the prospective aspect marker in Persian

According to Vendler (1957: 147), there are four classes of eventuality. Among these four classes, achievements are telic but unlike accomplishments do not mark duration. In this section, we shall sketch the incipient development of the progressive marker into prospective, a border category between aspect and evidentiality, with achievement verbs, as in (41):

(41) dâr-e   mi-oft-e
     PROSP-3SG   PROS-PRS.fall-3SG
     'It is about to fall down.'

The grammatical notion of prospective has received a fair amount of attention, both from a synchronic and a diachronic perspective, in a range of individual languages as well as in cross-linguistic studies (see e.g. Comrie 1976, Dahl 1985, Kuteva 2001 and Heine and Kuteva 2002). The previous research suggests that the prospective markers often evolve from desiderative predicates (e.g. 'want', 'love to') and locative concepts of proximity (e.g. locative adverbs such as 'near'; and directive motion verbs such as 'come'). However, some aspects of change that have been neglected in this area and are going to be discussed in this contribution include the effects of contextual motivation (metonymy), the cognitive impact of source event schemas (metaphoric extension), the modal meaning of the grammatical aspect (evidentiality), and pragmatic factors (warning). These factors have led prospectivity to be linguistically encoded using the Persian predicate *dâštan* as a source construction. The prospective aspect in Persian has been widely believed to have developed out of the verb *xâstan* 'want' (volition event schema) (Lambton 1979: 54, Naghzguy-Kohan 2011). However, what the previous studies on the origin of prospective aspect in Persian have failed to account for is the explicit trajectory of the development of the abstract grammatical concept of prospectivity out of the event schemas of progression. We start with the discussion of prospectivity in Section 4.1 and continue with a discussion of the characteristic features of prospective marker *dâštan* emerging from the metonymic component of progressive meaning in Persian in Section 4.2. Section 4.3 focusses on the pragmatic potential of the prospective, and Section 4.4 concludes that the semantic changes described in this section can be profitably described in terms of increase in speaker-orientation.

4.1 Prospective aspect: preliminaries

It is generally accepted in the literature that the prospective is an aspectual category which establishes a relation between a state and some subsequent event (Comrie 1976: 64). This prospective situation is symmetrical to the retrospective situation of resultative aspect which links a state at one time to a situation at an earlier time through its result. Typologically speaking, tense in languages is asymmetrically centered on the axis of present time, so that the lack of a direct correspondence between forms with perfect meaning and forms with prospective meaning is not surprising (cf. Comrie 1976: 64). The latter denotes a temporal phase closely before the initial boundary of the situation denoted by the main verb, with no implication that the situation does actually come about.

4.2 The prospective marker in Persian

The periphrastic prospective aspect in Persian consists of the auxiliary verb *dâštan* 'have' and a punctual achievement verb in simple present tense as in (42):

(42) *dâr-e   xafe   mi-š-e*
    PROSP-3SG   drowned   PROSP-PRS.become-3SG
    'S(h)e is about to drown'

On the basis of (42) and on what we have suggested about the development of non-core functions of the progressive aspect, we conclude that the prospective construction materializes when the progressive marker *dâštan* does not modify a durative verb as in the progressive construction, but an achievement verb. With the new meaning of ongoingness of a durative situation, the construction may acquire the meaning of prospective metonymically when applied to achievement events (e.g. *mordan* 'die', *oftâdan* 'fall', *residan* 'reach', *gozaštan* 'pass', *xafe šodan* 'drown' and so on). For the present purpose it may suffice to recall that achievements are instantaneous, that is, they are approaching an endpoint immediately. With reference to the progressive function of *dâštan*, the absence of event duration results in highlighting the beginning of the whole situation before it is borne out. In our view, based on our analysis of the development of the prospective function of the progressive, it is a metonymic relation that starts with contiguity in the linguistic world of the utterance which gives rise to the new conversational implicature. This mechanism of change can be referred to as context-induced reinterpretation.

4.3 Evidentiality from prospective aspect

In this section, we are going to investigate a secondary evidential meaning for the prospective in Persian, and its other subjectified pragmatic inferences.

The question which arises here is, why do languages encode the prospective notion? In order to address this question we share some observations about non-core meanings of the prospective construction that have a strongly pragmatic imprint, and appear to be related to the evidence on which the statement is based. Based on Persian data, we claim that the prospective construction represents a state of affairs witnessed by the speaker. This constitutes the distinction between the prospective meaning and the expression of straightforward future time reference. The prospective, as in (43), indicates the existence of a source of evidence (mostly eyewitness) for a given information, which the future lacks. With regard to the polysemous nature of *mi-*, recall that, in this construction, *mi-* affixed to punctual achievement verbs has a prospective function:

(43) dâr-e   mi-mir-e
     PROSP-3SG IMPF-PRS.die-3SG
     'S(h)e is about to die'

In (43), a situation is described in which someone alerts the addressee(s) to the already extant signs of some potential future situation: the event of someone dying. The prospective expression in (43) might well be read as a 'warning shout' to some third party to prevent the imminent situation. In this manner, this construction is applied to achievement situations in order to direct the attention of the addressee(s) to an expected event, which may still be prevented from coming about. Conversely, both (43) and (44) are unlikely to be expressed in situations which the speaker is remote from the event location. The prospective aspect marks the speaker's information source indicating how something is learnt directly:

(44) begir=eš   dâr-e   mi-oft-e
     PRS.hold=it PROSP-3SG   IMPF-PRS.fall-3SG
     'Hold it! It is about to fall.'

Both (43) and (44) clearly have evidential connotations invoked by the presence of the prospective aspect. The speaker deduces a possible future event on the basis of some visual evidence.

4.4 Increase in speaker-orientation

At the end of Section 2.3, we have indicated that the development of a prospective function out of a possessive function can be interpreted in terms of an increase in speaker-orientation, one of three dimensions of speech-act orientation together with hearer-orientation and orientation toward discourse itself (cf. Narrog 2012: 105).

The same can be said about the development of the prospective meaning with its evidential uses. While the progressive meaning reflects the speaker's temporal perspectivization of a state-of-affairs, the prospective goes one step further.

It reflects the speaker's extrapolating from a current state-of-affairs to a potential future, that is, irrealis state-of-affairs. As Narrog (2012: 278) writes, the prospective "is temporal in that the time of the event is later than the reference time. It is modal in that the embedded proposition is not factual, namely a prediction, and it is evidential in that the prediction is usually based on some kind of evidence." Thus, the prospective is a category on the transition from aspect to modality. Furthermore, modal, especially epistemic modal, and evidential categories are generally located higher on hierarchies of grammatical categories that reflect increased speech-act orientation (cf. Narrog 2012: 102–105). It is thus only fair to conclude that the history of Persian *dâštan* as described here is a case of increase in speaker-orientation, and accordingly, speech-act orientation.

5 The Auxiliation Dimensions Model

Auxiliation is the diachronic process through which auxiliaries develop out of lexical sources. The process is considered as an instance of grammaticalization in which the range of a morpheme advancing from a lexical to a grammatical status increases (Kuteva 2004: 1). The *Auxiliation Dimensions Model* proposed by Davari and Naghzguy-Kohan (forthcoming) is a descriptive model of auxiliaries outlined along three dimensions that delineates salient aspects of the process of auxiliation. Building on Heine's (1993) concept of auxiliation, we claim that the development of auxiliaries and their linguistic behavior, which has evoked numerous theoretical controversies in the past, can be considered in terms of their force, source, and their degree of auxiliation. The first dimension motivating the process is the force dimension, which refers to the grammatical function into which the auxiliary develops. In its absence, nothing would trigger the development of grammatical meanings to rise through auxiliary systems. Following Heine (1993), we argue that the most prominent forces of auxiliation in the Persian auxiliary system are the functions of tense, aspect and modality. The second dimension is the source of auxiliation. According to Heine et al. (1991) and Heine (1993) auxiliaries denoting abstract grammatical concepts that typically relate to temporal state (tense), temporal contours (aspect), and type of reality (modality), tend to develop out of lexical structures that denote such general concepts as location, motion, possession, activity, desire, posture and relation. As discussed by Heine (1993), generic verbs such as the following are common sources of grammaticalization:

a. location: be at, stay at,...
b. motion: go, come, move,....
c. possession: have, get, own,.....

However, Heine observes that these verbs are themselves part of more complex concepts called event schemas which are taken into account as the ingredients of the second dimension of the process of auxiliation, namely the source of auxiliation. Based on this model, the event schemas responsible for the development of auxiliaries in Persian are arranged in Tab. 1:

Tab. 1: The event schemas as the sources of auxiliation in Persian.

Conceptual form	Event schemas
'X is at Y'	Location
'X moves to/from Y'	Motion
'X does Y'	Action
'X wants Y'	Volition
'X becomes Y'	Change-of-state
'X is like Y'	Equation
'It is X that clause'	Evaluative
'X has Y'	Possession

The emergence of abstract grammatical concepts through concrete event schemas is related to the cognitive process by which stereotypical situations that are basic to human experience serve as a source for auxiliaries. Thus, the proper source for the expression of the grammatical concept is chosen.

In a last step, the *Auxiliation Dimension Model* specifies the formal changes throughout the process. The third dimension, degree of auxiliation, which is more language-specific, is related to the domain of formal changes. For determining the degree of auxiliation in Persian, the model focuses on ten Persian verbal features, which are listed in Tab. 2.

Based on the Persian auxiliary verbs and their verbal features, our dimension of auxiliation degree posits three degrees of the auxiliation process in Persian as manifested in morphological and phonological contents. Table 3 shows the three degrees of auxiliation corresponding to the formal status of the Persian auxiliaries.

Now we are in the position for analyzing the progressive marker *dâštan* 'to have' based on the *Auxiliation Dimensions Model*. As for the dimension of auxiliation force, we can conclude that it is a grammatical aspect, namely progressive. Furthermore, according to Heine's (1993) basic event schemas, the auxiliation source of progressive meaning is the possession event schema. The third dimension of the model, the degree of auxiliation, assigns the second degree of auxiliation to the Persian progressive marker, the verb *dâštan* 'have', since it loses its subjunctive, imperative, future and negated forms. Table 4 sums up the dimensions of auxiliation of the progressive aspect marker *dâštan* in Persian.

Tab. 2: Verbal features in Persian based on grammatical categories.

Grammatical category	Verbal feauture
Declarative Mood/Habitual & Progressive Aspect	mi-
Subjunctive Mood	be + PRS stem + Person endings
Imperative Mood	be + PRS stem
Present Tense	mi + PRS stem + Person endings
Past Tense	Past stem +-t (-d)
Future Tense	PRS stem xâstan 'to want' + subjunctive mood
Person and Number	Person endings
Passive Voice	Past participle + šodan 'to become' + person endings
Negation	na-/ne-

Tab. 3: Degrees of auxiliation in accordance with the formal status of the Persian auxiliaries.

The formal status of the auxiliary	Degree of auxiliation
Preserving verbal morphology and displaying a fully verbal morphosyntax	First degree
Losing part of or all verbal features, being fixed in a specific verbal form	Second degree
Losing the full phonological form	Third degree

Tab. 4: Auxiliation Dimensions of progressive aspect marker in Persian.

Persian progressive marker	Auxiliation dimensions
Progressive aspect	Auxiliation force
Possession event schema	Auxiliation source
Second degree	Auxiliation segree

6 Conclusion

The present study has investigated the development of the Persian periphrastic progressive aspect from its origins to its present-day core and non-core functions. As far as the origin of the progressive is concerned, we conclude that it has arisen through metonymic relations, which triggered new context-induced re-interpretation. The semantic potential of the verb *dâštan* 'have', that can be reinterpreted as 'ongoingness of a durative event', results in a conceptual shift from having a physical object to having the continuum of an action at a focal point of utterance. This semantic change can be understood in terms of increase in speaker-orientation that accompanies the process of grammaticalization. Besides the general tendency towards speaker-orientation, we also showed that distinct uses as an expression of the speaker's subjective attitude, that is, for interpretations that are not firmly grounded in the properties of a situation in the extra-linguistic world, but more in the subjective conceptualization of the speaker, developed. The whole set of changes described in this paper can be rendered as a grammaticalization chain as represented in (45):

(45) Chain of grammaticalization of *dâštan*
 locative ⟶ possessive ⟶ progressive ⟶ prospective

We also tried to provide an analysis of the auxiliation process through *Auxiliation Dimension Model* which is a descriptive model of auxiliaries outlined along three dimensions: the force, the source and the degree of auxiliation. By this model, we offered an account of gradual change which is crucial for grammaticalization considering critical factors. Within this cross-componential model of change, we focused on the functional inferences as the force dimension which is involved in expansion and change, through the acquisition of more abstract, indexical and procedural meanings. We also considered the nature and semantic properties of the source item, which is of key importance for the emergence of the target item in terms of the source dimension. Based on empirical observations of the Persian verbal features, and on the principle of decategorization in grammaticalization (Heine 1993: 55), we illustrated the degrees of morphosyntactic change which lexical verbs undergoing auxiliation exhibit. This includes loss or neutralization of morphological markers and of syntactic possibilities characteristic of the category of lexical verb. Based on the *Auxiliation Dimensions Model*, the progressive aspect was identified as the force for auxiliation, the possession schema as the auxiliation source, and we determined that the construction has a second degree of auxiliation.

Uncommon abbreviations

EMPH = emphasis; HAB = habitual; IMPERF = imperfect, ITER = iterative; NP = New Persian; PROSP = prospective.

References

Alomri, Abu-Mansur. 2009. *Moghaddameye Shahnameye Abumansuri*. In Karim Keshavarz, (ed.), *Hezâr sâl nasr-e Farsi [One thousand years of Persian prose]*. Tehran: Elmi Farhangi.
Anderson, Gregory D. S. 2006. *Auxiliary verb construction*. Oxford: Oxford University Press.
Bartholomae, Christian. 1904. *Altiranisches Wörterbuch*. Strassburg: Trübner.
Benveniste, Emile. 1966. *Problèmes de linguistique générale*. Paris: Gallimard.
Bybee, Joan L., William Pagliuca & Revere D. Perkins (1994). *The evolution of grammar: Tense, aspect and modality in the languages of the world*. Chicago: The University of Chicago Press.
Comrie, Bernard. 1976. *Aspect*. Cambridge: Cambridge University Press.
Croft, William. 1990. *Typology and universals*. Cambridge: Cambridge University Press.
Dahl, Östen. 1985. *Tense and aspect systems*. Oxford: Basil Blackwell.
Davari, Shadi & Mehrdad Naghzguy Kohan. Forthcoming. *The emergence of auxiliaries in Persian*.
Dehghan, Iraj. 1972. Dâštan as an auxilary in contemporary Persian. *Archiv Orientální* 40. 198–205.
Ghaani, Habib. 2009. *Parishan*. In Karim Keshavarz (ed.), *Hezâr sâl nasr-e Farsi [One thousand years of Persian prose]*. Tehran: Elmi Farhangi.
Ghomeshi, Jila. 2001. Control and thematic agreement. *Canadian Journal in Linguistics* 46(1–2). 9–40.
Gignoux, Philippe. 2003. *Ardavirafname*. Tehran: Institut Français de Recherche en Iran.
Givón, Talmy 1984. *Syntax: A functional-typological introduction*, Vol.1, Amsterdam & Philadelphia: John Benjamins.
Harley, Heidi. 2002. Possession and the double object construction. In Pierre Pica & Johan Rooryck (eds.), *Yearbook of linguistic variation*, Vol. 2. Amsterdam & Philadelphia: John Benjamins.
Hedayat, Sadegh. 1977 [1933]. *Alavie Khanum*. Tehran: Elmi Publication.
Heine, Bernd & Tania Kuteva. 2002. *World lexicon of grammaticalization*. Cambridge: Cambridge University Press.
Heine, Bernd, Ulrike Claudi & Friederike Hünnemeyer. 1991. *Grammaticalization: A conceptual framework*. Chicago: University of Chicago Press.
Heine, Bernd. 1993. *Auxiliaries: Cognitive forces and grammaticalization*. Oxford: Oxford University Press.
Heine, Bernd. 1997. *Possession: Cognitive sources, forces, and grammaticalization*. Cambridge: Cambridge University Press.
Heine, Bernd. 2002. On the role of context in grammaticalization. In Ilse Wischer & Gabriele Diewald (eds.), *New reflections on grammaticalization*. Oxford & New York: Oxford University Press.
Hengeveld, Kees. 2011. The grammaticalization of tense, mood and aspect. In Bernd Heine & Heiko Narrog (eds.), *The Oxford handbook of grammaticalization*, 462–472. Oxford: Oxford University Press.
Jamasp-Asana, Dastur Jamaspji Minocheherji. 1992. *Pahlavi texts (transcription, translation)*. Tehran: National Library of Iran.
Kayne, Richard S. 1993. Toward a modular theory of auxiliary selection. *Studia Linguistica* 47. 3–31.
Kent, Roland G. 1953. *Old Persian*. New Haven, Connecticut: American Oriental Society.

Khusru Ghubadiyani, Nasir. 2009. *Safar-nama*. In Karim Keshavarz (ed.), *Hezâr sâl nasr-e Farsi* [*One thousand years of Persian prose*]. Tehran: Elmi Farhangi.
Killie, Kristin 2004. Subjectivity and the English progressive. *English Language and Linguistics* 8(1). 25–46.
Kuteva, Tania & Mehrdad Naghzguy Kohan. 2011. On grammatical categories and linguistic categorization. Summer School on Iranian Linguistics, Universität Hamburg.
Kuteva, Tania. 2001. *Auxiliation: an enquiry into the nature of grammaticalization*. Oxford: Oxford University Press.
Lakoff, George & Mark Johnson. 1980. *Metaphors we live by*. Chicago: The University of Chicago Press.
Lambton, Ann K. S. 1979. *Persian grammar*. Cambridge: Cambridge University Press.
Mackenzie, D. N. 1986. *A concise Pahlavi dictionary*. London: Oxford University Press.
Naghzguy Kohan, Mehrdad. 2011. Auxiliary verbs and representation of aspect in Persian. *Adab Pazhuhi, a quarterly journal of Persian language and literature* 14. 93.
Narrog, Heiko 2012. *Modality, subjectivity, and semantic change*. Oxford: Oxford University Press.
Skjærvø, Prods O. 2002. *An introduction to Old Persian*. Revised and expanded 2nd edn. https://www.fas.harvard.edu/~iranian/OldPersian/opcomplete.pdf. (accessed 10 May 2013)
Stassen, Leon. 2009. *Predicative possession*. Oxford: Oxford University Press.
Steinkrüger, Patrick O. 1997. Zur Grammatikalisierung der *haben*-Verben im Katalanischen. *Sprachtypologie und Universalienforschung* 50(4). 329–338.
Storms, G. 1964. The subjective and the objective form in Modern English. *English Studies. Supplement presented to R. W. Zandvoort on the occasion of his seventieth birthday*. 57–63. Amsterdam: Swets & Zeitlinger.
Tabari, Mohammad ibn Jarir. 2009. *Tarjumiy-i Tafsir-i Tabari*. In Karim Keshavarz, (ed.), *Hezâr sâl nasr-e Farsi* [*One thousand years of Persian prose*]. Tehran: Elmi Farhangi.
Taleghani, H. Azita. 2008. *Modality, aspect and negation in Persian*. Amsterdam & Philadelphia: John Benjamins.
Windfuhr L. Gernot. 1979. *Persian grammar: History and state of its study*. The Hague: Mouton.
Zhukovski, Valentin A. 1899. *Asrr al-tawd f maqmt al-Shaykh Ab Sa'd*. Pitrbrgh: Pitrbrgh Dr al-Khalfah.

Carlos García Castillero
Grammaticalization as morphosyntax and representation: Mood from tense markers in the Old Irish and Romance conditional

Abstract: In some Western European languages, the combination of markers of future and imperfect gives rise to an expression which is used as both future-in-the-past, typically in reported speech, and conditional, typically in the apodosis of conditional sentences. This combination, which is usually called conditional, is found in Irish (e.g. Old Irish *no-regad* 'he would go'), Western Romance (e.g. Old Spanish *daria* 'he would give') and English. Whereas the English conditional is an analytical formation, the Romance synthetic form is the outcome of a process of univerbation from a previous periphrasis which can be found in Late Latin texts, and the Irish conditional is a synthetic form from the very beginning of its existence. This paper considers the change that goes from the temporal to the modal value of the conditional in the perspective of Functional Discourse Grammar. For the diachronic process leading to the Irish conditional, this paper proposes a process of morphologization different to the two main processes usually considered, namely, the creation of new morphemes from lexical items or from phonological variations. The term proposed for this type of morphologization is 'morpheme combination', according to which new morphemes are created by means of the combination of previously existing morphemes.

Keywords: future-in-the-past, conditional, Old Irish, morpheme combination, functional merger, morphologization

1 Introduction

This paper focuses on the diachronic process by which Irish and Western Romance conditional forms arose from the combination of the future and imperfect tense markers. By 'conditional form', or simply 'conditional', I understand the verbal form of these languages which is used in the main clause of conditional sentences to express counterfactual mood (i.e. the equivalent to the English *He would go*

Carlos García Castillero: University of the Basque Country, C/Tomás y Valiente s/n, 01008 Vitoria-Gasteiz, Spain, carlos.garcia@ehu.eus

DOI 10.1515/9783110519389-008

in *He would go home today, if he had time*), as well as in subordinate clauses to express future-in-the-past (e.g., *He told me that he would go home*).

There are actually very few studies on the diachrony of the Irish conditional form. Thurneysen (1946: 332), and McCone (1997: 85) are basically nothing more than a reference to the Western Romance form. While this is to some extent understandable, the fact that the same combination of tense markers expresses the same range of meanings in languages which use different formal strategies suggests that there is a relatively straightforward diachronic path for that change. I consider this change, in which the combination of future and imperfect tense markers becomes a mood marker, as the outcome of a process of grammaticalization, similar to that of temporal into conditional connectives considered by Heine and Kuteva (2002: 293), or to that of future tense markers into markers of epistemic modality (Heine and Kuteva 2002: 142–143).

The first main aim of this paper is to put forward a diachronic explanation valid for the Western Romance and Irish form which can also be assumed for other equivalent forms. For this purpose, Section 2 presents the basic formal and functional aspects of the Old Spanish conditional, as well as some possible Late Latin antecedents, and Section 3 offers a description of the Old Irish conditional. On the basis of the previous sections, Section 4 then establishes the process of grammaticalization of the combination of future and imperfect, paying special attention to the syntactic mechanism involved, a point which in my opinion has not been sufficiently addressed in previous studies of this change.

This diachronic account is examined in its functional and formal dimensions within the framework of Functional Discourse Grammar (Hengeveld and Mackenzie 2008). In Section 5 I consider the semantic aspect of the above process of grammaticalization as it occurs at the Representational Level. By its very design, Functional Discourse Grammar allows for a general consideration of grammaticalization in which a given semantic (representational) development may have various formal (morphosyntactic) consequences. Section 6 proposes the notion of 'morpheme combination' for the formal process involved in the rise of the Old Irish conditional.

As the second main goal of the paper, it is claimed that "morpheme combination", constitutes a type of morphologization which must be distinguished from processes in which independent words become affixal grammatical elements and also from processes in which phonological alternations are reanalysed as grammatical markers. This consideration leads to a broader definition of morphologization as a general diachronic process, a definition which includes the changes considered in previous accounts, but also the type of morphological change considered in this paper. Section 7 summarizes the main ideas of the paper.

2 The Western Romance conditional

In accordance with the basically diachronic approach of this paper, the Western Romance conditional is exemplified by means of Old Spanish forms (Section 2.3), where the basic temporal and modal values of the form are already clearly attested. In order to measure the chronological depth of this formation in the prehistorical development of Romance languages, some Late Latin periphrases commonly considered in the literature are also presented in Section 2.2.

2.1 Basic issues

The Western Romance conditional can be illustrated initially with the Spanish form *comería* 'I would eat', which represents a combination of the future ending on *-ré*, meaning 'I will eat' and the imperfect ending on *-ía* meaning 'I used to eat, was eating, ate'. The English expression *I would eat* represents the same tense combination in an analytic shape. All those formations, as well as the Irish conditional form seen later in Section 3, are instances of Thieroff's (2010: 11–12) "Western conditional", and interestingly their uses are basically the same, i.e. the temporal use of future- (or posterior-) in-the-past, typically in reported discourse, and modal use, typically in the apodosis of the conditional sentence.

This coincidence is all the more significant since such a combination of future and preterite can also be observed in another Western European language such as Basque. In Standard Basque, the future *ikusiko du* 's/he will see' is the base to which the preterital auxiliary of the expression *ikusten zuen* 's/he used to see' is added, resulting in expressions of reported speech like *(esan zidan) ikusiko zuela* '(s/he told me that) s/he would see'. Up to this point, the Basque combination of future and past is basically the same as in Irish, Western Romance and English. Unlike those languages, however, the Basque form is not used in conditional sentences, with the apodosis being expressed by a different verb form altogether (e.g. *joango balitz, ikusiko luke* 'if s/he went, s/he would see').[1]

---

[1] This Basque periphrasis of the future form in *-ko* (*etorriko*) and an auxiliary verb with the potential ending *-ke* (*luke*) is termed 'conditional' by Haase (2010: 638) (he uses the 1st person plural form *ikusiko genuke* 'we would see'), but such a form is not used in reported speech, where the expected statement would be *(esan zidan) ikusiko zuela / genuela* '(s/he told me) that s/he / we would see'.

Apart from geographic proximity, Western Romance and Irish conditionals therefore coincide also in their synthetic character and in their basic uses.² Moreover, both forms occupy a well-established place in their respective verbal systems, so that the diachronic processes leading to this form must have happened in the previous phases of those languages.

2.2 Late Latin antecedents

With the necessary prudence, the Post-classical and Late Latin use of the periphrasis of the infinitive with the imperfect of the verb *habere*, as in examples (1) to (3), can be taken as early evidence of its use in spoken varieties which would later become the Romance vernaculars. Each example is taken to represent a stage in the linguistic development assumed for the future-in-the-past. In example (1), it appears in a subordinate clause depending on a verb in the past tense; in example (2), the future-in-the-past does not depend on a past tense in the main clause, and furthermore it appears as an independent clause; finally, in example (3) it appears as the verb of the apodosis of a conditional sentence.

(1) *Tamen et creatori notum erat futurum. An non utique notum quod sub caelo et in terra eius habebat reuelari?* (Tertullian, *Aduersus Marcionem* 5.18.4)
tamen   et   creator-i   not-um   er-a-t
but   and   creator-DAT.SG   known-NOM.SG   COP-IMPF-3SG
futur-um   an   non   utique   not-um   quod
future-NOM.SG   POLQ   NEG   certainly   known-NOM.SG   COMP
sub   cael-o   et   in   terra   eius
under   sky-ABL.SG   and   in   earth-ABL.SG   3SG.GEN.SG
habebat   reuelari
have-IMPF-3SG   reveal-INF.PASS
'But yet to the Creator also the future was known. Did he not inevitably know that which beneath his heaven and on his earth was due to be revealed?'

---

2 A further parallel could be the so-called Latin (and Oscan-Umbrian) imperfect subjunctive (e.g. Lat. *amarem*, or *fatereris* in example (3)), which according to García Castillero (2000: 88–89) can be explained as the subjunctive in *-ē- of the (unreduplicated) Indo-European *s*-future.

(2) *Verbum autem domini manet in aeternum. Ecce quid ames, si uis manere in aeternum. Sed dicere habebas: unde possum apprehendere uerbum dei?* (Augustinus Hipponensis, *In Iohannis euangelium tractatus*, 7.1)

uerb-um	autem	domin-i	mane-t	in
word-NOM.SG	but	lord-GEN.SG	last/PRES-3SG	in
aetern-um		ecce	quid	ame-s	si
perpetual-ACC.SG		here is	what\ACC.SG	love/SBJV-2SG	if
ui-s		mane-re	in	in aetern-um	sed
will/PRES-2SG		last-INF.ACT	in	perpetual-ACC.SG	but
dice-re	habe-ba-s	unde	poss-um	apprehende-re
say-INF.ACT	have-IMPF-2SG	whence	can/PRES-1SG	can/PRES-1SG
uerb-um	de-i			
word-ACC.SG	god-GEN.SG			

'But the word of the Lord lasts forever. That is what you must love if you want to last forever. But you would / might say: whence can I learn the word of God?' (translation after Adams 2013: 662–663).

(3) *Sanare te habebat deus per indulgentiam, si fatereris* (Caesarius Arelatensis, *Sermones Caesarii uel ex aliis fontibus hausti*, 59,4)

sana-re	te	habe-ba-t	de-us	per
heal-INF.ACT	2SG.ACC	have-IMPF-3SG	god-NOM.SG	by means of
indulgenti-am	si	fate-re-ris		
indulgence-ACC.SG	if	confess-IMPF.SBJV-2SG		

'God would heal you out of indulgence if you confessed'

The periphrasis *habebat reuelari* in (1) is interpreted by Adams (2013: 661) as a "future-in-the-past", in which some additional modal nuance can be perceived. Note also that *habebat reuelari* appears in a syntactic context in which there is a negative verb of knowing and a polar interrogative marker (*an non* [...] *notum* [...]), two elements which will turn out to be relevant for the treatment of Old Irish as well.

Bourova (2005: 313) notes that the use of this Late Latin periphrasis with a potentiality value is less frequent, yet there are some instances, such as those in (2) and (3). With respect to these two examples, Adams (2013: 663) notes that

> [t]he imaginary speaker [i.e. the addressee implied in *dicere habebas* of (2)] is not presented as in a position to raise an imaginary objection at a point in the past, but rather has the potential to make the objection in the present. If this description is accepted, the example in the apodosis of a conditional construction cited above from Caesarius containing *sanare habebat* [i.e. example (3)] might be reclassified as expressing a potential in the present.

In other words, Adams points to the idea that the initial expression of the future-in-the-past, which can be justified in a complement clause depending on a verb in the past tense, comes to be used in environments in which it does not depend on a past tense. It is this new situation, in which the future-in-the-past is related to a present situation, in which the potentiality value develops and enables its use in the apodosis of a conditional construction.

2.3 The "Western conditional" in Old Spanish

The temporal meaning of the Western Romance conditional can be observed in the Old Spanish examples (4) and (5), whereas the modal value appears in (6). Example (4) is taken from López de Ayala's *Coronica del rey Pedro* (between the late 14th and early 15th centuries), and examples (5) and (6) come from the *Poema de Mio Cid* (between the late 11th and early 12th centuries, cited from Smith 1993: 43–44). The short expression *si non* before the conditional form *perderiemos* in example (6) must be understood as an elliptical condition which can be rendered more explicitly as 'if we did not act in this manner, [...]'. As noted by Company Company (2006: 407–408), from which (4) is taken, both the temporal and the modal uses are also present in Modern Spanish and other Romance languages.

(4) *E dixole luego el rey don Enrrique al dicho mossen Beltran que el gelas daria las villas que el rey don Pedro le prometiera* (Pedro I, 197.7b)
E   dix-o=le   luego   el   rey   don E.
and say/PRET-3SG=3SG.M   then   ART/M.SG   king   sir E.
al   dich-o   mossen B.   que   el
to/ART/M.SG   say/PTCP-M.SG   priest B.   COMP   3SG.M
ge-las=da-ría-ø   las   vill-as   que
DAT.3-ACC.3PL.F=give-COND-3SG   ART.F.PL.   town-F.PL   COMP
el   rey   don P.   le   prometie-r-a
ART/M.SG   king   sir P.   DAT.3SG   promise-PST.SBJV-3SG
'And then King Enrique said to the aforesaid Father Beltran that he would give him the towns that King Pedro had promised him'.

(5) *Martin Antolinez el pleito a parado que sobre aquelas archas dar le ien .vi. çientos marcos e bien gelas guardarien fasta cabo del año* (Cid 160–162)
M.A.   el   pleit-o   a   para-d-o
        ART/M.SG   arrangement-M.SG   AUX.3SG   arrange-PST.PTCP.M.SG
que   sobre   aquell-as   arch-as   da-r<le>ie-n
COMP   over   DEM.DIST-F.PL   chest-F.PL.   give-COND<DAT.3SG>-3PL

vi.çientos	marc-os	e	bien	ge-las=guarda-rie-n
600	mark-M.PL	and	well	DAT.3-ACC.3P.F=keep-COND-3PL
fasta	cabo	del		añ-o
until	end	of/ART/M.SG		year-M.SG

'Martin Antolinez has made the arrangement (so) that they would give him six hundred marks for those chests and that they would keep them for one year'

(6) *Non vos osariemos abrir nin coger por nada; si non, perderiemos los averes e las casas* (Cid 44–45)

non	vos=osa-rie-mos	abr-ir	nin	cog-er	por
NEG	DAT.2PL=dare-COND-1PL	open-INF	nor	take-INF	for
nada	si	non	perde-rie-mos	l-os	aver-es
nothing	if	NEG	lose-COND-1PL	ART-M.PL	possession-PL
e	l-as	cas-as			
and	ART-F.PL	house-F.PL			

'We would not dare open [the doors] for you or make you welcome at all; otherwise, we would lose our possessions and houses'

Example (5) is basically similar to (4) in the sense that it presents the future-in-the-past in an environment in which it depends on a past tense, but it includes the synthetic form *guardarien* 'they would keep' and the split form *dar le ien* 'they would give him'. The component that could be interpreted synchronically as an infinitive (i.e. *dar*) is separated from the inflectional marker *ien* by (and only by) clitic pronouns. Such split forms, also used in the parallel future form (e.g. *doblaruos he la soldada* 'I will double your salary', Cid 80) are found in all the Romance languages of the Iberian Peninsula, even in Modern Portuguese, as well as in some South Italian dialects. On this issue, see Company Company (2006: 359–371).

The use of such Western Romance future and conditional forms based on the periphrasis with *habeo* may well have begun in the 1st or 2nd centuries A.D., given its degree of development from the very beginning of the historical attestation of the Romance languages, and the presence of its assumed Latin equivalent at a relatively early date (Tertullian, the author of example (1), lived 160–230 A.D.).

3 The Old Irish conditional

The conditional form has been present in Irish (Celtic, Indo-European) verbal morphology from the Old Irish period onwards. This study is concerned with evidence from the Old Irish period, which covers approximately the 8th and

9th centuries A.D. The cursory description of the Old Irish verbal complex in Section 3.1 will provide the necessary notions to get some idea of the morphological constituency of the attested forms analysed in Section 3.2. Section 3.3 then considers these forms in their syntactic context in order to establish the functional profile of the Old Irish conditional.

3.1 A brief outline of the Old Irish verbal complex

Table 1 gives a somewhat simplified version of the theoretically possible slots in the template of the Old Irish verbal complex, which occupies the first position in the clause. It should be noted that the Old Irish verbal complex never has all those slots occupied at the same time. The table also serves to establish the basic rule for the position of the main stress in this structure: it falls on the first syllable of slot 3 if this slot is occupied by some element; if not, it falls on the first syllable of slot 4.

Tab. 1: Theoretical template of the Old Irish verbal complex.

1	2	3	4	5	6
Particle(s) / preverb a	Pronominal affix	Preverb(s) (a), b, c, d, e	Verbal stem	Verbal ending	Pronominal affix

For a detailed treatment of all the grammatical categories and forms expressed in the Old Irish verbal complex, see García Castillero (2012, 2013). The following preliminaries are important for understanding my argument in the next sections: (i) The verbal complex comprises all the possible finite verbal expressions in Old Irish, which therefore have an eminently synthetic nature. (ii) An Old Irish verbal complex may be simple (type (a), *canaid* 's/he sings', in Tab. 2) or compound, the latter being characterized by having at least one preverbal element in either slot 1 or 3. These preverbal elements are of two main types: On the one hand, lexical preverb(s) such as *for-* 'over'. They are located in slots 1 and/or 3 depending on a series of morphosyntactic properties such as clause type, and constitute a lexical compound when added to a simple verb, i.e. type (b), *for-cain* 's/he teaches', in Tab. 2. This form *for-cain* is a lexical compound of *canaid* 's/he sings' and the literal meaning of 'singing over', which is lexicalized as 'to teach', probably makes reference to the act of singing the lesson to (over) the students who had to repeat it. In contrast to these preverbs with lexical meanings, the conjunct particles, most of which only appear in slot 1, carry a grammatical meaning (basically clause type and/or negative polarity), e.g., the negative declarative particle *ní-*.[3] This combination of conjunct particle and simple verb is type (c), *ní-cain* 's/he doesn't sing', in Tab. 2. An element appearing in slot 1 can easily be identified by its relative position with respect to an infixed pronoun in slot 2. (iii) Slot 1 may include either a lexical preverb or a grammatical particle, but if both types of preverbal elements appear in the same verbal complex, then the conjunct particle(s) appear(s) in slot 1 and the lexical preverb(s) occupy/occupies slot 3. Since this situation is not found in the Old Irish examples given in this section, it will not be considered any further in this paper. Table 2 shows the constituency of some basic examples according to the template given in Tab. 1.

Tab. 2: Simple (*cainid* 'sings') and lexical compound (*for-cain* 'teaches') verbs in 3rd person singular present indicative active.

		1	2	3	4	5
a. Basically simple verb without pretonic elements	*can-aid* 's/he sings'				can	-id
b. Compound verb with a lexical preverb	*for-cain* 's/he teaches'	for-			can	-P[4]
b'. (b) + infixed pronoun	*for-dom-cain* 's/he teaches me'	for-	dom-[5]		can	-P
c. Simple verb with a pretonic particle	*ní-cain* 's/he does not sing'	ní-			can	-P
c'. (c) + infixed pronoun	*ní-m-cain* 's/he does not sing (to) me'	ní-	m-		can	-P

3.2 The form of the Old Irish conditional

The Old Irish conditional, also known as the "secondary future" in traditional grammar (e.g. Thurneysen 1946: 332), involves the addition of the imperfect marker(s) to the future stem (slot 4). The Old Irish imperfect must have an element

---

3 The acute in the Old Irish spelling serves to mark a long vowel, although this graphic device is not used consistently by Old Irish writers.
4 The superscript P indicates the palatalized character of the previous consonant, a feature which is marked in Old Irish orthography by the *-i-* before the final nasal of the stem *can-*.
5 The infixed pronoun form *-dom-* in *for-dom-cain* 's/he teaches me' (also *-dam-*) is decided by the phonotactic shape (i.e. (-)VC-) of the previous preverb (*for-*); as can be observed in the form *ní-m-cain* 's/he does not sing me', the infixed pronoun form used after the negative conjunct particle *ní-* (CV-) is *-m-*.

in slot 1, so that if the involved form already has at least one of the preverbal elements mentioned in the previous section, only the specific imperfect endings (slot 5) are added to the present stem; however, if slot 1 of the verbal complex is not yet occupied, the imperfect form adds the semantically void pretonic particle *no-* plus the imperfect endings (i.e. slot 1 + slot 5).

This section will only illustrate the forms included in the three examples of the next section, i.e. examples (7) to (9). There are several future formations in Old Irish, the main classification being the difference between weak and strong futures, constituting a lexical opposition similar to that in Germanic. A future qualifies as weak if it is formed with a suffix *-f-* attached to the present stem,[6] as in the form *indamsoirfad* 'whether [God] would deliver me' in (8), from the simple weak verb *soíraid* 'delivers'. The pretonic elements in *in-dam-* are the polar interrogative conjunct particle in^N- and the first person singular infixed pronoun *-dam-*, which occupy slots 1 and 2 respectively. The compound form *indamsoirfad* therefore represents type (c') in Tab. 2.

Every other future formation is considered strong, and most of them represent a Proto-Indo-European inheritance which can be found in other ancient Indo-European languages as well. An example of a strong future is the so-called *ē*-future, characterized by the root vocalism *-ē-*, as in the future *at-béla* 'will die', on the basis of which the conditional form *at-belad* 'he would die' in (7) is formed; the form *at-belad* implies a long root vowel, in spite of the lack of acute, and contrasts with the present form with a short vowel, in this case *at-baill* 'dies'. This verb is characterized by its leniting 3rd person singular neuter infix pronoun *-t-* attached to the lexical preverb *es-* 'from, away' (as if it were *es-t-* > *at-* in pretonic position) and originally meant 'to throw it (scil. 'the life') away'. The compound form *atbelad* therefore represents type (b') in Tab. 2.

Finally, an example of a conditional form with the preverb *no-* is *noregad* 'it would go, apply', given below in (9). This form belongs to the paradigm of the simple verb *téit* 'goes', and is based on the suppletive future stem which may be observed in *rig-mi* 'we shall go' (e.g. Wb 15c23); to that future stem, the imperfect markers of *no-teg-ed* 'he used to go' (e.g. Ml 29d9) are applied. The compound form *noregad* must be understood as an example of type (c) in Tab. 2. Table 3 includes the three Old Irish conditional forms the morphology of which is discussed in this section, i.e. *indamsoirfad*, *atbelad* and *noregad*.[7]

---

[6] The origin of this future suffix has been much debated. I simply refer to McCone's (1991: 176–180) treatment.

[7] Note that Tab. 3 does not illustrate every form given in Tab. 2, but mainly serves to illustrate the forms discussed in the next section.

Tab. 3: Present, future, imperfect and conditional forms of three Old Irish verbs.

		1	2	3	4	5
a. Simple verb *soiraid* 'delivers'	indicative present *soir(a)id* 's/he delivers'				soir	-(a)id
c'. Simple verb *soíraid* with pretonic particle and infixed pronoun	conditional *indam-soirfad* 'would he deliver me?'	in-	dam-		soir-f	-ad
b'. Compound *at-baill* 'dies' (with inf. pron.)	indicative present *at-baill* 'dies' conditional at-belad 'would die'	es- es-	t- t-		ball bēl	ᵖ -ad
a. Simple verb *téit* 'goes' c. Simple verb *téit* 'goes' with a pretonic particle	present indicative *tiagmi* 'we go' future *rigmi* 'we shall go' imperfect *no-teged* 'he used to go' conditional *no-regad* 'it would go'	no- no-			tiag rig teg reg	-mi -mi -ed -ad

In spite of the fact that the Old Irish conditional is a morphologically transparent formation, one should emphasize that it is a truly synthetic form, in accordance with the general character of the verbal complex noted in the previous section.

3.3 On the use of the Old Irish conditional

According to Thurneysen's (1946: 332) description, the Old Irish conditional has both a temporal and a modal use. The temporal use involves some reference to "an action which, when viewed from a definite point of past time, lay in the future", as in example (7). The modal use serves "to indicate that under certain conditions something could occur (*potential*), or –still more frequently– that something would, should, or could happen [...] or have happened under certain conditions which, however, remain unfulfilled (*modus irrealis*)"; examples (8) and (9) below illustrate this use. Notice that I have only included the apodosis of the conditional sentence in example (9). The morphology of the conditional forms *atbelad* in (7), *in damsoirfad* in (8) and *noregad* in (9) has been explained in the previous section.

(7) *asbert side* contra ezechiam *atbelad* (Ml 16c10, c. 850 A.D.)
    as-ber-t =side   contra ezechiam   at-bel-ad
    say-(DECL)say-PST.3SG.ACT=3SG.M   die/3SG/DECL-die\FUT-IMPF.3SG.ACT
    'he said to Hezekiah that he would die'

(8) *nífetar in damsoirfad dia fanacc* (Ml 90c19, c. 850 A.D.)
    ní-fet-ar   in-dam-soir-f-ad   dia   fanacc
    NEG.DECL-know-1SG   INTQ-1SG-deliver-FUT-3SG.IMPF   God\NOM.SG   or not
    'I don't know whether God would deliver me or not'

(9) [...] *robad dundsasad diant ainm panis tantum noregad* (Ml 118b6, c. 850 A.D.)
    ro-ba-d   du-nd=sasad
    PFV-(DECL)\COP.IMPF.SBJV-3SG   for-ART.M.DAT.SG=food\M.DAT.SG
    di-an-t=ainm   panis tantum
    for-REL-COP.PRES.IND.3SG=name\N:NOM.SG
    no-reg-ad
    IMPF-(DECL)go\FUT-IMPF.3SG.ACT
    '[for if he put *panem* only and did not put *meum*], it would apply only to the food called *panis*' (more lit. '[...], it would be only to the food called *panis* that it would apply')

In a sentence like (7), the conditional *atbelad* 'he would die', which is introduced by the preterite *asbert* 'he said', appears in "indirect speech complements with D[ependent] T[ime] R[eference]", a subtype of utterance predicates in Genee's (1998: 149) classification of sentential complements in Irish. Leufkens' (2013: 203) interpretation of the English conditional (say, *He said that he would come*) as "posterior-in-the-past" perfectly applies to this Old Irish form. The semantic implications of this temporal use have been made explicit by Leufkens (2013: 207–208) in her explanation of the optionality of tense copying or back-shifting in equivalent English structures of indirect reported speech, a process which the speaker can ignore (to say then *He said that he will come*) "when she believes in the truth of the original quote". Correspondingly, as Leufkens goes on to argue, "[i]f the current speaker does not commit herself to the quote's content (or does not have a strong opinion about it), she is more likely to use a back-shifted tense". This epistemic nuance constitutes the semantic basis for the modal uses of the conditional forms observed in the other Old Irish examples.

In (8), the conditional is introduced by the polar interrogative pretonic particle *in^N-* which depends on the present form *nífetar* 'I don't know', and expresses the doubts of the speaker about whether the state-of-affairs implied by the verb 'to deliver' will be achieved. This is an example of Genee's (1998: 205) "non-factual complement with knowledge C[omplement] T[aking] P[redicate]". In (9), the form *noregad* is in the apodosis of a conditional sentence. The basic condition stated in the protasis is not real. Rather, it is expressed by the past subjunctive, and the conditional form expresses the idea that the state-of-affairs referred to depends on the previous statement and is therefore only conjectural. The modal use of the conditional involves irrealis.

In the later development of the Irish language, the conditional assumes many functions of the subjunctive, and it may also appear in the conditional protasis (see McQuillan 2002: 196–197, Ó Baoill 2010: 285–286). This use of the Modern Irish conditional has a clear parallel in non-standard varieties of Modern Spanish, where it is perfectly normal to hear *Si sería rico, me iría de vacaciones* instead of standard *Si fuese rico, me iría de vacaciones*, both 'If I were rich, I would go on holidays'.

4 On the syntactic mechanism for the creation of the "Western conditional"

The basic diachronic development which is assumed in this paper is that established by Fleischman (1982: 64–66) for the Romance and Thurneysen (1946: 332) for the Irish conditional. Both scholars assume that the combination of the future and imperfect markers, the future-in-the-past, was initially used in subordinate environments such as the Late Latin example in (1), the Old Spanish one in (4) and the Old Irish one in (7), and that the basically temporal meaning gave way to the "modal sense" of the form. Much of this diachronic explanation is involved in Adams' (2013: 663) quote in Section 2 on the Late Latin examples (1) and (2), as well as in Leufkens' (2013: 207–208) explanation in Section 3, and has much in common with Narrog's (2012: 173–175) diachronic explanation of the epistemic use of the English form *should*. This development seems to be a case of Croft's (2000: 126–127) "hypoanalysis", a change in which "the listener reanalyses a contextual semantic/pragmatic property as an inherent property of the syntactic unit. In the reanalysis, the inherent property of the context [...] is then attributed to the syntactic unit, and so the syntactic unit in question gains a new meaning or function".

Interestingly, Croft refers to the Armenian example quoted by Bybee, Perkins, and Pagliuca (1994: 230–236). There the simple indicative present acquires subjunctive functions when its use is restricted to subordinate clauses and once the basic functions of the present indicative have been taken over by a new periphrastic progressive present form. The Armenian simple present form can also be used in main clauses, but it then has the modal value of "weak obligation" ('I am to' or 'I should'). This specific change is a further example of the possibility recognized by Bybee, Perkins, and Pagliuca (1994: 224) "that main clause uses can develop from subordinate clause uses". The difference with respect to the development assumed in this paper is that the conditional originates intrinsically in a subordinate clause. As recently stated by Vincent (2013: 124 fn.6) for the

Western Romance conditional, this interpretation implies "a grammaticalization pattern which originates in a subordinate context".

Viewed as a whole, the diachronic development of the combination of future and imperfect may be exemplified by the sequence of English expressions included in (10). The step that goes from (10a) to (10b) only represents the creation of the future-in-the-past when a statement made in the future tense is reported as uttered in the past, that is to say, when it depends on a main verb in past tense.

(10) a. *I will come* → b. *He said (that) he would come* → c. *If he had time, he would come*

In the sentence *He said (that) he would come* in (10b), the future- (or posterior-)in-the-past *would come* as a subordinate form has a tense value, determined by the main clause past form *He said (that ...)*. The rise of the modal implication of the future-in-the-past becomes clear when this form no longer depends on a past tense. When the form involved can be viewed as connected with the present, as suggested in the Late Latin and Old Irish examples of (2) and (8) respectively, the modal value of the form becomes prevalent, and the modal value appears in its use as a main clause with counterfactual value.

The step that goes from (10b) to (10c) involves a change in the syntactic status of the clause which includes the conditional, i.e. the future-in-the-past form which acquires modal value: in (10b) it appears in a complement clause, i.e. in a subordinate environment, whereas in (10c) it is the apodosis of the conditional sentence, i.e. it is a main clause in the strict sense of the term. To be sure, the real distance between these types of subordinate and main clauses is not very big. On the one hand, complement clauses are among the less subordinate ones, especially when the complement taking predicate is a verb of speech. On the other hand, the apodosis of the hypothetical conditional sentence semantically depends on the conditional protasis, in the sense that it cannot occur without the protasis. In other words, the complement clause is one of the subordinate clauses which is more main-clause like, whereas the hypothetical apodosis is perhaps one of the more dependent- or subordinate-like main clauses. Whatever the exact mechanism of syntactic change that enables the transition from one to another type of clause, it does not involve a major change.

In this sense, one is tempted to assume a process of insubordination, a syntactic change defined by Evans (2007: 367) as "the conventionalized main clause use of what, on prima facie grounds, appear to be formally subordinate clauses". The Old Irish example in (8), where the conditional form is in a polar interrogative clause (*in damsoirfad* lit. 'would God deliver me?') which depends on a verb of thinking in the present tense (*nífetar* 'I don't know') is a good candidate for this change, since the adduced polar interrogative clause could perfectly well appear by itself. Nevertheless, the main drawback of this line of explanation is that the conditional only rarely appears in completely independent clauses such as the Late Latin example (2) above, where *dicere habebas* neither depends on a main verb, as *non notum (erat) quod ... habebat reuelari* in example (1), nor is combined with a protasis, such as *sanare te habebat ... si fatereris* in example (3). The conditional seems to be a form which has a low degree of dependency, even though it apparently must lean on another clause, be it main or subordinate. According to the extant evidence, Evans' notion of insubordination applies to the "Western conditional" only in a very limited sense.

A final point worth making here concerns the possible areal influence in the rise of the "Western conditional". One of Fleischman's (1982: 64) arguments in her discussion of alternative hypotheses, namely, "the fact that a single form exhibits these two functions [i.e. the temporal and the modal] in a wide range of unrelated languages", points to a more or less expected semantic change from temporal to modal meaning. In spite of the fact that the Irish, English and Romance languages have been in more or less close contact for centuries in Europe, the same situation is more difficult to imagine in Late Antiquity and the Early Middle Ages, the period in which at least the Romance and the Irish conditionals must have originated. The insularity of the Irish language is a factor to be considered here. This is of course not to say that Irish speakers of say the 4th to 7th centuries had no contact at all with other languages, but it seems that the contacts were not intense enough as to give rise to such an innovation in the language.

Though I am inclined to assume a completely independent process, at least in Irish, it is certainly true that there is no definitive argument to exclude the possibility that the "Western conditional" arose as the outcome of an areal influence, triggered by a process of "grammatical replication", the term used by Heine and Kuteva (2005: 260–261) for "[...] transfer of grammatical structures from one language to another without involving any linguistic form". However, even in this case, the previous observations on the grammaticalization of two tense markers into a mood marker would still be valid.

5 From temporal to modal meaning in Functional Discourse Grammar

The grammaticalization of the combination of two tense markers into a mood marker delineated in the previous sections takes place at the so-called Representational Level in Functional Discourse Grammar. However, any consideration of the whole development, starting with the rise of the statement *He said that he would come* in (10b) above, requires mentioning two other levels assumed in Functional Discourse Grammar, namely, the Interpersonal and the Morphosyntactic Levels, which deal with the pragmatic and the formal components of the language respectively.

At the Interpersonal Level, the referential act included in the communicated content of (10b) takes the form of indirect speech (*(that) he would come*), and therefore consists of "the (reformulated) communicated content of an earlier discourse act" (i.e. of *I will come*), as stated by Keizer (2009: 847), who also notes that the indirect speech strategy implies only one Discourse Act, and not two, as in the case of direct reported speech. In the languages under discussion, i.e. Irish, Western Romance and even English, languages in which the use of participial and, in general, non-finite verbal forms is (i.e. diachronically has been) severely restricted, the consequence of reformulating the earlier discourse act for the Morphosyntactic Level is that a subordinated clause with a finite verb must be used, so that the main clause verb (i.e. *He said*) imposes its tense over the future of the reported utterance, as assumed by Comrie (1985: 114) precisely for the English conditional form. The diachronic consequence of the previous process[8] is that the past tense marker is literally added to the basic future tense form, thus giving rise to a future relative to a point in the past.

The diachronic process of reanalysis of a relative tense marker into a marker of irrealis, the modal value of the conditional form, connects the two characteristic operators of the state-of-affairs, which is a semantic category of the Representational Level defined by Hengeveld and Mackenzie (2008: 166) as "entities that can be located in relative time and can be evaluated in terms of their reality status". The reality status of a state-of-affairs forms part of objective epistemic possibility (Hengeveld 2004: 1195, Hengeveld and Mackenzie 2008: 174). The structural closeness which Functional Discourse Grammar acknowledges for the tense and modal values of the conditional form may therefore serve as an explanation for the straightforward diachronic connection between them. The clear differentiation between the Representational and the Morphosyntactic Levels allows for a separate consideration of the morphological consequences of the process of grammaticalization, a question which will be addressed in next section.

---

8 This is probably an instance of the dynamic relation between the different Levels of representation acknowledged in Functional Discourse Grammar, as suggested by Hengeveld and Smit (2009: 1126 fn.8).

6 Morpheme combination: towards a new definition of morphologization

The discussion in the preceding sections focused on the semantic and syntactic aspects of the diachronic process. The rise of the Irish and Western Romance (and even of the English) conditional involves the same basic process which includes two well-known and interrelated changes, namely, (a) the syntactic change that goes from the future-in-the-past in complement clauses to the hypothetical mood in conditional apodoses, and (b) the grammaticalization of two tense markers into one mood marker.

Change (b) is a good example of "merger", which Heine and Reh (1984: 43–44) define as the process by which "the meaning or function of two linguistic units merges into one new meaning/function which is different from that of the combined units". This notion of "merger" is one of the functional processes which Heine and Reh (1984: 44) explicitly distinguish from morphosyntactic processes such as "compounding", which "has the effect of combining two or more linguistic units into one single word" (Heine and Reh 1984: 32).

It is important to emphasize the distinction between the semantic (or representational) and the formal (or morphosyntactic) aspects of the change concerned. The assumption that there is basically the same functional or semantic process in which each language or language group (i.e. Irish, Romance and English) displays different formal strategies gives us a good opportunity to illustrate the general distinction between grammaticalization and morphologization, two general diachronic notions which very often go hand in hand, but which must be properly distinguished. In this respect, Joseph (2003: 475–478) observes that grammaticalization affects the functional status (from less to more grammatical) of one or more linguistic items, regardless of its formal status as a separate word or as an affixal element, whereas morphologization deals with the diachronic processes leading to affixal elements and, in general, morphological markers. In the "Western conditional", basically the same grammaticalization process (i.e. the "merger" defined above) has had different formal outcomes. The formal process that occurred in Irish is different from what can be observed in the Western Romance languages and, much more clearly, in English, where a periphrastic expression such as *would come* is used. In view of the formal description in section 3.2 above, the Old Irish conditional is the outcome of the mere combination of two already existing morphological elements, so that this conditional is a synthetic form from the very beginning of its existence.

Current treatments of morphologization consider two basic types of processes, depending on the lexical or phonological character of the linguistic feature which becomes a morpheme: see Joseph (2003: 473–475), Koefoed & van Marle (2004: 1582–1584), Wurzel (2004: 1600), Andersen (2010: 123–124). The first type of change is the well-known and frequent process of coalescence of formerly lexical elements, which concerns the set of phenomena usually considered in studies on grammaticalization and concisely summarised by Haspelmath (2011). The second type involves a morphophonological marker (e.g. the consonantal mutations precisely attested in the Insular Celtic languages from the very beginning of their historical attestation) which was initially the mere phonological reflex of a segmental morpheme: typically, the segmental morpheme disappears but its meaning comes to be expressed by its phonological consequence, which is no longer phonologically, but morphologically motivated. In addition to these sources of morphological elements, some other possible sources have been considered in the recent literature. Narrog (2004) proposes exaptation as a further process by which new morphemes can be created. In particular, Narrog (2004: 373–377) explains the rise of the Japanese causative forms -*asu* and -*sasu* from a previous lexical element used to mark transitive verbs, a process for which he adduces the parallel of e.g. the creation of causative morphemes from instrumental or means-and-manner verbal morphemes in some North-American languages. As a result of this interpretation in terms of exaptation, Narrog assumes that morphological elements of a lexical nature constitute a source of inflectional morphological elements.

For a semasiological classification of morphological changes, the case of the Old Irish conditional represents a type of morphologization different from these three types, a type in which the new morpheme is due to the combination of two previously existing morphemes. I propose the term "morpheme combination" for this morphologization process, which has a clear counterpart in Heine and Reh's semantic or functional "merger". This morphological change may certainly be considered as a subtype of Heine & Reh's "compounding" mentioned above. However, since the term "compound" is strongly associated with the combination of lexical elements such as stems or roots which give rise to new lexical elements, that is, a process of lexicalization, I think that it is more appropriate to use a different term for the diachronic process which involves the "composition" of inflectional elements. From a diachronic perspective, the linguistic elements on which the new morpheme is based in this case are neither lexical – whether independent of affixal – nor phonological. They are elements of the inflectional morphology of a language. The process of morpheme combination assumed for the Old Irish conditional is certainly not the most frequent one in diachronic morphology, but it is not completely unparalleled. Take, for instance, the Old Armenian use of the subjunctive aorist as a future: e.g., from *sirem* 'I love', the subjunctive aorist is *sirec^cic* 'I will love', where *c^c* reflects a voiceless alveolar aspirate affricate sound. The analysis of the subjunctive aorist as the combination of the aorist and subjunctive markers is straightforward in synchronic Old Armenian, where the subjunctive present is *siric^cem* (with suffix *-ic^c-*) and the indicative aorist is *sire^cci* 'I loved' (with suffix *-ec^c-*). The combination of the aorist *-ec^c-* and the subjunctive *-ic^c-* markers, which gives rise to the subjunctive aorist (*-ec^cic*), is used to express future tense, though it certainly can retain its literal meaning also, as reminded by Godel (1975: 38).

The consideration of a process such as "morpheme combination" as a further source of morphemes in the diachronic development of a language implies that the definition of morphologization should be more general than that of Joseph (2003: 472), who defines it as "a set of developments by which some element or elements in a language that are not a matter of morphology at one stage come to reside in a morphological component – or at least to become morphological in type – at a later stage". Similarly, Andersen (2010: 123–124) considers that "[t]hey [the processes of morphologization "from syntax" and "from phonology"] can be brought under a single definition of morphologization as 'types of change by which grammatical expressions or other expression elements become clitics or inflectional affixes or modifications'". Andersen's paper on morphologization is relevant at this moment because it includes a specific section on "Combinations of grams" (Andersen 2010: 136–137) as a part of "Changes in Inflectional Morphology". The two cases Andersen adduces are the Russian plural hortative resulting from the addition of the plural imperative ending *-t'e* to the basic hortative form (i.e. *po-govor'-im* + *-t'e* 'talk!' (pl.)) and the Modern Bulgarian narrative imperfect *piš-e-l* resulting from the addition of the *-l* marker of the Middle Bulgarian aorist narrative *pis-a-l* to the imperfect stem *piše-*. However, these new forms do not seem to involve a new meaning different from the two previous ones, in the sense that the meaning of each morphological element can still be analysed in the resulting form. These new forms do not involve a process of "merger" as defined by Heine and Reh (1984), and this is surely why they are considered by Andersen in the group of changes which affect inflectional paradigms. "Morpheme combination" is thus the combination of morphemes the function or meaning of which is merged, resulting in a new morpheme in the language concerned.

I therefore propose a wider definition of morphologization as every diachronic process leading to the creation of a morpheme, whether based on independent or dependent lexical elements, phonological features, or on the combination of previously existing morphemes which comes to express a new meaning.

7 Conclusion

The "Western conditional", despite having the same categorial composition and grammatical use in Irish, Romance and English, receives different formal expressions with respect to the synthetic vs. analytic opposition: whereas the forms in Irish and Romance are synthetic, English displays an analytic pattern. Viewed diachronically, the Germanic pattern has always been analytic, while it can safely be assumed that the Romance conditional originally comes from an analytic pattern, which can be observed in split formations such as the Old Spanish *dar le ien* 'they would give him' in example (5) in Section 2, whereas the Irish conditional, finally, has been synthetic from its very origin.

Grammaticalization of tense into mood markers, as a process occurring at the Representational Level of Functional Discourse Grammar, has therefore taken place in all three languages (or language families). In contrast, morphologization has occurred only in Romance, due to a process of coalescence, and in Irish, as the outcome of a process of "morpheme combination", but not in English. This observation can be considered in the light of Bybee, Perkins, and Pagliuca's (1994: 118) and, more recently, Bisang's (2004) contention that the specific morphosyntactic character of a language represents an important condition for the formal consequences of grammaticalization. Both the predominant isolating profile of the Asian languages Bisang refers to and, in a narrower perspective, the expression of grammatical categories through morphological means in the Western European languages considered in this paper, constitute a specific morphosyntactic environment which may determine some formal consequences of grammaticalization. In the specific case of the "Western conditional", I would contend that the analytic or synthetic nature of the form taken as basic, i.e. the future, determines the character of the derived and parallel form, i.e. the conditional.

Given that the current definitions of morphologization as a general diachronic process usually include the specific nature of the sources of the new morphemes, the recognition of a different diachronic process leading to the creation of a new morpheme calls for a broader definition of morphologization. The process of "morpheme combination" considered for the Irish conditional is not based on a previous independent (or dependent) lexical element or a concomitant phonological modification, but on the composition of two previously existing inflectional morphemes which develops a new function, semantically related to the previous ones, but different from them. With respect to the previous ones, this new definition of morphologization is more comprehensive and appropiate from a descriptive point of view. Further research should consider the possibility of including other processes such as subtraction, but this question lies outside the scope of this paper.

Assuming that the origin of the conditional is in the future-of-the-past created in reported discourse (or thinking), i.e., in subordinated complement clauses, the use of this form in the apodosis of conditional sentences represents a change in the syntactic status of the clause in which the conditional is used, in the sense that the new, grammaticalized use as a marker of irrealis appears in the syntactically main clause of the conditional sentence. Although it must be acknowledged that this is not a clear case of the process of insubordination proposed in the recent literature, the syntactic context of the assumed change certainly involves an initial stage of subordinate clause and a later stage of main clause. This question deserves further investigation.

Acknowledgments

This chapter is a revised version of a paper presented at the Workshop "The grammaticalization of tense, aspect, mood and modality from a functional perspective", held at the University of Amsterdam on the 18th–19th October 2013. This research was supported by project FFI-2011-27056 granted by the Spanish Government, and from the research group GIC 10/83, IT 486-10 (UFI 11/14 at the University of the Basque Country). I would like to thank the organizers of the workshop, who have accepted this paper and have made important suggestions on previous versions of the text. The responsibility for any remaining error or inaccuracies is solely mine.

Uncommon abbreviations

ACT = active, IMPF = imperfect, N3PL = no third person plural, NOTA = nota augens, PPRT = pretonic particle, POLQ = polar interrogative clause particle

Abbreviations used for the sources of the examples

Cid = Smith (1993), Ml = Stokes and Strachan (1901–1903:i.7–483), *Pedro I* = López de Ayala (1985), Wb = Stokes and Strachan (1901–03:i.499–712)

References

Adams, J. N. 2013. *Social variation and the Latin language*. Cambridge: Cambridge University Press.
Andersen, Henning. 2010. From Morphologization to Demorphologization. In Silvia Luraghi & Vit Bubenik (eds.), *Continuum companion to historical linguistics*, 117–146. London & New York: Continuum.
Bisang, Walter. 2004. Grammaticalization without coevolution of form and meaning: the case of TAM in East and mainland Southeast Asia. In Walter Bisang, Nikolaus P. Himmelmann & Björn Wiemer (eds.), *What makes grammaticalization? A look from its fringes and its components*, 109–138. Berlin & New York: Mouton de Gruyter.
Bourova, Viara. 2005. A la recherche du 'conditionel latin': les constructions *infinitif* + forme de *habere* examinées à partir d'un corpus électronique. In Johannes Kabatek, Claus D. Pusch & Wolfgang Raible (eds.), *Romanistische Korpuslinguistik II: Korpora und diachrone Sprachwissenschaft / Romance corpus linguistics II: corpora and diachronic linguistics*, 303–316. Tübingen: Günther Narr.
Bybee, Joan, Revere Perkins & William Pagliuca. 1994. *The evolution of grammar. Tense, aspect, and modality in the languages of the world*. Chicago & London: The University of Chicago Press.
Company Company, Concepción. 2006. Tiempos en formación romance II. Los futuros y condicionales. In Concepción Company Company (ed.), *Sintaxis histórica de la lengua española*. Primera Parte: *La frase verbal*, Vol. 1, 349–418. México D.F.: Fondo de Cultura Económica.
Comrie, Bernard. 1985. *Tense*. Cambridge: Cambridge University Press.
Croft, William. 2000. *Explaining language change: An evolutionary approach*. London: Longman.
Evans, Nicholas. 2007. Insubordination and its uses. In Irina Nikolaeva (ed.), *Finiteness: Theoretical and empirical foundations*, 366–431. Oxford: Oxford University Press.
Fleischman, Suzanne. 1982. *The Future in thought and language: Diachronic evidence from Romance*. Cambridge: Cambridge University Press.
García Castillero, Carlos. 2000. *La formación del tema de presente primario osco-umbro*. Vitoria-Gasteiz: Servicio Editorial de la Universidad del País Vasco.
García Castillero, Carlos. 2012. The paradigm of clause types in Old Irish: The morphological encoding of illocutionary force. In H. Craig Melchert (ed.), *The Indo-European verb. Proceedings of the Conference of the Society for Indo-European Studies, Los Angeles, 13–15 September 2010*, 61–72. Wiesbaden: Reichert.
García Castillero, Carlos. 2013. Morphological externalisation and the Old Irish verbal particle *ro*, *Transactions of the Philological Society* 111(1). 108–140.
Genee, Inge. 1998. *Sentential complementation in a functional grammar of Irish*. The Hague: Holland Academic Graphics (LOT International Series 7).
Godel, Robert. 1975. *An introduction to the study of classical Armenian*. Wiesbaden: Ludwig Reichert.
Haase, Martin. 2010. Mood in Basque. In Björn Rothstein & Rolf Thieroff (eds.), *Mood in the languages of Europe*, 633–643. Amsterdam & Philadelphia: John Benjamins.
Haspelmath, Martin. 2011. The gradual coalescence into 'words' in grammaticalization. In Heiko Narrog & Bernd Heine (eds.), *The Oxford handbook of grammaticalization*, 342–355. Oxford: Oxford University Press.

Heine, Bernd & Tania Kuteva. 2002. *World lexicon of grammaticalization*. Cambridge: Cambridge University Press.
Heine, Bernd & Tania Kuteva. 2005. *Language contact and grammatical change*. Cambridge: Cambridge University Press.
Heine, Bernd & Mechthild Reh. 1984. *Grammaticalization and reanalysis in African languages*. Hamburg: Helmut Buske.
Hengeveld, Kees. 2004. Illocution, mood, and modality. In Geert Booij, Christian Lehmann, Joachim Mugdan & Stavros Skopeteas (eds.), in collaboration with Wolfgang Kesselheim, *Morphologie / Morphology: Ein internationales Handbuch zur Flexion und Wortbildung / An international handbook on inflection and word-formation*, 2. Halbband / Volume 2, 1190–1201. Berlin & New York: Walter de Gruyter.
Hengeveld, Kees & J. Lachlan Mackenzie. 2008. *Functional Discourse Grammar: A typologically-based theory of language structure*. Oxford: Oxford University Press.
Hengeveld, Kees & Niels Smit. 2009. Dynamic formulation in Functional Discourse Grammar. *Lingua* 119. 1118–1130.
Joseph, Brian D. 2003. Morphologization from syntax. In Brian D. Joseph & Richard D. Janda (eds.), *The handbook of historical linguistics*, 472–492. Oxford: Blackwell.
Keizer, Evelien. 2009. The interpersonal level in English: reported speech. *Linguistics* 47 (1). 845–866.
Koefoed, Geert & Jaap van Marle. 2004. Fundamental concepts. In Geert Booij, Christian Lehmann, Joachim Mugdan & Stavros Skopeteas (eds.) in collaboration with Wolfgang Kesselheim, *Morphologie / Morphology: Ein internationales Handbuch zur Flexion und Wortbildung / An international handbook on inflection and word-formation*, 2. Halbband / Volume 2, 1574–1589. Berlin & New York: Walter de Gruyter.
Leufkens, Sterre. 2013. Time reference in English indirect speech. In J. Lachlan Mackenzie & Hella Olbertz (eds.), *Casebook in Functional Discourse Grammar*, 189–212. Amsterdam & Philadelphia: John Benjamins.
López de Ayala, Pero. 1985. *Coronica del rey don Pedro*, edición y estudio de Constance L. Wilkins y Heanon M. Wilkins. Madison: The Hispanic Seminary of Medieval Studies.
McCone, Kim. 1991. *The Indo-European origins of the Old Irish nasal presents, subjunctives and futures*. Innsbruck: Institut für Sprachwissenschaft der Universität Innsbruck.
McCone, Kim. 1997. *The Early Irish verb*. 2nd edn., revised with index. Maynooth: An Sacart.
McQuillan, Peter. 2002. *Modality and grammar: A history of the Irish subjunctive*. Maynooth: National University of Ireland.
Narrog, Heiko. 2004. From transitive to causative in Japanese (Morphologization through exaptation). *Diachronica* 21(2). 351–392.
Narrog, Heiko. 2012. *Modality, subjectivity, and semantic change. A cross-linguistic perspective*. Oxford: Oxford University Press.
Ó Baoill, Dónall P. 2010. Mood in Irish. In Björn Rothstein & Rolf Thieroff (eds.), *Mood in the languages of Europe*, 273–291. Amsterdam & Philadelphia: John Benjamins.
Smith, Colin. 1993. *Poema del Mio Cid*. Madrid: Cátedra.
Stokes, Whitley & John Strachan (eds.). 1901–1903. *Thesaurus Palaeohibernicus: A collection of Old Irish glosses, scholia, prose and verse*, with a suppl. by Whitley Stokes. Dublin: Dublin Institute of Advanced Studies.
Thieroff, Rolf. 2010. Moods, moods, moods. In Björn Rothstein & Rolf Thieroff (eds.), *Mood in the languages of Europe*, 1–29. Amsterdam & Philadelphia: John Benjamins.

Thurneysen, Rudolf. 1946. *A grammar of Old Irish*, revised and enlarged edition; translated from the German by D. A. Binchy & O. Bergin. Dublin: Dublin Institute of Advanced Studies.

Vincent, Nigel. 2013. Compositionality and change in conditionals and counterfactuals in Romance. In Silvio Cruschina, Martin Maiden & John Charles Smith (eds.), *The boundaries of pure morphology: Diachronic and synchronic perspectives*, 116–136. Oxford: Oxford University Press.

Wurzel, Wolfgang Ulrich. 2004. Morphologisierung: von der Phonologie zur Morphologie. In Geert Booij, Christian Lehmann, Joachim Mugdan & Stavros Skopeteas (eds.) in collaboration with Wolfgang Kesselheim, *Morphologie / Morphology: Ein internationales Handbuch zur Flexion und Wortbildung / An international handbook on inflection and word-formation*, 2. Halbband / Volume 2, 1600–1611. Berlin & New York: Walter de Gruyter.

Jimena Tena Dávalos
The end of a cycle: Grammaticalization of the future tense in Mexican Spanish

Abstract: This article discusses the grammaticalization of the analytic and synthetic future forms in Mexican Spanish from the perspective of Functional Discourse Grammar (FDG). The current distribution of Mexican Spanish indicates that the expression of future reference is shifting from synthetic to analytic, and that the synthetic form is losing its future function and is experiencing a process of further grammaticalization. Through a diachronic corpus analysis, the present study shows that the analytic future form has grammaticalized into an absolute tense marker. Similarly, the data indicates that the synthetic form has entered new semantic domains, among them epistemic modality. The observed grammaticalization of Mexican Spanish future forms can be adequately explained in terms of an increase in scope in the hierarchical layers of representation. Based on this evidence, it is argued that FDG can serve as a basis for predicting a set of linguistic principles that can help to understand the formation of future reference systems.

Keywords: grammaticalization, relative tense, absolute tense, immediate future, prospective aspect, epistemic modality, analytic future, synthetic future

1 Introduction[1]

Modern Spanish offers a number of resources to express future reference. The two constructions that are most commonly associated with future meaning are the synthetic form (SF), as in example (1), and the analytic form (AF), as seen in (2):

(1) Mañana   comeré   en   casa   de   María.
    tomorrow eat.FUT.1SG   in   house   of   Maria
    'Tomorrow I will eat at Marias's house

---

[1] I would like to express my immense gratitude to Hella Olbertz and Kees Hengeveld for their encouragement, guidance, assistance and their comments on the earlier versions of this paper, all of which served to greatly improve the present manuscript.

Jimena Tena Dávalos: University of Amsterdam, Amsterdam Center for Language and Communication, Spuistraat 210, 1012 VT Amsterdam, The Netherlands, jimenatd@hotmail.com

DOI 10.1515/9783110519389-009

(2) *Mañana   voy   a   comer   en   casa   de   María.*
    tomorrow   go.1SG to   eat.INF at   house   of   Maria
    'Tomorrow I am going to eat at Marias's house'

In current Mexican Spanish (and some other Latin American dialects), examples (1) and (2) can be treated as semantic equivalents because in this context it is possible to use the AF and the SF interchangeably.

Although both options are available to speakers of Mexican Spanish, numerous studies (Fleischman 1982, Gutiérrez 1995, Orozco 2005, Durán Urrea and Gradoville 2006) have shown that the choice between one form and the other may be influenced by non-linguistic factors such as geographical location, age, level of formality, and social background. The extent and frequency in which both future forms are used reveals much about the way in which Spanish is changing. Although in many dialects of Spanish both future forms share many of the same functions such as the expression of intention and prediction qualitative and quantitative studies (Sedano 1994, Gutiérrez 1995, Durán Urrea and Gradoville 2006) have demonstrated that over the past decades the AF has become the predominant form to express future reference in the Spanish dialects of Mexico, Colombia, Venezuela and Spanish spoken in the U.S.A. At the same time, the SF has increasingly become associated with modal functions (Bybee 1995: 451, Durán Urrea and Gradoville 2006) as observed in (3), where the epistemicity is reinforced by the preceding *no sé* 'I don't know' and where the use of the AF would result in an ungrammatical sentence as seen in 3b:

(3) *yo   no   sé   qué   tendrán   esas   cartas.*
    I   not   know.1SG   what   have.FUT.3PL   those   letters
    Yo   no   me   comprometo.
    I   not   refl.1SG   commit.1SG
    'I don't know those letters may contain. I don't commit myself.'
    (CREA, oral, s.d)

(3b) **yo   no   sé   qué   van   a   tener   esas*
     I   not   know.1SG   what   go.3PL   to   have.INF   those
     cartas.   Yo   no   me   comprometo.
     letters   I   not   refl.1SG   commit.1SG
     'I don't know what those letters are going to contain. I don't commit myself.'

The current distribution of the Spanish future form in some of the American dialects indicates that the expression of future reference is shifting from synthetic to analytic, and that the synthetic form is losing its future function and is experiencing a process of further grammaticalization.

The processes taking place are not unexpected; rather they appear to be in line with the predictions made by the model of Functional Discourse Grammar (FDG) as proposed by Hengeveld (2011: 580), in which grammaticalization in the field of TMA is explained as an increase in scope in relation to a layered hierarchical scale. According to this model, in the formation of future markers, modal expressions of intention or obligation and aspectual markers of prospectivity can acquire a posterior meaning and may, in turn, become absolute future tense markers, that can then further grammaticalize into markers of epistemic modality.

The pattern predicted by FDG has already been observed in the history of the Romance languages. Indeed, diachronic accounts of the future in Romance have demonstrated that the original synthetic Latin forms were replaced in Romance by analytic constructions. The aforementioned forms eventually agglutinated, leading, once more, to the formation of synthetic constructions. The observed pattern led Fleischman (1982: 110) to conclude that future reference is subject to a process of cyclical alternation between synthetic and analytic forms.

In this article I argue that in Mexican Spanish the cycle is shifting again. Through a diachronic corpus analysis I show that the analytic future form has grammaticalized into an absolute tense marker. Similarly, I demonstrate that the synthetic form has entered new semantic domains, among them epistemic modality. Finally, I argue that the observed grammaticalization of Mexican Spanish future forms can be adequately explained in terms of an increase in scope in the hierarchical layers of representation. I conclude that FDG can serve as a basis for predicting a set of linguistic principles that can help to understand the formation of future reference systems.

The present study is organized as follows: in Section 2, I give a brief diachronic account of the Spanish future reference forms, from Classical Latin until its present distribution. In Section 3, the theoretical background is presented, which includes an introduction to the model of FDG as well as a presentation of the concepts that will serve as the foundations of this paper. Section 4 presents my research questions and hypotheses which follow from the theoretical background sketched in Section 3. Section 5 develops the methodology of the corpus analysis. In Section 6 the results are presented, and in Section 7 the data is interpreted according to Functional Discourse Grammar. In Section 8 I discuss the results and pose some questions for further research. Finally, Section 9 presents the conclusions of this study.

2 Diachronic overview of Spanish future forms

In order to have better understanding of the cyclical nature of the Spanish future forms a diachronic overview of both forms will be presented in the following section, starting with a brief description of the origins of the synthetic future in Section 2.1. Followed by an overview of the analytic form in Section 2.2. Finally a description of what is known about the current distribution of the future forms in Mexican Spanish is given in Section 2.3.

2.1 From Latin to Romance

Classical Latin used suffixally inflected verb forms to express future reference, as in *ama-bo* 'love-FUT.1.SG, *ama-bis* 'love-FUT.2.SG'. However, these synthetic future forms were not preserved in any of the Romance languages; instead, as Fleischman (1982: 113) states, they were replaced by analytic constructions that involved the Latin auxiliary *habere* plus an infinitive form (Lat. *amare habeo* 'I have to love' > 'I shall love'), which spread across a large part the Roman-speaking territory and eventually fused to form new inflected forms in a least the following modern Romance languages: Italian, French, Spanish, Portuguese, Occitan and Catalan (Dahl 2000: 318).

The development of *habere* from an auxiliary to a future tense marker is one of the paradigm examples of the process of cyclical alternation between synthetic and analytic forms. Although the details of this process fall outside the scope of the present paper, I will provide a general account of this change, as this antecedent will lead to a better understanding of the current changes in Spanish future reference.

The verb *habere* in Latin was a verb of possession or belonging which could only introduce a nominal object, an explanation of how this construction came to acquire future overtones is offered by Pinkster (1987), who suggests that when *habere* was modified by a gerundive (a purposive non-finite form), this construction could in some context have a possibility or a necessity reading. Pinkster observed that in this type of construction the gerundive could be replaced by the infinitive and as such *habere* + infinitive became an alternative to *habere* with gerundive, especially in verbs of communication (e.g. 'tell', 'say'). The possibility to combine *habere* with an infinitive is seen as the crucial element in the development of *habere* into a future auxiliary. The first example of *habere* modifying an infinitive was found in the writings of Cicero in 80 B.C., and has been interpreted by Pinkster depending on the context (1987: 207–208) as having a similar meaning to the modal verb *posse* 'can' and also *debere* 'must'. By the second half of the 2nd century A.D., the construction *habere* with an infinitive was found with more frequency, as observed in the writings of the writer Tertullian. According to Pinkster (1987: 206), it is during this period that the first examples of this construction with a modal nuance can be found. Finally, by the second half of the 3rd century A.D. *habere* was already interpreted as a future auxiliary by the Romans. During its transformation the *habere* construction covered a range of meanings and was used with complete freedom; as such Pinkster (1987: 207) hypothesizes that a widening of selection restrictions on the part of *habere* facilitated its development into an auxiliary verb. As can be observed from the timeline sketched out by Pinkster (1987) the early appearance of the infinitive + *habere* construction may explain why this construction can be claimed to be the precedent of the synthetic future form of some Romance languages.

After *habere* was reanalyzed as a future auxiliary this form commenced a transformation that culminated in the birth of the modern synthetic future forms found in most of the Romance languages. This was a slow process that spanned a number of centuries, and a number of theories have been put forward about the stages of this evolution (Fleischman 1982). With respect to Spanish it is generally argued that due to frequency of use the forms of the auxiliary *habere* were phonologically reduced to mostly monosyllabic forms. For example, the first person plural form *habemus*, lost the stem (*hab*)-*emus* and all that remained was the weak form (*h*)*emos*, which agglutinated to the infinitival verb *amar-emos* (Penny 1991: 163–164). It is at this point that we are able to place the birth of "the new future form" in Spanish and most of the (Western) Romance languages (see Dahl 2000: 318, quoted above).

2.2 The 'go' + infinitive future

It is not uncommon for languages to offer more than one resource for expressing futurity. According to Bybee et al. (1991: 18–19) common sources of future forms include: (i) aspectual markers, (ii) verbs or constructions with agent-oriented meaning, such as 'desire', 'obligation' and in some cases 'ability' (iii) temporal adverbs and (iv) movement verbs with goal oriented modality, such as 'come' and 'go'. With respect to the latter, cross-linguistic studies carried out by Bybee et al. (1994: 253) suggest that the most frequent and consistent lexical forms of future grams are in fact movement verbs. An explanation for this frequency is also provided by Bybee et al. (1994: 268), who claim that the semantics of movement toward a goal can be and is metaphorically interpreted as moving forward in time as well as space, making the transition to future easier and more direct than the evolution from agent oriented modalities as observed in the evolution of *habere*.

Spanish, French and Portuguese all developed goal-oriented 'go' constructions that have now grammaticalized as future tense auxiliaries. According to Fleischman (1982: 78–85), the use of 'go' constructions in these languages developed quite late, and it is therefore likely that it was an independent development in the different Romance languages.

According to Fleischman (1982: 78) in Spanish the 'go' + infinitive construction began to acquire a temporal meaning in the 13th century. This claim is supported by Yllera (1980: 171), who adds that during that century the construction was used as a prospective marker, which she refers to as *futuro próximo* 'near future'. Fleischman (1982: 79) states that by the 16th century it was attested as a temporal marker in literary discourse and polite conversation. From this moment onwards, the use of the analytic construction has been on the rise, to the extent that, by most accounts, the analytic form is considered the dominant exponent of future temporality in a large part of the Spanish speaking world (Lope Blanch 1972; Gutiérrez 1995; Durán Urrea and Gradoville 2006).

2.3 The present state of future reference in Mexican Spanish

A number of studies have examined the distribution of the future tense in Mexican Spanish. Moreno de Alba (1997) studied the distribution of the future forms in the dialect of Mexico City's educated population. In this quantitative study he concluded that the morphological future was the dominant form to express future reference amongst educated speakers, but that it was nonetheless a form in decline. In a more recent study Lastra and Martín Butrageño (2008) examined the current distribution of the analytic and synthetic future forms in a sociolinguistic corpus of Mexico City. Their analysis demonstrated that although the synthetic form is still widely used in Mexico City, it is significantly less frequent than the analytic form. Specifically, they found that the use of the synthetic future is most common in sentences where the analytic form is not an option such as in the expression of suppositions or concessives. Lastra and Martín Butrageño's (2008) study provides strong evidence for the claim that the analytic future is taking over the domain that was previously reserved for the synthetic construction, including the expression of distant future as well as unspecified temporal proximity and the expression of warnings and promises. Additionally, they found that age and level of education also affected the relative frequency of both future forms. Overall, younger speakers tended to use the synthetic future less frequently than older speakers. At the same time amongst people with higher levels of education, the synthetic future was more preserved, however, even in this group the analytic form was the predominant one. Similar results were obtained by Gutiérrez (1994) who analyzed the distribution of the future forms in the dialect of Morelia, Michoacán, a city located in the proximities of Mexico City. His participants were divided into three groups according to their level of education (primary, secondary, and higher education). His results indicated that the analytic form was the most frequent in all groups, but that it was relatively least frequent amongst the higher education group, more frequent in the primary education group, and most frequent amongst those with secondary education.[2] The evidence thus far suggests that the analytic form is the predominant form in Mexican Spanish and that it has intruded into the domain of the synthetic form.

A brief diachronic account of the future forms in Spanish seems to incontrovertibly support the hypothesis that future reference in Spanish follows a cyclical pattern. The fact that a change which occurred in Late Latin (more than a millennium ago) is now repeating itself is certainty intriguing. Moreover, it seems to in part confirm the cross-linguistically observed paths of development of future morphemes (Bybee 1995, Bybee et al. 1991).

3 Theoretical background

In this section I will introduce the theory of Functional Discourse grammar, which constitutes the basis for the analysis made in the present work. In Section 3.1 the theory's approach to gramaticalization will be presented. Section 3.2 explores de gramaticalization paths of TMA components. Finally in Section 3.3 the basic notions used for my analysis will be defined.

3.1 Functional Discourse Grammar and grammaticalization

Functional Discourse grammar (FDG) as presented by Hengeveld and Mackenzie (2009) is a top-down model of grammar which is organized according to four different levels of representation; the Interpersonal Level (pragmatics), the Representational Level (semantics), the Morphosyntactic Level (morphosyntax) and the Phonological Level (phonology). Furthermore, according to FDG, grammatical categories are organized in layers which are ordered in terms of their

---

2 Though it would be expected that the primary school group have a higher frequency than the secondary school group, Gutiérrez's results might be explained as being due to an age factor. It is likely that the speakers with primary education only were older than the rest of the participants, therefore it is not unlikely that they exhibited a more conservative behavior.

pragmatic or semantic scope. At the Representational Level, the model includes four different semantic layers, as shown in the following representation:

(4) configurational property > state of affairs > episode > propositional content

Hengeveld (2011) explains that Tense, Mood, and Aspect (TMA) are assigned to these layers depending on their semantic scope. Aspect is divided into two categories. The first category, located at the level of configurational properties,[3] concerns the aspectual distinctions that specify the internal temporal constituency of a state of affairs. The second category, on the other hand, quantifies over the state-of-affairs as a whole. Similarly, tense is divided into two categories; relative and absolute tense. The former locates a single state-of-affairs in time in relation to another, whilst the latter places the episode (i.e. a set of states-of-affairs) in time in relation to the moment of speaking. Finally, modality is organized in four different subcategories, distinguishing participant-oriented modality at the layer of the configurational property, event-oriented modality at the layer of the state-of-affairs, objective epistemic modality at the layer of the episode, and subjective epistemic modality at the layer of the propositional content (for more details see Hengeveld this volume).

According to the hypothesis made by FDG, Hengeveld (2011: 593) concludes that TMA expressions will develop as a result of increase in semantic scope, along the hierarchically organized layers of semantic organization. Thus, it is hypothesized that grammaticalization of TMA elements will follow the pattern in (4). An example of this cline can be observed in the grammaticalization of English *will*, described by Hengeveld (2011: 583) on the basis of Bybee et al. (1991), which begins with a lexical predicate. This element then develops into a modal of intention/obligation (participant-oriented modality, at the layer of the configurational property), transforms later into a relative tense marker (at the layer of the state of affairs), that eventually becomes an absolute tense marker (at the layer of the episode) and in a final stage acquires an inferential reading (at the layer of the propositional content).

3.2 The origins of tense and its further destinations

According to the model of FDG, the two potential sources for tense include aspect markers and markers of participant-oriented modality (Hengeveld 2011: 593).

---

[3] "Situational concept" in Hengeveld (2011), but "configurational property" in all other publications.

In the case of aspect markers it is stated that these elements have their origins in predicates that, as mentioned above, may or may not be verbal in nature. I will only focus on verbal predicates here as they are the only ones relevant for the present discussion. Among the lexical verbs that may turn into aspectual markers are phrasal verbs that can potentially grammaticalize into ingressive and egressive aspect markers. Additionally, metaphorical or metonymical extensions of the original meaning of lexical verbs may give rise to aspectual categories. Such is the case of the auxiliary *go to* construction in English; which originally implied a movement forward in space. In this respect Hengeveld (2011: 584) states: "The prospective interpretation is a result of the metaphorical extension of the meaning of forward moment in space in the direction of an object, to the meaning of forward moment in the direction of an event". Once a verb has grammaticalized into an aspectual maker, it may then move further up the scale and turn into a tense marker and ultimately transform into an epistemic modal.

The modal origin of tense follows a similar path as the one described above, that is, according to FDG, potential sources for tense are volitional or deontic markers which by their very nature imply a sense of posteriority. They are therefore productive elements in the formation of futures.

3.3 Prospective aspect, relative tense and absolute tense

As noted in the introduction, the present article argues that the grammaticalization of future reference in Spanish follows the predictions established by the model of Functional Discourse Grammar. As such I expect, at least in the case of the analytic form, to see an evolution from a prospective marker, into a relative tense, and then into an absolute tense. Therefore it is important to establish what is meant by each of these terms. Prospective aspect is defined in this paper as a future event resulting from, or determined by a present circumstance. In this sense, it is understood that prospective aspect possesses an imminent dimension as explained by Fleischman (1982: 103–127). In example (5) the future event apparently can be predicted on the basis of a given behavior by *the composer*:

(5) *They played the Grieg Concerto every time the composer was going to have an attack* (BYU-BNC, fiction, 1989)

The distinction between relative and absolute tense is understood here in relation to the reference point with respect to which an event is located in time.

In example (6) the reference point for the future event is an earlier moment in the past:

(6) *I didn't know that I was going to have to sell my house for twenty five thousand less than all my neighbours* (BYU-BNC, oral, 1999)

Absolute tense is seen here as locating the event in relation to the moment of speaking, whereas relative tense is seen a locating the event in relation to a temporal reference point established in the utterance itself or in its context:

(7) *the firm cancelled the trip to Moscow that Elaine and I were going to take in June* (BYU-BNC, misc., s.d.)

4 Research questions and hypothesis

The research questions guiding this study are whether or not predictable patterns can be observed in the diachronic development of future reference forms, and if the model of Functional Discourse Grammar correctly explain the diachronic development of future reference in Mexican Spanish.

In the light of the previous comments it is predicted that the development of the future forms in Spanish, both analytic and synthetic, can be interpreted in terms of scope increase along the hierarchical layers of semantic organization. As such it is hypothesized that the analytic future grammaticalized first into a relative tense marker and then into an absolute tense marker. On the other hand, it is predicted that the temporal use of the synthetic future is decreasing. Based on what is known about the development of futures, a likely path is its development into a marker of epistemic modality, which would correspond to a higher stage in the hierarchy in (4).

It is evident that any language change, (e.g. the grammaticalization of the future forms from Latin to Romance) is unique and involves a particular constellation of facts and circumstances. Nonetheless, by testing the predictions of a model such as the one proposed by FDG, it may be possible to provide evidence for the claim that these changes follow predictable patterns.

5 Methodology

In this section I will describe the methodology used in the study. Starting with a description of the material in Section 5.1, followed by a description of the data collection in Section 5.2, this methodological section will end with the way in which the data was analyzed (Section 5.3).

5.1 Material

The empirical evidence used in this study was drawn from two extensive online corpora provided by the Real Academia Española, namely the diachronic corpus of Spanish known as CORDE (*Corpus Diacrónico del Español*) and the contemporary corpus of Spanish known as CREA (*Corpus de Referencia del Español Actual*). Both corpora include a variety of written text from all around the Spanish speaking world. The CORDE includes texts from the earliest documented history of Spanish up until 1974. The CREA is composed of written and oral texts from 1975 to 2004. For the purpose of this study only the Mexican files from the CORDE and the CREA were included, with the exception of the data from the 15th century which was taken from the Spanish files, when due to evident historical reasons there was no Mexican data available.

In order to give a full account of the current distribution of future reference in Mexican Spanish, both oral and written files of the CREA were analyzed for this period. It is generally assumed that what speakers do orally is only much later reflected in their writings, so studying the oral variety for the latest period studied allows us to include a further virtual time period by comparing written and spoken texts from the period 1975–2004.

5.2 Data collection

The data was organized and analyzed in periods of one hundred years, except for the last period, which only includes data from 1975 until 2004, because 1975 is the starting point for the CREA corpus.

In order to achieve full comparability, the search for both analytic and synthetic futures was restricted to instances with the third person singular and plural. Whereas in the first two centuries it was hard to find sufficient examples, there was large amount of relevant cases specifically in the nineteenth and twentieth centuries. So, in order to extract the examples in that period each search was randomly filtered so as to select approximately 30 examples. The data was then coded according to a set of criteria that will be described in the following section.

5.3 Data analysis

5.3.1 Synthetic future

The data for the synthetic future was coded according to the expression or future reference and epistemic modality. Items coded as expressing future reference were those in which the situation was predicted to occur after the moment of speech, as in example (8) where the temporal interpretation is reinforced by the presence of the adverbial phrase *año mil diez,*

(8) *alimentar a los siete mil millones de seres humanos que habrán en el año dos mil diez*
 será   el   mayor   desafío   del   siglo   veintiuno.
 be.FUT.3SG the   biggest challenge of-the century twenty-one
 'Feeding the the seven thousand million humans that will be there in the year 2010, will be the biggest challenge of the twenty first century.' (CREA, oral, 1999)

Items coded as expressing epistemic modality were those in which the analytic form referred to a speaker's evaluation about the proposition that was made, as in example (9). In order to determine if an item did indeed express epistemic modality, the following additional criteria were considered: (i) expression of supposition as in examples (9) and (10), (ii) the expression of concession (Bybee 1995: 452) as illustrated in (11), and (iii) the presence of epistemic adverbials as seen in (12):

(9) *Pregúntenles a sus tíos, a Julián o a Francisco,*
 ellos lo   recordarán   tan   bien   como   ahora   lo
 they   it   remember.FUT.3PL   as   well   as   today   it
 recuerdo   yo
 remember.1sg   I
 'Ask your uncles Juliano or Franscisco, they will remember it as well as I now remember it.' (CREA, fiction, 1973)

(10) *creo   que   dijo   que   no,   entonces   o*
 believe.1SG   that   said.3SG   that   no   then   or
 habrá   dicho   que   sí [...]
 AUX.FUT.3SG   said   that   yes
 'I think (she) said no, then or she will have said yes [...]'
 (CREA, oral, s.d)

(11) *Visiblemente irritado el alcalde de la capital mexicana señaló:*
 "Podrá   ser   la   embajadora   de   España,   pero
 can.FUT.3SG be.INF   the   ambassador.FEM   of   Spain   but
 nadie   está   autorizado   a   decir   mentiras."
 nobody   be-being.3SG   authorized   to   tell.INF lies
 'Visibly irritated the mayor of the mexican capital pointed out; "She may be the embassador of Spain, but nobody is authorized to tell lies".' (CREA, press, 2004)

(12) Seguramente habrá   espacio de   opinión sobre
    certainly   there-be.FUT.3SG   space   of   opinion about
    temas   de   la   agenda   política   que   han
    subjects of   the   agenda   political which AUX.3PL
    quedado   pendientes
    remained   pending
    'Surely there will be space to give an opinion about the topics in the
    political agenda that are pending' (CREA, press, 1997)

5.3.2 Analytic future

The analytic form was coded according to the expression of motion, aspect and future. Instances coded as expressing motion were those in which *ir* is a transparent verb of motion as in (13) were the directional adverbial reinforces the meaning of spatial advance.

(13) *Porque la vida es una fuente de alegría, sabe Zaratustra;*
    pero donde la   canalla   va   a   beber, todas las
    but   where the   mob   go.3SG   to   drink.INF   all the
    fuentes   están   envenenadas.
    sources   be-being.3PL   poisoned
    'Because life is a source of happiness, knows Zaratustra; but here the
    mob goes to drink all the sources are poisoned.' (CORDE, fiction, 1940)

Instances coded as expressing prospective aspect where those in which the state of affairs was related to some subsequent situation (Comrie 1976: 65), where the basis of what is known at the time of speaking could be used to predict the occurrence of the state of affairs as seen in example (14) where supposition is made based on the evidence of what is being witnessed.

(14) [Description of an indigenous show with a stick which is being kicked
    like a football; the writer is amazed by the elegance of the player]
    Y   muchas veces   parece   que   le   va   a   dar
    and   many   times   seem.3SG   that   him   go.3SG   to   give.INF
    en   la   cabeza,   y   cuando   menos   catamos   acude
    on   the head   and   when   least   look.1PL   come.3SG
    con   el   un   pie   y   lo   recoge...
    with   him   the   foot   and   it   get.3SG
    'And many times it seems that the stick is going to hit him on his head,
    and when we least expect it he comes with his foot and gets it ...' (CORDE,
    history, 1609)

Instances coded as expressing future where those in which the situation was set to occur at some point after the moment of speech as seen in example (15a) where the context leads us to infer that the uncle is not death yet and therefore it is not until sometime after the moment of speech that his inheritance will be known. Furthermore, in this example is possible to replace the analytic form with the synthetic form, as seen in (15b), without altering the meaning of the sentence, as such, interchangeability also helped to determine if an item could be coded as expressing future reference.

(15) a. *Por eso te pido, a nombre de mis hermanos y en el mío propio, que apenas sepas*

qué	es	lo_que	va	a	heredar=te		mi
what	be.3sg	what	go.3SG	to	leave.INF=you.DAT		my

tío,	nos	avises		para	que	nosotros
uncle	us.ACC	inform.SBJV.2SG		so	that	we

sepamos	qué	es	lo_que	no	nos	va
know.SBJV.1PL	what	be.3SG	what	not	us.ACC	go.3SG

a	tocar
to	touch.INF

(15) b. *Por eso te pido, a nombre de mis hermanos y en el mío propio, que apenas sepas*

qué	es	lo_que	te	heredará	mi	tío,
what	be.3sg	what	you.DAT	leave.FUT.3SG	my	uncle

nos	avises		para	que	nosotros	sepamos
us.ACC	inform.SBJV.2SG		so	that	we	know.SBJV.1PL

qué	es	lo_que	no	nos	tocará
what	be.3SG	what	not	us.ACC	touch.FUT.3SG

'This is why I ask you, in the name of my brothers and in mine, that as soon as you know what my uncle is going to leave to you, you inform us, so that we know what is we are not going to get.' (CREA, fiction, 1979)

Finally items were coded as ambiguous when both a lexical or aspectual interpretation was possible as observed in (16) where the reflexive pronoun *se* could refer to *confesar* thus implying reference to the beginning of a confession and therefore an aspectual reading. Alternatively, the pronoun could also refer to the verb *ir*, implying movement towards the confessional box, therefore making a lexical interpretation possible.

(16) *Muchos omnes e mugieres son que en su vida non han memoria nin se acuerdan de peccados, mas antes*

```
quando    se       van      a     confessar,
when      REFL.3   go.3PL   to    confess.INF
```
dizen al confessor: – "Padre, preguntadme, ca yo non me acuerdo de quantos peccados.
'There are many men and women who in their lives don't have memories neither do they remember their sins, but rather,
when they go to confession / when they are going to confess
they say to the confessor: – "Father, ask me, because I do not remember which sins I have committed".' (CORDE, sermons, 1411)

As suggested by Heine and Narrog (2012) ambiguous examples are to be expected, especially during the transitory stage of the gramaticalization cline.

Crucial elements in the context that help to determine how to categorize each item from the database are, firstly, the compatibility of the subject with movement and, secondly, the presence of time modifiers.

6 Results

In this section I will start by presenting the results for the synthetic form (Section 6.1). This will be followed by a presentation of the analytic data (Section 6.2).

6.1 Diachronic evolution of the synthetic future form in Mexican Spanish

The results from the data on the synthetic form are summarized in Tab. 1. As can be observed, up until the 15th century the only function of the synthetic construction was that of a future reference marker. Modal uses of the synthetic form began to emerge in the 16th century. As illustrated in (17) where the synthetic form *habrá* is used to make a supposition about the number of people that live in the village:

```
(17) Hay            desta        ciudad   allá         sesenta   leguas,
     there-be.3SG   from-this    city     [to]-there   sixty     miles
     adonde   dicen     habrá           treinta    vecinos:
     where    say.3PL   there-be.3SG    thirty     inhabitants
```
sobre esta villa hay diferencias entre Francisco de Ibarra, gobernador de aquellas partes, y esta audiencia.

'There are from this city to there approximately seventy leagues, where they say there may be thirty inhabitants. With respect to these villages there are differences between Francisco de Ibarra, governor of those lands, and this council.' (CORDE, legal text, 1525)

However, as Tab. 1 indicates, the predominant function of the synthetic form continues to be that of a future reference marker. It is only in the data corresponding to the most recent period (1975–2004) that we can see a slight increase in the modal function of the synthetic construction. From the data it is possible to speculate that the epistemic uses will become more frequent, however, as with any case of grammaticalization this will be a slow and gradual process.

Tab. 1: Diachronic development of the synthetic future form.

Period	Future	Ambiguous	Modal	Totals
1400–1500	29	1		30
1500–1600	29		1 (supposition)	30
1600–1700	27	1	1 (2 supposition, 1 concessive)	28
1700–1800	30		2 (1 supposition, 1 concessive)	32
1800–1900	26	1	4 (3 supposition, 1 concessive)	31
1900–1975	24		6 (4 supposition, 2 concessive)	30
1975–2004 written	23		8 (5 supposition, 2 epistemic adverb, 1 probability)	31
1975–2004 oral	24		7 (4 supposition, 1 epistemic adverb, 1 concessive)	31

6.2 Diachronic data of the analytic future form in Mexican Spanish

The results from the analytic data, summarized in Tab. 2, show that from the 15th century up until the 17th century the main meaning of the *ir a + infinitive* construction was that of spatial advance. During this period, uses of the construction with a prospective meaning began to emerge, however, these early examples mostly included animate subjects, and the actions described did not contradict the movement meaning encoded in the lexical use of *ir*. Similarly, it is during these early stages that ambiguous examples between lexical and prospective are more common. The data from the 18th century seem to indicate a period of transition in which both meanings, the lexical and the prospective, were used at equal rates. By the 19th century however, the prospective meaning of *ir a* + infinitive had become the predominant function of the construction. Simultaneously, it is during this period that the analytic form started to be used as an expression of immediate futurity.

From the 20th century onwards the use of the analytic form with a lexical meaning is very rare. Simultaneously, at the beginning of this century we can observe the first instances of the analytic construction used as an absolute tense marker. The data from the end of the 20th until the present date clearly shows that the analytic construction has grammaticalized into a future tense auxiliary, moreover, the distribution of this form in current Mexican Spanish shows that the predominant function of the analytic construction is that of indicating future reference. However, the aspectual meaning has not disappeared yet. This is to be expected given that grammaticalization occurs in gradual stages (Heine and Narrog 2009) and as such various forms and uses can co-exist during transition periods.

As expected, a difference was found between the frequency of the aspectual, immediate future and absolute future in the oral and written corpus (corresponding to the period between 1975–2004). It is evident from what can be observed in Tab. 2 that the analytic form with an absolute future reading is more widespread in oral speech. This is not surprising since written speech tends to be more conservative, however, it does help to illustrate more accurately the current situation of Mexican Spanish.

Tab. 2: Diachronic development of the analytic future form.

Period	Motion	Ambiguous	Aspect	Immediate future	Future	Unclear	Totals
1400–1500	22	4	2	–	–	2	30
1500–1600	21	6	3	–	–	–	30
1600–1700	13	4	6	–	–	–	23
1700–1800	8	5	7	–	–	–	20
1800–1900	4	2	17	3	–	4	30
1900–1975	1	0	18	7	1	3	30
1975–2004 written	3	–	12	4	9	2	30
1975–2004 oral	–	0	4	7	18	1	30

7 Analysis

The results from the present study permit us to trace a sequence in the semantic development of both of the synthetic (Section 7.1) and analytic future forms (Section 7.2) of Mexican Spanish. The observed patterns appear to confirm the hypothesis that the grammaticalization of future morphemes from a given source move in predictable paths.

7.1 Synthetic future

With respect to the diachronic evolution of the synthetic form we can distinguish two periods, the first in which the synthetic form only functioned as an absolute tense (1400–1500) and a second period in which the synthetic form began to acquire the new semantic function of epistemic modality (starting in the 16th century). The shift into the realm of modality, however, proceeds slowly. The predominant function of the synthetic form in Mexican Spanish remains the expression of futurity. However, the data does indicate that the modal uses of the synthetic future are becoming more frequent and will possibly increase in the years to come. The increasing association of the synthetic future with modal uses such as the expression of probability (as seen in (17)) or supposition is in line with the predictions made by the model of FDG. Likewise, the path of development that this form has taken corroborates Bybee et al's (1991) cross-linguistic observation that the expression of epistemic modality is characteristic of future forms that have undergone long periods of development. This claim is further supported by the fact that the items coded as modal (in our data) are not interchangeable with the analytic form, as observed in (18) where (18a) is clearly a supposition relating to the a present situation and (18b) is a prediction about a future occurrence.

(18) *Todavía falta que obscurezca señor... presidente. Mire, le traje una cerveza fría y estas tortas,*
 'It is still a while until it gets dark sir...president. Look, I brought you a cold beer and these sandwiches,'
 a. *pienso que tendrá hambre ...*
   think.1SG that have.FUT.3SG hunger
   'I think you may be hungry' (CREA, fiction, 1995)
 b. *pienso que va a tener hambre ...*
   think.1SG that go.3SG to have.INF hunger
   'I think you are going to become hungry'

7.2 Analytic future

With respect to the diachronic evolution of the analytic future form, it was possible to trace four stages of development. As predicted by the model of FDG, the analytic form had its origins in a lexical movement verb as seen in (19), where the 'go to' construction unambiguously implied a movement of the subject from one place to another, as evident from the use of the adverbial expressions *al monte* and *al mar.*

(19) e   es   asý   como   el   que   va   a   pescar   peçes
      and   is   so   like   the   who   go.3SG to   fish.INF fishes
      al   monte   o   el   que   va   a   buscar   liebres
      to-the mountain   or   the   who   go.3SG to   seek.INF hares
      al   mar.
      to-the sea

'and it is like the one who goes to the mountain to fish and goes to the sea to catch hares' (CORDE, fiction, 1430)

Following the developmental path predicted by the model of FDG during the second stage of development, the analytic construction became an aspectual marker. The second stage began during the 15th century where the first examples of the construction with aspectual overtones started to appear, as mentioned previously, these early examples were still compatible with the motion encoded in *ir* as illustrated in (20) where an aspectual reading is favored due to the placement of the clitic (clitic climbing) *le van a hablar* 'they are going to speak him' rather than *van a hablarle* 'they go to speak to him' and yet due to the human subject the movement reading is also plausible.

(20) ¡Y   qué   sobervio   se   haze   en   sus   preguntas,
     and   what   arrogant   REFL.3   make.3SG   in   his   questions
     qué   desabrido   en   lo_que   ha   de   responder,   qué
     how   bland   in   what   have.3SG   to   answer.INF   what
     presuntuoso   está   a   los   que   le   van
     boastful   be-being.3SG   to   the   who   to.DAT   go.3PL
     a   hablar!
     to   speak.INF

'And how arrogant is the way he behaves when questioning, how bland in what he has to answer and how boastful he is to those who are going to talk to him!' (CORDE, fiction, ca. 1500)

It is not until the 18th century that the first non-compatible examples can be found as observed in (21) where the inanimate subject of the sentence *castigo* 'punishment' rules out a lexical reading.

(21) *Estad,   pues,   seguros   de   que   haré*
    be.IMP.PL   therefore   certain.PL   of   that   do.FUT.1SG
    respetar   vuestras   personas   en   el   castigo   que
    respect.INF   your.PL   persons   in   the   punishment   which
    se   va   a   ejecutar.
    REFL.3   go.3SG   to   carry-out.INF
    'Be therefore assured that I will have your persons respected in the punishment that is going to be carried out.' (CORDE, fiction, 1780)

By the 19th century the analytic form was used predominantly as an aspectual marker. In the third stage of development the analytic construction began to express imminent futurity as seen in (22) and (23) where the immediacy is reinforced by the temporal expressions *al rato* 'later' and *en lo sucesivo* 'from now on', respectively.

(22) – *Puedo volver al rato.*
    – *Fíjate   que   al_rato   va   a   ser   peor,*
      imagine.IMP   that   later   go.3SG   to   be.INF   worse
      porque   va   a   estar   dormido
      because   go.3SG   to   be-being.INF   asleep
    '– I can come back later'.
    – I think later is going to be worse because he is going to be sleeping'
    (CREA, fiction, 1979)

(23) *Sí, licenciado –contestó–; vaya a tomarse su descanso. Y ya lo sabe: desde esta noche se queda aquí conmigo. Ahorita mero mando que le preparen el gabinete que ocupaba Luisito,*
    porque   usté,   en   lo   sucesivo,   va   a
    because   you.FORMAL   in   the   following   go.2SG.FOMAL   to
    ser   mi   secretario.
    be.INF   my   secretary
    'Yes, sir –he answered– go have a break. And you know: from this evening onward you stay with me. Right now I have the office prepared that belonged to Luisito, because from now on you are going to be my secretary.' (CREA, fiction, 1926–1928)

Finally, in the fourth stage the analytic future has grammaticalized into an absolute tense marker as can be observed in (24) and (25). This is evident from the fact that the periphrastic construction appears frequently in conjunction with absolute temporal adverbials, such as *el próximo siglo* in (24) and *el próximo año* in (25).

(24) Sin embargo, la historia, la nueva historia se está escribiendo, y esta
historia que hoy ustedes, todavía los vencedores,
van	a	ser	para	el	próximo	siglo	aquellos
go.3PL	to	be.INF	for	the	next	century	those
que	va	a	condenar	esta	historia		
whom	go.3SG	to	condemn.INF	this	history		

'However, history, the new history is writing itself, today you are the winners, but in the next century you are going to be the ones that are going to be condemned by this history.' (CREA, oral, s.d)

(25) Un primer escenario que está siendo ya publicado por varias vías de comunicación
es	que	el	próximo	año	se	van	a	pagar
is	that	the	next	year	REFL.3	go.3PL	to	pay.INF
ciento	ochenta	mil		millones	de	pesos	por	el
hundred	eight	thousand		millions	of	pesos	for	the
concepto	de	intereses	a	la	deuda	pública.		
concept	of	interests	to	the	debt	public		

'A first scenario that has already been published in several media is that next year one hundred and eight million pesos are going to be paid of interest for public debts.' (CREA, oral, 1999)

From the analysis of the data it can be concluded that there are predictable patterns in the diachronic development of futures, and furthermore, that in Mexican Spanish the synthetic form is experiencing an ongoing change towards the domain of modality, whilst the analytic future has grammaticalized into an absolute tense. Perhaps the best illustration of the present situation of the future forms is shown in (26), where both forms appear in the same sentence, the difference being, evidently, that future reference is being expressed by the AF (*van a circular*) whereas the SF is used to express epistemic modality (*sabrán*):

(26)
El	día	de	mañana	van	a	circular	ya	
the	day	of	tomorrow	go.3PL	to	circulate.INF	already	
todos	los	automóviles		normalemente.	Como	sabrán	ustedes	
all	the	cars		normally	as	know.2PL	you.PL	
el	día	de	hoy	pues	pues		no	circularon,
the	day	of	today		DISCOURSE-MARKER		not	circulated.3PL

'Tomorrow all vehicles are going circulate normally again. As you will know today they didn't.' (CREA, oral, s.d.)

8 Discussion

The evidence from the corpus shows that in current Mexican Spanish the analytic future has grammaticalized into an absolute tense marker. Furthermore, as proposed by the theory of FDG the observed grammaticalization path from a motion verb to an aspectual marker to a posteriority marker and finally to a future marker can be explained in terms of an increase along the hierarchical layers of semantic organization. However, according to the general hypothesis of FDG as presented in Hengeveld (2011) it is expected that aspect markers will develop into relative tense markers before becoming absolute tense markers. As observed in our data this was not the case. Instead, we saw a development from immediate future to absolute future. The concept of immediate future does not fit with the description of relative tense given in Section 3.3 above, because the relativity of tense can only be assessed from a temporal viewpoint other than the present. As such it is very well possible that a study of the imperfective past form of the construction, *iba/iban a* + infinitive 'was/were going to' could yield evidence of a relative tense function of this construction. However, I refrained from including this form in the present study because it would affect the comparability of the analytic future with the synthetic future.

In the case of the synthetic future it appears it is now entering the last phase of the stages predicted by Functional Discourse Grammar, that is, its meaning is shifting to become an epistemic modal.

Although my investigation has provided some interesting results they must be taken with care. The relatively small number of tokens collected per century does not allow testing for chance significance. Therefore a future study is needed in order to provide more robust results. Furthermore, although this study allows to observe a diachronic development of the synthetic and analytic futures along the grammaticalization cline it is important to note that working with an open corpus as done in this study does not allow us to determine if in Mexican Spanish the synthetic form is more frequent than the analytic form when used to mark temporal reference. The fact that the synthetic future has experienced an increase in its use as a modal marker, however, allows us to infer that speakers use the analytic form more frequently to express future reference than the synthetic form. However, in order to arrive at a definite conclusion a further synchronic study comparing frequency of occurrence would have to be carried out.

The story of the future is far from over and many questions remain to be studied. If Fleischman's theory of the cyclical nature of the future is correct it will not be long before the dominant analytic form begins to morph into a synthetic one. Indeed, Fleischman (1982: 152) reports that in some rural areas of El Salvador, Panama and rural Mexico the analytic form has begun to show signs of agglutination (*Tú va=comer* 'you go=eat' instead of *Tú vas a comer* 'you go to eat'). Thus, it could be predicted that this analytic form may eventually become a synthetic form. If this were to occur it would constitute an unprecedented case in the Romance paradigm, as it would be the first instance of the fusion of a verb with a preposed auxiliary thus potentially leading to prefixation. Consequently, it would inform us about the direction in which Spanish syntax is shifting. In the light of this observation, it would be wise to continue investigating the future reference of Spanish in this direction.

9 Conclusions

Evidence from this study shows that in Mexican Spanish the synthetic future has acquired modal overtones, furthermore the corpus shows that this the non-temporal usage is becoming more frequent, although, as mentioned before, the primary function of the synthetic form is still the expression of future reference. Similarly, the data collected in the present study has allowed us to trace a four stage process in the grammaticalization of the analytic form; from lexical form to prospective marker to imminent future and finally absolute future. Therefore it seems correct to say that "developments in the domain of tense and aspect can be fruitfully interpreted in terms of scope increase along hierarchically organized layers of semantic organization" as indicated by Hengeveld (2011: 593). Following the theory of FDG it was predicted that before becoming an absolute future the analytic form should have bygone a relative tense stage, the data from the present study does not allow us to confirm this claim. This finding, however, does not necessarily contradict the theory of FDG, given that there may be evidence to support an intermediate stage between the expression of prospectively and the expression of absolute future reference.

The evolution of future reference in Mexican Spanish provides evidence for the claim that there are predictable patterns in the diachronic evolution of the future. Furthermore, it confirms the idea that FDG can serve as a model to predict a set of linguistic universals with respect to the formation of future reference.

References

Bybee, Joan. 1995. Spanish tense and aspect from a typological perspective. In P. Hashemipour, R. Maldonado & M. van Naerssen (eds.) *Studies in language learning and Spanish linguistics in honor of Tracy Terrell*, 442–457. San Francisco: McGraw Hill.

Bybee, Joan, Revere Perkins and William Pagliuca. 1991. Back to the future. In Elizabeth Closs Traugott & Bernd Heine (eds.), *Approaches to grammaticalization*, Vol. 2, 17–58. Amsterdam & Philadelphia: John Benjamins.

Bybee, Joan, Revere Perkins and William Pagliuca. 1994. *The evolution of grammar: Tense, aspect, and modality in the languages of the world*. Chicago: The University of Chicago Press.

Dahl, Östen. 2000. The grammar of future time reference in European languages. In Östen Dahl (ed.), *Tense and aspect in the languages of Europe*. 309–361. Berlin & New York: Mouton de Gruyter.

Davies, Mark. Online. *BYU-BNC*. (Based on the British National Corpus from Oxford University Press). http://corpus.byu.edu/bnc/ (accessed December 2015).

Durán Urrea, Evelyn & Michael Gradoville. 2006. Variation in the future tense of New Mexican Spanish, in: Taryne Hallett, Simeon Floyd, Sae Oshima, and Aaron Shield (eds.) SALSA Proceedings XIV. *Texas Linguistic Forum* 50. http://studentorgs.utexas.edu/salsa/proceedings/2006.htm (accessed February 2014).

Fleischman, Suzanne. 1982. *The future in thought and language: Diachronic evidence from Romance*. Cambridge: Cambridge University Press.

Gutiérrez, Manuel. 1994. La influencia de "los de abajo" en tres procesos de cambio lingüístico en el español de Morelia Michoacan. *Language problems and language planning* 18(3). 257–269.

Heine, Bernd & Heiko Narrog. 2009. Grammaticalization and linguistic analysis. In Bernd Heine & Heiko Narrog (eds.), *The Oxford handbook of linguistic analysis*. 401–424. Oxford: Oxford University Press.

Hengeveld, Kees. This volume. A hierarchical approach to grammaticalization.

Hengeveld, Kees. 2011. The grammaticalization of tense and aspect. In Bernd Heine & Heiko Narrog (eds.), *The Oxford handbook of grammaticalization*, 580–594. Oxford: Oxford University Press.

Hengeveld, Kees & J. Lachlan Mackenzie. 2009. Functional Discourse Grammar. In Bernd Heine & Heiko Narrog (eds.), *The Oxford handbook of linguistic analysis*. 367–400. Oxford University Press.

Lastra, Yolanda & Pedro Martín Butragueño. 2008. Futuro perifrástico y futuro morfológico en el corpus sociolingüístico de la Ciudad de México. Paper read at the XV International Conference of the ALFAL, Montevideo, 2008.

Lope Blanch, Juan M. 1972. *Estudios sobre el español de México*, México D.F.: Universidad Nacional Autónoma de México.

Moreno de Alba, José. 1977. Vitalidad del futuro de indicativo en la Norma Culta del Español hablado en México. In Juan M. Lope Blanch (ed.), *Estudios sobre el español hablado en las principales ciudades de América*, 129–146. México: Universidad Nacional Autónoma de México.

Pinkster, Harm. 1987. The strategy and chronology of the development of future and perfect tenses in Latin. In Martin Harris & Paolo Ramat (eds.) *Historical development of auxiliaries*, 193–185. Berlin & New York: Mouton de Gruyter.

Real Academia Española. Online. *Corpus diacrónico del español* (CORDE). http://www.rae.es (accessed September 2014–January 2015).

Real Academia Española. Online. *Corpus de referencia del español actual* (CREA). http:// www. rae.es. (accessed September 2014–January 2015).

Sedano, Mercedes 1994. El futuro morfológico y la expresión *ir a* +infinitivo en el español hablado de Venezuela. *Verba* 21. 225–240.

Yllera, Alicia. 1980. *Sintaxis histórica del verbo español: las perífrasis medievales.* Zaragoza: Departamento de Filología Francesa. Universidad de Zaragoza.

Aude Rebotier
The grammaticalization of tenses and lexical aspect – the case of German and French perfects

Abstract: This article aims at describing the role of lexical aspect in the evolution of perfects along their grammaticalization processes into past tenses in German and French, focussing on evidence in the present state of the two languages. It considers both the semantic evolution, i.e. the stages from adjectival constructions to tense via resultatives and similar, and the formal evolution, i.e. the loss of agreement of the past participle, and changes with respect to auxiliary selection. The investigations yield the following results: (i) Both French and German perfects are still evolving semantically and formally, although at least in some of their uses they can already be considered as tenses. (ii) Throughout the grammaticalization process a relaxation of restrictions on lexical aspect takes place. However, the role of lexical aspect is more significant in German, where the perfect evolves into a past tense, as opposed to French, where it turns into a past perfective. (iii) In spite of the persistent agreement of the participle, the grammaticalization of the French perfect seems to be more advanced than that of the German perfect. There is no one-to-one matching between the formal and the semantic stages of grammaticalization.

Keywords: perfect, past tense, lexical aspect, resultative, grammaticalization, French, German

1 Introduction[1]

In this section I will first introduce the problem examining the literature about the role of lexical aspect in the grammaticalization of tenses and in particular

---
[1] I would like to thank Hella Olbertz, Kees Hengeveld and Heiko Narrog for their thorough comments on the content as well as on their invaluable help with my English.

Aude Rebotier: Université de Reims Champagne-Ardenne, UFR Lettres et Sciences humaines, 57 rue Pierre Taittinger, 51096 Reims Cedex, France, aude.rebotier@univ-reims.fr

DOI 10.1515/9783110519389-010

a hypothesis presented in Leiss (1992), and then give my view on lexical aspect, since it slightly differs from Vendler (1967) and from Leiss (1992).

1.1 Lexical aspect and the grammaticalization of tenses: the scope of this study

Correlations between aspectuality and temporality have often been noticed. The famous definition of aspect by Comrie (1976: 3) has a temporal component: "Aspects are different ways of viewing the internal temporal constituency of a situation" (hence some authors define aspect as belonging to temporality, for example Klein 1994: 14). It is also known that aspect can have secondary temporal meanings (Leiss 1992: 238; Bhat 1999: 93; Dahl 2000: 16). However, the link between lexical aspect and the emergence of new tenses has been studied less frequently. An interesting theory has been proposed by Leiss (1992), according to whom the compatibility of tense with lexical aspect changes in the course of the grammaticalization of tenses. She claims that tense is a fully-developed category as soon as it admits all kinds of aspectual verbs, but as long as this is not the case, it is a transitional category in the process of becoming a fully developed temporal category (Leiss 1992: 237). In this study I will follow Leiss, but I will not restrict myself to considering just verbs but study them in the contexts in which they are used. The capacity of combining with all kinds of lexical aspect can be seen as a case of semantic bleaching, one of the main criteria for grammaticalization mentioned in the literature, which "correlates with a generalization of the contexts in which the gram [i.e. grammatical morpheme, A. R.] can be used" (Bybee et al. 1994: 6). Part of those contexts are the aspectual characteristics of the lexical content of the sentence in which the new verbal form is used.

Perfects are the source of past tenses in a great number of languages. The reduction of lexical aspectual restrictions in this grammaticalization process, as predicted by Leiss's hypothesis, has often been mentioned in the literature, namely when the resultative becomes a perfect with current relevance, "anterior" in my terminology (Bybee et al. 1994: 69; Dahl and Hedin 2000: 393; Lindstedt 2000: 368). However, we can suppose that lexical aspect continues to be relevant in later stages of grammaticalization, since it still plays a role in contemporary French and German in the choice of the auxiliary ('be' or 'have') with intransitive verbs. The continuing choice between two auxiliaries can be viewed as a criterion for the degree of grammaticalization (Askedal 2010, see Section 3.1 below). In this article I aim at describing the role played by lexical aspect in the evolution of perfects all along the path of their grammaticalization into past tenses. To this end, I will consider not only semantic evolution, but also the reflection of grammaticalization in form.

Leiss's theory is mainly based on German, a language that lacks grammatical aspect. The comparison with French will allow for testing how lexical aspect interacts during the grammaticalization process with the grammatical aspect borne by French past tenses. This comparison is particularly interesting because French and German perfects have very similar morphologies (with two auxiliaries) and they both have reached an advanced stage on the grammaticalization path. The evolution of the perfects has been studied cross-linguistically (Bybee, Perkins and Pagliuca 1994, Lindstedt 2000, Drinka 2001), but without focussing on German and French. Many studies have been dedicated to the evolution of the perfect in French (Caudal and Vetters 2007), in Romance languages (Squartini and Bertinetto 2000), in German (Leiss 2007) or in Germanic languages (Askedal 2010), but comparisons between German and French are incidental. Other studies compare the tenses (Weber 1954, Confais 1995), or the perfect (Schaden 2007) in German and in French, but do not deal with the process of grammaticalization.

A further issue is Leiss's statement according to which atelic ('imperfective' in Leiss's 1992 terms) verbs form the "grammatical vanguard" in the emergence of tenses (Leiss 1992: 233). This is the case for future tenses: in Slavic and early Germanic languages (Gothic, Old High German), the periphrastic future is an imperfective future, restricted to additive (i.e. imperfective or atelic) verbs (Leiss 1992: 240).[2] Only in a second stage did it admit all kinds of verbs in German. But contrary to this, perfects are primarily compatible only with non-additive (perfective or telic) verbs (Leiss 1992: 236). I will try to explain this contradiction.

However, before examining the case of the perfect, a short presentation of lexical aspect will be needed, in order to explain the way I will deal with this domain.

1.2 Lexical aspect

I assume that lexical aspect is a property of verbal expressions, which Klein (1994: 168) calls the "lexical content" of the utterance, and not that of the verb

---

[2] In Leiss's approach (1992: 32–35), aspect in Slavic Languages and lexical aspect in other languages are of the same nature, with the difference that only the former allows a choice between the two perspectives (since almost every perfective verb has an imperfective correspondent). She distinguishes between *additive* (imperfective and atelic) and *non-additive verbs* (perfective and telic). In fact, Slavic aspect is often described as a "grammaticalized lexical aspect" (Dahl 1985: 89), whose temporal effects are very similar to those of purely lexical aspect (Bertinetto and Delfitto 2000: 210).

alone. This lexical content will be represented here by taking the infinitive as the point of departure. The two categories of lexical aspect we need here are telicity (Garey 1957, Klein 1994), and transformativity (Zifonun et al. 1997), which I will consider one by one.

Telic verbal expressions are bounded, as described in Garey (1957). That is, they have an inherent terminal point. Their main features are the following two.

(i) They have an inherent duration, although not always the same (Klein 1994: 212). This duration, when it is not reduced to the terminal point (Vendler's achievements), can be expressed by "in x time", whereas the duration of atelic expressions can be expressed with "for x time". English *sing* is atelic, because there is no intrinsic boundary; you can *sing for five minutes*, not *in five minutes*. *To sing the song* is telic, because it must cease once you have reached the last note of the song. You can *sing the song in five minutes*.

(ii) They cannot be used to designate the subparts of whole the process, whilst all parts of a process designated by atelic expressions are similar and can be referred to with the same expression, i.e. atelic expressions are 'divisible' (Leiss 1992: 47–48). Garey's (1957) test is based on that property: "Si on *verb*ait, mais a été interrompu tout en *verb*ant, est-ce qu'on a *verb*é?" [If one was *verb*ing, but was interrupted while *verb*ing, has one really *verb*ed?] (Garey 1957: 105)[3]. If the answer is positive, the verbal expression is atelic. Vendler's states and activities are both atelic; accomplishments and achievements are telic. His description of the accomplishments *run a mile* and *draw a circle* corresponds to properties (ii) and (i):

> (...) if someone stops running a mile, he did not run a mile; if one stops drawing a circle, he did not draw a circle. But the man who stops running did run, and he who stops pushing the cart did push it. (...) Thus we see that while running or pushing a cart has no set terminal point, running a mile and drawing a circle do have a "climax", which has to be reached if the action is to be what it is claimed to be. (Vendler 1967 [1957]: 100)

Let us now turn to transformativity. Transformative (also: change-of-state, transitional, terminative) verbal expressions designate a process leading to a new situation (which may be a new location). *To die* is transformative because it expresses the transition from the state *alive* to the state *dead*. Transformativity is an important factor for the selection of the auxiliary for the perfect of intransitive

---

3 Comrie (1976: 44) proposes a similar test for English.

verbs (see Section 3.1 below). The following linguistic tests are based on the past participle:
(i) Transitive verbs in transformative expressions allow a stative passive, i.e., a construction with 'be' (1c) expressing the resulting state of the active (1a) or dynamic passive version (in (1b), with auxiliary *werden* 'become'):

(1) a. *Sie zerstören die Stadt.*
       they destroy the town
       'The destroy / are destroying the town.'
    b. *Die Stadt wird zerstört.*
       the town becomes destroy.PTCP
       'The town is being destroyed.'
    c. *Die Stadt ist zerstört.*
       the town is destroy.PTCP
       'The town is in ruins.'

With non-transformative expressions, the 'be' construction is either impossible or synonymous with the dynamic passive (Bobillon et al. 1987: 236; Zifonun et al. 1997: 1864, 1872–1874). The test is the same in French, but yields a less clear result because the stative passive and the dynamic passive are formally identical, since both use 'be' as an auxiliary.
(ii) In German, the participle of intransitive verbs can be used as an attribute in a noun phrase (2), which is not possible with non-transformative expressions (3):

(2) *das ein.geschlafene Kind*
    the fall.asleep.PTCP child
    'the sleeping child'

(3) **das geschlafene Kind*
    the sleep.PTCP child
    'the slept child'

As examples (2) and (3) show, transformativity is often obtained in German by prefixes (*schlafen* 'to sleep' / *einschlafen* 'to fall asleep'). In (2), the prefix *ein-* expresses inchoativity. Inchoativity is always transformative, here the process leads from a waking state into sleep, a new situation. Given the relevance of derivational verbal morphology, studies on German tend to make reference to transformative verbs rather than to transformative expressions or situations. However, they often admit that complements, especially place adverbials are also relevant (Duden 9: 442, Bobillon et al. 1987: 240). Consider the use of the participle of motion verbs. When used alone, they yield a non-transformative expression but in combination with an indication of the target a transformative one. The expression can be used attributively only in the latter case, illustrated in (5):

(4) *der   gelaufene   Junge
    the   run.PTCP   boy
    'the run boy'

(5) der   aus   dem   Zimmer   gelaufene   Junge
    the   out.of the   room   run.PTCP   boy
    'the boy who has run out of the room' (Thieroff 1992: 24)

Transformative expressions can be seen as a subclass of telic expressions, i.e. "those which have a well-defined result-state as part of their inherent meaning" (Dahl and Hedin 2000: 390).[4] Transformative expressions are always telic, since the beginning of the new state is an inherent terminal point of the process. But a telic expression can be non-transformative: French *faire une heure de musique* 'spend an hour making music' is telic, since if you are interrupted during such an hour reserved for music you did not spend an hour playing music; but it has no resulting state.[5] German *ausläuten* (stop ringing) is also telic but non-transformative, according to the test with the participle:

(6) Die   Glocken   haben   ausgeläutet
    the   bells   have   stop.ringing.PTCP
    'the bells have stopped ringing'

(7) *die   ausgeläuteten   Glocken
    the   stop.ringing.PTCP   bells
    (Zifonun et al. 1997: 1866)

As Fig. 1 shows, Vendler's categories do not account for the concept of transformativity.

---

4 Other authors who make an explicit difference between telic and transformative are Vet (1980: 62, 71 *non duratif / transitionnel*), Klein (1994: 85, 212 *d.-definite content / 2-state lexical contents*) and Zifonun et al. (1997: 1865–1867, *telisch / transformativ*).
5 *Faire une heure de musique* 'to spend an hour making music' is nearly synonymous with *faire de la musique pendant une heure* 'to make music for an hour'. This example suggests that it is legitimate to consider the whole lexical content of the sentence and not only the verb, the objects and the place complements when examining lexical aspect: *to make music* is atelic, but *to make music for an hour* is telic. In other words, aspect would not concern only the verb and its arguments, i.e. the configurational property, as in Hengeveld (this volume).

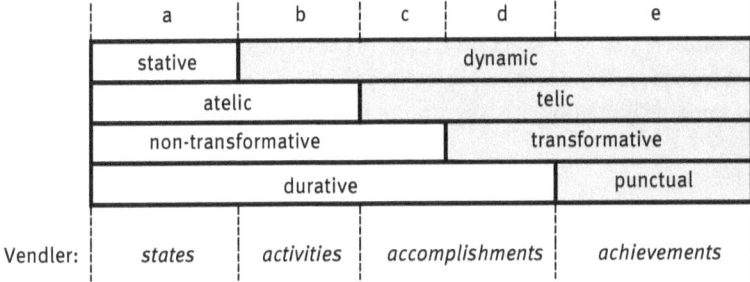

Fig. 1: The four main categories of lexical aspect and the corresponding terms in Vendler (1967 [1957]).

The letters heading the columns correspond to the results of the inclusion of transformativity in the Vendlerian classification, which can be exemplified by the following verbs and expressions: (a) *believe*, (b) *sing, run*, (c) *faire une heure de musique* 'spend an hour making music', (d) *die, draw a circle*, (e) *reach the top*.

As we will see, it is the telicity and transformativity of the whole sentence that interacts with the aspect borne by the French tenses and by the resultative respectively (see Section 2.2). The aim of this paper is to investigate how lexical aspect intervenes in the different stages of the semantic evolution of the perfect in German and in French (Section 2) and in the two formal criteria of grammaticalization for perfects proposed by Askedal (2010), i.e. auxiliary selection and past participle agreement (Section 3). This paper ends with my conclusions on the degrees of grammaticalization of the perfect in the two languages (Section 4).

2 The semantic evolution of the perfect and lexical aspect

In this section, I will first set out the grammaticalization paths of perfects and describe them in detail (Section 2.1) and will then examine the role played by lexical aspect in this process (Section 2.2).

2.1 The stages of the grammaticalization of perfects

Most linguists (Bybee et al. 1994: 61–69; Squartini and Bertinetto 2000: 406; Lindstedt 2000; Hengeveld, this volume) agree on the stages that lead from adjectival constructions to a past tense in different languages, with slight variations: (i) adjectival construction (ungrammaticalized construction) (Section 2.1.1), (ii) resultative (perfect) (Section 2.1.2), (iii) anterior (perfect) (Section 2.1.3), and (iv) past tense (preterite or past perfective) (Section 2.1.4). The presentation of these developments will end with a synthesis (Section 2.1.5).

2.1.1 Adjectival constructions

Adjectival constructions with 'have' are attested in the earliest stages of Romance and Germanic languages. The past participle is a deverbal adjective which functions as object complement (with 'have'). 'Have' is a full verb, with a possessive meaning:

Old High German:
(8) phīgboum   habēta   sum   giflanzōt-an
    fig.tree [ACC.M.SG] had someone plant.PTCP-ACC.M.SG
    in   sīnemo   wīngarten.
    in   his   vineyard
    'Someone had a fig tree planted in his vineyard.' (Tatian, quoted by Askedal 2010: 565)

Latin:
(9) in   ea   provincia   pecunias   magnas
    in   this province   money.ACC.F.PL   great.ACC.F.PL
    collocatas   habent.
    invest.PTCP.ACC.F.PL   have.IND.PRS.3PL
    'They have great capital invested in that province.'
    (Cicero, quoted by Bybee et al. 1994: 68)

Adjectival constructions are still common in modern languages:

French:
(10) La   voiture   a   les   phare-s   allumé-s.
     the   car   has   the.PL   headlight[M]-PL   turn.on.PTCP.M-PL
     'The car's headlights are on.'

German:
(11) 42   Weichen   allerdings   können   nicht   mit   Strom   beheizt
     42   points   however   can.3PL   not   with   current   heat.PTCP
     werden,   sie   haben   Propangasbrenner   eingebaut.
     become.INF   they   have.3PL   propane.burners   integrate.PTCP
     'However, 42 points cannot be heated with current, they have propane burners integrated.' (Leiss 1992: 187)

As 'have' allows using adjectives as object complement, adjectives with the copula are subjects complements.[6] Past participles can be used in such structures with a passive meaning:

(12) Les   phare-s   sont   allumé-s.
     the   headlight[M]-PL are   turn.on.PTCP.M-PL
     'The headlights are on.'

However, there is no direct ungrammaticalized forerunner of the 'be' perfects in Latin, since the 'be' construction with past participle was already a perfect in the passive or with deponent verbs. In Old High German, in contrast, such active adjectival constructions seem to have existed, with a possible alternation between 'be' and 'become' (Leiss 1992: 160).

2.1.2 Resultative[7]

The next stage can already be considered a perfect. The resultative expresses a present state as the result of a previous action (or a past state as the result of a previous action, when the auxiliary is in a past tense). The main feature is that the grammatical subject of 'have' or 'be' has to be the semantic subject of the verb in the past participle.
(i) With 'have', this means that the agent has to be mentioned, whereas there is no need for this in adjectival constructions, which only express a property of the object. This means that, in contrast to (10), (13) is a perfect.

(13) Le   conducteur a   allumé   les   phare-s.
     the   driver   has turn.on.PTCP   the.PL headlight[M]-PL
     'The driver has turned the headlights on.'

Whereas in (10) it can be either the driver or somebody else who turned the headlights on, in (13), in the perfect, the grammatical subject necessarily refers to the driver. Thus, the participle is no longer an object complement, and the lexical meaning of 'have' has faded. The subject (*le conducteur*) and the object (*les phares*) are the subject and the object of the verbe *allumer* and not those of 'have', which has become an operator and cannot be modified (Hengeveld, this

---

6 As the French name for these functions (*attribut du sujet* and *attribut de l'objet*, respectively) suggests, in both cases a property – expressed by the past participle – is assigned to the referent of the subject or object.
7 Some authors do not mention this stage and consider resultative uses of perfects as part of the anterior. Lindstedt (2000) thus uses the term *resultative* for the first, fully ungrammaticalized stage. Bybee et al.(1994: 68) call *resultatives* adjectival constructions like example (7).

volume). Moreover, in contemporary French and English, the past participle must immediately follow the verb, which is not the case in adjectival constructions with 'have'.

(ii) With 'be', only formulas with intransitive verbs can evolve into perfects. With transitive verbs, the subject of 'be' is not the semantic subject of the participle, and the whole has a passive meaning, as in example (12) above. The innovation of the Modern Romance perfect was to give the past participle, which had a passive meaning in Latin, an active meaning (Drinka 2003: 115).[8] However, 'be' in resultative perfects is closer to the copula than auxiliary 'have' is to full verb 'have', since there is no change in word order.[9]

Dahl (1985: 135) states that very few languages have a specific form devoted to the expression of the resultative. In most languages, the resultative is only one of the possible uses of the perfect. Indeed, there is no ancient stage of the French perfect with an exclusively resultative meaning attested (Caudal and Vetters 2007: 123). This still is the case in German and in French: one of the possible readings of (13) above, as well as (14) and (15) below, is resultative, namely when these sentences mean that the headlights are on and that the speaker is here, respectively.

(14) *Der   Redner   ist   angekommen.*
 the   speaker   is   arrive.PTCP
 'The speaker has arrived.' (Thieroff 1994: 102)

(15) *Le   conférencier   est   arrivé.*
 the   speaker[M].SG   is   arrive. PTCP.M.SG
 'The speaker has arrived.'

In all the three sentences (13), (14) and (15), it is impossible to use 'still' to indicate that the state persists (Bybee et al. 1994: 65), which shows that the participle can no longer be read as a deverbal adjective as in (10) above.

---

[8] In Old High German, too, passive 'be' constructions with a participle seem to have existed before active ones (Leiss 1990: 161).
[9] Dik (1987: 58) calls copula auxiliarization (which occurs in the 'be' perfect and in the passive) an *expansion*, i.e. a "process whereby some grammatical element receives an extra, equally grammatical function", which in the case of 'be' is "a gradual expansion into the domain of the verbal paradigm". The source (copula) and the target (auxiliary) of this process are closer to each other than in grammaticalization proper.

(13) a. ??*Le   conducteur   a   toujours   allumé   les*
        the   driver   has   still   turn.on.PTCP   the.PL
        phares.
        headlight.M.PL
        'The driver has still turned the headlines on.'

(14) a. ??*Der   Redner   ist   immer noch   angekommen.*
        the   speaker   is   still   arrive.PTCP
        'The speaker has still arrived'

(15) a. ??*Le   conférencier   est   toujours   arrivé.*
        the   speaker[M].SG   is   still   arrive. PTCP.M.SG
        'The speaker has still arrived'

(10) a. *La   voiture   a   toujours   les   phare-s   allumé-s.*
        the   car   has   still   the.PL   headlight[M]-PL turn.on.PTCP.M-PL
        'The car's headlights are still on.'

2.1.3 Anterior

The anterior is the prototypical stage of a perfect, and is sometimes itself called "perfect". It expresses "continuing relevance of a previous situation" (Comrie 1976: 56) or "a past action with current relevance" (Bybee et al. 1994: 61).

The anterior is said to correspond to the different uses of the English present perfect. Two main further uses are added to the resultative use: the continuative perfect, illustrated in (16), which describes "a situation that started in the past but continues into the present" (Comrie 1976: 60), and the experiential perfect, illustrated in (17), in which "a given situation has held at least once during some time in the past leading up to the present" (Comrie 1976: 58):

(16) *We've lived here for ten years.* (Comrie 1976: 60).

(17) *Bill has been to Amerika.* (Comrie 1976: 59)

In both uses, the past event is viewed from the present.

Authors that do not deal with English often fail to mention the anterior, as do Leiss (1992) in her treatment of the German perfect, and Caudal and Vetters (2007) when dealing with the French perfect; in both publications, the authors only distinguish between uses as resultatives and as tenses. Conversely, some authors do distinguish between the continuative and the experiential perfect. The latter is said to be more tense-like, i.e. more advanced in the grammaticalization process (Squartini and Bertinetto 2000: 406; Lindstedt 2000). The French and German perfects do not have continuative uses.

2.1.4 Past tense

In German and in French, the perfect has reached one further stage: it allows a temporal adverb which locates the event itself in time rather than the resulting state, nor does the temporal adverb concern a time-span stretching to the time of the utterance as in (16):

(18) a. *Am   7.   Januar   1986   hat   es   geschneit.*
        PREP.DET 7th   January   1986   has   it   snow.PTCP
    'It snowed on January 7th 1986' (Thieroff 1994: 102)
   b. *Le   7   janvier   1986,   il   a   neigé.*
       The   7   January   1986   it   has   snow.PTCP
    'It snowed on January 7th 1986'

In French, such a combination has been possible marginally, with some kinds of temporal adverbs, since the 15th century, and widened in a decisive way in the second half of the 17th century (Vetters and Caudal 2007: 125–134):

(19) *au   commencement   de   ces   guerres,   je   luy*
      at.the   beginning   of   these   wars   I   him.DAT
      ai   donné   mon   enseigne.
      have   given   my   flag
    'At the beginning of these wars, I gave him my flag'
    (Monluc, 1592, quoted by Vetters and Caudal 2007: 134)

From a typological perspective, Dahl and Hedin (2000: 393) state that cross-linguistically, "current relevance interpretation is reluctantly combined with explicit specifications of time". The English translation with a perfect (like in 18c) is not correct in that case (see, however, Walker 2008).

(18) c. **It has snowed on 7th January 1986.*

Many grammars and linguistic studies mention two different uses of the perfect in German and in French: as a resultative and as a tense. The latter can be substituted with a past tense, preterite in German and *passé simple* in French, and is commonly held to be a full tense (Bybee et al. 1994: 69 for a typological view, Vet 1980: 83 for French; Helbig and Buscha 2001: 135 and

Thieroff 1994: 101 for German). (18a) and (18b) illustrate the temporal use, the substitution is possible:

(20) a. *Am   7.   Januar   1986   schneite   es.*
       PREP.DET   7th   January   1986   snow.PST   it
       'It snowed on January 7th 1986' (Thieroff 1994: 102)
    b. *Le   7   janvier   1986,   il   neigea.*
       the   7   January   1986   it   snow.PST.PFV
       'It snowed on January 7th 1986'

Yet in several respects, the French and German perfects have not yet fully developed into past tenses. They are often said to retain some nuances that indicate their origin and, in particular, to be less appropriate than synthetic tenses for narrative sequences of events. Some authors even conclude that the perfect in these languages is not grammaticalized (Confais 1995: 56). In both languages, the perfect developed in the presence of a simple past, the preterite in German and the *passé simple* in French. The predecessors of these simple past tenses in Classical Latin and in High Old German, respectively, had both perfect aspect and past tense uses. When the periphrastic perfect appears, it competes with the synthetic tense, and nowadays both tenses continue to coexist.

Dahl (1995: 365) characterizes the situation in German as a "singular situation of competition between the perfect and the old preterite", because the grammaticalization of the perfect into a past tense has not yet been achieved. For French, the same point has been made by Caudal and Vetters (2007: 134), who, furthermore, observe that the *passé composé* still possesses some properties of a resultative, and, in particular, of a present tense. Indeed, in some contexts the French perfect still is dispreferred, particularly when there is no link between the past event and the time of utterance. In a previous study, I compared the uses of French past tenses that could be replaced by a *passé simple* (among which the perfect) in a Wikipedia corpus (Rebotier 2014a). The results show that simple past and perfect, even when the latter is used as a tense, are not used in exactly the same contexts, and that some syntactic, semantic and textual factors are statistically relevant.[10] Thus, the perfect shows a negative correlation with syntactic patterns in which the subject follows the verb, a structure that is not very common in French and occurs mainly in narration. Conversely, the perfect has a positive correlation with fully

---

[10] The study concerned only two verbs, *naître* 'be born' and *mourir* 'die', primarily in biographies. The relevant variation I found does not only concern the difference between the perfect and the *passé simple*, but there was also variation with respecto to other possible tenses, particularly the historical present, which is also very frequent in biographies.

specified dates (day, month and year), which occur, in this corpus, preferentially in the introduction, i.e. in the part of the biography that is not narrative.

2.1.5 Synthesis

The evolution of the perfect into a past tense seems to be more advanced in French. Weber (1954: 63) already noticed that the link between the speech time and the past event is by far stronger in the German than in the French perfect. In his cross-linguistic study on tense and aspect, Dahl (1985: 130) states that the German perfect is clearly a perfect, whereas the French perfect is a perfective (Dahl 1985: 70), that is, a past tense with perfective aspect. This difference can be explained by the fact that the sentences used by Dahl to state the uses of each verbal form belong to a colloquial level. In French, the synthetic past tense (*passé simple*), which competes with the perfect, has almost completely disappeared from spoken language and is mainly used in narrative written texts. Therefore, Squartini and Bertinetto (2000: 422) contend that in "French vernaculars" the perfect has reached the last, purely aoristic stage, whereas in "standard French" it is still between the perfectal and the aoristic stage.

Figure 2 summarizes the evolution of the perfect. In standard French and German, it is beyond the anterior, but maybe not at the last stage yet.

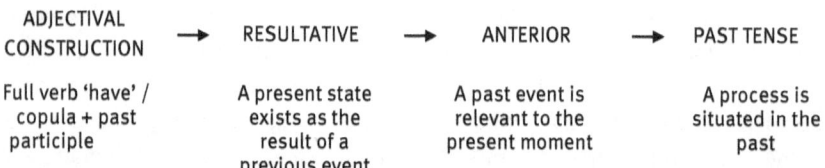

Fig. 2: The grammaticalization of perfects.

2.2 The role of lexical aspect in the grammaticalization of the perfect

The first stages of the evolution of perfects, i.e. the adjectival constructions and the resultative, express a resulting state, which is only possible with transformative expressions ("change-of-state verbs" in Bybee et al. 1994: 69; "verbs with an inherent result" in Dahl and Hedin 2000: 392). When the perfect extends to non-transformative verbs, the form must be reinterpreted, and it becomes an anterior or a tense. Some authors explain that not all verbs are allowed with an anterior: according to Bybee et al. (1994: 69), there is a restriction to dynamic (i.e. non-stative) predicates, whereas Lindstedt (2000: 368) claims that the restriction obtains with telic predicates.[11] The form can combine with all kinds of lexical aspect only at the last stage, when the perfect has developed into a full tense. In both views, Bybee's and Lindstedt's, the perfect becomes accessible to larger groups of verbal expressions, from the right to the left of the cells in Fig. 1. According to our hypothesis, aspectual lexical constraints are loosening in the grammaticalization process:

> If we apply the term 'current relevance' here [to an anterior, A. R.], it does not mean primarily that the direct result of the event is valid, rather it means that the event has repercussions of some kind for the participants of the discourse situation. In contrast to the prototypical cases of resultative perfects above, these repercussions are *not directly derivable from the meaning of the verb*. (Dahl and Hedin 2000: 391–392) [the emphasis is mine]

Grammaticalization means that the form becomes more and more independent of the lexicon, that is, in the case of tenses, of lexical aspect.

Furthermore, the stepwise evolution could explain the contradiction mentioned in the introduction. The German future first admitted atelic expressions only, because it came into existence as an imperfective future. The perfect first admitted transformative expressions only, because it was started out as a resultative, i.e. a phasal aspect, rather than a tense. The construction applies to non-transformative (and later to atelic) expressions only when the form really is becoming a past tense, during the last stages. Thus atelicity is associated in both cases with the precise stage of emergence of past or future tenses.

It is known that (lexical or grammatical) aspect can indirectly express temporal meaning. Imperfectivity or atelicity is regulary associated with present reference, perfectivity or telicity / transformativity with past or future reference. In Slavic languages, perfective verbs in the present always refer to the future. In German, a similar effect of lexical aspect has been noticed (Saltveit 1960: 55, Schecker 1988: 144, Leiss 1992: 226): telic expressions ('perfective' / 'non-additive' verbs in their terminology) refer by default to the future when used in the present without any specific temporal information. According to Leiss (1992: 236), the role of the perfect originally was to enable perfective verbs to refer to the present, and that of the future, to enable imperfective verbs to refer to the future.[12] Actually,

---

[11] Lindstedt's "material bound", required by the resultative and present in what he calls "telic situations", corresponds to transformativity in my terminology, while his "temporal bound", required by the current relevance perfect, i.e. anterior, corresponds to telicity.

[12] Saltveit's statement that 'perfective verbs' always refer to the future, either in the present tense or in the future tense, was the origin of the dispute about the German future, as a temporal or a modal form, which had recent interesting developments, although less linked with lexical aspect (see Rebotier 2006).

atelic expressions are more often used in the future tense than telic ones when referring to the future (Rebotier 2005: 463).[13]

Cross-linguistic studies highlight in particular the relation between past tenses and perfectivity, because past events are most naturally seen as a whole. In languages that possess aspectual categories but no tense, or have a minimal tense system, imperfective aspect typically has present (or non-past) reference and perfective aspect past reference (Dahl 1985: 79, 2000: 16; Bhat 1999: 93). The evolution of the perfect shows that, conversely, in the emergence of tenses, the leading categories of lexical aspect are those which are less able to entail past reference without tenses, i.e. atelic/non-transformative ones.

However, there is an important difference between French and German perfects. In French, in addition to the temporal meaning, past tenses convey grammatical aspect, i.e. there is a perfective and an imperfective past. The grammaticalized perfect fits into this system: it becomes a perfective past that competes with the *passé simple*, and it contrasts with the imperfective past, *imparfait*. I will elaborate on this point in the remainder of this section.

Perfectivity in French (unlike in Slavic languages) is the grammatical counterpart of lexical telicity. All verbs are compatible with all past tenses, but the use of the simple past or the perfect with an atelic expression causes a reinterpretation: the verbal expression necessarily receives a telic reading. For example, when there is a time span is assigned to the atelic process, it thereby becomes telic. Consider (21) and its variants for the different readings of *hésiter* 'hesitate':

(21) a. *Il   hésitait   devant la   porte.*
       he   hesitate. PAST.IPFV.3SG before the   door
       'He was hesitating before the door.'
   b. *Il   hésita   devant la   porte.*
       he   hesitate. PAST.PFV.3SG before the   door
       'He hesitated (for a moment) before the door.'
   c. *Il   a   hésité   devant la   porte.*
       he   has   hesitate.PTCP   before the   door
       'He hesitated (for a moment) before the door.'

In example (21a) with the imperfective past, the reading is atelic, whereas in the perfective variants, with the *passé simple* and the perfect, (21b) and (21c),

---

[13] Among 156 utterances referring to the future without a modal verb: 70.5% of the telic ones are in the present and 70.5% of the atelic ones are in the future; 73.4% of the utterances in the present and only 52.3% of thoses in the future are telic.

respectively, only a telic reading is available. The perfect or *passé simple* may also cause an inchoative interpretation.

(22) a. A   quinze   ans   j'   avais   la   jaunisse.
        at   fifteen years I   have. PAST.IPFV.1SG   the   jaundice
        'At 15 I had jaundice'
    b. A   quinze   ans   j'   ai   eu   la   jaunisse.
        at   fifteen years I   have. PRS.1SG have.PTCP   the   jaundice
        'At 15 I caught jaundice'
    c. A   quinze   ans   j'   eus   la   jaunisse.
        at   fifteen years I   have. PAST.PFV.1SG   the   jaundice
        'At 15 I caught jaundice'

The verb used in all three versions of (22) is *avoir* 'have', but with simple past (22c) or perfect (22b), the most obvious meaning is 'to catch jaundice', i.e. the inchoative of 'have jaundice'. Inchoative expressions are necessarily telic, as already mentioned in the discussion of examples (2) and (3) above.

Thus the grammaticalization of the perfect in French means a diachronic shift from transformativity – in the first uses of the construction as resultative – to telicity, yielding a perfective past tense with telicizing effects on lexical aspect. In this process, transformativity in the first stages is a lexical constraint on grammatical form, as the resultative can be used only with transformative expressions, whereas telicity in the last stage is a grammatical constraint on lexical semantics, because the lexical expressions have to be interpreted in a telic way. The grammaticalization of the French perfect is also a grammaticalization of aspect.

In German, there is no grammatical aspect, except for the resultative use of the perfect, which may be called a phasal aspect: the preterite is aspectually neutral and so is the perfect, as soon as it can be considered a tense. For example, it is possible to have a continuous meaning with the German perfect (23a), which would be impossible with the French perfect (23c). In French, the expression of continuity requires the *imparfait* (23b).

(23) a. Um   elf   Uhr   hat   es   immer   noch   geschneit.
        at   eleven   o'clock   has   it   allways still   snow. PTCP
        'At eleven o'clock, it was still snowing' (Thieroff 1994: 105)
    b. A   onze   heures,   il   neigeait   toujours.
        at   eleven   o'clock   it   snow. PAST.IPFV still
        'At eleven o'clock, it was still snowing'
    c. *A   onze   heures,   il   a   neigé   toujours.
        at   eleven   o'clock   it   has   snow.PTCP   still
        'At eleven o' clock it still snowed.'

The difference between (22a) on the one hand and (22b)–(22c) on the other must be expressed, as in English, with two different verbs; German expresses aspectual differences by means of the lexicon, i.e. by means of lexical aspect. The following example exactly parallels the French example in (22):

(24) a. *Mit   fünfzehn   hatte   ich   Gelbsucht.*
       with   fifteen   have.PAST.1SG   I   jaundice
       'At 15 I had jaundice'
   b. *Mit   fünfzehn   bekam   ich   Gelbsucht.*
      with   fifteen   get.PAST.1SG   I   jaundice
      'At 15 I caught jaundice'
   c. *Mit   fünfzehn   habe   ich   Gelbsucht   bekommen.*
      with   fifteen   have.PRS.1SG   I   jaundice   get.PTCP
      'At 15 I caught jaundice'

Because German tenses bear no aspectual meaning, lexical aspect is not modified by grammatical aspect and has more influence: the atelicity of *schneien* 'snow' and of *Gelbsucht haben* 'have jaundice' in (23), the telicity of *Gelbsucht bekommen* 'catch jaundice' in (24) is not affected by the conjugation. This means that the grammaticalization of the German perfect implies only a loss of aspectual restrictions, from transformativity at the first stage (resultative) to aspectual neutrality at the last stage (past tense).

With respect to lexical aspect, the grammaticalization of the perfect implies a loss of lexical restrictions in both languages: at the first stage (resultative), only transformative expressions are allowed; and at the last stage (past tense or past perfective), all kinds of expressions are compatible with the tense. In French (past perfective), they receive a telic interpretation, whereas in German (past tense) lexical aspect remains unaffected. This difference is reflected in the two divergent ways at the last stage of Fig. 3 (Dahl 1995: 361; Bybee et al. 1994: 105).

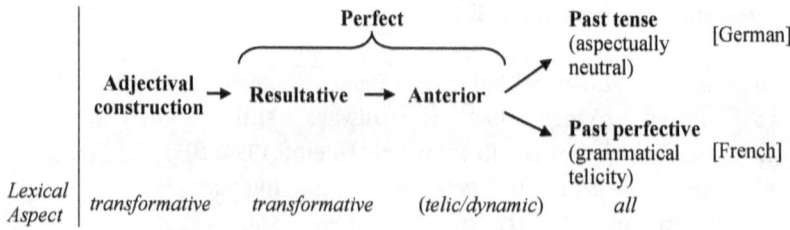

Fig. 3: Aspect in the grammaticalization of perfects.

3 The formal criteria of grammaticalization of the perfect and lexical aspect

Askedal (2010) considers two formal criteria of grammaticalization for the perfect: the loss of agreement of the past participle, and the change from two auxiliaries to only one, namely 'have'. Combining the two parameters, he gives the following typology for Germanic languages (Tab. 1), from the least (I.) to the most grammaticalized (IV.) perfects.[14]

Tab. 1: Typology of Germanic perfects (Askedal 2010: 566).

	Intransitive verbs[15]	Transitive verbs	
I.	BE + agreement	HAVE + agreement	Old High German, Norse
II.	BE + agreement	HAVE + no agreement	Norwegian (Nynorsk), Faroese
III.	BE + no agreement	HAVE + no agreement	German, Dutch, Frisian
IV.	HAVE + no agreement	HAVE + no agreement	English, Swedish, Icelandic

Table 1 raises an important question: according to these two formal criteria, the English perfect (type IV) would be more advanced in grammaticalization than the German perfect (type III). This cannot be the case if we consider the uses of both perfects, since the English perfect has not gone beyond the stage of an anterior. This means that, although these two criteria may indeed be signs of formal grammaticalization, they are not linked to a specific stage of contentive grammaticalization. Formal and semantic evolution do not have to occur at the same pace.

Yet, one important point is that both auxiliary selection and agreement are associated with lexical aspect, as will be shown in Section 3.1, on auxiliary selection, and Section 3.2. on agreement. The relation between the two will be discussed in Section 3.3.

---

14 According to Bybee et al. (1994: 68–69), the same criteria are relevant in Romance languages.
15 The column title is a simplification: only intransitive verbs can have 'be' as an auxiliary in German, but 'be' is not the only auxiliary for intransitive verbs. I reproduce the table from Askedal (2010), translated into English.

3.1 Auxiliary selection

In French and German, the selection of the auxiliary 'have' or 'be' is mainly lexical: it depends on the verb that is used in the perfect, which may be considered a case of unfinished formal grammaticalization. Indeed, the generalization of 'have' can be seen as a sign of grammaticalization: it indicates that the original differentiation between the two verbs 'have' and 'be' is no longer relevant, and that the auxiliary has lost its original meaning or function, and expresses a grammatical meaning in combination with the participle. Nevertheless, the evolution cannot to be reduced to the change from two auxiliaries to one but will turn out to be more complex.

In adjectival constructions, 'have' expresses possession and 'be' is the copula. When the construction becomes a perfect, there are three factors that are relevant for the distribution of the auxiliary: transitivity (Section 3.1.1), lexical aspect (Section 3.1.2) and the degree of (semantic) grammaticalization (Section 3.1.3).

3.1.1 Transitivity

Transitivity is an important factor, since in both languages only intransitive verbs form their perfect with 'be'. Transitive verbs must use 'have'. When the 'have' construction becomes a perfect, the object is no longer an object of 'have', but an object of the verb in the past participle. The opposition between 'be' and 'have' with transitive verbs then becomes an opposition between passive (12) and perfect active (13):

(12) Les   phare-s   sont   allumé-s.
     the   headlight[M]-PL are   turn.on.PTCP.M-PL
     'The headlights are on.' or 'The headlights are beeing turned on.'

(13) Le   conducteur   a   allumé   les   phare-s.
     the   driver   has   turn.on.PTCP   the.PL   headlight[M]-PL
     'The driver has turned the headlights on.'

Additionally, the 'have' perfect can be used also for intransitive verbs.

3.1.2 Lexical aspect

The second factor, lexical aspect, can only play a role when the perfect has reached at least the stage of an anterior and also admits non-transformative verbs. The differentiation concerns only the intransitive verbs.

Intransitive transformative verbs,[16] i.e. verbs expressing a change of state or a change of location for the subject, are traditionally said to take the auxiliary 'be' in French (Riegel et al. 1999: 252; Wilmet 2003: 341) as well as in German (Zifonun et al. 1987: 1872; Schanen and Confais 1989: 133). Other intransitive verbs mainly take 'have'. However, the rule is more appropriate for German than for French, because in contemporary French, many verbs take 'have' although they express a change of location or a change of state. Examples are *exploser* 'explode' or *grandir* 'grow up':

(25) a. *La   bombe   a   explosé.*
       the   bomb   has   explode.PTCP
   b. *Die Bombe   ist   explodiert.*
       the bomb   is   explode.PTCP
       'The bomb has exploded'

(26) a. *Elle   a   grandi   en   Afrique.*
       she   has   grow.up.PTCP   in   Africa
   b. *Sie   ist   in   Afrika   aufgewachsen.*
       she   is   in   Africa   grow.up.PTCP
       'She has grown up in Africa'

There are fewer exceptions in German: the transformative verbs of beginning and ending take auxiliary 'have', and the non-transformative verb *bleiben* 'remain' as well as copular *sein* 'be' take auxiliary 'be'. The examples (25b) and (26b), however, follow the rule mentioned above, i.e. as transformative intransitive verbs they take auxiliary *sein* 'be'.

On the other hand, the auxiliary may vary in German with a given verb depending on the lexical aspect of the sentence. More specifically, a verb of motion expresses a non-transformative event when the activity is considered as such, but a transformative one when there is a goal mentioned. Therefore, it may take *haben* 'have' in the first case (27a) and must take *sein* 'be' in the second case (27b):

(27) a. *Wir   sind   /   haben   den   ganzen   Tag   geritten*
       we   are   /   have   the   whole   day   ride.PTCP
       /   geschwommen.
       /   swim. PTCP
       'We have been riding / swimming all the day'

---

16 All grammars speak of verbs rather than of verbal expressions or situations. As we will see, the auxiliary depends in part on the verb itself and in part on the aspect of the lexical content of the whole sentence.

b. *Wir   sind   in-s   Nachbardorf*
   we   are   in-the.ACC.N.SG   next.village[ACC.N.SG]
   geritten / geschwommen.
   ride.PTCP / swim.PTCP
   'We have ridden / swum to the next village' (Thieroff 2009: 300)

This alternation is also possible with verbs other than motion verbs, when a motion reading is imposed on them by means of an adverbial expression of change of location. Consider the following example with the verb *klappern* 'rattle':

(28) a. *Der   Motor   hat   geklappert.*
        the   motor   has   rattle.PTCP
        'The motor rattled.'
   b. *Sie   sind   mit   einem   alten   Auto   durch   Deutschland*
        they   are   with   a   old   car   through   Germany
        geklappert.
        rattle.PTCP
        'They went rattling through Germany with an old car'.

There is no such difference in French: the auxiliary is *avoir* 'have' in both cases:

(29) a. *Nous   avons   nagé   toute   la   journée.*
        we   have.PRS.1SG   swim.PTCP   all   the   day
        'We have been swimming all the day'
   b. *Nous   avons   nagé   jusqu' au   village   voisin.*
        we   have.PRS.1SG   swim.PTCP   to.the   village   next
        'We have swum to the next village'

These examples show that the choice of the auxiliary is determined lexically in French and is more meaningful in German. This seems to indicate that the process of grammaticalization is more advanced in French. In German, however, there is also a certain trend toward lexical fixation. As we can see in (27a), the auxiliary 'be' is always possible, also in non-transformative uses of the verbs. Moreover, not all motion verbs allow both auxiliaries. Many of them make their perfect only with 'be':

(30) a. *Wir   sind   den   ganzen   Tag   gefahren   / gelaufen*
        we   are   the   whole   day   drive.PTCP   / run.PTCP
        / gebummelt.
        / stroll.PTCP
        'We have been driving / running / srolling all the day'

b. *Wir   sind   ins   Nachbardorf gefahren   / gelaufen*
   we   are   in-the   next.village drive.PTCP / run. PTCP
   / gebummelt.
   / stroll. PTCP
   'We have driven / run / strolled to the next village' (Thieroff 2009: 300)

According to Duden 9 (2011: 443), the verbs *gehen* 'to go' and *reisen* 'to travel', which only take 'be', once allowed the auxiliary 'have'. The *Duden* compilers summarize the situation as follows: "Insgesamt nimmt bei den Bewegungsverben die Perfektumschreibung mit *sein* immer mehr zu, auch wenn diese ohne Richtungsangabe verwendet werden" [All in all, the perfect-periphrasis with *sein* 'be' for verbs of motion is increasing, also when they are used without a direction complement] (Duden 9 2011: 442).[17]

3.1.3 Grammaticalization stage

The third factor concerns some intransitive French verbs which can appear with both auxiliaries. The difference is not the lexical aspect of the verbal phrase, but the meaning of the perfect. With those verbs, 'be' may express resultativity, whereas 'have' is used when the perfect is an anterior or a tense (Leeman-Bouix 2005: 110). However, the situation is not that simple: in (31) both *avoir* 'have' (31a) and *être* 'be' (31b) are compatible with a time adverbial dating the process, which shows that they have a temporal function:

(31) a. *Le   livre   a   paru   en   décembre.*
        the   book   has   appear. PTCP in   december
        'The book appeared in December.'
     b. *Le   livre   est   paru   en   décembre.*
        the   book   is   appear. PTCP in   december
        'The book appeared in December.'

In general, however, *être* 'be' is preferably used for the expression of a present resulting state (32), this being compatible with time adverbials dating this state, such as *depuis décembre* 'since December' in (32b).

---

[17] A slight change in the formulation for *bummeln* 'stroll' illustrates this fact: "The verb *bummeln* (...) is used in the perfect nowadays *also* with *be*" in the 4th edition (1985) has become in the 7th (2011) "[is used] *predominantly* with *be*" (*auch schon* and *überwiegend* respectively; the translation and emphasis are mine).

(32) a. *Le   livre   est   paru.*
      the   book   is   appear.PTCP
      'The book has appeared.'
   b. *Le   livre   est   paru   depuis   décembre.*
      the   book   is   appear.PTCP   since   december
      'The book is available since December.'

The opposition between the two auxiliaries has been reinterpreted: it no longer depends on the kind of verb or verbal phrase (in terms of transitivity and transformativity), but on the meaning of the perfect, 'have' indicating the most tense-like uses. Such an opposition has also been identified for languages where 'have' is the only perfect auxiliary, such as Icelandic (Askedal 2010: 569), and English:

(33) a. *He is gone.*
    b. *He has gone.* (Bybee et al. 1994: 63)

However, the situation is different in English, because *is gone* is not a perfect, and it admits the modification by the adverb of duration *still*, i.e. *He is still gone*. The corresponding French expression *Il est parti* would not allow the modification by *encore / toujours* 'still', even in its resultative meaning. As mentioned above in 2.1.2 in relation to examples (13)–(15), this test shows that *est parti* and *est paru* can be considered perfects, even in their resultative meaning, rather than adjectival constructions. A further argument is that there is a non-resultative 'be' perfect in French with both verbs.

Thus, the auxiliary 'be' resists the competition with 'have' in some resultative uses of the perfect. Yet, this opposition of the auxiliaries is on the decline, too: more and more French verbs that once expressed such an opposition by means of the two auxiliaries tend to allow 'have' in resultative uses as well or can even be used with 'have' only (Leeman-Bouix 2005: 111; Wilmet 2003: 341). There is, again, a trend in French towards lexical fixation: each verb comes to have one auxiliary only.

In sum, the 'be' perfect seems to be less grammaticalized than the 'have' perfect. The latter has extended to both transitive and intransitive verbs and to all kinds of lexical aspect. 'Be', on the other hand, is the marked auxiliary: it can only be used with intransitive and (mainly) transformative verbs. Furthermore, 'be' is preferentially associated with the most ancient stages of the perfect: with transformative expressions and in resultative uses.

3.2 Agreement of the past participle

In the first stage of the grammaticalization of perfects as represented in Figs. 2 and 3, that of the adjectival constructions, the adjectival participle is a subject complement or an object complement, and it agrees in number and gender with the subject and the object, respectively. The loss of agreement can be seen as part of the process of grammaticalization (Askedal 2010: 555, Marchello-Nizia 2006: 116), since it breaks the predicative relationship between subject and participle (with auxiliary 'be') or between object and participle (with auxiliary 'have'). Loporcaro (1995: 154) also mentions several authors from the 1960s who make similar assertions about Romance languages.

Although this criterion seems to be useless in languages like German, where agreement on predicative adjectives has also disappeared, Askedal (2010: 572) argues that in Germanic languages, the agreement of the past participle disappears earlier than adjectival agreement. German has lost the participle agreement that was still present in High Old German.[18] A few Germanic languages, Nynorsk and Faroese, have kept subject agreement when the auxiliary is 'be', but all of them have lost agreement with auxiliary 'have'. Bessler (1995: 275) makes a similar observation about Romance languages: all those that use the auxiliary 'be' have kept subject agreement, whereas with 'have' object agreement is not always present, and is even very infrequent when the object follows the verb. This confirms the difference between the perfect with 'be' and the perfect with 'have'. The former is less grammaticalized than the latter, since the agreement disappears earlier with 'have' than with 'be'.

In French, subject agreement is still required when the auxiliary is 'be'. With the auxiliary 'have', object agreement has disappeared when the object follows the participle, but it is still required by the grammatical norms when the object precedes the participle. From these properties, Askedal (2010: 579) concludes that, with respect to the perfect, French is much more conservative than any modern Germanic language and corresponds to the stage of High Old German as regards the grammaticalization of the perfect. However, this conclusion only concerns the formal evolution of the perfect in these languages and ignores the functional aspects of grammaticalization, i.e. the semantics and the use of the perfect. Viewed from a functional perspective, the French perfect cannot be said to be any less grammaticalized than the German perfect. Loss of agreement cannot be considered a criterion to assess the degree of grammaticalization. Loporcaro (1995: 154–158) introduces some counterexamples among Romance languages: the absence of agreement does not necessarily imply the existence of a grammatical

---

18 Consider example (8), repeated here as (i): the ending -*an* of the participle indicates a masculine singular accusative, which agrees with the noun *phīgboum*.

(i) phīgboum habēta sum giflanzōt-an in sīnemo wīngarten.
 fig.tree [ACC.M.SG] had someone plant.PTCP-ACC.M.SG in his vineyard
 'Someone had a fig tree planted in his vineyard.'

periphrasis. Conversely, the persistence of agreement does not necessarily indicate that no grammaticalization has occurred or that the grammaticalization is less advanced than in another language where agreement has disappeared.

In addition, agreement is no longer stable in contemporary French: its decline is most obvious with the auxiliary 'have' (Audibert-Gibier 1992: 9, Brissaud-Cogis 2008: 421). In Rebotier (2014b), I studied the agreement of the past participle with the auxiliary 'have' in a corpus of readers' comments of French online newspapers (2010–2011). Two main conclusions can be drawn from that study:

Firstly, there is agreement in about half of the cases in which it is required: this confirms that there is a growing gap between norm and usage. The main deviation from the norm is the absence of agreement (41.8% of all occurrences where an agreement was expected). Consider (34), where the past participle *vu* fails to agree with the object *la pièce de théâtre*:

(34) la   pièce   de   théâtre   que   j'   ai   vu
     the   play[F.SG]   of   theatre   REL   I   have.PRS.1SG   see.PTCP.M.SG
     hier   au   soir   a [sic]   la   TV
     yesterday   at.the   evening   at   the   TV
     'The play I saw last night on TV.'(Reader of the *Figaro*, 2010)

The second most frequent deviation consists in a "wrong" subject agreement, which constitute 69% of all occurrences of agreement against the norms, i.e. the participle with *avoir* 'have' agrees with the subject, which should only be the case when the auxiliary is *être* 'be'. In (35), the past participle *semblée* incorrectly agrees with the feminine subject *cette scène*:

(35) cette   scène   m'   a   semblé-e   choquant-e
     this.F.SG   scene[F.SG]   me.DAT   has   seem. PTCP-F.SG shocking-F.SG
     et   violent-e
     and   violent-F.SG
     'This scene seemed shocking and violent to me' (Reader of the *Figaro*, 2010)

There is thus a tendency to treat the perfect with 'have' like the perfect with 'be', regardless of the different original meanings of the two auxiliaries. Both trends (no agreement or the same agreement with both auxiliaries) are a sign of increasing grammaticalization.

Secondly, I checked the influence of several morphological, syntactic and semantic parameters of agreement in this corpus. The rate of agreement is significantly lower when the sentence contains an element that would make a resultative reading impossible: a time adverb, such as *hier au soir* 'last night' in (34), or an infinitive, a manner adverb, and some complements.

This means that agreement is more often neglected when the resultative meaning, the most ancient use of this form, is excluded, which confirms that the loss of agreement and the grammaticalization of the perfect are interrelated. Moreover, agreement is more stable with transformative verbs such as *élire* 'elect', *donner* 'give', *trouver* 'find', *prendre* 'take', *poser* 'ask', *forcer* 'force' and *perdre* 'lose', even when the perfect has no resultative meaning in the sentence.

3.3 Discussion

Both formal characteristics investigated, auxiliary selection and agreement, allow for a refinement in the discussion of the current situation of the perfects in French and German. In both languages they are still evolving, which means that the grammaticalization of the perfect is continuing in both languages. Firstly, we noticed that there is a tendency towards a purely lexical determination of auxiliary 'have' or 'be'. Secondly, the agreement of the participle in French, which is a remnant of the original syntactic relations, is about to become obsolete. These formal changes are linked with lexical aspect, since transformative expressions are relatively resistant to the evolution, with respect to both the continuing intrusion of auxiliary 'have' into the domain of intransitive verbs and the loss of participle agreement.

There are some differences between the two languages, however. As yet, auxiliary selection is more sensitive to lexical aspect in German than in French. In French, we observe a generalization of *have* as the auxiliary of the perfect: no more than thirty verbs take the auxiliary *be* in contemporary French; in fact, it is probable that 'have' is in the process of ousting auxiliary 'be', in the same way as it did in English and Spanish. In German, the trend to lexical fixation is less strong, and to the degree that it does occur, auxiliary 'be' tends to be associated with motion verbs, i.e. with verbs that are potentially transformative. The difference may just confirm that the German perfect is less grammaticalized than the French perfect, but it can also be due to a typological difference between German and French. According to Bhat (1999: 182), "languages that give greater prominence to aspect than to tense develop a perfective form from an earlier perfect construction [...], whereas languages that give greater prominence to tense than to aspect develop past [...] forms from their perfect". In this view German, as a language without grammatical aspect, would have to be a tense-prominent language, and French an aspect-prominent language. However, apart from the fact that Bhat (1999: 180) seems to consider French to be a tense-prominent rather than an aspect-prominent language, this analysis fails to take into account that the perfectives stemming from perfects in Romance languages are *past* perfectives or aorists, i.e. associations of tense and aspect.[19] In my view the explanation presented in Abraham (1999), is more appropriate. In Abraham's view, there is a competition between tense and aspect. "Descending languages" express time from the point of view of the person involved in the action, i.e. through grammatical aspect. As opposed to descending languages, both German and Latin are what he calls "ascending languages", insofar as they give prominence to tense. But German has some descending features, especially because it developed a lexical aspect in the form of verbal prefixation when it lost the flexional aspect of Proto-Indo-European. This distinction corresponds to the difference presented in Section 2.2 above: lexical aspect is more important in German than in Romance languages, and the grammaticalization of tenses would be restrained in German by the strong lexical aspect. This sensitivity to lexical aspect impedes the formal simplification of the perfect to 'have' + participle. Therefore, it is more probable that the grammaticalization of the perfect will be reflected in form earlier in French than in German.

4 Conclusion

The example of the French and German perfects confirms the hypothesis that the grammaticalization to tense is accompanied by a relaxation of restrictions on lexical aspect: as the form becomes grammatical, it is more and more independent from the lexicon. The use of the perfect is first restricted to transformative expressions and then gradually becomes compatible with all kinds of lexical aspect. German and French perfects have reached this stage. Moreover, transformativity is still relevant for describing the evolution once all kinds of verbal expressions are admitted, since it affects the evolution of both auxiliary selection and/or agreement in contemporary German and French. Transformativity turns out to be relevant all along the evolution of the perfects, for formal phenomena as well as for the semantic evolution.

We can make Leiss's theory that atelic (or: imperfective) verbs are crucial in the emergence of tenses more specific: transformative expressions take the lead in the creation of the perfect, but non-transformative expressions take the lead in the process of its grammaticalization into tense.

---

[19] This simplification originates in Bybee et al. (1994: 83) who uses just "perfective" for reference to the perfective past, with the precision that "many of our perfective grams are restricted to the past, and for the rest the perfective use typically refers to past events".

The last part of the evolution is different in the two languages. In French, the grammaticalization of the perfect leads to the emergence of both tense and grammatical aspect, i.e. past and perfective. All aspectual expressions are compatible with past perfective, although, when atelic, they may receive a telic reading. The historical evolution of the perfect is a shift from lexical transformativity to grammatical telicity. German has no grammatical aspect, and the perfect in this language becomes a mere past tense through grammaticalization. Lexical aspect is not constrained by the grammatical morphemes and can be expressed freely; an atelic expression in the perfect, for example, may have a continuous meaning. The different aspectual structure of German and French explains why the grammaticalization of the French perfect is easier, since lexical characteristics are less intrusive, and why the grammaticalization of the German perfect seems to be less advanced than that of the French perfect.

The case of the perfects also confirms Hengeveld's statement (this volume) that "an element that moves up a contentive scale will either move up the formal scale as well or stay where it is at the formal scale": in comparison to the German perfect, the contentive grammaticalization of the French perfect is more advanced, but its formal grammaticalization is less advanced. Both are semantically more grammaticalized and formally less grammaticalized than the English perfect. Yet, in both languages, formal and semantic grammaticalization is progressing in the same direction.

The stages of semantic evolution are almost the same as those described in Hengeveld (this volume), and can be viewed as scope increase concerning the grammaticalization into tense as well as (in French) into grammatical aspect. However, the case of the French and German perfect is more complex insofar as it involves the grammaticalization of two different verbs, 'have' and 'be', whose evolutions are mutually related. They tend to become allomorphs of the perfect auxiliary in complementary distribution, but what triggers their distribution still reflects their incomplete grammaticalization into tense auxiliaries.

As for the formal evolution, both verbs can be viewed as operators from the resultative stage onwards. However, in the present case, the change from lexeme to operator (defined as an element that cannot be modified), which is general and cross-linguistically relevant, goes hand in hand with other changes, above all the loss of agreement and of differential auxiliary selection. The formal grammaticalization thus turns out to be gradual: both perfects are still evolving formally in the stage of past tenses. Moreover, the formal evolution can be explained by semantic factors such as lexical aspect and the interpretation of the perfect, i.e. the grammaticalization stage on the contentive scale. The present case is illustrative of the fact that in the process of grammaticalization contentive and formal evolution cannot move in opposite directions.

References

Abraham, Werner. 1999. How descending is ascending German? On the deep interrelations between tense, aspect, pronominality, and ergativity. In Werner Abraham & Leonid Kulikov (eds.), *Tense-aspect, transitivity, and causativity* (Studies in Language Companion Series 50), 253–292. Amsterdam & Philadelphia: John Benjamins.

Askedal, John Ole. 2010. Periphrastische Passiv- und Perfektkonstruktionen in den germanischen Sprachen. Unterschiedliche Grammatikalisierungsstufen und ihre areale Distribution. *Germanistische Linguistik* 206–209b. 553–586.

Audibert-Gibier, Monique. 1992. Etude de l'accord du participe passé sur des corpus de français parlé. *Langage et société* 61. 7–30.

Bhat, D. N. Shankara. 1999. *The prominence of tense, aspect and mood*. Amsterdam & Philadelphia: John Benjamins.

Bessler, Paul. 1995. L'accord du participe passé dans les langues romanes: une approche morphosyntaxique. *The Canadian journal of linguistics*, 40 (3). 269–296.

Bobillon, Jean-Marc, Martine Dalmas, Jean-François Marillier & Marcel Vuillaume. 1987. Transformativität und Intransformativität. Zur Interpretation deutscher Passivsätze. In Centre de Recherces en Linguistique Germanique de l'université de Nice (C.R.L.G.) (ed.) *Das Passiv im Deutschen*, 235–255. Tübingen: Niemeyer.

Brissaud, Catherine & Danièle Cogis. 2008. L'accord du participe passé. Reconsidération d'un problème ancien à la lumière de données récentes sur l'acquisition. In Jacques Durand, Benoît Habert & Bernard Laks (eds.), *Congrès mondial de linguistique française*, Paris 9–12 juillet 2008, 413–424. Paris: EDP Sciences.

Bybee, Joan, Revere Perkins & William Pagliuca. 1994. *The Evolution of grammar: Tense, aspect and modality in the languages of the world*. Chicago: The University of Chicago Press.

Caudal, Patrick & Carl Vetters. 2007. Passé composé et passé simple: sémantique diachronique et formelle. In Emmanuelle Labeau, Carl Vetters & Patrick Caudal (eds.), *Sémantique et diachronie du système verbal français* (Cahiers Chronos 16). 121–155. Amsterdam & New York: Rodopi.

Comrie, Bernard. 1976. *Aspect*. Cambridge: Cambridge University Press.

Confais, Jean-Paul. 1990. *Temps-mode-aspect: les approches des morphèmes verbaux et leurs problèmes à l'exemple du français et de l'allemand*. Toulouse: Presses universitaires du Mirail.

Dahl, Östen. 1985. *Tense and aspect systems*. Oxford: Blackwell.

Dahl, Östen. 1996. Das Tempussystem im Deutschen im typologischen Vergleich. In Ewald Lang & Gisela Zifonun (eds.), *Deutsch – typologisch*, 359–368. Berlin & New York: Mouton de Gruyter.

Dahl, Östen & Eva Hedin. 2000. Current relevance and event reference. In Östen Dahl (ed.) *Tense and aspect in the languages of Europe*, 385–401. Berlin & New York: Mouton de Gruyter.

Dik, Simon C. 1987. Copula auxiliarization: how and why? In Martin Harris & Paolo Ramat (eds.), *Historical development of auxiliaries*. 53–84. Berlin & New York: Mouton de Gruyter.

Drinka, Bridget. 2001. The formation of periphrastic perfects and passives in Europe: An areal approach. In Barry J. Blake & Kate Burridge (eds.), *Historical Linguistics 2001: Selected papers from the 15th International Conference on Historical Linguistics, Melbourne, 13–17 août 2001*, 105–128. Amsterdam & Philadephia: John Benjamins.

Dudenredaktion. 1985. *Duden – Richtiges und gutes Deutsch: Wörterbuch der sprachlichen Zweifelsfälle*. 3., neu bearbeitete und erweiterte Auflage (Der Duden in 10 Bänden, Bd. 9). Dieter Berger, Günther Drosdowski & Otmar Käge (eds.). Mannheim: Dudenverlag.

Garey, Howard B. 1957. Verbal aspect in French. *Language* 33. 91–110.
Helbig, Gerhard & Joachim Buscha. 2001. *Deutsche Grammatik: ein Handbuch für den Ausländerunterricht.* Berlin & New York: Langenscheidt.
Hengeveld, Kees. This volume. A hierarchical approach to grammaticalization.
Klein, Wolfgang. 1994. *Time in language.* London & New York: Routledge.
Leeman-Bouix, Danielle. 2005 [2002]. *Grammaire du verbe français.* Paris: Armand Colin.
Leiss, Elisabeth. 1992. *Die Verbalkategorien des Deutschen.* Berlin & New York: De Gruyter.
Lindstedt, Jouko. 2000. The perfect – aspectual, temporal and evidential. In Östen Dahl (ed.), *Tense and aspect in the languages of Europe,* 365–383. Berlin & New York: Mouton de Gruyter.
Loporcaro, Michele. 1995. Grammaticalizzazione delle perifrasi verbali perfettive romanze e accordo del participio passato. *Archivio glottologico italiano* 80(1–2). 144–167.
Marchello-Nizia, Christiane. 2006. *Grammaticalisation et changement linguistique.* Louvain: De Boeck Université.
Rebotier, Aude. 2005. Les Temps verbaux en allemand et en français et les phénomènes aspectuels. Comparaison de deux systèmes. PhD thesis. Grenoble: Université Grenoble 3 Stendhal.
Rebotier, Aude. 2006. Le Futur de l'allemand. *Corela* 4 (1). http://corela.edel.univ-poitiers.fr/index.php?id=445.
Rebotier, Aude. 2011. Les emplois stéréotypiques des temps narratifs en français. *Textes et contextes* 5. http://revuesshs.u-bourgogne.fr/textes&contextes/document.php?id=1256.
Rebotier, Aude. 2014a. The passé simple takes a step back; who steps in? Narrative tenses for *naître* and *mourir* in French and in Italian. In Jacques Bres & Emmanuelle Labeau (eds.), *The evolution of verbal systems* (Sciences pour la communication 108), 7–54. Bern: Peter Lang.
Rebotier, Aude. 2014b. French participle agreement with *avoir*: current trends as an indication of grammaticalization. In Jacques Bres & Emmanuelle Labeau (eds.), *The evolution of verbal systems,* 115–144. Bern: Peter Lang.
Riegel, Martin, Jean-Christophe Pellat & René Rioul. 2004. *Grammaire méthodique du français.* Paris: Presses universitaires de France.
Saltveit, Laurits. 1960. Das sogenannte deutsche Futur und die adäquate Methode. *Beiträge zur Geschichte der deutschen Sprache und Literatur* 87. 227–234.
Schaden, Gerhard. 2007. La sémantique du parfait. Étude des "temps composés" dans un choix de langues germaniques et romanes. PhD thesis. Paris: Université Paris 8.
Schanen, François & Jean-Paul Confais. 1989. *Grammaire de l'allemand: formes et fonctions.* Paris: Nathan.
Schecker, Michael. 1988. Über die Zukunft des Futur, oder: Tempus und Zeit im Standarddeutschen. In U. Maas (ed.) *Geteilte Sprache: Festschrift für Rainer Marten,* 131–173. Amsterdam: Grüner.
Squartini, Mario & Pier Marco Bertinetto. 2000. The simple and compound past in Romance languages. In Östen Dahl (ed.), *Tense and aspect in the languages of Europe,* 403–439. Berlin & New York: Mouton de Gruyter.
Thieroff, Rolf. 1992. *Das finite Verb im Deutschen. Tempus – Modus – Distanz.* Tübingen: Narr.
Thieroff, Rolf. 2009. Perfekt. In Elke Hentschel & Maria Vogel (eds.), *Deutsche Morphologie,* 296–310. Berlin & New York: de Gruyter.
Vendler, Zeno. 1967 [1957]. Verbs and times, In Zeno Vendler. *Linguistics in philosophy.* 97–121. Ithaca: Cornell University Press [Reprint of: Verbs and times. *The Philosophical review* 66. 143–160].

Vet, Co. 1980. *Temps, aspects et adverbes de temps en français contemporain. Essai de sémantique moderne.* Genève: Droz.

Walker, Jim. 2008. The footballer's perfect – Are footballers leading the way? In Eva Lavric, Gerhard Pisek, Andrew Skinner, and Wolfgang Stadler (eds.), *The linguistics of football*, 295–303. Tübingen: Gunter Narr.

Weber, Hans. 1954. *Das Tempussystem des Deutschen und des Französischen. Übersetzungs-und Struktuurprobleme.* Bern: Franke.

Wilmet, Marc. 2003 [1997]. *Grammaire critique du français*, 3rd edn. Bruxelles: Duculot.

Zifonun, Gisela, Ludger Hoffmann, Bruno Stecker & Joachim Ballweg. 1997. *Grammatik der deutschen Sprache.* Berlin & New York: de Gruyter.

Hella Olbertz and Wim Honselaar
The grammaticalization of Dutch *moeten*: modal and post-modal meanings

Abstract: This chapter provides a synchronic and diachronic description of the Dutch modal *moeten*, which means 'must' in Modern Dutch. The synchronic description combines Narrog's (2005) distinction between volitive and non-volitive modality with Hengeveld's (2004) approach to modality, which subcategorizes modal distinctions according to their domains and their targets. It is shown that *moeten* can be used to express all of these distinctions, although it is rare in the function of objective epistemic modality. The diachronic description focuses on deontic *moeten* and post-deontic non-modal meanings. It consists of two parts, the first describing the Old Dutch *moeten* 'may' and its development into an expression of optative illocution in Middle Dutch, as well as its semantic shift to modal necessity. In this context Nuyts' (2011, 2013) claim, according to which *moeten* has been undergoing a process of degrammaticalization from Middle Dutch onward, is critically evaluated. The second part of the diachronic description of *moeten* is dedicated to a 20th century innovation which consists of the use of *moeten* in an imperative-like construction. The chapter ends with a synthesis of the changes undergone by *moeten* from Old Dutch onward making use of the Functional Discourse Grammar approach to grammaticalization (Hengeveld this volume).

Keywords: modal necessity, modal possibility, optative, imperative, degrammaticalization, Dutch

1 Introduction[1]

As opposed to most other Germanic languages, such as English, German, or Danish (Mortelmans, Boye and van der Auwera 2009), Modern Dutch has only

---

[1] We are grateful to Kees Hengeveld, Heiko Narrog and an anonymous reviewer for their valuable comments. Hella Olbertz gratefully acknowledges financial support from the grant no. 2014/00034–5 received from the São Paulo Research Foundation (FAPESP).

Hella Olbertz: University of Amsterdam, Amsterdam Center for Language and Communication, Spuistraat 134, 1012 VB Amsterdam, The Netherlands, h.g.olbertz@uva.nl
Wim Honselaar: University of Amsterdam, Slavic Department, Spuistraat 134, 1012 VB Amsterdam, The Netherlands, w.j.j.honselaar@uva.nl

one auxiliary expression of modal necessity, *moeten*.² As a consequence, *moeten* is highly polysemous, i.e. it can express almost any kind of modal necessity of both the non-epistemic and the epistemic type. With the deontic modals of most other Germanic languages (except English), it shares the property of being able to occur without a lexical verb in a number of contexts, such as in that of directional movement. Consider the following examples from Dutch (1a), German (1b) and Danish (1c) quoted from Mortelmans, Boye and van der Auwera (2009: 25, 29, 45):

(1) a. *Zij   moet   naar   huis.*
       she   must.PRS   to   home
    b. *Sie   muss   nach   Hause.*
       she   must.PRS   to   home
    c. *Hun   skal   hjem.*
       she   must.PRS   home
    d. **She must home*
       'She has to go home'

The difference between Dutch, German, Danish and also Swedish (Lissan Taal-Apelqvist pers. com.) is, however, that Dutch allows the independent use of *moeten* with eventive subjects, as shown in example (2):

(2) *Moet   dat   dan,   vraag   ik,   gelukkig   worden?*
    must.PRS that   then   ask.PRS.1SG I   happy   become.INF
    'Is that really necessary, I ask, to be happy?'
    (DRAPAC 28 MtH)

The wide applicability of deontic *moeten* as a lexical verb has led to the idea that *moeten* might be in the process of degrammaticalization (Nuyts 2011: 180; 2013: 131–132).³

On the other hand, *moeten* has an innovative auxiliary use which is far more grammaticalized than the grammatical expressions of modal necessity in other Germanic languages. Consider the following example:

(3) *Moet   je   horen   wat   ze   nu   weer*
    must.PRS.SG   you   hear.INF   what   they   now   again

---

2 In fact, there is a second one, *dienen te* 'need, ought to', which covers rule based necessity only and appears exclusively in very formal written contexts, such as legal texts and instructions.
3 Nuyts (2014: 369–379) presents an explanation of this "degrammaticalization" in terms of iconicity, which is, however, too much dependent on the Cognitive Grammar view on deontic modality to be helpful in this context.

bedacht   hebben
invented.PTCP   AUX.PRS.PL
'Now listen what they have been contrieving now!'
(DRAPAC 20 AF)

In this construction *moeten* has developed beyond the modal domain proper into an expression of an imperative-like illocution (or "sentence mood" in the terms of Narrog 2005, 2012, this volume).

Our contribution will explain the property illustrated in (2) and focus on the grammaticalization of *moeten* within and beyond modality, thus providing an account of the case illustrated in (3). It is the aim of this paper to describe the grammaticalization of *moeten* making use of an approach to the grammaticalization of modals presented in Hengeveld (this volume). In order to account for this process adequately, we will first describe the modal uses of *moeten* from a synchronic perspective and then discuss both its semantic and its syntactic development from a diachronic perspective, in the course of which we will show that, in a certain sense, there is a kind of "degrammaticalization" of *moeten*, but not in the way Nuyts (2011, 2013) proposes. The synchronic data used in this paper will consist of a corpus of 20th century literary prose of 3.156.483 words, which has been drawn from the *Dutch-Russian Amsterdam Parallel Aligned Corpus* (DRAPAC), and the *Corpus Hedendaags Nederlands* 'Corpus of Modern Dutch' (CHN), provided online by the Institute for the Dutch Language (INT). For the diachronic section of this paper we will use the online diachronic dictionaries of the INT.

Section 2 of this study will be dedicated to the description of the modal functions of *moeten* in Modern Dutch making use of a categorization of modality that is inspired by Hengeveld (2004, this volume). In Section 3, we will consider the diachrony of *moeten* discussing both the semantic and syntactic developments as well as the potential degrammaticalization of this modal. Section 4 will deal with the use of the innovative post-modal *moeten* and explain the restrictions on this use. Section 5 will discuss the grammaticalization of modal and post-modal *moeten* from a Functional Discourse Grammar perspective, and Section 6 will be dedicated to our conclusions.

2 The modal meanings of *moeten*

Our point of departure is the definition of modality provided by Narrog (2005: 697), according to which "the expression of a state of affairs is modalized if it is marked for being undetermined with respect to its factual status, i.e. it is neither positively nor negatively factual". We interpret the concept of "state of affairs" as used here in a non-technical sense and read it as including propositional contents, too. Our classification of modality makes use of Hengeveld's (2004) distinction between domains and targets of modal evaluation. The domains include facultative, deontic and (objective and subjective) epistemic modality, and the targets are (i) primary participants (mostly agents) in events, (ii) events, and (iii) propositional contents. We will, therefore, distinguish, for instance, between participant-oriented and event-oriented deontic modality. However, we will deviate from Hengeveld (2004) at one point: instead of his presentation of the domain of modal evaluation as forming one whole, we rather prefer the distinction used by Narrog (2005) between those domains that have "an element of will" in the source of modality, and those that have not.[4] We therefore follow Narrog in making a basic distinction between "volitive" and "non-volitive" modal domains, the former including deontic and boulomaic and the latter inherent, circumstantial and epistemic modal distinctions. Furthermore, we make use of the concept of "episode" (cf. Hengeveld this volume), which we consider to be basically a "tensed state of affairs". The most important modal distinctions that result from this approach and can be expressed by *moeten* are represented in Tab. 1, in which the bracketed numbers refer to the examples to be given below.

Tab. 1: Modal distinctions expressed by *moeten*.

Target	Domain	
	volitive	non-volitive
participant	*deontic* (4)	*inherent* (9)
event	*prescriptive deontic* (5–6)	*circumstantial* (10)
episode	*evaluative deontic* (7–8)	(*objective epistemic*)
proposition	–	*subjective epistemic* (11)

The general idea of the schema in Tab. 1 is that its vertical orientation reflects the increasing scope of the modalization: in the case of participant-oriented modality,

---

[4] The "element of will" can concern any source of modalization, be it an individual or some norms or rules, which, in the end, are always manmade. Narrog (2005: 683–685) refers back to Jespersen (1924), who first introduced this distinction between different types of what he named "mood" as well as to Heine (1995) and Palmer (2001), who have reintroduced this distinction before him.

the modal is supposed to modify the relation between the predicate and its arguments; event-oriented modals modify a non-tensed state of affairs and may take participant-oriented modals in their scope; episode-oriented modals modify a state of affairs that can be located in time and may take event-oriented modals in their scope, and proposition-oriented modals modify propositional contents and as such can take all the lower elements in their scope. We will provide evidence for these scope relations in the discussion of the volitive domain.

Examples (4)–(11) illustrate the different uses of *moeten* listed in Tab. 1. The example (4) illustrates the case of participant-oriented deontic (volitive) modality, which concerns the necessity that is imposed by either some person or some general rule on a specific human participant in the state of affairs referred to.

(4) *Hij schreef mij eens dat wij niet hard moesten*
    he write.PST.SG me once that we not hard must.PST.PL
    zijn in ons oordeel over haar.
    be.INF in our judgement about her
    'He wrote me once that we shouldn't be hard in our opinion about her.'
    (DRAPAC 24 HH)

The fact that the modal is in the past tense is due to past tense copying (*consecutio temporum*) from the main clause, which does, however, not affect the principled posterior orientation of the modalized expression (cf. Laca 2014: 82).

We now turn to the event-oriented volitive category, i.e. prescriptive deontic modality, as referred to in Tab. 1. In this case the source of the modal necessity consists of general or institutional norms, laws, as well as any type of instructions, whereas the target is some state of affairs, the primary argument of which refers either to a second order entity, or to an inanimate or non-specific animate first order entity. Example (5) illustrates the second order entity type:

(5) *Milieuvriendelijk en -bewust gedrag moet*
    environment_friendly and _conscious behaviour must.PRS.SG
    worden gestimuleerd
    AUX.INF stimulated.PTCP
    'Environment-friendly and -conscious behaviour must be stimulated'
    (CHN, Press 2010)

Example (6) is another example of prescriptive deontic modality. In this example the source is Government Information and the target is a state of affairs, because the referent of the first argument is a group of people which is identifyable but not specific. This means that the potential referents know that they are meant, but the writer of the text does not know who they are (Hengeveld and Mackenzie 2008: 36).

(6) Ook   uitzendkrachten,   vrijwilligers of   stagiairs,   moeten
    also   temporary_employees   volunteers   or   trainees   must.PRS.PL
    zich   kunnen   identificeren   met   een   origineel   identiteitsbewijs.
    REFL.3   can.INF   identify.INF   with   a   original   proof_of_identity
    'Even temporary employees, volunteers, or trainees must be able to identify
    themselves with an original ID'
    (*Informatie van de Rijksoverheid*, internet)

This example furthermore illustrates the fact that event-oriented modality can have participant-oriented modality in its scope, in this case participant-oriented possibility, expressed by *kunnen* 'can', because the individuals in question are required to take the necessary measures in order to be able, in concrete cases, to produce an ID.

As opposed to prescriptive deontic modality, evaluative deontic modality[5] has its source in a personal view on what is considered necessary. This modal distinction can scope over prescriptive deontic modality. In (7) *moeten* has an auxiliary expression of prescriptive deontic possibility *mogen* 'may' in its scope:

(7) *Wie   zo   denkt   'houdt   niet   van   en   is*
    who   like_this   think.PRS.SG   care.PRS.SG   not   for   and   is
    tegen   joden'   en   is   een   anti-semiet,   die   men
    against   jews   and   is   a   anti-semite   who   INDEF.PRON
    straffeloos   zo   moet   mogen   noemen.
    unpunished   like_this   should.PRS.SG may.INF   call.INF
    'Who thinks like this 'is not fond of and is against jews' and is an anti-semite, whom one should be allowed to refer to as such without being punished.'
    (CHN, Essay 1995)

In addition, evaluative deontic *moeten* can concern a state of affairs in the past:

(8) [An accusation of murder]
    Ze   hadden   een   ander   doelwit   moeten   uitzoeken.
    they   have.PST.PL   a   different   target   must.INF   choose.INF

---

[5] In Olbertz and Gasparini Bastos (2013) this distinction has been referred to as one between "objective" and "subjective" deontic modality. However, given that "subjective deontic modality" is not subjective in the strict sense of the term, we prefer the labels "prescriptive" and "evaluative" here.

*Bram was niet schuldig.*⁶
Bram was not guilty.
'They should have chosen a different target. Bram was not guilty.'
(DRAPAC 61 LdW)

This does not mean that the obligation expressed by the modal concerns the past state of affairs, rather the state of affairs remains posterior to the modalization (Lyons 1977: 824). However, both the modalization and the state of affairs are anterior to the moment of speaking, i.e. the moment at which the evaluation takes place (Narrog 2008: 288).⁷ What (8) expresses is the speaker's opinion that in the past there was a necessity for the state of affairs *een ander doelwit uitzoeken* 'chose a different target' to occur, and that neither the modalization through *moeten* nor the state of affairs are real, as indicated by means of the pluperfect tense marking. Given the fact that the evaluation in (8) concerns a past state of affairs, we account for this use in FDG by making use of the "episode", which corresponds to (sets of) tensed states of affairs.

Let us now turn to the non-volitive semantic domain, where we will start again with participant-oriented modality working downwards toward the propositional modalization. The participant-oriented non-volitive necessity is basically inherent, that is to say, it finds its origin in physical or psychological needs of an animate individual, and does, indeed have a restricted applicability, including "nutrition and excretion", as Narrog (2012: 10) aptly remarks. But in Dutch it includes also weeping, yawning, and laughing as in the following example:

(9) *Anna,   even   alles   vergetend,   moest   lachen*
    Anna   for_a_bit   everything   forgetting   must.PST.SG   laugh.INF
    om   deze   zeldzame   vorm   van   bijgeloof   in_het_kwadraat.
    about   this   rare   form   of   superstition   squared
    'Anne, for a moment forgetting everything, couldn't help but laugh about this rare form of utter superstition.'
    (DRAPAC 36 TdL)

---

6 In (7) the past form of the auxiliary *hebben* 'have' one would normally require the past participle form of the auxiliary verb *moeten*, which does indeed exist, because Dutch modal verbs are not defective. However, the Dutch *moeten* has the infinitival form because it is followed by the infinitive of a main verb. In the combination with an infinitival full verb modal and aspectual verbs never have a participial form due to the rule *infinitivus pro participio*, which Dutch has in common with German (cf. e.g. IJbema 1997 for more details).
7 We are grateful to Heiko Narrog for pointing this out to us.

Turning to event-oriented necessity, we find circumstantial necessity as the non-volitive distinction at this level. As Narrog (2012: 10) observes, it is indeed difficult to find truly circumstantial cases of necessity which do not allow for a deontic reading, but they do exist: in the case quoted in the following example, the necessity depends on the rising sea level, an objective factor exterior to the event in question:

(10) *Volgens Van Ravenswaay is het [industriële] park*
 according_to Van Ravenswaay is the industrial park
 belangrijk vanwege de stijgende zeespiegel, waardoor
 important because_of the rising sea_level whereby
 sowieso moet worden uitgeweken naar het zuiden
 anyway must.PRS.SG AUX.INF swerved.PTCP to the south
 van het land.
 of the country
 'According to Van Ravenswaay the [industrial] park is important because of the rising sea level, due to which the park will have to be relocated to the South of the country anyway.'
 (CHN, Press 2010)

The remaining distinction to be discussed is subjective epistemic necessity, because we have not found any case of objective epistemic necessity expressed by *moeten*. Usually, objective epistemic necessity is expressed in Dutch by means of adjectival expressions. As opposed to subjective epistemic cases of *moeten*, objective epistemic *moeten* is motivated by objective calculations.[8]

---

[8] Occasionally, however, *moeten* can fulfil that function, too, as shown in the following example suggested to us by Kees Hengeveld (in 2015):
(i) *Hij is in januari 2000 geboren, dus hij moet nu 15 zijn.*
 he is in januari 2000 born so he must.PRS.SG now 15 be.INF
 'He was born in January 2000, so he must be 15 by now.'
At first glance, the concepts "objective" and "epistemic" seem to be incompatible, since "epistemic" generally presupposes the individual evaluation of the external world rather than a description of the external world. However, cases of objective epistemic *moeten*, such as the one exemplified here, are possible in situations in which the speaker – until the moment of speaking – did not realize that the given state of affairs is indeed necessarily the case.

Example (11) illustrates the expression of subjective epistemic necessity by means of *moeten*:

(11) *Bij   deze   woorden   kon   ik   een   glimlach, die*
     at   these   words   can.PST.SG   I   a   smile   which
     iets   zeer   kwetsends   moet   gehad   hebben,
     something   very   offensive   must.PRS.SG   had.PTCP   have.INF
     niet   onderdrukken.
     not   suppress.INF
     'At these words I couldn't suppress a smile, that must have had a very offensive effect.'
     (DRAPAC 18 ME)

Hengeveld (1988: 236–237) provides a number of tests for subjectivity, the most generally applicable ones are the following two: (i) subjectively modalized expressions are bound to declarative illocution, objectively modalized expressions are not, and (ii) subjectively modalized expressions cannot be contained in hypothetical sentences, objectively modalized expressions can. Now let us compare (11) to a (somewhat simplified) adjectival expression of the same content (12):

(12) *Het   is   waarschijnlijk   dat   de   glimlach   iets   zeer*
     it   is   probable   that   the   smile   something   very
     kwetsends   had.
     offensive   have.PST.SG
     'It is likely that the smile had a very offensive effect.'

When questioning both expressions, then (11a) is marginally acceptable as an echo question in reaction to (11), whereas (12a) is grammatical and acceptable without such a restriction.

(11) a. ??*Moet   de   glimlach   iets   zeer   kwetsends*
        must.PRS.SG   the   smile   something   very   offensive
        gehad   hebben?
        had.PTCP   have.INF
        'Must the smile have had a very offensive effect?'

(12) a. *Is   het   waarschijnlijk   dat   de   glimlach   iets   zeer*
        is   it   probable   that   the   smile   something   very
        kwetsends   had?
        offensive   have.PST.SG
        'Is it likely that the smile had a very offensive effect?'

Let us now apply the second test mentioned in (ii) above, which consists in using the subjective and the objective epistemic modal expressions in a conditional apodosis:

(11) b. ??*Als de glimlach iets zeer kwetsends gehad*
　　　　　if　the　smile　something　very　offensive　had.PTCP
　　　　　moet　　　　　hebben,　heb　　　　　ik　met　je　te　doen.
　　　　　must.PRS.SG　have.INF　have.PRS.1SG　I　with　you　to　do.INF
　　　　　'If the smile must have had a very offensive effect, I pity you.'

(12) b. *Als het waarschijnlijk is dat de glimlach iets*
　　　　　if　it　probable　　　is　that　the　smile　something
　　　　　zeer kwetsends had,　　　heb　　　　　ik　met　je
　　　　　very　offensive　have.PST.SG　have.PRS.1SG　I　with　you
　　　　　te doen.
　　　　　to do.INF
　　　　　'If it's likely that the smile had a very offensive effect, I pity you.'

Again, the subjective epistemic expression in (11b) is awkward, whereas the objective modal expression in the conditional clause in (12b) is fine. The conclusion is therefore that the epistemic use of *moeten* is virtually restricted to the subjective type, i.e. to the expression of the commitment to the truth of a proposition either by the speaker or a different subject referent.[9]

We have shown in this Section that *moeten* is able to express any kind of volitive and non-volitive distinction of modal necessity. As the volitive distinctions discussed here are all of a deontic nature, we will, henceforward, refer to the volitive domain as "deontic domain". The remainder of this paper will be dedicated exclusively to the deontic domain, which is the one that gave rise to the imperative-like *moet je* construction, which is the focus of this paper.

---

9 Although, as a general rule, the subject in such cases refers to the speaker, this is not necessarily the case:

(i)　*Volgens　　　Irene　moet　　　　zijn　algemene　indruk　　　wel　　　juist*
　　　according_to　Irene　must.prs.sg　his　general　　impression　indeed　correct
　　　zijn　　geweest.
　　　be.inf　been
　　　'According to Irene his general impression must have been correct.'

3 The diachrony of deontic *moeten*

In this section we will consider the diachronic semantic and syntactic development of deontic *moeten* with the first and foremost aim to find out if the predictions with regard to grammaticalization implied in Tab. 1 can be confirmed. In addition, we will also take a glance at the development of the independent, i.e. lexical variant of *moeten* in order to challenge Nuyts's (2011, 2013) claim. We will first present the relevant data in Section 3.1 and discuss these data in Section 3.2.

3.1 Diachronic data

This section will make use of the data provided in the four historical dictionaries of Dutch, made available online by the INT.[10] We will first look at the semantic development of *moeten* from the first attestations onward and then consider the development of lexical uses of *moeten*.

In the first attestations of Old Dutch (approx. 950–1150) *moeten* (in the form of *mozon*) primarily expressed participant-oriented possibility 'may':

(13) That   se   blîuen   mozon   in   [g]odes   riche.
     that   they   stay.INF   may.PRS.PL in   god.GEN   empire
     'That they may stay in God's empire.'
     (*Mittelfränkische Reimbibel*, 1151–1200, ONW)

This meaning of *moeten* can still be found in Middle Dutch (approx. 1200–1550):

(14) Die   man   bat   hem ...,   dat   hi   met   hem
     that   man   asked.PST.SG   him   that   he   with   him
     moeste   varen,   maer   Jhesus   ontseid   hem
     may.PST.SG   sail.INF   but   Jesus   forbid.PST.SG_it   him
     'This man asked him permission to sail with him but Jesus denied it.'
     (*Rijmbijbel*, ms 1300–1350?, MNW)

---

10 According to the information provided by the INT, The Old Dutch Dictionary (ONW) covers the period from ca. 500 to 1200, the Early Middle Dutch Dictionary (VMNW) the period from ca. 1200 to 1300, the Middle Dutch Dictionary (MNW) that from 1250 to 1550 and the Modern Dutch Dictionary (WNT) from 1500 to 1976 (however, the entry on *moeten* dates from 1907). Given the overlap between Early Middle Dutch and Middle Dutch, we will lump the two together under the heading of "Middle Dutch".

Most cases are similar to (14) in having specific human referents for the primary participant slot, and are therefore expressions of participant-oriented modality. However, in contexts of laws and instructions, *moeten* is also used with non-specific human referents, i.e. as an expression of event-oriented deontic possibility, as illustrated in (15):

(15) *Dat   men   voortaan   gheen   brandewijn   sal   moeten*
     that   one   henceforth   NEG   brandy   shall.PRS.SG   may.INF
     tappen
     serve.INF
     'That henceforth no brandy may be served'
     (*Wfr. Stadsrechten*, 1536, WNT)

In addition, this example is illustrative of the fact that from the 16th century onward *moeten* is used in the sense of deontic possibility only in the combination of *moeten* with some kind of negation.[11] As an expression of deontic possibility, *moeten* gradually comes to be substituted in early Modern Dutch by *mogen* 'may', which in Old Dutch had the exclusive function of expressing physical ability and was still relatively rare as an expression of deontic possibility in Middle Dutch (Duinhoven 1997: 409–410).

In addition to the strictly modal meanings, *moeten* had developed an optative function from Middle Dutch onward:

(16) *Onse   here   moete   met   u   wesen*
     our   lord   must.PRS.SUBJ.SG   with   you   be.INF
     'May our Lord be with you'
     (*Spiegel Historiael*, ca. 1350, MNW)

This optative function of *moeten* has been lost in the 18th century and is presently expressed by the subjunctive paradigm of the verb *mogen* 'may', which was infrequent in this function in Middle Dutch (Duinhoven 1997: 408).

We now turn to the first attestations of deontic necessity expressed by *moeten* in Medieval Dutch. As opposed to what we have seen so far, these are of the participant-oriented (17) as well as of the event-oriented (18) type, and there is no way of assessing which was first.

---

11 For an overview of diachronic changes between necessity and possibility in other languages, see Narrog (2012: 185–199), who emphasizes the role of negation in this process, as proposed by, among others, Goossens (1987) for English and Bech (1951) for German.

(17) Gi   muet   allene   [bute]n   staen.
     you   must.PRS.SG   alone   outside   stand.INF
     'You must stay outside alone.'
     (*Reinaert E*, 1276–1300, VMNW)

(18) sijn   aes   moet   sijn   uersch   ende   leuende
     its   bait   must.PRS.SG   be.INF   fresh   and   alive
     'its bait must be fresh and alive'
     (*Der Naturen Bloeme*, 1287, VMNW)

In the period between the 15th and the 18th centuries, deontic modality expressed by *moeten* gradually becomes predominantly an expression of deontic necessity. By then the participant-oriented is only a bit more frequent than event-orientation: out of the 17 unambiguous cases of deontic necessity, 10 are participant-oriented and 7 are event-oriented. Example (19) illustrates the former and (20) the latter:

(19) Sonder   sneven   moetti   mijn   hoge   gebod   volbringen
     without   hesitate.INF   must.PRS.SG_he   my   high   order   fulfil.
     'Unwaiveringly he must fulfil my high assignment'
     (*De sevenste bliscap van Maria*, 1445–1465, MNW)

(20) Men   moet   Gode   meer   gehoorsaem   zijn   dan
     one   must.PRS.SG   god   more   obediant   be.INF   than
     den   menschen
     the   men
     'One must be more subserviant to God more than to men'
     (*Statenbijbel*, 1688, WNT)

In 18th century Dutch, we also find cases of *moeten* in the evaluative deontic necessity function, which we classified as episode-oriented in Tab. 1 in Section 2. As mentioned earlier, evaluative deontic necessity modalizes either a modalized state of affairs or an anterior one. The latter is the case in the following example:

(21) Een   schurk,   die   al   lang   moest   zyn
     a   scoundrel   who   already   long   must.PST.SG   be.INF
     opgehangen   geworden,
     hanged.PTCP   AUX.PTCP
     'A scoundrel, who should have been hanged long ago,'
     (*Willem Leevend*, 1784–1785, WNT)

As regards the independent use of *moeten*, in Early Middle Dutch already *moeten* in its deontic necessity meaning can be used independently as long as directional movement is implied, such as illustrated in the following example:

(22) *Wi   moeten   int   helsce   vier.*
     we   must.PRS.PL   in_the   infernal fire
     'We must [go] into the infernal fire.'
     (*Rijmbijbel*, 1285, VMNW)

The use of independent *moeten* of the type illustrated in this example has become very frequent in Modern Dutch. As would be expected, independent *moeten* occurs primarily with human referents as primary arguments, a situation that remains basically unchanged in Middle Dutch.[12] In early stages of Modern Dutch (1500–today), however, we find independent uses of *moeten* in its deontic necessity meaning in (metaphorical) directional movement contexts, now more frequently with inanimate referents:

(23) *Daer   most   een   drinckpeningh   off*
     there   must.PRS.SG   a   gratuity   off
     'A gratuity must [be deducted] from it'
     (*Boere-klucht*, 1612, WNT)

About two hundred years later, there are also cases of event-oriented deontic modality that are unrelated to movement, where the first argument refers to an event rather than to an object:

(24) *Hij   zou   zeker...   trotsch   worden;   en   dat*
     he   would.SG   certainly   haughty   become.INF   and   that
     moet   niet
     must.PRS.SG   not
     'He would certainly become haughty and that must not [happen]'
     (*Maurits Lijnslager*, 1808, WNT)

---

12 However, in the examples quoted in VMNW, there are also two cases with non-animate referents, one of which is the following:
(i) *Want   alle   dinc   mu^{o}t   wi^{e}der   tu^{o}t   sinre   naturen*
    for   all   thing   must.PRS.SG   again   to   its   nature
    'For everything must [return] to its nature'
    (*Moraalboek*, 1270–1290)

In Modern Dutch, *moeten* can be used independently also in clear cases of evaluative deontic necessity:

(25) [*En je kunt nu eenmaal niet een vrijhandelsakkoord sluiten en daarbij bepaalde sectoren uitsluiten.* 'And you just cannot conclude a free trade agreement and at the same time exclude certain sectors.']
Maar   achteraf   bekeken   had   dat   misschien
but   from_back   viewed.PTCP   AUX.PST.SG that   perhaps
wel   gemoeten.
indeed   must.PTCP
'But looking back maybe this should have [happened] indeed.'
(CHN, Press, 2003)

Now we have seen five phenomena of diachronic change within the deontic domain of *moeten*: (i) the increasing prominence of deontic necessity meaning, (ii) the concomitant loss of the deontic possibility meaning, a process that was parallelled by (iii) the increasing use of *moeten* in other than participant-oriented functions, (iv) the loss of the optative, and (v) the gradual broadening in terms of different uses of *moeten* as a lexical verb.

3.2 Discussion

In this section we will start with the last case of diachronic change mentioned above, the expansion of *moeten* as an independent lexical verb, and then discuss the other changes.

Nuyts (2011: 161; 2013: 126) shows, on the basis of corpus analysis, that the independent use of *moeten* has increased between Old Dutch and Modern Dutch from 0% in Old Dutch to 5% in written Modern Dutch and 10.5% in spoken Modern Dutch. This ratio in Modern Dutch is confirmed by an analysis of a section (165,879 words) of our own written corpus. The semantic distribution yields the picture represented in Tab. 2. In addition, Tab. 2 shows that 94% of the independent uses of *moeten* express directional movement, and that almost all of these are directed towards specific human referents, i.e. are expressions of participant-oriented modality.

Tab. 2: Independent use of *moeten* in Modern Dutch literature (165,879 words).

Total *moeten*:	635		
	of which independent:	35 (5.57%)	
		of which directional movement:	33 (94.0%)
		of which participant-oriented:	30 (85.7%)

Nuyts (2011, 2013) proposes to view this process, as well as similar processes in the case of *kunnen* 'can' en *mogen* 'may', as one of "degrammaticalization", but he also shows that the case of the Dutch modals does not fit the concept of "degrammaticalization" as it stands. The most influential study of degrammaticalization, Norde (2009), defines the relevant type of "degrammation" as a shift (i) from grammatical to lexical content or (ii) from more grammatical to less grammatical content (Norde 2009: 133). Therefore, Nuyts (2011: 179–180; 2013: 132) introduces the concept of "primary degrammaticalization", which is supposed to account for cases of partial loss of auxiliary properties, irrespective of possible semantic changes.

Our hypothesis with respect to the rise of the independent lexical uses of *moeten* is, however, that deontic *moeten* was first lexicalized in the context of directional movement in participant-oriented contexts, where it would always be read as 'must go to', as in example (22). On analogy to the participant-oriented cases, lexical *moeten* would then also be used when the primary participant refers to an inanimate object as in (23), which becomes more frequent from the 17th century onward. Later on, on analogy to the movement cases, lexical *moeten* came to be used incidentally in non-movement contexts.[13] This means that there is just a gradual and analogical process of lexicalization, for which Nuyts does not provide anything but a new label.

As regards the semantic processes, the gradual expansion of deontic *moeten* in general to event-oriented and later episode-oriented contexts, which we have described in Section 3.1, confirms our expectations with regard to the increasing scope of *moeten*. However, this expectation is not borne out with respect to deontic necessity: in this context we would have expected *moeten* to start off with participant-orientation and then spread to event-orientation, but the fact is that both develop in parallel. A possible explanation may be related to the fact that the expression of deontic necessity was taken over from Old Dutch *sullan* 'shall' (Modern Dutch *zullen*), when this ceased to express deontic necessity and came to express future tense exclusively. The Old Dutch dictionary (ONW) entry of *sullan* mentions twelve cases of deontic necessity, ten of which are participant-oriented, one is event-oriented and one is doubtful. Another possible explanation may be in the very nature of deontic necessity: the source of deontic necessity probably more often is a "collective will" i.e. general rules rather than the will of an individual, and deontic necessity from a general source can be equally targeted to states of affairs and to participants in states of affairs.

A further aspect in the development of *moeten* that calls for an explanation is the loss of the optative function, which could in fact be analyzed as a true case of "degrammation" in Norde's (2009) terms, because the optative is

---

[13] For a diachronic study of this problem see Honselaar and Olbertz (2016).

generally regarded as a sentence type or sentence mood, to be associated with illocution rather than with modality (Levinson 1983: 42; Hengeveld 2004: 1191; Hengeveld and Mackenzie 2008: 71). We believe that the "retraction"[14] of *moeten* from the illocutionary domain can be explained through the loss of the function of deontic possibility. As we have seen, this was the most prominent function of *moeten* until the 15th century and most probably the source of the development of the optative (van der Auwera and Plungian 1998: 107, 112–113), the first occurrence of which dates from the 13th century. The most probable explanation of this process is the following: when the possibility function of *moeten* gradually gave way to the necessity function, the optative function shifted together with the expression of deontic possibility to the – by then innovative – modal auxiliary *mogen*.

As we will show in the next section, *moeten* has recently come to fulfil a new illocutionary function; this time it is one which is more in line with the semantic specialization of volitive *moeten* to the domain of deontic necessity.

4 A new illocutionary function of *moeten*

This section deals with the imperative-like construction with *moeten*, which we will preliminarily refer to as the *moet je* construction, exemplified in (3) in the introduction to this chapter, which we repeat here for convenience.

(3) Moet je horen wat ze nu weer
    must.PRS.SG you hear.INF what they now again
    bedacht hebben
    invented.PTCP AUX.PRS.PL
    'Now listen what they have been contrieving now!'
    (DRAPAC 20 AF)

Occasionally we find, instead of the informal second person pronoun, *je*, the neutral plural pronoun *jullie* or the rather formal singular pronoun *u*:

(26) [speaker wants primary schoolteachers to be experts in certain subjects rather than being generalists]
    Moet u zich eens voorstellen
    must.PRS.SG you.FORMAL REFL.2.FORMAL MIT imagine.INF

---

14 Haspelmath (2004: 33–35) defines "retraction" as a process consisting of the loss of manifestations of higher degrees of grammaticalization of a given lexical item.

wat	daar	voor	didactische	en	pedagogische	impuls
what	there	for	didactic	and	pedagogical	impulse

van uitgaat!
from emanate.PRS.SG

'Imagine what a didactic and pedagogical impulse this produces!'
(CHN, Press, 2003)

The *moet je* construction appears in the 20th century DRAPAC corpus from the 1940s onward. In the literature it has been mentioned in the 1950s already by Droste (1956: 33), who refers to this construction as 'invitation' and relates it to the imperative. Apart from this, the *moet je* construction has not received much attention in the literature on Dutch modals, with the notable exception of Janssen (2006).[15] Our aim in this section is to pin down the exact interactional function of the *moet je* construction, which obviously is similar but not equal to the imperative. This section will be organized as follows: in 4.1 we will present the form of the *moet je* construction and in 4.2 we will explain this form in relation to the function of this construction.

4.1 The form of the *moet je* construction vs the imperative

Like the imperative, the *moet je* construction is not tensed, which implies that *moeten* is obligatorily present tense marked (Droste 1956: 33; Janssen 2006: 337). Thus the past tense variant of (27a), namely (27b), is ungrammatical.

(27) a. [*Ik reed me daar op een avond door de Westgaag en opeens zag ik er een midden op de weg zitten. Ik probeerde nog af te remmen maar het was al te laat, hij sprong recht in mijn gezicht, zo van de grond af,* 'One evening I was cycling through the *Westgaag* and suddenly I saw one [a skunk] sitting in the middle of the street. I tried to brake but it was too late: he jumped right into my face, from the streetlevel,'

moet	je	nagaan,	terwijl	ik	op	een	hoge
must.PRS.SG	you	imagine.INF	while	I	on	a	high

fiets zat.
bicycle sat.PST.SG

'just imagine, while I was sitting high on a bicycle.'
(DRAPAC 29 MtH)

---

[15] Nuyts, Byloo and Diepeveen (2007: 167) quote an example of this construction and, without taking note of its specific properties, interpret it as a *sterk advies* 'strong piece of advice' (2007: 168). Nuyts (2011, 2013) does not mention the *moet je* construction at all.

b. *moest   je   nagaan,   terwijl   ik   op   een   hoge
   must.PST.SG   you   imagine.INF   while   I   on   a   high
   fiets   zat.
   bicycle   sat.PST.SG
   'just imagined, while I was sitting high on a bicycle.'

A second property that the *moet je* construction shares with the imperative is its addressee-orientation, i.e. the subject in the construction with *moeten* must always have a second person referent. Therefore the 1st person plural variant of (28a), i.e. (28b), is ungrammatical as it stands, although interpretable as a deontic question.

(28) a. [Talking about World War II: one of two imprisoned members of the Dutch resistance is telling how they passed their time talking about their work while waiting for their execution]
   Moet   je   je   voorstellen   hoe   we
   must.PRS.SG   you   REFL.2SG   imagine.INF   how   we
   daar   zaten
   there   sat.PST.PL
   'Just imagine how we were sitting there'
   (DRAPAC, 38 HM)
   b. *Moeten   we   ons   voorstellen   hoe   we
   must.PRS.PL   we   REFL.1PL   imagine.INF   how   we
   daar   zaten
   there   sat.PST.PL
   'Must we imagine how we were sitting there'

A third property the *moet je* construction shares with the imperative is the position of the finite verb, which must always be sentence initial. (29b), where the pronoun is in sentence initial position, is interpretable, but only as a declarative participant-oriented deontic expression.

(29) a. [During an interview, Pieter van den Hoogenband, Dutch swimming champion, shows the interviewer his first swimming certificate, gained at the age of five]
   Moet   je   dit   zien
   must.PRS.SG   you   this   see.INF
   'Just take a look at this'
   (CHN, Press, 2011)
   b. ≠*Je*   moet   dit   zien
   you   must.PRS.SG   this   see.INF
   'You must see this'

Now let us turn to the properties that distinguish the *moet je* construction from the imperative. First, the *moet je* construction must always contain a pronoun referring to the addressee: compare (30), which exemplifies the *moet je* construction, with the imperative in (31).

(30) a. *moet   je   hier   ruiken*
        must.PRS.SG you   here   sniff.INF
        'take a sniff at this!'
        (DRAPAC 27 MtH)
    b. **moet   hier   ruiken*
        must.PRS.SG   here   sniff.INF
        'must sniff at this'

(31) *Ruik   eens... dit   is de   geur   van   heiligheid.*
     sniff.IMP   MIT   this   is the   smell   of   sacredness
     'Just take a sniff ... this is the smell of sacredness.'
     (CHN, Press, 2011)

Secondly, the *moet je* construction allows only unstressed addressee pronouns (Droste 1956: 33) as shown in (32), while imperatives allow emphatic pronominal reference to the addressee for the exclusive purpose of contrastive focus marking (33).

(32) a. *Moet   je   eens   luisteren, Marco.*
        must.PRS.SG you   MIT   listen.INF Marco
        'Listen, Marco!'
        (CHN, Press, 2006)
    b. **Moet   jij   eens   luisteren, Marco.*
        must.PRS.SG you.EMPH   MIT   listen.INF Marco
        'Must you listen, Marco.'

(33) [—*Hoor nou eens even* ... 'Now just listen ...']
     — *Nee,   luister   JIJ   nou   eens   even!*
        no   listen.IMP   you.EMPH   PRT   MIT   MIT
     '— Now YOU just listen!'
     (E. Proper and S. van den Eynden, *Vals profiel*. 2010, internet)

Thirdly, the *moet je* construction is bound to positive polarity, as shown in (34a) and (34b), while imperatives may be negated as, can be gathered from example (35).

(34) a. *Moet   je   kijken!*
        must.PRS.SG you   look.INF
        'Look!'   (DRAPAC 38 HM)

b. *Moet   je   niet   kijken!
   must.PRS.SG you   not   look
   'Don't you want to look!'

(35) Kijk   niet   Eddy,   kijk   niet
     look.IMP not   Eddy   look.IMP not
     'Don't look, Eddy, don't look!'
     (CHN, *Van hier en daar en overal*, 1986)

Fourthly, the *moet je* construction does not admit a temporal modifier such as *morgen* 'tomorrow' in the state of affairs it has in its scope (36), while such a modification is possible in the case of imperatives (37).

(36) a. [*"Als lucht ben je onzichtbaar en overal.* ' "Being air, you are invisible and you are everywhere.']
        Moet   je   je   eens   indenken, eekhoorn."
        must.PRS.SG   you   REFL.2SG   MIT   imagine   squirrel
        'Just imagine, squirrel." '
        (DRAPAC 56 TT)
     b. *Moet   je   je   morgen   eens   indenken, eekhoorn.
        must.PRS.SG   you   REFL.2SG   tomorrow MIT   imagine   squirrel
        'Imagine tomorrow, squirrel." '

(37) Kom   morgen   maar   terug.
     come.IMP   tomorrow   MIT   back
     'Come back tomorrow.'
     (CHN, Press, 2004)

Finally, the use of the *moet je* construction is restricted to verbs of physical and mental perception, that of the imperative is not. Consider the imperative of the verb *come* in (38a) and the application of the same verb to the *moet je* construction in (38b), which yields an ungrammatical result.

(38) a. *"Henri,   kom   eens   hier   [..]" riep   hij.
        Henri   come.IMP   MIT   here   shouted.PST.SG   he
        ' "Henri, just come here [...]" he shouted.'
        (DRAPAC 48 GR)
     b. *Henri,   moet   je   eens   hier   komen
        Henri   must.PRS.SG   you   MIT   here   come.INF
        'Henri, must you just come here'

From the examples we have seen so far, we can gather that the lexical restriction is such that it allows for all kinds of perception; (i) visual: *zien, kijken* 'look' (cf. examples (29) and (34), respectively), (ii) auditive: *horen, luisteren* 'listen' (cf. examples (3) and (32), respectively), (iii) olfactory: *ruiken* 'sniff' (cf. example (30)), and (iv) mental: *nagaan*, reflexive *voorstellen* and reflexive *indenken* 'imagine' (cf. examples (27), (28), and (36), respectively).

In the following section, we will show that despite these numerous restrictions, the *moet je* construction can be viewed as a grammaticalized expression of an illocutionary distinction.

4.2 The function of the *moet je* construction: immediate perception imperative

We have shown in Section 4.1 that *moet je* behaves like a positive imperative requiring from the addressee the perception of some state of affairs. This perception, i.e. the perlocutionary effect of the imperative, needs to be realized immediately at utterance time, this is why temporal marking is excluded, hence "immediate perception" is required.

The impossibility to stress the addressee in this construction is related to the fact that there is obligatory focus marking elsewhere, i.e. on the element expressing the required perlocutionary effect. This may be the verb, as in the following example:

(39) *Moet   je   eens   KIJKEN*
     must.PRS.SG you   MIT   look.INF
     'Just LOOK!'
     (CHN, Press, 2005)[16]

However, whenever there is additional information present specifying the object to be perceived, such as the noun phrase *dit tolletje* 'this little tol' in the following example, then this element is in focus:

(40) *moet   je   DIT   TOLLETJE   zien*
     must.PRS.SG you   this   tol.DIM   see.INF
     'Look at THIS LITTLE TOL!'
     (CHN, Press, 2005)

Elements such as the noun phrase in (40), the demonstrative pronoun *dit* 'this' in example (29) and the locative adverb *hier* 'here' in example (30) always have

---

16 In this case, the verb is the only possible element to be stressed, because mitigating particles, such as *eens* in this case, cannot be stressed (Elffers 1997: 60). For the use of particles in Dutch imperatives and the like cf. Vismans (1994).

deictic reference to an entity present in the situation of the interaction. As a general rule, we can therefore establish that this construction always requires focus marking on the most focal element expressed in the construction.[17]

What we have not explained so far is the incompatibility of the *moet je* construction with negation. The function of this construction is to draw the attention of the interlocutor to something to be perceived, this attention drawing is a type of linguistic action, i.e. in terms of Hengeveld and Mackenzie (2008: 47) it is the realization of a "discourse act". As such it cannot be negated, very much in the same way as a performative speech act cannot be negated.

Given the properties described in this section, we will refer to this construction as the "immediate perception imperative".[18]

5 The grammaticalization of deontic *moeten*

In this section we will account for the diachronic development of deontic *moeten* and for its synchronic scope relations within the framework of Functional Discourse Grammar (Hengeveld and Mackenzie 2008, 2010), in which such a development can be accounted for in a straightforward way, as shown in Hengeveld (2011, this volume).

Functional Discourse Grammar (FDG) is conceived as a top-down layered model of the grammatical competence of speakers in view of verbal interaction as the main function of language. The highest components of the grammar consist of an interactional pragmatic and a semantic level, where the former governs the latter. Each of these components has an internal structure of

---

17 Janssen (2006) refers to the *moet je* construction as "focus construction". The situation becomes more complex in the case of mental perception, where, depending on a number of contextual factors either the object to be perceived or the verb can be in focus:
(i) *moet*   *je*   *je*   MIJN   SITUATIE   *eens*   *voorstellen!*
     must.PRS.SG   you   REFL.1SG   my   situation   MIT   imagine.INF
     'Just imagine MY SITUATION!'
(ii) *moet*   *je*   *je*   *mijn* *situatie* *eens*   VOORSTELLEN!
     must.PRS.SG   you   REFL.1SG   my   situation   MIT   imagine.INF
     'Just IMAGINE my situation!'
Obviously, prosodic factors play an important role in the pragmatics of the *moet je* construction, but we will not go into details here. We are indebted to Cecilia Odé for discussion and suggestions in this field.
18 This post-modal development confirms the unproven claim made by Bybee, Perkins and Pagliuca (1994: 210) that deontic necessity can develop into imperativity; see also van der Auwera and Plungian (1998: 96) and Narrog (2012: 159–160, this volume).

hierarchical layers that corresponds to linguistic scope relations. We have seen the internal structure of the semantic level ("representational level" in Functional Discourse Grammar) on the vertical axis in Tab. 1: (i) participant-oriented modality operates on the predicate and its arguments ("configurational property" in FDG), (ii) event-oriented modality operates on the state of affairs, (iii) episode-oriented modality operates on (a set of) states of affairs that can be freely located in time, (iv) proposition-oriented modality operates on a propositional content, which can be located in neither time nor space but can be evaluated in terms of truth.

The interactional pragmatic level is called the "interpersonal level" in FDG and has a hierarchical structure, too. The highest layer is the individual "discourse act", which may or may not equal a clause. The discourse act basically consists of the illocution and the content to be communicated.[19]

In the representations given in Tabs. 3 and 4, the interpersonal level is abbreviated as IL and the representational level as RL. Within each level, the relevant internal hierarchical layers are given, and the arrows indicate the expected direction of change. The boldfaced layers and arrows correspond to the changes that have actually taken place. The modal meanings are given in italics and the numbers refer to the example(s) given for each type in the course of this paper.

Table 3 represents the Medieval development of *moeten* as an expression of deontic possibility, before these meanings definitively shifted to the modal *mogen* in the 18th century.

Tab. 3: Historical development of *moeten* in the function of deontic possibility (12th–18th c.).

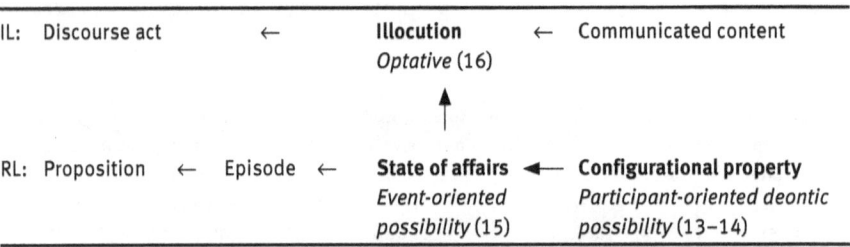

The case of *moeten* as an expression of deontic necessity, represented in Tab. 4, is different for the simple reason that a more differentiated development has taken place within the – semantic – representational level.

---

[19] For more details on the theory of Functional Discourse Grammar, see Giomi (this volume).

Tab. 4: Historical development of *moeten* in de function of deontic necessity (13th–20th c.).

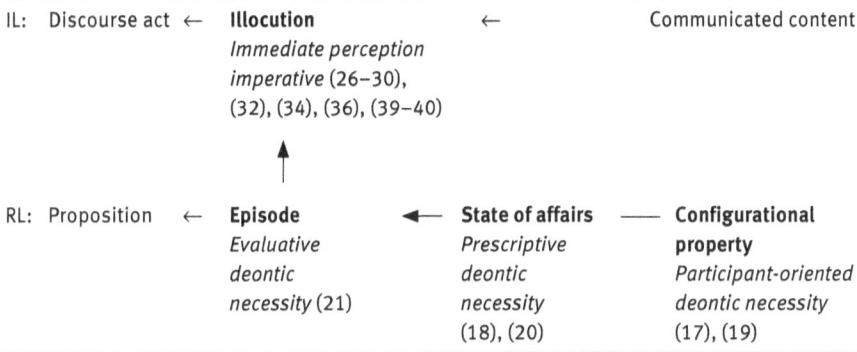

A further important point of divergence is that in this case the diachronic data do not reflect any historical development from participant-oriented modality to event-oriented modality, which is marked by the fact that there is no arrow but a dash between the configurational property and the state of affairs. Nevertheless, the mutual ordering of these elements correctly reflects the fact that despite of the lack of diachronic evidence, there is a synchronic scope relation between participant-oriented and event-oriented modality such that the latter scopes over the former, rather than the other way round.

This analysis provides additional evidence for the development of grammaticalization within and across levels in Functional Discourse Grammar (Hengeveld this volume).

6 Conclusion

In this paper we have shown that in Modern Dutch *moeten* expresses all kinds of deontic and non-deontic modal meanings, among which objective epistemic modality is rather marginal. Modern Dutch *moeten* also has a lexical version, which we interpret as a case of lexicalization, rather than degrammaticalization. Viewed from a diachronic perspective, deontic *moeten* developed twice from semantics proper to the domain of illocution: in Medieval Dutch it developed from deontic possibility to optative illocution, and in 20th century Dutch it developed from deontic necessity to imperative illocution, giving rise to the "immediate perception imperative". Although the results of the first development shifted in the 18th century to a new expression, i.e.

mogen 'may', both developments are interesting cases of what according to Narrog (2012: 160) "can be taken as a paradigm example of increased speech act orientation." Narrog (2012, this volume) presents quite a number of similar diachronic changes. Whereas Narrog prefers to represent these changes with the emphasis on their graduality, we have chosen the Functional Discourse Grammar approach (Hengeveld this volume) which emphasizes the stepwise hierarchical layering to be observed in the development of *moeten* from both a synchronic and a diachronic perspective.

Uncommon abbreviations

DIM = diminutive, EMPH = emphasis, FDG = Functional Discourse Grammar, IL = interpersonal level, INT = Institute for the Dutch Language, MIT = mitigation, PRT = particle, RL = representational level.

Corpora

[CHN] *Corpus Hedendaags Nederlands*. Leiden: Institute for Dutch Lexicology (INL).
    https://portal.clarin.inl.nl/search/page/search (accessed 14 January 2015)
[DRAPAC] *Dutch-Russian Amsterdam Parallel Aligned Corpus*. Amsterdam: Department of Slavic Studies, University of Amsterdam.
[MNW] *Middelnederlandsch Woordenboek*. Leiden: Institute for the Dutch Language (INT).
    http://gtb.inl.nl/ (accessed 14 April 2014)
[ONW] *Oudnederlands Woordenboek*. Leiden: Institute for the Dutch Language (INT).
    http://gtb.inl.nl/ (accessed 14 April 2014)
[VMNW] *Vroegmiddelnederlands Woordenboek*. Leiden: Institute for the Dutch Language (INT).
    http://gtb.inl.nl/ (accessed 14 April 2014)
[WNT] *Woordenboek der Nederlandsche Taal*. Leiden: Institute for the Dutch Language (INT).
    http://gtb.inl.nl/ (accessed 14 April 2014)

References

Bech, Gunnar. 1951. Grundzüge der semantischen Entwicklungsgeschichte der hochdeutschen Modalverba. *Historisk-filologiske meddelelser* 32(6). 1–28.
Bybee, Joan, Revere Perkins & William Pagliuca. 1994. *The evolution of grammar. Tense, aspect, and modality in the languages of the world*. Chicago & London: The University of Chicago Press.
Droste, Flip G. 1956. *Moeten. Een structureel semantische studie*. Groningen & Djakarta: J. B. Wolters.
Duinhoven, A. F. 1997. *Middelnederlandse syntaxis synchroon and diachroon*. Vol. 2. *De werkwoordgroep*. Groningen: Martinus Nijhoff.
Elffers, Els. 1997. De onaccentueerbaarheid van modale partikels. In Els Elffers, Joop van der Horst & Willem G. Klooster (eds.), *Grammaticaal spektakel*. 59–70. Amsterdam: Vakgroep Nederlandse Taalkunde.

Giomi, Riccardo. This volume. The interaction of components in a Functional Discourse Grammar account of grammaticalization.

Goossens, Louis. 1987. Modal tracks: the case of *magan* en *motan* In Anne-Marie Simon-Vandenbergen (ed.), *Studies in honour of René Derolez*, 216–236. Ghent: Universiteit Gent.

Haspelmath, Martin. 2004. On directionality in language change with particular reference to grammaticalization. In Olga Fischer, Muriel Norde & Harry Perridon (eds.), *Up and down the cline – the nature of grammaticalization* (Typological studies in language 59), 17–44. Amsterdam & Philadelphia: John Benjamins.

Heine, Bernd. 1995. Agent-oriented vs. epistemic modality: some observations on German modals. In Joan Bybee & Suzanne Fleischman (eds.), *Modality in grammar and discourse* (Typological studies in language 32), 17–53. Amsterdam & Philadelphia: John Benjamins.

Hengeveld, Kees. 1988. Illocution, mood and modality in a Functional Grammar of Spanish. *Journal of Semantics* 6. 227–269.

Hengeveld, Kees. 2004. Illocution, mood and modality. In Geert Booij, Christian Lehmann & Joachim Mugdan (eds.), *Morphology: a handbook on inflection and word formation*. II, 1190–1202. Berlin & New York: Mouton de Gruyter.

Hengeveld, Kees. 2011. The grammaticalization of tense and aspect. In Bernd Heine & Heiko Narrog (eds.), *The Oxford handbook of grammaticalization*. 580–594. Oxford: Oxford University Press.

Hengeveld, Kees. This volume. A hierarchical approach to grammaticalization.

Hengeveld, Kees & J. Lachlan Mackenzie. 2008. *Functional Discourse Grammar: a typologically-based theory of language structure*. Oxford: Oxford University Press.

Hengeveld, Kees & J. Lachlan Mackenzie. 2010. Functional Discourser Grammar. In Bernd Heine & Heiko Narrog (eds.), *The Oxford handbook of linguistic analysis*. 367–400. Oxford: Oxford University Press.

Honselaar, Wim & Hella Olbertz. 2016. The use of Dutch *moeten* without an infinitive: a case of degrammaticalization? In: Anne Bannink & Wim Honselaar (eds.), *From variation to iconicity. Festschrift for Olga Fischer on the occasion of her 65th birthday*. 185–201. Amsterdam: Pegasus.

IJbema, Aniek. 1997. Der IPP-Effekt im Deutschen und Niederländischen. *Groninger Arbeiten zur germanistischen Linguistik* 40. 137–168

Janssen, Theo A. J. M. 2006. Focusconstructies als *kijk eens* en *moet je eens kijken*. *Nederlandse Taalkunde* 11(4). 332–365.

Jespersen, Otto. 1924. *The philosophy of grammar*. London: G. Allen & Unwin.

Laca, Brenda. 2014. Epistemic modality and temporal anchoring. *Revista virtual de estudos da linguagem*. Special issue 8. 76–103.

Levinson, Stephen C. 1983. *Pragmatics*. Cambridge: Cambridge University Press.

Lyons, John. 1977. *Semantics*. Cambridge: Cambridge University Press.

Mortelmans, Tanja, Kasper Boye & Johan van der Auwera. 2009. Modals in the Germanic languages. In Björn Hansen & Ferdinand de Haan (eds.), *Modals in the languages of Europe: a reference work* (Empirical approaches to language typology 44), 11–69. Berlin & New York: Mouton de Gruyter.

Narrog, Heiko. 2005. Modality, mood, and change of modal meanings: a new perspective. *Cognitive Linguistics* 16(4). 677–731.

Narrog, Heiko. 2008. The aspect modality-link in the Japanese verbal complex and beyond. In Werner Abraham & Elisabeth Leiss (eds.) *Modality–aspect interfaces. Implications and typological solutions* (Typological studies in language 79), 279–307. Amsterdam & Philadelphia: John Benjamins.

Narrog, Heiko. 2012. *Modality, subjectivity, and semantic change. A cross-linguistic perspective*. Oxford: Oxford University Press.
Narrog, Heiko. This volume. Relationship of form and function in grammaticalization: the case of modality.
Norde, Muriel. 2009. *Degrammaticalization*. Oxford: Oxford University Press.
Nuyts, Jan. 2011. Degrammaticalisatie van de Nederlandse modale hulpwerkwoorden. *Verslagen & mededelingen van de Koninklijke Academie van de Nederlandse taal- en letterkunde* 121(2). 155–182.
Nuyts, Jan. 2013. De-auxiliarization without de-modalization in Dutch core modals: a case of degrammaticalization? *Language Sciences* 36. 124–133.
Nuyts, Jan. 2014. Zelfstandig gebruikte modalen: een functioneel perspectief. *Nederlandse Taalkunde* 19(3). 351–373.
Nuyts, Jan, Pieter Byloo & Janneke Diepeveen. 2007. *Mogen* en *moeten* en de relaties tussen deontische modaliteit en modus. *Nederlandse Taalkunde* 12(2). 153–174.
Olbertz, Hella & Sandra Gasparini Bastos. 2013. Objective and subjective deontic modal necessity in FDG: evidence from Spanish modal auxiliary expressions. In J. Lachlan Mackenzie & Hella Olbertz (eds.), *Casebook in Functional Discourse Grammar*, 277–300. Amsterdam & Philadelphia: John Benjamins.
Palmer, F. R. 2001. *Mood and modality*, 2nd ed. Cambridge: Cambridge University Press.
van der Auwera, Johan & Vladimir A. Plungian. 1998. Modality's semantic map. *Linguistic Typology* 2. 79–124.
Vismans, Roel. 1994. *Modal particles in Dutch directives. A study in Functional Grammar*. Amsterdam: IFOTT.

Name index

Abraham, Werner 268
Adams, J. N. 195, 196, 204
Adelaar, Alexander 120, 122
Andersen, Henning 208, 209, 210
Anderson, Gregory D. S. 168
Anduganov Ju. V. 149
Ansaldo, Umberto 30, 82
Arends, Jacques 116
Ariel, Mira 105
Askedal, John Ole 242, 243, 247, 248, 259, 264–266
Audibert-Gibier, Monique 266
Auwera, Johan van der 85, 273, 274, 289, 295

Bakker, Dik 3, 30
Bartens, Raija 134
Bartholomae, Christian 165
Bech, Gunnar 284
Benveniste, Emile 58, 165
Bertinetto, Pier Marco 243, 247, 252, 254
Bessler, Paul 265
Bhat, D. N. Shankara 242, 256, 268
Bisang, Walter 4, 30, 80, 82, 210
Bobillon, Jean-Marc 245
Boland, Annerieke 14, 44, 65
Bolinger, Dwight 46
Borges, Robert 111, 126–128
Börjars, Kersti 105
Bourova, Viara 195
Boye, Kasper 3, 31, 45, 273, 274
Brems, Lieselotte 22
Brissaud, Catherine 266
Bugaeva, Anna 153
Buscha, Joachim 253
Butler, Christopher S. 40
Bybee, Joan L. 3, 6, 14, 18, 24, 30, 40, 47, 58, 64, 76, 79, 82, 89, 99, 101, 104, 106, 142, 145, 168, 204, 210, 216, 219, 221, 222, 226, 232, 242, 243, 247–252, 254, 255, 259, 264, 268, 295
Byloo, Pieter 290

Carlin, Eithne B. 116
Caudal, Patrick 243, 250–253
Cinque, Guglielmo 14, 94
Clark, Robin 79
Cogis, Danièle 266
Cohn, Abigail C. 116
Collinder, Björn 140, 153
Company Company, Concepción 196, 197
Comrie, Bernard 47, 120, 142, 181, 182, 206, 227, 242, 244, 251
Confais, Jean-Paul 243, 253, 261
Conners, Thomas J. 118, 122
Connolly, John H. 49
Contini-Morava, Ellen 55
Cornish, Francis 49
Croft, William 204
Csepregi, Márta 142
Cuvalay-Haak, Martine 44
Cuyckens, Hubert 154

Dahl, Östen 47, 181, 218, 219, 242, 243, 246, 250, 252–256, 259
Dasher, Richard B. 39, 40, 47, 53, 84, 134
Davari, Shadi 3, 7, 9, 163, 184
Davidse, Kristin 22
Dehghan, Iraj 165
Denison, David 22
Diepeveen, Janneke 290
Diewald, Gabriele 82
Dik, Simon C. 2, 40, 44, 92, 95, 250
Donner, Kai 149
Dossena, Marina 58, 61
Drinka, Bridget 243, 250
Droste, Flip G. 290, 292
Dudas, Karen Marie 116
Duinhoven, A. F. 284
Durán Urrea, Evelyn 216, 220

Elffers, Els 294
Erdal, Marcel 148
Evans, Nicholas 6, 135, 154, 205
Ewing, Michael C. 118

Fleischman, Suzanne 203, 205, 216–220, 223, 237
Foley, William A. 14, 40
Fox, Anthony 134

García Castillero, Carlos 194, 198
Garey, Howard B. 244
Gasparini-Bastos, Sandra 44, 278
Geis, Michael L. 46
Gelderen, Elly van 3, 45, 78, 93, 105
Genee, Inge 202, 203
Ghesquière, Lobke 22
Ghomeshi, Jila 168
Giannakidou, Anastasia 68
Gil, David 118, 119
Giomi, Riccardo 3, 5, 8, 296
Gipper, Sonja 149
Givon, Talmy 172
Godel, Robert 209
Goossens, Louis 80, 284
Gotti, Maurizio 58, 59
Gradoville, Michael 216, 220
Grández Ávila, Magaly 19, 20, 25
Greenberg, Joseph 6
Grice, Paul 46, 53
Gutiérrez, Manuel 216, 220

Haase, Martin 194
Hagoort, Pieter 117
Hajdú, Péter 137, 145, 149–152
Hanazono, Satoru 81
Hanenberg, Stanley 121
Harder, Peter 3, 31, 45
Haspelmath, Martin 105, 208, 289
Hattnher, Marize Mattos Dall'Aglio 17, 50, 136, 137, 150
Hedin, Eva 242, 246, 252, 254, 255
Heine, Bernd 4, 6, 9, 24, 39, 40, 47, 48, 50, 51, 52, 54, 55, 56, 63, 76, 78, 82, 103, 104, 105, 164, 168, 169, 172, 173, 178, 181, 184, 185, 187, 192, 206, 207, 229, 231, 276
Helbig, Gerhard 253
Helimski, Eugene 140, 143, 144, 148, 149
Hengeveld, Kees 5–8, 13–15, 17, 18, 21–23, 39–46, 49–51, 55, 58, 92, 95, 112, 114, 115, 126, 129, 134, 137, 141, 142, 150, 192, 207, 217, 221–223, 236, 237, 246, 247, 250, 269, 273, 275, 276, 277, 280, 281, 289, 295–298
Himmelmann, Nikolaus P. 118
Hirayama, Teruo 88
Honselaar, Wim 7, 8, 288
Hopper, Paul J. 3, 45, 76, 83, 134, 178

IJbema, Anniek 279

Jalava, Lotta 6, 135, 137, 138, 140, 142, 146, 147
Janhunen, Juha 134, 138, 143, 148, 153, 156
Janssen, Theo 290, 295
Jespersen, Otto 84, 276
Johanson, Lars 142
Johnson, Mark 169
Joseph, Brian D. 208, 209

Kagan, Olga 115
Kailuweit, Rolf 40, 45
Kaltenböck, Gunther 103
Keizer, M. Evelien 14, 21, 24, 30, 31, 44, 45, 206
Kent, Ronald G. 148, 170, 171
Kerslake, Celia
Killie, Kristin 179
Kim-Renaud, Young-Key 81
Kiparsky, Paul 105
Klein, Wolfgang 242, 243, 244, 246
Koefoed, Geert 208
König, Ekkehard 47
Kroon, Sjaak 117
Krug, Manfred 24
Künnap, Ago 153
Kuteva, Tania 4, 24, 28, 51, 54, 56, 78, 82, 104, 168, 172, 181, 184, 192, 206

Labanauskas, Kazys 134, 135, 138, 140, 142, 143, 145–147, 150, 152
Lakoff, George 169
Lambton, Ann K.S. 168, 181
Lamiroy, Béatrice 82
Langacker, Ronald W. 83
LaPolla, Randy J. 40, 92, 94
Lastra, Yolanda 220
Leeman-Bouix, Danielle 264, 265
Lehmann, Christian 24, 30, 46, 76, 77, 106

Leinonen, Marja 142
Leiss, Elisabeth 7, 242–244, 248–251, 255
Lester, Leland A. 58
Lestiono, Riski 122
Leufkens, Sterre 202, 203, 204
Levinson, Stephen 289
Lewis, M. Paul 116
Lim, Lisa 30, 82
Lindstedt, Jouko 142, 242, 243, 247, 249, 252, 255
Lope Blanch, Juan M. 220
Loporcaro, Michele 265, 266
Lyons, John 76, 279
Lyublinskaya, M. D 140

Mackenzie, J. Lachlan 13, 14, 17, 24, 39–44, 46, 49–51, 55, 58, 92, 114, 169, 192, 207, 221, 277, 289, 295, 296
Malchukov, Andrej L. 134, 135, 140, 143, 145, 149, 154, 156
Marchello-Nizia, Christiane 265
Markopoulos, Theodore 64
Marle, Jaap van 208
Martín Butragueño, Pedro 220
Maslova, Elena 105
Matasović, Ranko 45
Matras, Yaron 112, 113, 115, 127
Matthews, George Hubert 14
McCone, Kim 192, 200
McQuillan, Peter 203
Mikola, Tibor 134, 138, 144, 148, 149, 152, 153, 154, 155
Moreno de Alba, José 220
Mortelmans, Tanja 273, 274
Mulder, Walter de 82
Muysken, Pieter 111
Myhill, John 118

Naghzguy-Kohan, Mehrdad 163, 181, 184
Narrog, Heiko 2, 4, 6–9, 14, 18, 30, 45, 76, 77, 81, 83, 84–95, 101–103, 134, 135, 138, 141, 149, 155, 163, 164, 179, 183, 184, 204, 208, 209, 229, 231, 273, 275, 276, 279, 280, 284, 295, 298
Nicolle, Steve 45, 105
Nikolaeva, Irina 137
Norde, Muriel 103, 288

Nuyts, Jan 44, 273–275, 283, 287, 288, 290
Nykiel, Jerzy 2

Ó Baoill, Dónall 203
Odé, Cecilia 295
Olbertz, Hella 7, 8, 17, 24–26, 29, 44, 278, 288

Pagliuca, William 18, 64, 204, 210, 243, 295
Palmer, F. R. 76, 276
Perkins, Revere D. 18, 64, 204, 210, 243, 295
Perrot, Jean 152
Pinkster, Harm 218, 219
Polinsky, Maria 115
Pollock, Jean-Yves 14

Quirk, Randolph 58, 96

Ravindranath, Maya 116
Rebotier, Aude 5, 7, 253, 256, 266
Reesink, Ger P. 4
Reh, Mechthild 4, 76, 78, 207, 210
Rhee, Seongha 81
Riegel, Martin 261
Rijn, Marlou van 3, 30
Rizzi, Luigi 14
Robbeets, Martine 135, 154, 156
Roberts, Ian 3, 45, 78, 79, 83, 93, 105
Robson, Stuart 116, 118, 119, 120
Rocci, Andrea 65
Róna-Tas, András 148
Roussou, Anna 3, 45, 83, 93, 105

Sakel, Jeanette 113, 115, 127
Salminen, Tapani 136–138, 140, 145, 150, 151, 153
Saltveit, Laurits 255
Schaden, Gerhard 243
Schanen, François 261
Schecker, Michael 255
Schotel, Henk 117
Schwenter, Scott A. 28
Sedano, Mercedes 216
Siegl, Florian 140, 143, 148
Siewierska, Anna 3, 30
Skjærvø, Prods O. 169–171

Smit, Niels 207
Souza, Edson Rosa Francisco de 23, 45
Squartini, Mario 243, 247, 252, 254
Stassen, Leon 172, 173
Stolz, Thomas 104
Storms, G. 179
Sweetser, Eve 22

Tabor, Whitney 45
Taleghani, H. Azita 167
Tena Dávalos, Jimena 8
Terent'ev, V. A. 148
Tereščenko, N. M. 135, 140, 146, 147, 152, 153
Thieroff, Rolf 193, 246, 250, 252, 253, 258, 262, 263
Thompson, Sandra 79
Thurneysen, Rudolf 192, 200, 201, 203
Traugott, Elizabeth Closs 3, 18, 30, 39, 40, 45, 47, 53, 58, 61, 76, 83, 84, 104, 134, 178

Van Valin, Robert D. jr. 14, 40, 92, 94
Vander Klok, Jozina 118, 119, 120, 122, 128
Velde, Freek van de 34
Vendler, Zeno 180, 242, 244, 247
Verbov, G. D. 142, 148
Vet, Co 44, 246, 253
Vetters, Carl 243, 250–253
Villerius, Sophie 8
Vincent, Nigel 105, 204
Vismans, Roel 294
Visser, Fredericus T. 58
Vovin, Alexander 149
Vruggink, Hein 116, 117, 122

Wagner-Nagy, Beáta 140, 143, 148
Waldenfels, Ruprecht von 63
Walker, Jim 252
Wanders, Gerry 22, 23, 45
Weber, Hans 243, 254
Wilmet, Marc 261, 265
Windfuhr, L. Gernot 168
Wolfowitz, Clare 117, 118
Wrenn, Charles Leslie 58
Wurzel, Wolfgang Ulrich 208

Yagmur, Kutlay 117
Yakpo, Kofi 121, 128
Yllera, Alicia 220
Yuzawa, Kōkichirō 90
Zhukovski, Valentin A. 165
Zifonun, Gisela 244–246, 261
Zwicky, Arnold M. 46

Language index

Ainu 153
Ancient Greek 63
Armenian 203, 208–209

Bulgarian 66, 209-210
Basque 145, 172, 193

Chamus 56

Dutch 7, 8, 10, 112, 117, 122, 123, 127, 128, 130, 273–298

Enets languages 140–141, 143, 148, 152, 153, 157
Enets, Forest 142–143, 148
English 5, 18, 21, 24, 31, 43, 56–59, 61, 63, 67, 69, 76, 79, 82, 86, 93, 95, 116, 117, 119, 140, 145, 165, 172, 175, 191, 192, 193, 202–207, 210, 222, 223, 244, 252, 259, 264, 269, 273, 274, 284
Éven 145, 149

French 5, 7, 10, 165, 218, 219, 241–270

German 5, 7, 10, 165, 241–270, 273, 274, 279, 284
Germanic 9, 10, 200, 210, 243, 248, 259, 265, 266, 273–274
Gothic 243

Hidatsa 14, 15

Indonesian Javanese 112, 116, 120–128

Japanese 1, 7, 8, 75–103, 135, 149, 208
Javanese 8, 9, 111–130

Kamass 149
Khanty 142
Komi 142
Korean 80–81

Late Latin 191–196, 203–205, 221
Latin 6, 10, 194, 197, 217, 218, 224, 248, 249, 250, 253, 268

Mansi 142
Middle English 58–61
Middle Persian 165–167, 169, 171
Modern Greek 56, 63–69
Modern Irish 191–194, 203, 206, 207, 210
Modern Persian 165–187

Nenets languages 140–141, 143, 148, 151–153, 157
Nenets, Forest 142, 148, 153
Nenets, Tundra 6, 9, 133–157
Nganasan 143, 148, 152, 157

Old English 57–58, 79
Old High German 243, 248–250, 259
Old Irish 6, 9, 191, 192, 195, 197–205, 208, 209
Old Persian 165, 170, 171
Old Spanish 9, 191–193, 196, 203, 210

Portuguese 23
Proto-Samoyedic 138, 139, 141–143, 148–149, 152–155

Romance 6, 9, 10, 191–194, 196, 197, 203–208, 210, 217–220, 224, 237, 243, 248, 250, 259, 265–268
Russian 140, 165, 209

Samoyedic languages 134–157
Selkup 143, 149, 153, 157
Slavic languages 66, 243, 255, 256
Spanish 6, 7, 8, 9, 18, 25–29, 42, 193, 196, 203, 212, 215–237, 267
Spanish, Ecuadorian Highland 26, 28–29
Spanish, Mexican 8, 9, 215–237
Spanish, Pensinsular 28–29
Sranan Tongo 111, 112, 117, 122–123, 126–128, 130
Surinamese Dutch 127, 128, 130
Surinamese Javanese 111–130
Swahili 50–55
Swedish 274

Tatar 149
Tok Pisin 55–57, 69
Tswana 56
Tungusic languages 145, 149
Turkic languages 148
Turkish 142

Udmurt 142
Uralic languages 133, 135–138, 142–143, 149, 156, 157

Yurakaré 149

Zulu 56

Subject index

absolute tense 7, 17, 18, 27, 114, 215, 217, 222–224, 231, 232, 234–236
absolute time 17
achievement 163–164, 180–183, 244
aktionsart *see* lexical aspect
approximation 17, 24, 96, 97
areal influences 205, 206
aspect 1, 4, 7, 8, 9, 10, 14, 27, 44, 95, 99, 111–114, 120–122, 128–129, 164, 168, 169, 178, 179, 180, 181, 184, 185, 186, 222–223, 242, 243, 247, 254–263, 267–269 *see also* durative, habitual, inchoative, imperfective, iterative, perfect, perfective, phasal aspect, progressive aspect, prospective aspect, proximative aspect, resultative
assumed information 17, 23, 29, 31, 42, 43, 49, 50, 53, 55, 56, 61, 69, 82, 105, 133, 136, 140, 146, 153, 183, 255, 277, 283, 294
auditive 135–137, 152–157, 294
auxiliary 'be' 261, 262, 263, 264, 265, 268
auxiliary 'have' 250, 260, 261, 263, 265, 266, 267
auxiliation 163, 164, 169, 176, 177, 184–187
Auxiliation Dimension Model 169, 184, 185, 187
auxiliation force 185, 186
auxiliation source 185–187

borrowability 113, 130
borrowability hierarchy 111
borrowing 113, 115, 122, 129, 149
bridging context 9, 47, 48, 50–54, 57, 60, 64–67, 70

category climbing 91
causal clauses 16, 23, 98, 118, 119, 121, 135, 140, 141, 144, 154, 155, 157, 175, 176, 192, 204, 205, 207, 211
conative modality 122, 127, 130
Conceptual Component 41, 42, 49, 53, 55, 60, 62
conceptual metaphor 169

conditional 16, 85, 98, 282
conditional verb form 6, 9, 191–211
    see also future-in-the-past
context generalization 54, 78, 82, 155
Contextual Component 39–43, 48–55, 70
conventionalization 39, 40, 46–55, 63, 69, 70

decategorialization 78, 80, 81
declarative 23, 164, 167–168, 186, 199, 281, 291
degrammaticalization 75, 102, 103, 105, 106, 273, 274, 275, 287–288, 298
deontic modality 44, 93, 95, 96, 98–101, 157, 274, 276, 277, 278, 285–286
direct non-visual evidential 137, 152 *see* auditive
domain of modal evaluation 276
durative 163, 180, 182, 187

epistemic modality 19, 20, 65–68, 94–101, 115, 192, 216–219, 224–226, 229–237, 273
epistemic modality, objective 17, 20, 114, 273, 276, 298
epistemic modality, subjective 17, 20, 63, 114, 222, 276
evidential 6, 9, 89–90, 96, 98, 103, 133–157, 182–184 *see also* auditive, indirect evidentiality, inferential evidentiality, reportative, similative evidential

facultative modality 19–20, 58, 276
Functional Discourse Grammar 5, 8, 9, 10, 13–15, 39–41, 92, 114, 191–192, 206, 207, 210, 215, 217, 221–223, 236, 273–275, 296–298
functional merger 191
future 6, 8, 9, 18, 27, 33, 34, 41, 51, 56–58, 61–67, 81, 89, 94, 113, 114, 119, 120, 121, 124, 125, 128, 130, 133, 137–139, 142–146, 150, 156, 157, 183, 184, 186, 191–197, 200–206, 207, 209, 211, 215–237, 243, 255, 256, 288

future, analytic 215, 217, 220, 224, 227, 230, 231, 232, 233, 234, 235, 236
future, synthetic 9, 215, 218, 219, 220, 224, 225, 229, 230, 232, 236, 237
future-in-the-past 61, 191, 192, 194, 195, 196, 203, 204, 205, 207–211

generalized invited inference 47, 53
Grammatical Component 39, 41, 43, 48, 49, 50, 54, 68, 70
grammaticalization, criteria of 30–31, 78–79, 105–106, 242, 247, 259
grammaticalization, degree of 23, 76, 106, 242, 266
grammaticalization, direction of 4, 44–46, 75, 103–106, 114–115, 128
grammaticalization, formal 3–5, 29–34, 75–76, 77–82, 101–106, 141–148, 242–243, 259–269
grammaticalization, functional 3–5, 18, 25–26, 31–34, 75, 82–106, 134, 141–145, 267–269
grammaticalization, parameters of 5, 75, 77–79, 80–82

habitual 87, 98, 114, 157, 165–168, 171, 178, 186, 188
heritage language 111–112
hierarchical structure 2, 8, 13, 16, 34, 44, 91–93, 114, 215, 296
hypoanalysis 204

immediate perception 294–297
imminent future 55, 183, 220, 234, 237
imperative illocution 41, 64, 289–295, 297
imperfective 93–101, 164–165, 176, 236, 243, 255–257, 269
inchoative 174, 257
indirect evidentiality 140, 142
inferential evidentiality 43, 90–91, 94–98, 100, 151, 222
inferred information 133, 140, 145
insubordination 6, 9, 133–135, 138, 152–156, 205, 211
intersubjectification 22, 45, 83–84
iterative 165, 188

layering 7, 8, 13, 14, 75, 94, 97, 98, 102, 298
lexical aspect 7, 10, 241–247, 254–269
see also achievement, punctual, telic, terminative, transformative

matter, replication of 111–113
metonymy 164, 165, 169, 174, 178, 179, 181
mirativity 17, 29–31, 140
modal necessity 10, 58–62, 68, 97, 101, 142–143, 273, 277, 282–289
modal possibility 10, 273,
modality 1, 8, 9, 17–20, 24, 43–44, 63, 75–115, 121–124, 127, 133–157, 181–184, 193, 196, 273–298 see also conative modality, deontic modality, domain of modal evaluation, epistemic modality, facultative modality, modal necessity, modal possibility, non-volitive modality, target of modal evaluation, volitive modality
morpheme combination 191, 192, 207, 209–211
morphological type 4, 13, 30, 31
morphologization 191–193, 207–211
Morphosyntactic Level 45, 206–207, 221

narrative mood 141–142
necessitative 137–139, 142–146, 150, 152, 156–157
negation 24, 79, 93–101, 136, 144, 146, 167, 186, 284, 295
non-verbal predicate 136, 138, 141
non-volitive modality 7, 87, 93–94, 273, 276, 279–280, 282

obligative 137, 138, 139, 145, 150, 157
obligatorification 78, 80
optative illocution 273, 297

parallel path hypothesis 3–4, 30–31
participle 9, 27, 133–134, 138–151, 155–157, 165, 186, 241, 244–250, 259–260, 265–268, 279
participle agreement 247–259, 264–268
past tense 10, 28, 32, 61, 62, 137, 142, 146, 147, 150, 168, 186, 194, 196, 197, 204, 207, 241–243, 247–270, 277, 290

pattern, replication of 111–113, 128
perfect 5, 7, 10, 120–121, 133, 137–141, 156, 169, 182, 241–269
perfective 66, 93–101, 114, 121, 165, 241, 243, 248, 254–258, 268–269
phasal aspect 17, 44, 94–96, 98–101, 114, 130, 223, 257
possessive progressive 7, 163
probabilitative *see* similative evidential
progressive aspect 121, 125–129, 163–187
prospective aspect 9, 111, 121, 124–126, 128, 133, 144, 168, 179–183, 215–237
proximative aspect 41, 51–53
punctual 180–183

reanalysis 47, 53, 83, 133–135, 140–147, 151, 154–155, 174, 176–177, 205–207, 219
relative tense 7, 17–18, 44, 61, 114, 207, 215, 222–224, 236–237
relative time 17, 207
reportative 17, 24–25, 61, 94–98
reported speech 6, 191, 193, 194, 202–203, 206
Representational Level 15–18, 22–26, 29, 32, 33, 42–44, 50–51, 61–62, 114, 192, 206–207, 210, 221, 296–298
resultative 7, 26, 32, 114, 133, 139–142, 156–157, 242, 247–255, 257–258, 264–269

scope 1, 2, 4, 7–9, 13–16, 18, 21, 22, 29, 34, 44, 45, 62, 68, 77, 78, 81, 91, 93–99, 103, 104, 106, 114, 115, 128, 129, 139, 141, 144, 147, 148, 211, 215, 217, 218, 221, 222, 224, 237, 242, 269, 276–278, 288, 293, 296, 297
similative-evidential 137–139, 145–150, 152, 156–158
speech-act orientation 8, 75, 83–85, 91, 101, 106, 134, 156, 164, 179, 183–184, 298
stability 111–113, 130
state-of-affairs 15, 17–20, 24, 25, 27, 32, 33, 50, 51, 59, 61, 63, 65–67, 69, 90, 91, 97, 114, 115, 128, 129, 179
subjectification 22, 45, 83–84
subjectivity 77, 83, 163, 180, 281
switch context 47, 54–56, 61, 63, 66, 70, 174–176, 178

target of modal evaluation 276
telic 180, 243–244, 246, 255–258, 269
temporary possession 172–173, 177
terminative 244
transformative 244–246, 254–258, 261–269

univerbation 78, 191

verbal complex 198–201
verbalization 9, 107, 133, 134, 147, 151, 155, 156
volitive modality 7, 43, 93–94, 96–97, 276–278, 280, 282, 289

word order 82, 115, 118, 174–175, 250